# GROWTH AND CRISIS IN THE SPANISH ECONOMY: 1940–93

*Growth and Crisis in the Spanish Economy: 1940–93* appraises the turbulent development of the Spanish economy over the last fifty years and places current economic problems in their historical context. The author examines the economic, political and social problems inherited from the Franco era and their evolution into the present. The book includes:

- a detailed discussion of economic development under Franco, including the boom years of the 1960s followed by the decline of the early 1970s;
- an analysis of the decade of economic crisis which only ended in 1985;
- an evaluation of the economic successes achieved by the González government during the second half of the 1980s;
- an examination of the causes and effects of the economic crisis in the early 1990s;
- an analysis of why, despite serious attempts to revitalize the industrial sector, Spain still has one of the highest levels of unemployment in the OECD.

The book is easily accessible, well illustrated with graphs and has over 100 tables. It will be a valuable guide for those interested in the dramatic contemporary history and future of the Spanish economy.

**Sima Lieberman** is Professor of Economics at the University of Utah, USA. He has taught at a number of institutions around the world and has spent considerable time in Spain. In 1992 he received the title of *Knight Commander* from King Juan Carlos I for his work on the Spanish economy.

# ROUTLEDGE STUDIES IN THE EUROPEAN ECONOMY

1 *Growth and Crisis in the Spanish Economy: 1940–1993*
  Sima Lieberman

2 *Work and Employment in Europe: A New Convergence?*
  Peter Cressey and Bryn Jones

3 *The Italian Economy in the 1990s*
  Edited by Homa M. Scobie

# GROWTH AND CRISIS IN THE SPANISH ECONOMY: 1940–93

*Sima Lieberman*

London and New York

First published 1995
by Routledge
11 New Fetter Lane, London EC4P 4EE

Simultaneously published in the USA and Canada
by Routledge
29 West 35th Street, New York, NY 10001

© 1995 Sima Lieberman

Typeset in Sabon by Solidus (Bristol) Limited

Printed and bound in Great Britain by
T.J. Press Padstow, Cornwall

All rights reserved. No part of this book may be reprinted or
reproduced or utilized in any form or by any electronic,
mechanical, or other means, now known or hereafter
invented, including photocopying and recording, or in any
information storage or retrieval system, without permission in
writing from the publishers.

*British Library Cataloguing in Publication Data*
A catalogue record for this book is available from the British Library

*Library of Congress Cataloguing in Publication Data*
Lieberman, Sima, 1927–
Growth and crisis in the Spanish economy : 1940–93 / Sima
Lieberman.
  p.   cm.
Includes bibliographical references and index.
ISBN 0-415-12428-X
1. Spain—Economic conditions—1918–1975.
2. Spain—Economic conditions—1975–    I. Title.
HC385.L463    1995
330.946′082—dc20             95-2227
                              CIP

ISBN 0-415-12428-X
ISSN 1359-7957

To two distinguished Spanish scholars,

**Ramón Martín Mateo**, former Rector of the University of Alicante, Spain

and

**Andrés Pedreño Muñoz**, Rector of the University of Alicante, Spain

# CONTENTS

*List of graphs* ix
*List of tables* xi
*Acknowledgements* xvi

INTRODUCTION: FIVE DECADES OF SPANISH
ECONOMIC HISTORY 1
*References* 16

1 THE SPANISH ECONOMY UNDER THE FRANCO REGIME 17
   *The Spanish economy in the 1940s* 26
   *The Spanish economy in the 1950s* 38
   *The National Stabilization Plan of 1959* 51
   *References* 55

2 STIMULANTS AND IMPEDIMENTS IN THE ECONOMIC
   BOOM OF THE 1960s 57
   *The beginning of economic recovery at the end of 1961* 63
   *Continued economic growth and the renewal of state dirigisme* 67
   *The Franco regime in the mid-1960s* 86
   *The crisis of 1967 and the balance of the 1960s* 89
   *An evaluation of Spain's economic growth in the 1960s* 96
   *Was Spain's industrialization history typical of Western*
      *European experience?* 103
   *Did the Spanish economy move toward a free market system*
      *in the 1960s?* 113
   *References* 116

3 THE 1970s: THE ENDING OF SPAIN'S ECONOMIC
   MIRACLE YEARS AND THAT OF THE FRANCO ERA 118
   *The last years of General Franco's life: 1970–5* 119
   *From monarchy without a monarch to the beginning of*
      *the reign of Don Juan Carlos I: The economic crises*
      *of the late 1970s* 160
   *The transition to democracy: 1977, 1978* 175

## CONTENTS

| | |
|---|---|
| *The clouded dawn of the new democracy* | 187 |
| *References* | 191 |

**4 ECONOMIC CRISIS IN THE 1980s: 1980–5** — 192
- *Review of the Spanish economy at the start of the 1980s* — 192
- *The fall of the UCD Government* — 208
- *The Spanish economy under UCD leadership* — 211
- *Spain's industrial structure in the early 1980s* — 231
- *Spain and the European Community: 1975 to 1982* — 238
- *The last UCD attempts to rescue the economy* — 243
- *The first three years of the PSOE Government: 1983–5* — 248
- *References* — 259

**5 ECONOMIC RECOVERY DURING THE SECOND HALF OF THE 1980s** — 260
- *Structural evolution of the Spanish economy: 1970–85* — 260
- *Spain's entry into the European Community* — 269
- *Spain's bank crisis of 1977–85 and the financial problems of the country's industrial firms* — 276
- *Criticisms of the first Felipe González Administration* — 281
- *The OECD economies in 1986* — 283
- *The new Spanish economic miracle* — 290
- *Crisis, recovery and industrial policy* — 294
- *Global economic trends and the Spanish economy, 1987–90* — 305
- *Conclusion: The economic achievements of the PSOE Government during the second half of the 1980s* — 330
- *References* — 332

**6 THE RETURN OF ECONOMIC CRISIS AND THE CHALLENGES OF THE EARLY 1990s** — 334
- *The Spanish economy in 1991* — 334
- *The Spanish economy in 1992* — 339
- *The Spanish economy in 1993* — 348
- *Stopping Spain's deindustrialization* — 356
- *References* — 360

| | |
|---|---|
| *Bibliography* | 361 |
| *Index* | 366 |

# GRAPHS

### Chapter 1

| | | |
|---|---|---|
| 1 | Wholesale price index: 1940–59 | 34 |
| 2 | Evolution of the Spanish GDP: 1940–58 | 35 |
| 3 | Relationship between Spanish exports and national income: 1950–9 | 43 |

### Chapter 2

| | | |
|---|---|---|
| 4 | Bank credit and the money supply: 1956–61 | 66 |
| 5 | Bank credit and prices: 1956–63 | 67 |
| 6 | Price indices: 1962–7 | 82 |
| 7 | Imports: 1963–6 | 84 |
| 8 | Exports: 1963–6 | 85 |
| 9 | Cost of living: 1965–9 | 95 |
| 10 | Spain's foreign trade: 1964–9 | 96 |
| 11 | Evolution of the GNP for selected countries: 1955–79 | 98 |
| 12 | Industrial production trends in selected countries: 1960–80 | 99 |
| 13 | Investment as a percentage of GDP, selected countries: 1955, 1965, 1972 | 102 |

### Chapter 3

| | | |
|---|---|---|
| 14 | Investment index: 1962–72 | 133 |
| 15 | Utilization of productive industrial capacity: 1968–72 | 135 |
| 16 | Spain's foreign trade: 1964–72 | 137 |
| 17 | Evolution of the domestic industrial output and its annual growth rates: 1960–73 | 146 |
| 18 | Trend of the index of industrial orders: 1970–4 | 153 |

### Chapter 4

| | | |
|---|---|---|
| 19 | Evolution of the components of Spain's GDP: 1970–88 | 246 |

# GRAPHS

## Chapter 5

| | | |
|---|---|---|
| 20 | Evolution of real industrial output: 1971–84 | 263 |
| 21 | Evolution of investment in Spain's secondary sector: 1978–84 | 264 |
| 22 | Spain's index of industrial production: 1984–9 | 292 |
| 23 | Annual percentage changes in the prices of consumer goods over their level in the previous year in major OECD countries: 1984–9 | 309 |

## Chapter 6

| | | |
|---|---|---|
| 24 | Evolution of Spain's GDP and industrial production: 1971–92 | 341 |
| 25 | Cyclical behaviour of the Spanish economy: 1972–92 | 342 |
| 26 | Spain's GDP per inhabitant as a percentage of the EC's GDP per inhabitant: 1960–92 | 344 |
| 27 | Real GDP convergence trends, Spain–EC: 1984–92 | 345 |
| 28 | Evolution of Spain's investment and GDP: 1983–92 | 346 |
| 29 | Evolution of Spain's employment and unemployment between 1985 and 1992 | 348 |
| 30 | Rate of unemployment as a percentage of the active population: 1985–93 | 349 |
| 31 | US dollar prices of a barrel of Arabian Light Oil: 1973–93 | 351 |

# TABLES

### Introduction

| | | |
|---|---|---|
| 1 | Spanish GDP per capita: 1960–88 | 11 |
| 2 | Growth rates of real GDP per inhabitant: Spain, EC-12 | 12 |
| 3 | Indicators of Spanish economic recovery during the period 1985–9 | 13 |

### Chapter 1

| | | |
|---|---|---|
| 4 | Spanish industrial production indices: 1929–51 | 18 |
| 5 | Import-substitution indicators: 1941–58 | 38 |
| 6 | Distribution of industrial plants according to persons employed: 1958 | 45 |
| 7 | Industrial productivity in some European countries: 1960 | 50 |

### Chapter 2

| | | |
|---|---|---|
| 8 | Indices of industrial production: 1960 and 1961 | 64 |
| 9 | Indices of industrial employment and numbers of registered unemployed: 1960 and 1961 | 65 |
| 10 | Tourism in Spain: 1955–64 | 71 |
| 11 | Spanish emigration to Europe and emigrants' remittances | 72 |
| 12 | Foreign capital investment in Spain: 1959–64 | 72 |
| 13 | Per capita income of selected pole provinces in 1964 | 78 |
| 14 | Industrial production indices: 1963 and 1964 | 80 |
| 15 | Industrial production indices: 1964–6 | 90 |
| 16 | Annual rates of growth of real GNP, selected countries | 97 |
| 17 | Spain, composition of the gross industrial product in 1960 and 1972 | 100 |
| 18 | Productivity indices, selected countries: 1969 | 100 |
| 19 | Indices of industrial productivity, net production per employed person: 1963–70 | 101 |
| 20 | Rates of growth of industrial output: 1913–73 | 104 |

TABLES

## Chapter 3

| | | |
|---|---|---|
| 21 | Annual percentage changes in real GNP and in prices | 120 |
| 22 | Comparative rates of growth of the industrial GDP: 1960–6, Spain, EC and Japan | 121 |
| 23 | Relative contributions by Spanish industries to the aggregate industrial value added: 1954, 1960, 1970 | 122 |
| 24 | Average size of the labour force in industrial firms in Spain and in selected countries | 125 |
| 25 | Spain's foreign trade: 1970–1 | 131 |
| 26 | Selected economic indicators: 1971–2 | 132 |
| 27 | Industrial investment in 1972: Percentage variation 1972/1971 | 134 |
| 28 | Percentage annual increases in Spain's external trade: 1969–72 | 136 |
| 29 | Principal components of imports: 1971–2 | 138 |
| 30 | Principal components of exports: 1971–2 | 138 |
| 31 | Evolution of the relative weight of industrial sectors in the value of aggregate industrial output: 1960–72 | 147 |
| 32 | Physical growth of selected Spanish industries: 1960–72 | 148 |
| 33 | Industrial productivity levels in selected European countries: 1960 | 149 |
| 34 | Dollar value of the gross industrial product per employed person in ten selected European countries in 1960 and 1970 | 151 |
| 35 | Evolution of the composition of the industrial gross value added: 1960–70 | 152 |
| 36 | Percentage change in the value of key industrial variables: 1971–4 | 155 |
| 37 | Annual percentage increases in the rates of inflation in selected countries: 1974 and 1975 | 161 |
| 38 | Unemployment rates at the end of 1975 in selected countries | 162 |
| 39 | Percentage annual changes in productivity growth in selected countries: 1974 and 1975 | 162 |
| 40 | Net effect of taxes and transfers on household incomes: 1970–7 | 182 |
| 41 | Employment trends in Spain: 1960–77 | 182 |
| 42 | Spain's foreign trade: 1973–9 | 190 |
| 43 | Spain's balance of payments: 1978 and 1979 | 190 |

## Chapter 4

| | | |
|---|---|---|
| 44 | Structure of Spanish demand: 1973–80 | 193 |
| 45 | Percentage annual rates of change in consumption: 1967–80 | 194 |
| 46 | Characteristics of industrial foreign trade in the EC countries and in Spain: 1975 | 197 |
| 47 | Characteristics of Spanish industrial sectors: 1975 | 197 |

## TABLES

| | | |
|---|---|---|
| 48 | Spanish industrial demand: 1971–86 | 199 |
| 49 | Annual rates of growth of the foreign trade of Spanish industries: 1971–86 | 200 |
| 50 | Spanish international competitiveness indices: 1976–8 | 205 |
| 51 | Selected Spanish macroeconomic trends: 1977–80 | 211 |
| 52 | Percentage share of selected weak-demand industrial products in total national industry: selected countries, early 1970s | 212 |
| 53 | Comparative consumer price trends: 1977–80 | 214 |
| 54 | Employment trends: 1976–80 | 214 |
| 55 | Spain's external accounts: 1979–81 | 219 |
| 56 | Annual percentage changes in key variables in seven major OECD countries: 1980–2 | 221 |
| 57 | Fixed investment, job creation and public subsidies in preferential industrial zones: 1981 and 1982 | 231 |
| 58 | Percentage distribution of numbers of industrial firms per size group: 1980–4 | 232 |
| 59 | Distribution of firm sizes in terms of their value added: 1980–4 | 233 |
| 60 | R & D activities of Spanish industrial firms: 1975–84 | 235 |
| 61 | Industrial technological coverage ratios: 1975–84 | 235 |
| 62 | Coefficients of indebtedness for public and private firms: 1982–4 | 236 |
| 63 | Cost of borrowing for public and private firms: 1982–4 | 237 |
| 64 | Cost of borrowing by industrial subsector: average 1982–4 | 238 |
| 65 | Spain's external accounts: 1983 and 1984 | 253 |
| 66 | Key Spanish macroeconomic variables: 1982–4 | 254 |

### Chapter 5

| | | |
|---|---|---|
| 67 | Composition of Spain's GDP: sectoral percentages, 1970–85 | 260 |
| 68 | Evolution of key variables in Spain's industrial sector: 1970–85 | 261 |
| 69 | Trends in Spain's industrial foreign trade: 1971–85 | 266 |
| 70 | Spain's industrial trade with the European Community: 1975–85 | 266 |
| 71 | Spain's industrial production: 1976–86 | 267 |
| 72 | Foreign trade balance of Spain's industrial sectors: 1975–86 | 267 |
| 73 | Evolution of Spain's industrial structure: 1975–86 | 268 |
| 74 | Imports and exports as a percentage of GNP, selected countries: 1968–80 | 275 |
| 75 | Per capita import and export values in Spain and in EC-10 countries: 1980 | 275 |

## TABLES

| | | |
|---|---|---|
| 76 | Average annual rates of growth of real imports and exports in Spain and in the industrialized countries: 1960–79 | 276 |
| 77 | Evolution of real interest rates and of the annual rate of growth of bank credit to the private sector: 1975–85 | 278 |
| 78 | Rates of growth of real GNP in the OECD area: 1985 and 1986 | 283 |
| 79 | Rates of interest in the OECD countries: 1985 and 1986 | 284 |
| 80 | Unemployment rates in the OECD area: 1985 and 1986 | 285 |
| 81 | Index of private consumer goods prices: 1985 and 1986 | 285 |
| 82 | Percentage annual change in per unit labour costs in OECD countries: 1985 and 1986 | 286 |
| 83 | Current account balances, selected countries: 1985 and 1986 | 286 |
| 84 | Spain's balance of payments in 1984, 1985 and 1986 | 289 |
| 85 | Growth in employment and wages: 1983–6 | 289 |
| 86 | Key economic industrial indicators: 1985–9 | 293 |
| 87 | Trends in Spain's industrial structure: 1975–86 | 295 |
| 88 | R & D investment efforts in selected OECD countries: 1983–90 | 298 |
| 89 | Receipts and spending of R & D funds in selected countries | 298 |
| 90 | Scientific output in Spain and other countries: 1982–90 | 300 |
| 91 | Trends in the numbers of patents registered in Spain and in other countries: 1982 and 1988 | 300 |
| 92 | Technological coverage ratios in Spain and selected OECD countries | 301 |
| 93 | Technological coverage ratios in high technology and other industries: 1987 | 302 |
| 94 | Annual percentage production increases in Spain's industries: 1985–8 | 304 |
| 95 | Annual increases in the rate of growth of real GNP in selected OECD countries: 1986 and 1987 | 307 |
| 96 | Indices of consumer goods prices in selected OECD countries: 1986 and 1987 | 308 |
| 97 | Unemployment and consumer prices inflation rates in OECD countries: 1987 and 1988 | 309 |
| 98 | Annual percentage change in GNP growth in the OECD area: 1988 and 1989 | 311 |
| 99 | Annual changes in the index of consumer goods prices: 1989 and 1990 | 312 |
| 100 | Annual changes in domestic industrial outputs: 1987 | 314 |
| 101 | Relative contribution of various cost groups to the level of inflation: 1985–8 | 320 |
| 102 | Percentage contribution of each cost group to the rate of inflation: 1985–8 | 320 |
| 103 | Spain's external accounts: 1986–8 | 321 |

TABLES

| | | |
|---|---|---|
| 104 | Rates of unemployment in various OECD nations: 1967–88 | 323 |
| 105 | Percentage of long-term unemployed persons in total unemployment: 1979 and 1985 | 323 |
| 106 | Annual percentage changes in the indices of industrial production: 1986–9 | 327 |
| 107 | Spain's external accounts: 1989 and 1990 | 329 |
| 108 | Spain's foreign trade: 1989 and 1990 | 329 |

## Chapter 6

| | | |
|---|---|---|
| 109 | Percentage annual changes in Spanish investment in industrial equipment and transport goods: 1990 and 1991 | 335 |
| 110 | Structure of the Spanish GDP by sectors: 1970–91 | 335 |
| 111 | Spain's employment structure and unemployment rate: 1970–91 | 336 |
| 112 | Evolution and structure of gross national saving: 1988–92 | 340 |
| 113 | Differences in the evolution of consumer prices and labour costs in Spain and the central countries of the EC: 1988–91 | 345 |
| 114 | Differentials between the Spanish rate of inflation and that in other countries and areas: 1988–92 | 347 |
| 115 | Percentage annual change in consumer goods prices in various countries: 1991, 1992 and 1993 | 350 |
| 116 | IMF estimates of annual percentage GDP change in industrialized countries: 1991, 1992 and 1993 | 352 |
| 117 | Key economic variables in Spain and in the EU countries: 1990–3 | 355 |

# ACKNOWLEDGEMENTS

I am thankful to **Carlos de Reparaz Madinaveitia, Jesús María San Martín Aldazabal, Luis Antonio Vida Sánchez** and **Luis Vida Giménez** for providing me with data and materials I could not have found in the United States.

# INTRODUCTION
## Five decades of Spanish economic history

For any economy, at any time, political and economic conditions inherited from earlier periods of time strongly affect current public and private decisions which bear on its political and economic future. The past and the future are interrelated through the possibilities of the present, and the latter is a product of past experience. An understanding of the political and economic evolution of Spain during the last five decades is essential to a good comprehension of the problems faced by the Spanish economy at the start of the 1990s.

It was Spain's misfortune to synchronize courageous efforts to modernize her political, social and economic institutions with the occurrence of catastrophic global economic developments. The attempts of the government of the Second Republic to improve the country's land tenure and educational systems and to do away with archaic neo-feudal institutions which anchored Spain to technological and economic backwardness were hampered by the Great Depression of the early 1930s and by the impact throughout Europe of fascist and Nazi ideologies. Spain's renewed resolve to democratize and modernize her society following the death of General Francisco Franco in 1975 occurred at a time when inflation and unemployment were growing in economically advanced countries as the result of the raw materials and energy crises of the early 1970s.

Spain's contemporary economic conditions must be studied in the light of past economic and political conditions and of past internal and external economic and non-economic developments. The policy of economic autarky embraced by General Franco during the long period 1939 to 1959 brought stagnation to the Spanish economy in the 1950s at the time when most of Western Europe was experiencing rapid economic growth. Franco's early dedication to autarky reflected both the dictator's enthusiasm for Mussolinian nationalist ideology and the realities of the post-Civil War economy considerably weakened by the effects of the Great Depression and by the human and non-human losses inflicted on Spain by the long and cruel civil war. Warfare had seriously damaged Spain's industrial installations and the country's infrastructure. It crippled the country's agriculture and left Spain with insufficient exchange reserves. Entrepreneurs and skilled workers who had supported the Republic fled Spain and deprived its economy of significant human resources.

World War II and the immediate consequences of its outcome strengthened General Franco's commitment to autarky. The war had seriously reduced Spanish imports of foodstuffs, raw materials and energy products and had limited Spanish exports. Following the end of the war, France, the United Kingdom and the United States imposed on Spain an economic embargo which the newly established United Nations sanctioned. Spain was not only deprived of any Marshall Plan aid, but its foreign trade was crippled. It was not until the early 1950s that Spain started obtaining foreign economic assistance, largely from the United States.

In order to understand the causality flows which characterized the years of serious economic crisis and those of dramatic economic recovery of the Spanish economy in the 1980s it is necessary to observe the country's political and economic evolution under both the Francoist regime and the succeeding democratic monarchy. Salient economic and political events clearly indicate that if we observe the entire post-Civil War period, extending from 1939 to the present, we can easily conclude that Spain and its major institutions evolved during four principal subperiods.

Strong autarkic policies dominated the Spanish economic scenario in the period 1939 to 1959, a period which ended with the enactment by the government of the Stabilization Plan of 1959. As will be observed in detail, this initial phase of Francoist rule was marked by severe internal and external economic disequilibria. During these years, the Spanish people suffered from food, energy and capital equipment shortages. Spain's agricultural sector was unable to increase its output to satisfy the domestic demand for food and the government appeared more interested in financing glorious and costly industrial projects than in raising and diversifying agricultural production. The government's efforts to implement an import-substitution programme by raising the public deficit, its attempts to appeal to workers who had lost their independent trade union federations by granting them significant salary and wage increases, and inelastic foodstuff and productive input supplies resulted inevitably in a succession of waves of price inflation and led to important economic policy changes in 1959. A rising deficit of Spain's balance of trade and the gradual depletion of the country's foreign exchange reserves further spurred the authoritarian regime of General Franco to modify its economic policy at the end of the 1950s.

The National Stabilization Plan of 1959 announced the beginning of a decade of rapid economic growth. This growth in the 1960s was further stimulated by the impact on Spanish economic life of booming Western European economies. The average annual real rate of growth of the Spanish Gross Domestic Product in the 1960s attained 7%, a rate of growth which Spain had never experienced before. According to the prominent Spanish economist, Professor Enrique Fuentes Quintana, it was the Stabilization Plan of 1959 and not the Development Plans of the 1960s which launched the 'Spanish economic miracle' of that decade (García Delgado, J.L., ed., 1988, 4–5).

The two major goals of the Plan were to achieve a faster pace of domestic economic growth and the restoration of external economic equilibrium. The attainment of such goals necessitated the achievement of internal price stability. To contain inflation, the Plan strongly limited public and private credit, ended governmental subsidies to the public enterprises and imposed ceilings on the growth of overall government spending. The Plan also established a new, single dollar rate for the Spanish peseta so as to encourage Spanish exports and relaxed existing restrictions on the entry of foreign capital. The Plan in effect attempted to put an end to Spain's traditional inward-oriented economic policies, policies which the Franco administration had buttressed until then through an extensive network of protectionist regulations aiming to reserve the domestic market exclusively to Spanish products. The Plan constituted an important initial post-Civil War step away from high protection and autarky.

The Plan was a recognition by the Francoist authorities that it was no longer possible for the Spanish economy to continue growing in isolation. It was an admission that Franco's policies had resulted in constantly rising costs of production and increased technological backwardness. It became clear to government economists that the sole demand of a domestic market of limited acquisitive capacity could no longer be counted upon to provide industrial modernization and the achievement of economies of scale. The Plan expressed the desire of Spain's contemporary industrial and financial bourgeoisie to partially and prudently open the domestic economy to the rest of the world and to liberalize the country's foreign trade.

The economy started experiencing rapid economic growth as of 1961. The controlled liberalization of imports increased the inflow of badly needed foreign capital equipment, equipment which soon allowed an increase in levels of production and of productivity. Spanish firms, eager to improve their productive processes, invested as much as they could in the acquisition of such imports. Expanding imports were also supported by rising exports made possible by the liberalization of Spain's foreign trade. The country's balance of payments was strengthened by expanding foreign investment in Spain, by remittances from Spanish workers who had migrated to other countries and, in a major way, by Spain's rapidly rising exports of tourist services. Tourism was becoming Spain's great export in the 1960s.

Spain's expanding industrial activity offered jobs to masses of Spaniards who had remained unemployed or underemployed until then. The agricultural sector and the female population were important pools of unemployed labour. During the 1960s, these workers either migrated to other European countries or were employed by the expanding domestic industries. The numbers of Spanish female workers increased by more than one million between 1960 and 1970 (Ibid., 14). These newly employed workers became an important contributing factor in the process of Spanish economic growth in the 1960s and played an important role in strengthening aggregate domestic demand in that decade.

Spanish economic expansion in the 1960s was however restricted by a number of political and economic factors. For largely political reasons, government authorities were not willing to move to a true market economy. The growth potential of the domestic economy was diminished by the continuation of governmental controls and by the maintenance of a commercial policy designed to preserve most of the government's protection apparatus. The tariff of 1960 remained highly protective. In order to assure their professional survival, government officials insisted on retaining their administrative powers; these powers covered the award of privileged credits, the granting of favourable tax treatment to certain firms and the officials' ability to reduce or limit competition. These officials also succeeded in safeguarding their discretionary powers to raise wages and to impede employers' dismissals of redundant workers. The maintenance of such powers was vital to the survival of the Franco regime; they had allowed the government to buy labour peace and, in a political environment which had outlawed both strikes and the right of workers to organize independent trade unions, had avoided major workers' insurrections. Government officials feared that the establishment of a free labour market could lead to a workers' revolt. Functionaries in charge of economic planning also did their best to limit the process of economic liberalization; what the Development Plans of the 1960s tried to achieve was economic growth without political and economic democracy. Finally, vested private interests supported much of the pre-1959 *dirigisme* which had protected their privileged status in the Spanish economy.

Other factors further restricted Spanish economic growth in the late 1960s. Most of the increase in domestic production was consumed at home and Spain's export performance remained weak. Though exports registered annual increases of as much as 14%, Spain's export capacity remained relatively insignificant largely because of the very low initial level of Spanish exports. The international competitiveness of Spanish exports was also weakened by the high wage increases mandated by the government in this period. As a result, Spain's trade balance in goods registered a deficit throughout the decade, though this deficit was easily covered by the surpluses showing in the services and transfers balances.

A major flaw in Spain's commercial policy in the 1960s was its emphasis on the development of import-substituting industries; it largely ignored the potential of expanding foreign trade as an agent of economic growth. The basic idea followed by the authorities was that the principal role of the country's exports was to pay for imports needed by the import-competing industries. Concurrently, public finance was largely used to pay wages and salaries in the public sector while the government failed to provide an adequate growth in the supply of public goods needed by an expanding economy.

Inadequate industrial expansion in the 1960s caused the migration of over 700,000 Spaniards to other European countries, while about 200,000 workers remained unemployed in Spain during the course of that decade (Ibid., 21). This meant that during the decade of the country's 'economic miracle', nearly one million Spanish workers were unable to find employment in their own country.

The decade of accelerated economic growth of the 1960s was followed by the decade of economic crisis of the 1970s. Paralysis plagued the Spanish economy until the middle of the 1980s. At the start of the 1970s, large American balance-of-payments deficits caused the US dollar reserves of third countries to grow rapidly, increased the internal liquidity of their economies and boosted their spending. Between 1970 and 1973 Spain was able to accumulate reserves amounting to 5.8 billion US dollars; concurrently, internal credit in Spain expanded at an annual rate of 30% (Ibid., 25). The first years of the decade were marked by large increases in consumption and investment spending in Spain, and the resulting demand-pull inflation produced an increase in the prices of consumer goods which attained an annual rate of 14% just before the occurrence of the international oil crisis in December 1973. Spain's rate of inflation surpassed the rates of the EC countries.

The early 1970s witnessed also a deterioration of Spain's terms of trade as raw materials and energy products prices increased in relation to the prices of manufactured goods. Although the terms of trade also deteriorated for most industrially advanced countries in Europe, Spain's high dependency on imports of crude oil had such an inflationary impact on Spanish domestic prices that consumer prices rose at an annual rate of 18% in 1975 while the Spanish balance of payments which had shown a surplus of US$ 500 million in 1973, registered a deficit exceeding US$ 3 billion one year later (Ibid., 26).

It was not only the impact of higher import prices which strengthened inflation in Spain. The Spanish government's practice of indexing wages and salaries in relation to the rate of inflation also fed inflationary pressures. During the late years of the Franco regime the government had followed the practice of determining wage and salary increases by applying the formula $\Delta \dot{w}_t = \Delta \dot{p}_{t-1} + 2/3\ (\Delta \dot{p}_{t-1})$ points, with $\Delta \dot{w}_t$ being the rate of wage and salary increase in year t and $\Delta \dot{p}_{t-1}$ being the rate of inflation in the year t–1. Such practice brought to Spain the highest increase in the real cost of labour among all of the OECD countries. The demand-pull inflation plaguing the Spanish economy was soon converted into a serious cost-push type of inflation. Rapidly rising costs of production diminished the competitiveness of Spanish exports and intensified the country's external deficit.

In order to contain inflation, the government took the usual counter-inflationary measures to weaken aggregate demand. The Spanish authorities adopted restrictive monetary and fiscal policies, policies which at a time of acute cost-push inflation caused a sharp fall in entrepreneurial profits and a decline in private investment. Many firms in Spain were unable to survive the decline in their profits; other firms tried to keep afloat by accumulating debt. Firms able to obtain credit were favoured at the time by the fact that real rates of interest were negative given the pace of inflation; the benefits of increased indebtedness ceased in the early years of the 1980s when real interest rates increased sharply; firms which had borrowed in the 1970s on the basis of variable interest loans experienced increased financial burdens in the early 1980s.

In the 1970s Spain, lacking domestic oil sources and facing large import price increases, shocked by two major oil price crises in the same decade, experiencing rapidly rising real labour costs, highly dependent on deteriorating foreign markets and burdened by a public sector unable to supply the domestic economy with the public goods needed for continued economic growth appeared to be fated to economic retrogression. Economic development was further impeded by a very inequitable and inefficient taxation system which failed to provide the government with sufficient funds to finance a productive public sector. Large scale tax evasion and the development of an 'underground economy' were traditional features of a traditional Spain.

Concurrently, government intervention in the economy remained high and impeded any movement of the domestic economy toward a free market system. Often incompetent public officials retained large discretionary powers in permitting or denying the establishment of new industrial enterprises and in the award of privileged credit and favourable tax treatment. Spain attempted to imitate the example of 'indicative planning' given by France, but, in Spain, government economic guidance was often the product of bureaucratic discretion and not the result of carefully and firmly established criteria. The Francoist bureaucracy remained wedded to a rigidly regulated labour market which limited the ability of firms to dismiss excessively large and redundant labour forces and impeded their modernization. As a result of all these factors, the Spanish economy, particularly in the late 1970s, was subjected to growing inflation, rapidly growing unemployment and a declining rate of economic growth.

The assassination of Admiral Carrero Blanco in December 1973, the man General Franco had designated to be his successor, and the subsequent illness of the dictator, froze governmental action and impeded the enactment of appropriate measures to contain the inflationary pressures generated by the sharp increase in the price of imported crude oil. Until April 1975 the government limited itself to 'camouflaging' the economic impact of the oil crisis in Spain. It tried to keep the consumption prices of energy products from rising by subsidizing the consumption of such products. To compensate for the adverse income effects of declining Spanish exports, it attempted to boost internal demand by authorizing inflationary salary and wage increases; it then tried to minimize the resulting inflation through price controls. The unavoidable consequences of such policies was an increase in the domestic consumption of subsidized energy products, an expanding internal public deficit and a sharp deterioration of the country's external position. The government appeared to cling to the belief that the crisis would soon disappear and that it would not be long until the price of imported crude oil would be back to its pre-crisis level.

In April 1975 this course of policy was discontinued and restrictive monetary and fiscal measures were enacted by the government. General Franco died in November 1975 and soon afterwards Spain's new King, Don Juan Carlos I, announced Spain's return to democracy. As in the early 1930s, Spain decided to democratize and to modernize her political, social and economic institutions at a time of international crisis. Nevertheless, until the national elections of June 1977 the government's economic position remained very passive in face of rising economic difficulties. Monetary and fiscal policies remained too permissive and wages and salaries continued to be overindexed. By June 1977, inflation in Spain had reached an annual rate of 25.4% and Spain's foreign debt had risen to US$ 12 billion (Ibid., 35). Spain's economic performance in that year was much poorer than that in the countries of the EC. (NB. EC is used throughout for convenience (not EEC or the current EU). The membership of the European Community increased from six to twelve countries during the period covered in this book.)

The Pact of the Moncloa of June 1977 was the government's first serious attempt to follow a policy of adjustment to the crisis. The Pact was signed by representatives of all the Spanish political parties seated in the national Parliament. Leaders of Spain's Right and Left recognized in 1977 that a return to economic stability and increased productive efficiency were the *sine qua non* of the viability of the country's recently established pluralist democracy.

The Pact of the Moncloa enumerated a number of economic adjustment measures that would be implemented by the government in order to rescue the Spanish economy from disaster. These measures took account of both the internal and the external positions of the economy. Internally, the rate of inflation had to be reduced; externally, the balance of payments had to be strengthened. In order to attain such goals, the economy had to undergo extensive reform. A major provision of the Pact was that the *dirigisme* of the Franco era had to be abandoned and Spain had to move to a market economy such as existed in the EC nations. More immediately, steps had to be taken to improve the productive efficiency of the sectors of the economy that had been most seriously damaged by the crisis.

The government's new economic policies purported to reduce the rate of expansion of the money supply, to reduce public spending for consumption purposes while increasing public investment, to encourage the growth of Spanish exports by allowing a free float of the Spanish peseta in the foreign exchange markets and to reduce the permitted rate of growth of wages and salaries.

The Pact detailed new ways of formulating the government's budget and controlling public spending. It provided for fiscal reform to improve the country's inequitable and inefficient tax system; tax reforms stipulated the imposition of personal income taxes, of income taxes to be paid by business organizations and the introduction of a 'value added' sales tax. The Pact mandated the government to supervise the financial health of financial institutions and to free the latter of the dense network of regulations imposed on them by the Franco regime.

The European Community was an important market for Spain. In 1971, at the time the Community comprised only six countries, Spain sold one-third of its exports to the EC countries and bought one-third of its imports in those countries (Donges, J.B., 1976, 99). The EC market was particularly important to Spain at a time when that country's exports were mostly constituted by agricultural products. Although Spain's balance of trade with the EC registered continuing deficits, the country benefited from such trade because it was able to acquire in the EC area the capital goods Spain needed to modernize and expand her industries. The benefits of such trade were understood by the Spanish government. As early as June 1970, it had signed a Preferential Commercial Agreement with the EC.

The full adhesion of Spain to the EC, effective 1 January 1986, was the continuation of the policy course embraced by Spain's leadership in 1977. Already in 1985, Spanish expectations that the country was about to become part of the European Community triggered the beginning of

## INTRODUCTION

a period of spectacular economic recovery from the latter half of 1985, a recovery which was maintained during the rest of the 1980s. This recovery was mostly based on the hope of Spanish entrepreneurs that Spanish exports to the Community market would expand and on the resulting increase in Spanish private investment. Realizing that in the future domestic products would have to face increased foreign competition in the national market, Spanish firms became eager to invest to improve their production efficiency.

To so-called 'socialist' government of Felipe González came to power in 1982. It pursued with renewed vigour the process of economic liberalization initiated in 1959 by the National Plan of Stabilization. As noticed, this process had been maintained by the adjustment policies stipulated by the Moncloa Pact of 1977, policies which further opened up the Spanish economy to the rest of the world and more particularly, to the economies of Western Europe. The government of Felipe González decided to completely abandon Spain's traditional reliance on protection and moved to integrate completely the Spanish economy into that of the European Common Market in 1985 and in 1986. Spain entered the EC as a full partner and adhered to the Community's Single European Act as this came into force between 1987 and the end of 1992. The process of economic integration was strengthened in 1989 when Spain agreed to participate in the European Monetary System.

Since the 1950s, Spain thus moved slowly, gradually, but in an irreversible fashion, away from the closed, highly regulated economy presided over by General Franco to an open, market-system type of economy. This move was not interrupted by the economic crises of the 1970s and by serious internal economic problems plaguing Spain in the years 1977 to 1985. In spite of such problems, and largely because of them, the González government placed Spain firmly inside the enlarging European Community.

The various Spanish governments that were formed following the death of General Franco, though marked by differences in political views, shared a common belief in their desire to ensure continuing Spanish economic growth. They all condemned inflation, protection and government intervention in the economy. Since 1975, Spain's political leaders, regardless of party, have sought price stability instead of inflation, economic liberalization instead of protection and the internal allocation of economic resources through a market system in lieu of governmental intervention.

These were the convictions which were strongly maintained by the government of Felipe González. During the difficult years of 1982 to 1985, this government steadily opposed solutions to the domestic problems created by the energy crises and by the collapse of the international Bretton Woods monetary and exchange systems which would favour inflation, protection and the abandonment of the country's move to a free market system. Patiently, it strove to integrate the Spanish economy into the EC economic system, even though such integration required of Spain a commitment to costly measures of structural reform.

The Spanish commitments to economic liberalization and an open market economy were more difficult to achieve in the 1980s than in the booming 1960s. In the latter decade, the goal of liberalization had for sole purpose Spanish participation in the benefits of the global economic boom. Spanish economic reforms did not have to be timed by mandatory deadlines. The pace of liberalization processes was dictated by the then existing Spanish government. In the 1980s, the pace of economic liberalization and that of the opening of the economy were set by an internationally agreed timetable for Spain's integration into the unified EC market as defined by the Single European Act. In that decade, Spain was forced to implement major economic reforms during a relatively short period of time to bring her economy closer to the economies of the central EC countries.

In the early 1980s, both the government and the people of Spain were eager to have Spain become part of the European Common Market. The enthusiasm for full membership in the EC had both political and economic reasons. Spaniards wanted to leave behind those times when most of Western Europe considered Spain to be an anomalous quasi-fascist country in Europe, a pariah country which politically, economically and culturally was more part of Africa than of Western Europe. They also realized that the future of a small- or medium-size European nation such as Spain could not be economically promising if that country chose to remain outside the EC. They further understood that even if Spain should receive *de jure* full membership in the Community, the country would never become a *de facto* full EC member as long as Spanish national income and wealth remained well below the average income and wealth levels prevailing in most other Community member countries.

In order to reduce the large income and wealth differentials which still set Spain apart in 1982 from the EC averages, the existing gap in Gross Domestic Product per inhabitant which separated Spain from the Community had to be reduced as rapidly as possible. In order to accomplish this goal, the Felipe González government felt that Spain would have to follow economic policies similar to those pursued in the advanced countries of the Community. The principal idea was to move to a coordination and convergence of Spain's economic policies with those of the leading EC nations. As Table 1 below indicates, the Spanish government succeeded in reducing the Spain–EC gap in Gross Domestic Product per inhabitant, even though in 1988 GDP per head in Spain was still only 75% of the corresponding average for the EC-12.

INTRODUCTION

Table 1 Spanish GDP per capita (percentage of the average for the EC-12): 1960–88

| Year | Per capita GDP | Year | Per capita GDP |
|---|---|---|---|
| 1960 | 59.1 | 1975 | 79.9 |
| 1961 | 62.6 | 1976 | 77.9 |
| 1962 | 65.4 | 1977 | 77.9 |
| 1963 | 68.1 | 1978 | 76.4 |
| 1964 | 68.3 | 1979 | 73.8 |
| 1965 | 69.5 | 1980 | 73.7 |
| 1966 | 71.3 | 1981 | 72.9 |
| 1967 | 71.4 | 1982 | 73.0 |
| 1968 | 72.0 | 1983 | 73.0 |
| 1969 | 73.9 | 1984 | 72.4 |
| 1970 | 73.3 | 1985 | 72.1 |
| 1971 | 73.9 | 1986 | 72.5 |
| 1972 | 76.2 | 1987 | 74.2 |
| 1973 | 77.1 | 1988 | 75.0 |
| 1974 | 79.1 | | |

Source: 'Las Tres Preguntas Clave de los Años Noventa', *Papeles de Economía Española*, 41/1989, p. xii

In order for Spain to come closer to the average GDP per inhabitant level obtained by the EC as a whole, the strategy of her government in the medium-run emphasized the attainment of greater internal and external stability and a better coordination and convergence with the economic policies of the major EC countries. This was to be achieved through budgetary policies which would reduce both the size of the public sector and that of the public deficit, as well as through an effort to strengthen Spain's export capacity, not by means of periodic devaluations of the home currency, but by achieving relative internal price stability and lower costs of production. The necessary structural reforms within the domestic economy were to be guided by a free price mechanism and not by governmental regulations. The González government strove from the time it came to power to obtain a rising growth rate of real GDP per inhabitant by means of economic policies that were to be compatible with those of the central EC nations. This goal was only partially achieved during the early 1980s.

On the whole, the strategy of the Spanish government in the 1980s was successful. By 1989, Spain's real GDP per inhabitant had reached 76% of the corresponding EC-12 level (*Papeles de Economía Española*, 41/1989, xiv). Spaniards were hopeful that their country would be able to catch up with the EC average level by the year 2,000.

This expectancy was and remains too optimistic. Table 2 shows that for the relatively prosperous period 1985 to 1989 Spain's growth rate of

*Table 2* Growth rates of real GDP per inhabitant: Spain, EC-12
(annual percentage increase)

|  | 1980–4 | 1985–9 | 1980–90 |
|---|---|---|---|
| EC-12 | 0.94 | 2.86 | 1.89 |
| Spain | 0.80 | 4.25 | 2.51 |
| Rate differential, Spain–EC | –0.14 | 1.39 | 0.62 |

Source: *Papeles de Economía Española*, 41/1989, p. xv

real GDP per inhabitant exceeded that of the EC-12 by 1.39%. Considering that during the period 1985 to 1989 the population of the European Community grew by 0.27% while that of Spain expanded in those years by 0.42%, the differential in the growth rate of real GDP per inhabitant during those five years is only 1.24%.

The relative index level of Spanish real GDP per inhabitant stood in 1989 at 76% of the corresponding EC-12 average. To attain an index level of 100 in the year 2,000, Spain's real GDP per inhabitant would have to show a rate of growth for the period 1989 to 2,000 which would exceed the corresponding EC growth rate by 31.6%. This means that on an annual basis Spain's growth rate of real GDP per inhabitant would have to exceed the EC rate by 2.53%. In fact, during the prosperous years of 1985 to 1989 the differential was only, as noted, 1.24%. Moreover, the growth rate attained by Spain in those five years was brought about by Spain's departure from her aims of achieving greater policy coordination and convergence with the leading EC nations (Ibid., xv).

If it is assumed that for the period 1989 to 2,000 Spain's growth rate of real GDP per inhabitant will exceed the corresponding EC rate by only 1%, Spain in the year 2,000 would stand at a relative index level of real GDP per inhabitant of only 85%. This figure in turn is based on the assumption that economic conditions will not deteriorate for Spain in the course of the period 1989 to 2,000.

Still, it is clear, as Table 3 indicates, that the adjustment policies implemented by the Felipe González government showed that this government attained remarkable success during the second half of the 1980s. Starting during the second half of 1985, Spain's economy recovered from a decade-long period of crisis relatively late. However, the pace of Spanish economic recovery exceeded the recovery rate in the EC countries. The Spanish recovery was largely the product of the economic policies of the Spanish Socialist Workers Party (PSOE) which had come to power in 1982. This government not only continued the adjustment measures stipulated by the Moncloa Pact of 1977, but made them more effective. In spite of its designation as 'socialist', the Felipe González government made great efforts to establish in Spain a capitalist

*Table 3* Indicators of Spanish economic recovery during the period 1985–9
(annual changes in percentages)

| Indicator | 1985 | 1986 | 1987 | 1988 | 1989 |
|---|---|---|---|---|---|
| Growth of internal demand | 2.9 | 6.1 | 8.5 | 7.7 | 7.6 |
| Investment (growth rate) | 3.4 | 14.7 | 17.3 | 14.8 | 14.6 |
| Investment (% of GDP) | 18.8 | 19.8 | 21.8 | 23.6 | 25.5 |
| Private consumption | 2.4 | 3.6 | 5.5 | 5.8 | 5.5 |
| Public consumption | 4.6 | 5.7 | 8.7 | 4.6 | 5.5 |
| Growth of production (GDP at market prices) | 2.3 | 3.3 | 5.5 | 5.3 | 4.9 |
| Agriculture and fishing | 3.1 | −9.1 | 9.6 | 3.7 | −1.0 |
| Construction | 2.2 | 5.9 | 10.4 | 12.5 | 13.0 |
| Industry | 2.1 | 5.6 | 5.1 | 4.2 | 4.4 |
| Services | 2.3 | 3.4 | 4.8 | 5.2 | 5.0 |
| Growth of employment | −0.9 | 2.2 | 3.1 | 2.9 | 4.0 |
| Unemployment rate | 21.6 | 21.2 | 20.5 | 19.5 | 17.0 |
| Changes in real salaries and wages per capita | −0.2 | 0.4 | 2.2 | 1.6 | 0.2 |
| Entrepreneurial profits | 3.0 | 2.3 | 5.8 | 7.0 | 4.2 |
| Increase in foreign investment (% of GDP) | 1.5 | 2.3 | 2.6 | 2.3 | 3.9 |
| Reduction of the public deficit | −7.0 | −5.7 | −3.6 | −3.0 | −2.0 |

*Source*: Papeles de Economía Española, 41/1989, p. xx

free market economy. Although a member of the Spanish socialist party, Felipe González, as Head of the Spanish Government, showed that in matters of economic policy he was a stronger 'free market enthusiast' than Ronald Reagan, the then President of the United States. The move to a free market system in Spain was to be assisted by greater internal price stability, by a return to external equilibrium, by the structural and technological modernization of a number of economic sectors such as industry and transport and by the creation of more efficient financial markets. The Spanish government succeeded in reducing the internal rate of inflation and in obtaining external balance. Fiscal measures designed to strengthen private investment in the country were enacted in 1985.

These adjustment measures were buttressed by the then existing global economic boom, a boom resulting both from the fall in the world price of crude oil and from the depreciation of the US dollar whose nominal value had fallen by 32% in relation to the Spanish peseta in the period

1985 to 1988. This propitious external economic climate was further sustained by Spain's full participation in the EC. The country's entry at the beginning of 1986 induced Spanish firms to increase their investment in new capital equipment in order to improve their competitiveness in the EC market and opened Spain to a massive entry of foreign capital.

These various developments rapidly strengthened Spain's internal aggregate demand and launched the process of Spanish economic recovery during the latter half of the 1980s. During these years, Spanish aggregate demand rose at an annual rate of between 7% and 8%, while real investment expanded annually at rates exceeding 14%. While investment in Spain represented only 18.8% of the country's GDP in 1985, it grew to 25.5% of GDP by 1989.

It was this rapid increase in internal aggregate demand which constituted the launching pad of Spain's economic recovery after 1985. During the latter half of the 1980s, the annual growth of Spain's GDP evaluated at market prices surpassed GDP growth in all other EC or OECD countries. Concurrently, the Spanish economy in this period created more than 1.5 million jobs and experienced a fall in the unemployment rate from 21.5% in 1985 to 16% in 1989. The second half of the 1980s brought to Spain a true 'economic miracle'.

A brief study of Spanish economic policy during the five decades which followed the end of the country's civil war in 1939 reveals that in this period the Spanish government effected two major changes in the direction of such policy. Both changes reflected the country's need to adjust to serious economic difficulties caused by external, as well as internal problems. The first dramatic change in official economic policy was embodied in the National Stabilization Plan of 1959. It practically ended General Franco's earlier pursuit of authoritarian autarky. Looking at the 1940s and 1950s, Professor Eduardo Merigó succinctly summarized Spain's economic and political problems at that time:

> Despite a period of growth and industrialization begun in the years of neutrality during World War I and pursued in the 1920s, depression, political upheavals, and the Civil War had meant that in 1940 Spain was economically more backward than ten years earlier. The proportion of the active population engaged in industrial activities had declined to 22% (the level of 1920), while that in agriculture had risen to over 50% ... Yet at the same time, agricultural production was 20% to 30% lower in the 1940s than in the 1920s. Output only recovered pre-war levels during the 1950s, and it was not until the 1960s that the same could be said of productivity. Overall output, which had fallen by 25% during the 1930s, grew at an annual rate of only 1.25% in the 1940s. Consequently, by 1950, it was still some 10% below its 1930 level.

## INTRODUCTION

And GDP per caput, at $300 in 1954, the first year for which comparable data are available, was barely 40 per cent of the average for OECD Europe.

The Spanish regime had established the institutional pattern of a corporate state superimposed on an administration which was basically Napoleonic, highly centralized, and rather inefficient. The absence of democracy was thus apparent not only in the suppression of human rights and democratic political processes, but also in the existence of a number of institutions and a legal system without equivalent in other Western market economies.

It would be difficult, however, to understand Spanish economic performance in the first two decades of the post-war period without taking one further factor into account: the fascist, nationalistic ideology considered economic growth as an essential aim. Its purpose may well have been power rather than welfare, but the growth objective was patently clear. The authoritarian nature of the regime, together with a regressive tax system, made it possible to generate a fairly high level of capital accumulation which, despite an inefficient allocation of resources, permitted, in the early stages, relatively high output growth rates.

Merigó, E., 1982, pp. 554–5

The principal contribution of the Stabilization Plan of 1959 to Spain's economic welfare was probably its weakening effect on fascist doctrine. It was preceded by significant changes in the composition of the government. The new decision makers were better educated men than their predecessors and though they still clinged to *dirigisme* in economic activities, they were willing to abandon the earlier policy of autarky and to slowly open Spain's doors to world trade. The success of their policies was bolstered during the 1960s by the global economic boom prevailing during that decade, and more particularly, by the rapid economic growth of the EC countries.

The oil crisis of 1973 announced the end of European post-World War II 'economic miracles'. General Franco died in November 1975 and Spain moved slowly toward a system of political democracy. The first free elections in Spain's post-Civil War period took place in June 1977. Recognizing the urgency of implementing solutions to the problems caused by a rapidly deteriorating economy, Spain's political leaders agreed in the same year to adopt new adjustment policies which would allow the economy to survive the energy crisis. They signed the Moncloa Pact of 1977. In the following year, Spaniards voted in favour of a new Constitution which established in Spain a political system of democratic monarchy. The Constitution of 1978 clearly expressed the people's will to build a new, dynamic European Spain dedicated to economic modernization and greater social justice.

This book purports to help its readers acquire a good understanding of Spain's economic problems in the 1980s, of the adjustment policies pursued by the Spanish government and of the outcome of such policies. Because economic problems and the nature of economic policies in a given country at a given time are the result of past economic experience, and form the base of that country's economic future, this study examines the evolution of Spain's economic performance during the four decades which preceded 1980. Following the analysis of Spain's economic crisis and recovery in the 1980s, the study will also present to the reader the author's thoughts regarding the short-term future of Spain's economy.

## REFERENCES

Donges, J.B., *La Industrialización en España, Políticas, Logros, Perspectivas*, Barcelona, Oikos-Tau Ediciones, 1976.

García Delgado, J.L., ed., *España Economía*, Madrid, Espasa Calpe, S.A., 1988. See article by Fuentes Quintana, E., 'Tres Decenios de la Economía Española en Perspectiva', pp. 1–78.

Merigó, E., 'Spain', in Boltho, A., ed., *The European Economy, Growth and Crisis*, Oxford, Oxford University Press, 1982, pp. 554–80.

*Papeles de Economía Española*, 'Las Tres Preguntas Clave de los Años Noventa', vol. 41, 1989, pp. v–xliii.

# 1

# THE SPANISH ECONOMY UNDER THE FRANCO REGIME

Many Spanish economists have interpreted the course of economic policy followed by General Franco's governments as showing two distinct phases. The first corresponds to a period of economic autarky in which the Spanish economy remained practically closed to the world and which extended from the end of the Civil War to 1959 when the seriousness of Spain's economic problems induced the Franco regime to accept economic reforms. This initial phase of Francoist administration ended with its approval of the National Stabilization Plan of 1959. The second stage was marked by a slow liberalization of economic activity in the country and by a very gradual opening of the Spanish economy. This phase covers the period 1960 to 1975 when the death of General Franco brought to Spain a new political and economic orientation.

Professor José Luis García Delgado believes that a better understanding of Franco's economy justifies the view that this economy passed through three phases. The first covers the period 1939 to 1949. This was a period of economic stagnation, of blind adherence to the goal of autarky and of extensive government regulations and strict control of any form of economic activity. The second phase covers the 1950s and ends with the enactment of the Stabilization Plan. The final phase extends over the 1960s and ends with the assassination of Admiral Carrero Blanco in 1973, the death of Franco's chosen political heir, marking the ultimate failure of Franco's political and economic systems. Professor García Delgado considers the years 1974 and 1975 as being already part of a transition period which guided Spain to a new democratic system (García Delgado, J.L., 1986, 171).

According to García Delgado, the wisdom of the government's pursuit of economic autarky by means of extensive controls in the 1940s started being challenged by the government formed in 1951. This scholar views the 1950s as forming an important watershed period during which Spain's authorities gradually abandoned the goal of autarky. It was this change in economic orientation that made the

National Stabilization Plan of 1959 possible. The last phase of Francoist economic rule is characterized by the implementation of measures of gradual economic liberalization, though government *dirigisme* does not disappear.

García Delgado refers to the first period of Franco's rule as 'the night of Spanish industrialization', a period during which Spanish industrial production stagnated and was unable to surpass the level it had attained in 1929. This economist bases his conclusions on indices of Spanish industrial production calculated by Professor Albert Carreras (Carreras, A., 1984, 127–57). These figures are shown in Table 4. The indices computed by Professor Carreras differ from those calculated by the National Institute of Statistics (INE) though both studies use 1929 as base year. Contrary to what is shown by the INE data, the indices of Carreras show that post-Civil War Spanish industrial output only exceeded that attained in 1929 in the year 1950.

García Delgado notes that while Greece, Italy and Yugoslavia (countries with relatively poor economies seriously damaged by World War II) succeeded during the period 1946 to 1950 in doubling, or nearly doubling, the index of their industrial production, Spain barely succeeded

Table 4 Spanish industrial production indices: 1929–51 (1929 = 100)

| Year | Carreras | INE |
|---|---|---|
| 1929 | 100.00 | 100.00 |
| 1930 | 105.32 | 101.20 |
| 1931 | 94.45 | 98.70 |
| 1932 | 93.64 | 94.70 |
| 1933 | 92.58 | 91.00 |
| 1934 | 94.71 | 98.60 |
| 1935 | 97.86 | 103.30 |
| 1939 | — | 72.30 |
| 1940 | 83.92 | 96.30 |
| 1941 | 78.50 | 94.40 |
| 1942 | 83.73 | 104.70 |
| 1943 | 86.64 | 112.20 |
| 1944 | 91.39 | 114.10 |
| 1945 | 86.86 | 106.00 |
| 1946 | 96.69 | 125.30 |
| 1947 | 95.12 | 128.10 |
| 1948 | 99.60 | 130.90 |
| 1949 | 97.74 | 124.30 |
| 1950 | 106.77 | 142.10 |
| 1951 | 111.68 | 150.50 |

Source: García Delgado, J.L., 'Estancamiento Industrial e Intervencionismo Económico Durante el Primer Franquismo', in Fontana, J., ed., *España Bajo El Franquismo*, Barcelona, Crítica, 1986, p. 174

in multiplying her industrial production index by 1.1 in the same period. García Delgado finds that for the longer period 1936 to 1950 Spain's industrial activity stagnated and the Spaniards' welfare level declined. This conclusion is shared by other Spanish scholars (Prados de la Escosura, L., 1984, 152).

For García Delgado, the night of Spanish industrialization was particularly tragic because it represented not only the end of a long and sustained period of slow economic growth which was maintained from the last third of the nineteenth century to the end of the first third of the twentieth, but also because it widened the gap separating the growth path of Western European economies from that of Spain. It forced Spain into greater relative economic backwardness. The decade of the night of Spanish industrialization proved also to be catastrophic for Spanish political, social and cultural life. The Franco government banned political parties, did away with independent labour unions, deprived workers of their legal right to strike, fixed salaries and wages and lost to emigration valuable human capital.

The tragic situation of the Spanish economy in the 1940s was observed by Josep Fontana and Jordi Nadal, two outstanding Spanish economic historians:

> the new regime [under Franco] was launched under the double banner of social reaction and economic isolationism.
>
> Apart from the nationalism, and indeed xenophobia, of the new government, it was external circumstances which made an isolationist policy inevitable. The outcome of the Civil War brought the complete loss of the gold reserves accumulated during the 1914–18 period and the burden of large debts to Germany and Italy. The Second World War, coming immediately afterwards, drastically reduced the invisible assets of the balance of payments (emigrants' remittances and capital imports). Under such conditions from 1939 onwards imports could only be financed by the equivalent exports. The problem was made even worse by an inflationary internal policy and the maintenance of overvalued exchange rates, retained for traditional prestige reasons, which put obstacles in the way of the export of home products ... calculated in gold pesetas at fixed value, the total (exports plus imports) of Spanish foreign trade, which already had decreased to 35.9% in 1931–35 as compared with 1926–30 = 100, reached bottom in 1940–44 (29.7%) ... This drastic reduction in foreign trade was the dominant factor of the whole economy...
>
> Fontana, J. and Nadal, J., 1976, pp. 503–4

Fontana and Nadal interpret the economic situation of the Spanish economy in the 1940s as García Delgado does. The two economic historians find that 'the national income was still, up to and including 1950, below the 1935 level, while the per capita income fell to even lower levels, due to the increase in population which, in spite of everything, had taken place' (Ibid., 507). Indeed, Spain's population increased during the 1940s, even though agricultural production had not yet recovered its pre-war level; a major reason for such increase was the cessation of emigration from Spain during the years of World War II.

The weak performance of the Spanish agricultural sector in the 1940s was caused by a number of factors. Warfare, a depleted Spanish treasury and a decline in world supplies forced Spain to import much less nitrogenized fertilizers and phosphates than in the period 1931 to 1935; Spain's farmers also faced serious shortages of quality seeds and of agricultural machinery; finally, government controls mandated for many years relatively low official foodstuff prices and agricultural producers therefore lacked any interest in expanding their crops. Fontana and Nadal note that it was only after a disastrous grain harvest in 1945 that the government allowed a substantial increase in grain prices in order to encourage grain producers to increase their output. During the entire 1940s food shortages were so serious that imports of foodstuffs from abroad had to be boosted. Given the limited means to pay for such imports and in spite of the government's interest in industrial growth, the authorities had to restrict imports of industrial machinery, of raw materials and of energy products. Thus, Spanish imports of raw cotton during the first half of the 1940s represented only 74.2% of their 1931–5 level; they stood at only 57.1% of the pre-war level during the balance of the decade (Ibid., 506). Given the enormous excess demand for foodstuffs, the internal terms of trade between agricultural and industrial products changed in favour of the former. While hunger plagued the urban masses, owners of large landed estates increased their wealth. The acquisition of land in the 1940s became a favoured form of investment for the wealthy. Concurrently, the pro-industrialization stance of the government also benefited industrial interests at the expense of rural and urban workers. The 1940s thus witnessed a redistribution of national income in favour of both industrialists and large agricultural producers to the detriment of workers. Exploitation of the latter by the former became more intense with the abolition of independent labour unions and with population growth. In addition, the government's fiscal reforms of 1941 further intensified the misery of the masses because indirect taxes on consumption were raised more steeply than direct taxes. This is why Fontana and Nadal conclude that:

> the civil war was won by the champions of an anti-bourgeois and anti-urban revolution, inspired by the purest spirit of nationalism. Their most representative figure was the smallholding farmer of the

centre and north, paragon of the virtues of the race; beside him, sharing the benefits of victory, stood the majority of the clergy, the big landowners and the industrial and financial oligarchy. In the other camp, the vanquished, were the day-labourers of Andalusia and Extremadura, the petty bourgeoisie and the industrial proletariat of Catalonia and the Basque Country, who, during the vile republican era had dared to challenge the sacred unity of the fatherland. Hardly was the civil war over than war broke out between the nations which had supported one side and those which had supported the other, and this contributed to broadening the rift between victors and vanquished within Spain.

Ibid., p. 503

Distinguished economic historians agree with García Delgado that 1951 brought a significant change in the direction of Francoist economic policy (Carr, R. and Fusi, J.P., 1979, 55–7). This change followed the first massive popular protest against the government's economic policies; in spite of threatened brutal police repression, a general strike took place in Barcelona in March. Fontana and Nadal describe the economic situation in Spain at that time:

In 1951 the failure of a decade of economic isolationism became apparent. War damage could no longer be blamed for the disastrous economic situation. It was now clear to all that the policy adopted since 1939 had failed to recover Spain's economic strength. Taking as a basis 1935 = 100, the national income, in fixed-value pesetas, was only 89 in 1950 (i.e. 11% less than in 1935), whilst prices reached 570 (which means that they had increased almost six times). The maladjustment between the rapidly rising prices and the wages rigidly controlled by the Ministry of Labour produced the first great mass movement to disturb the social peace of the national-syndicalist state...

Fontana, J. and Nadal, J., 1976, p. 512

On 18 July 1951 General Franco changed the composition of his government but kept in it old Falangist leaders strongly attached to the course of the economic policies of the 1940s. The new men charged with the task of implementing improved policies supported a slow move to a market economy; they also realized quite clearly that Spanish economic growth required large imports of capital goods and that such imports could only be financed by foreign aid. Without massive imports of capital equipment, it would be impossible for any Spanish government to attempt to integrate the country into the global economy. Without the assistance of foreign aid, Franco's rule had to end in failure. The advent of the Cold War between the United States and the Soviet Union saved

Franco's crumbling regime. The United States government, pleased by Franco's posturing as a strong enemy of communism, agreed to extend economic aid to Spain in exchange for the American use of military bases in Spain, bases which would be of great strategic value to the American military in the event of war breaking out between the two superpowers. The United States concluded a mutual defence agreement with Spain in 1953. The Eisenhower administration then proceeded to supply Spain with foodstuffs, fodder, fertilizers and raw materials such as cotton. American aid to the Franco regime started making the latter more acceptable to the governments of the 'free world'. Spain acquired membership in the United Nations in 1956. Concurrently, American economic aid helped Spanish industrial output to reach and surpass production levels attained in 1935; it also allowed the growth of agricultural production.

Franco's retention of some old Falangists as cabinet members in the new government limited the extent of economic reform the government was able to carry out. These men were dedicated to the preservation of the economic policy course of the 1940s. Among the most prominent Falangists retained in the government were José Luis Arrese y Magrá, the Secretary-General of the only legal political party in Spain under Franco, the quasi-fascist National Movement, as well as Spain's Minister of Housing from 1957 to 1960 and José Antonio Girón de Velasco, Minister of Labour in the 1950s.

The inflationary policies pursued by both the government and the private banks further impeded the acceleration of economic growth. The banks were allowed to create unlimited volumes of credit and their indiscriminate lending fuelled the country's price inflation. In turn, the government financed the National Industrial Institute, the INI, a gigantic holding company created in 1941 to further national economic self-sufficiency and to develop defence industries, by issuing short-term bonds which were immediately redeemable at the Bank of Spain; between 1951 and 1959 the government sold about 22 billion pesetas worth of these bonds and their redemption strengthened the inflationary process in the country (Ibid., 514).

The Ministry of Labour concurrently allowed wage increases to prevent a serious deterioration of workers' purchasing power. The resulting price–wage spiral was strengthened in 1956 when frosts destroyed most of Spain's exportable citrus crop, thereby weakening the country's export capacity. In order to maintain a minimum level of indispensable capital goods imports, the government practically exhausted its foreign exchange holdings in 1957. It also tried to contain labour strife by granting workers new wage increases.

Renewed strike activity caused by prices rising faster than total production caused General Franco to alter once again the composition of his government in February 1957. Falangists were replaced by better educated technocrats belonging to the secret Rightist and religious group known as *Opus Dei*. Among the new men coming to power were Alberto Ullastres, a former professor of economic history, who became Minister of Commerce, Mariano Navarro Rubio, appointed Minister of Finance, and Laureano López Rodó, also a university professor chosen to head the Technical Secretariat of the Presidency of the Government. These men agreed to follow a liberal economic policy which would bring the Spanish economy closer to a market system. They favoured tax reform, the suppression of the existing system of multiple exchange rates, a devaluation of the peseta and a more effective containment of domestic inflation.

Workers, too, pushed for significant economic reforms. New strikes broke out in Asturias in March 1958 and labour unrest extended to the Basque region and to Catalonia. The government appeased the workers by enacting the 'Law of Collective Agreements' which ended the power of the Ministry of Labour to determine wages; henceforth, wages were to be determined by negotiation between employers and selected employees. By the end of the 1950s, the men of *Opus Dei* had left far behind the old ideals of the 1940s.

Indeed, a number of significant economic reforms succeeded each other with amazing rapidity in both 1957 and 1958. In April 1957, the government abolished the complicated system of multiple exchange rates and devalued the peseta. Tax reform followed at the end of the year. Spain became an associate member of the OEEC in January 1958 and acquired full membership in the International Monetary Fund and in the International Bank for Reconstruction and Development. The new technocrats in power succeeded in transforming the earlier closed economy based on government-controlled foreign trade into a partially open economy with part of its foreign trade liberated from government controls. The enactment of the National Stabilization Plan in the summer of 1959 became the most significant economic act taken by a Francoist government during the entire period 1939 to 1959.

This Plan had its origin in a memorandum sent by the Spanish government to both the IMF and the OEEC on 30 June 1959. It enumerated proposed measures the Spanish government intended to take to improve the national economy. These measures were intended to achieve internal and external economic equilibrium and included fiscal and monetary reforms. Both international organizations gave their support to the contents of the document and to help Spain achieve the proposed goals they provided Spain with a loan of 546 million US dollars (Tamames, R., 1979, 429). The Plan was published in July. It pursued two main goals: first, it tried to establish the foundations of a process of balanced Spanish economic growth; and second, it purported to help the Spanish economy to integrate with greater ease into the global economy. Internal and external equilibria required price stability. Price stabilization was to be achieved by curtailing aggregate demand. In order to reduce such demand, the Plan called for the limitation of both public and private spending. The Plan enumerated a number of needed changes in monetary policy. The government was not to issue new government securities which could be immediately redeemed by their holders at the Bank of Spain. The redemption feature of existing public securities was an important cause of inflation because it allowed the unchecked expansion of bank credit. The Plan thus announced the limitation of bank credit extended to the private sector. Equally important, the Plan also announced that Spanish importers would be mandated to deposit in the Bank of Spain, previous to the act of importation, a sum equivalent to 25% of the value of their imports. Fiscal reforms centred on the reduction of public spending.

To the goals of containing the growth of aggregate demand, of attaining price stability and of reducing the country's propensity to import, the National Plan of Stabilization added as an important government objective the achievement of external equilibrium. It announced the liberalization of Spanish imports of a number of commodities and revealed that state trading would be gradually delegated to the private sector. Bilateral trade was to be replaced by global trade. External equilibrium was to be attained through the enactment of a new tariff system, by liberalizing imports of capital and by establishing a realistic, single exchange rate for the peseta. In order to conform with IMF directives, a gold value of the peseta was defined as 0.0148112 grams of fine gold, a value which established an exchange rate of 60 pesetas for the US dollar. Multiple exchange rates governing both Spanish imports and exports disappeared. The new peseta–dollar rate constituted a depreciation of the peseta intended to discourage Spanish imports and to boost the country's exports.

The Plan of Stabilization attempted to boost the inflow of foreign capital into Spain by facilitating foreign investment in the country and by granting amnesty to all Spaniards who had illegally accumulated wealth abroad and who were willing to repatriate such wealth; capital held abroad by Spaniards could be brought back to Spain without fear of government prosecution. The framers of the Plan of Stabilization clearly understood that a massive entry of foreign capital into Spain was the most effective way of obtaining external equilibrium.

Although the leading Spanish decision makers of the 1960s did not hesitate to support liberalizing economic reforms, they remained reluctant to embrace a true market economy in which government *dirigisme* would either become minimal or disappear altogether. Given the fact that these men had careers anchored to the large apparatus of government intervention, that their power and prestige were tied to their ability to allocate resources and extend credit, their strategy was to liberalize Spanish economic activity while retaining significant government control over such activity. Though willing to allow a slow liberalization of Spanish economic life, they opposed any democratization of the existing political regime.

The government technocrats of the 1960s, men such as Laureano López Rodó, embraced 'indicative economic planning', as developed by the French, as a way to maintain *dirigisme* in spite of the trend toward economic liberalization. The formulation of three-year indicative plans allowed a large bureaucracy to retain power and prestige and to claim credit for the fact that during the decade 1960 to 1970 the Spanish Gross National Product increased at a rate of 7.5% per year, the highest annual rate of growth of GNP in Europe, and that during the same period per capita income rose from $ 300 to $ 1,500 (Carr, R. and Fusi, J.P., 1979, 59).

The method of planning, even the organizational structure of the planning agency, were copied from the French model, although the administration of these plans was very much influenced by old Spanish traditions. The plans were the product of López Rodó's 'Commissariat for the Plan', initially a small agency attached to the Office of the Presidency of Government and subsequently transformed into a large 'Ministry for the Planning of Development'. These organizations formulated the Development Plans for the periods 1964–7, 1968–71 and 1972–5. The principal goal of these plans was to increase productive private investment and largely ignored income redistribution and the reduction of regional imbalances, particularly because the latter measures were thought of as slowing down the increase in private investment. Because the government technocrats could not request increases in public investment, they chose to follow a model of growth which was based on an unequal distribution of income and on regional imbalances. This was certainly the strategy presented in Plan I. Plans II and III gave some emphasis to social objectives and some importance to the redistribution of personal income and to regional planning to help the poorer areas of the country. However, their framers remained loyal to the strategy of unbalanced growth and to the belief that rapid growth in the wealthier regions of Spain would eventually benefit the poorer ones. They adopted the French concept of '*pôles de croissance*', poles of growth, standing for the idea that the government would invest in the development of infrastructure in such poles and grant tax benefits to firms establishing themselves in those areas. The poles were areas that had already experienced industrialization, not economically backward regions.

While the government technocrats claimed that Spain's economic successes in the 1960s were largely the product of the plans, many criticisms were directed at these plans (Ibid., 61). Critics pointed out that the plans sacrificed social improvement for the sake of economic growth; that they neglected the housing problems caused by the large movement of people from the countryside to the industrial urban centres; that they had failed to develop a more humane and just society by ignoring the need for a redistribution of personal income and that they kept in Spain a regressive system of taxation; finally, the point was made that the government deliberately allowed the profits–wages gap to widen in order to obtain the support of the wealthy élite, the people who were able to bring about a rise in private investment.

1973 dealt a mortal blow to Spanish economic planning. The beginning of the energy crisis in October 1973 and the assassination of the President of the Government, Admiral Luis Carrero Blanco on 20 December of that year suddenly imposed on the country an economic and a political crisis. Given the uncertain political and economic future of Spain, both the government leadership and the people lost interest in planning. A projected fourth plan covering the period 1976 to 1979 was never presented to the *Cortes*, Spain's Parliament. Following the death of General Franco on 20 November 1975, the Minister for Planning, Joaquín Gutiérrez Cano, was dismissed in the course of the government change of 13 December of the same year and no successor was appointed. The Ministry for the Planning of Development was abolished a few weeks later and its bureaucracy was transferred to a new, smaller agency serving both the Ministry of the Interior and the Office of the Presidency of Government. The end of Spain's planning experience coincided in time with the termination of the country's economic miracle of the 1960s.

From the vantage point that has allowed us to gain a brief overview of the evolution of Spain's economy during the thirty-seven years of General Franco's rule, let us now examine the component subperiods in greater detail.

## THE SPANISH ECONOMY IN THE 1940s

From 1 February 1938, the day when General Franco formed his first government, until the constitution of his fourth in the summer of 1951, Spain's economy remained characterized by three main aspects: a high degree of government interventionism; the pursuit of autarky; and acute inflation accompanied by stagnating production. The term 'stagflation', coined by economists in the 1960s, succinctly describes the condition of the Spanish economy during the period of World War II and during the immediate post-war years. These years of economic stagnation, and in certain cases even of economic retrogression, have been explained in terms of the damage inflicted by the Civil War on domestic capital equipment, particularly on Spain's means of transport, as due to the country's loss of its gold reserves as well as to Spain's inability to import foodstuffs, fertilizers, fuel and badly needed capital equipment during the entirety of the 1940s. Apologists of the Franco regime have also pointed out that in the immediate post-World War II years, the victorious nations chose to ostracize the Franco government and forced the Spanish head of state to embrace autarky until the early 1950s when the development of the Cold War between the United States and the Soviet Union induced the American government to support the Spanish government as an ally in the anti-communist campaign.

These developments colour however only part of Spain's economic picture in the 1940s. The most important part of the latter shows the 'Caudillo' eager to please and to unite around him the victors of 1939, all of them strong conservatives and traditionalists representing Spain's social élites. The victorious Right included the high officials in the Roman Catholic Church and in the military, the large landowners and the financial and industrial oligarchy (Fontana, J. and Nadal, J., 1976, 503). With the strong support given him by Spain's political Right, General Franco emerged from the Civil War as the country's autocrat whose absolute powers could not be limited by law because he ruled Spain *'por la Gracia de Dios'*. A strong nationalist, and very much influenced by Mussolini's fascism, the Caudillo started his long reign with a dogmatic belief in the virtues of national economic and military self-sufficiency.

Professors Carr and Fusi have noted what was peculiar in General Franco's dedication to strong autarky:

> What distinguished Spanish economic policy from that of other Western European states was that state *dirigisme* and autarky were seen as an ideal and *permanent* solution, not only as a response to the post-war crisis. The economists of the regime did not seek to justify autarky in economic terms, as had the protectionists in the nineteenth century. It was presented and defended as a political ideal; the recipe for a stable society and a suitable policy for an 'imperial military state'.
>
> Carr, R. and Fusi, J.P., 1979, p. 51

It was Franco's will to industrialize Spain regardless of cost, even at the expense of an impoverished agricultural sector and at a time when hunger plagued most Spaniards, so that Spain would operate as a completely closed economy, independent of the world's economic and political uncertainties. Franco succeeded in the 1940s in imposing his politico-economic dogma on a people physically and emotionally weakened by a long and brutal civil war and confused and intimidated by a new global war whose ends they could not understand.

Spain's political and economic history under Franco's rule is basically a history centring on the hegemonic powers of the dictator. Franco's ability to retain such powers for thirty-seven years, in spite of the outcome of World War II, was undoubtedly linked to his clever posture as a strong anti-communist crusader who was needed as an ally by the United States during the long Cold War period. It was also a product of his acumen in relying on lieutenants who were devoted to him. Though Franco changed the composition of his government ten times during his long tenure as Chief of State, and although the distribution of ministerial portfolios between Falangists, the military and conservative Catholics varied from Cabinet to Cabinet, Franco's chosen government leaders remained loyal to the Caudillo's politico-economic faith.

The Francoist dogma placed exceptional powers in the hands of the Chief of State who, like a seventeenth-century absolutist monarch, felt that he had been chosen by God to rule dictatorially. The powers of the Caudillo did not have to be legitimated by the will of the people as expressed by their votes in free elections; the Chief Executive did not base his power on universal suffrage. It was only natural that the new politico-economic dogma, highly influenced by its prophets in Berlin and in Rome, rejected as dangerous to its social order any freedom of speech, the existence of political parties and independent trade unions, the freedom of the press and the right of workers to strike. Franco adopted the Nazi *'Führerprinzip'*, the idea that in exchange for the government's maintenance of the institution of private ownership private entrepreneurs would obey the dictates of the government. Finally, following the example of all past and contemporary dictatorships, the Francoist dogma emphasized the need for continuous surveillance by strong security forces to maintain 'law and order' and to assure the survival of the regime. Any opposition to the Caudillo's will had to be destroyed.

General Franco changed the composition of his government three times between the beginning of 1938 and mid-1951. His first government was constituted in the city of Burgos on 1 February 1938, and consisted of twelve ministers, most of them being either military officers or high-ranking members of the Falangist party. The Ministry of the Interior, renamed subsequently Ministry of Governance, was given to Franco's brother-in-law, Ramón Serrano Suñer, a man with strong pro-Nazi inclinations.

The government's composition was changed on 9 August 1939. Serrano Suñer was retained as Minister of Governance. The new Cabinet remained in power until the end of World War II, acting mostly as an advisory group to the Chief of State who was the sole decision-maker in all matters considered by him as 'urgent'. This Cabinet favoured a process of reconstruction and development financed by large public deficits and by a rapid increase in the money supply. As a result, the index of consumer prices, given 1935 as the base year, climbed to 745.3 in 1951 (Tamames, R., 1979, 395). This government also pretended to improve the country's tax system in 1940 but it remained highly regressive.

Probably anticipating a German military defeat, Franco in 1942 decided to remove strongly pro-German Falangists from leading positions in government. He ended the political career of his brother-in-law and transformed members of the *Falange* into government functionaries without executive power. The Spanish government then abandoned officially its declared position as a 'non-belligerent' and proclaimed Spain to be a 'neutral' country.

Following the end of World War II, and with the Potsdam Conference under way, Franco decided to change the composition of his government once again on 18 July 1945. The new Cabinet was to remain in power until 18 July 1951. The new government, known as the 'government of autarky', tried to reinforce the country's self-sufficiency strategy and moved to silence workers' and students' demonstrations against the regime. In spite of the show of force by the authorities, the first serious strikes since the end of the Civil War developed in Catalonia and in the Basque Region and there were student demonstrations in Madrid and in Barcelona. Workers and students protested the intensification of inflation and the development of black markets in the country.

Two industrial laws, both enacted in 1939, clearly expressed the strong support given by the Franco regime to economic autarky. The first of these laws was the Law of Protection and Development of National Industry of 24 October 1939. The preamble to this law stressed 'the capital importance in the life of the nation of the availability in the home territory of industries necessary for war and of the primary resources indispensable for life' (Boletín Oficial del Estado, 1939). It further added that the post-Civil War economy would have to engage in 'considerable efforts to liberate Spain from imports of foreign products, which could be produced or manufactured in the area of our nation'. An important objective of the law was to induce Spanish private enterprise to produce most goods which until then had been imported; it was thought that the failure of Spanish producers to do so in the past was due to a lack of proper incentives; the government in 1939 believed that it could provide these incentives in the form of economic privileges. These privileges were to be extended to domestic firms that would be declared to be of 'national interest' (Ibid., Article I). Firms so designated by the government were to receive for a period of fifteen years significant advantages: their taxes would be reduced by as much as 50%; they were entitled to acquire land under the power of eminent domain; they could import needed machinery and equipment under special customs treatment; and the government guaranteed a minimum return of 4% on invested capital when the latter did not exceed one billion pesetas. Should the declared dividends of these firms exceed 7% of their capital, one half of the excess would have to be paid to the government.

A major flaw in this law was that it penalized efficient firms able to earn high dividends; another major weakness was the fact that the award of the coveted designation of firm of national interest was entirely left to the discretion of bureaucrats whose decision reflected more political than economic considerations. Even when the administrative decision was entirely free of bias, it was seldom made in the light of careful studies of opportunity costs and benefits.

The second industrial law was that of 24 November 1939, known as the Law of Regulation and Defence of National Industry. The law purported to 'create a prosperous national economy, freed of dependence on the exterior, able to reevaluate national primary resources'. Article 10 of this law provided that all public enterprises and all private firms receiving any type of economic benefit from the government would use exclusively in their production and distribution processes domestically produced inputs, except when needed inputs were not produced or were not available in Spain, or when, though available, domestic inputs were not of suitable quality. The law forced many Spanish enterprises, both public and private, to purchase domestically produced inputs at prices much higher than those prevailing in world markets.

Another major goal of the early Franco administration was to create a state holding company, modelled after the Italian *Istituto per la Ricostruzione Industriale*, and able to develop large-scale industrial enterprises which the private sector was unable to finance and to manage. The *Instituto Nacional de Industria* (INI), the National Institute of Industry, was established by a law of 25 September 1941, in order to 'propel and finance, in the service of the nation, the creation and reappearance of our industries, specially those which will have as principal end the solution of the problems imposed by the needs of defence of the nation or which will direct themselves to the development of our economic autarky, able to offer to Spanish saving a safe and attractive investment'. INI was thus assigned the task of industrializing the country in order to increase its military power and to render it more independent of foreign resources and products. In time, the military role of INI tended to weaken, specially in the post-World War II period when Spain started obtaining foreign military assistance from the United States. Its role as a major agent of industrialization persisted. The INI was endowed by the government in 1941 with 50 million pesetas; the cumulative government endowment rose to 54,650 million pesetas in 1976, while the aggregate value of its investments amounted in that year to 105,500 million pesetas (Schwartz, P. and González, M.J., 1978, 2). The number of manufacturing and financial enterprises it controlled or participated in grew rapidly over the years.

These laws clearly reflected the ideology of both General Franco and of their draftsman, Franco's first Minister of Industry and Commerce and his lifelong friend, Juan Antonio Suanzes. Suanzes directed the INI between 1941 and 1963. A naval officer trained as an engineer, he had severed his ties with the military in 1932 to take a position with the *Sociedad Española de Construcción Naval*, an affiliate of the British firm Vickers. Following the outbreak of civil war, Suanzes promptly joined the forces of General Franco. During his entire public life, Suanzes remained hostile to political liberalism and never ceased supporting the totalitarian state. Like Franco, he favoured the achievement of a Spanish autarkic economy; above all, he wanted a rapid expansion of the domestic industrial output that was to be obtained by providing the country with import-competing industries. If rising costs of production should adversely affect the country's export industries, the government would protect the latter by means of subsidies and by entering into bilateral commercial treaties with other countries. He supported the anti-liberal and anti-Marxist social doctrines of the Roman Catholic Church as expressed in encyclicals such as the *Syllabus*, the *Cuadrogesimo Anno* and the *Divini Redemptoris* which favoured associations of employers and their employees; he supported the government's control of such associations to further the interests of the state. As an engineer, he glorified the achievement of 'technical optimality' which he believed could only be achieved by means of centralized control of the economy. His enthusiasm for 'totalitarian' production led him to favour the total self-sufficiency of the domestic economy in order to avoid production bottlenecks. He overlooked the fact that policies of import-substitution generally result in an increase in the imports of capital goods. At a time when most Spaniards were poorly nourished, poorly clothed and poorly housed, Suanzes advocated that imports of foodstuffs and of consumer goods had to be sacrificed in order to allow larger imports of capital goods. Finally, this man firmly believed that only production by large, vertically integrated firms, was technically efficient.

The importance attached by both General Franco and Suanzes to the industrializing role of INI is evidenced by the fact that this agency was initially responsible only to the President of the Government, so that Suanzes, as head of INI, could operate free of ministerial interference. It was only in March 1968 that the INI became a branch of the Ministry of Industry.

In the 1940s, most INI investments centred on the production of fuels, fertilizers and electric power. These investments were not always carefully planned. For instance, the INI created a National Enterprise for Aluminium, a large consumer of electric power, before it developed its two major electric power companies, ENDESA and ENHER. Another major creation of the INI was the National Enterprise Calvo Sotelo which specialized in the production of liquid fuels and carburants. The

Calvo Sotelo company initiated shortly after its establishment in 1942 a detailed study concerned with the location of refineries, methods of production, input needs and market demand. The study was submitted to the government and the latter presented it to the Parliament, the *Cortes*. The latter gave the plan the force of law by approving a 'plan for the national production of liquid fuels, lubricants and connected industries'. The plan contemplated the installation of four large industrial complexes. The government authorized a credit of 1,993 million pesetas for the building of these facilities (Lieberman, S., 1982, 173).

The government also attempted to achieve a higher level of self-sufficiency in the production of fertilizers. In February 1940, firms producing nitrogenous products were designated as national interest industries. The E.N. Calvo Sotelo started producing nitrogenous fertilizers which allowed the share of the INI in the domestic production of fertilizers to expand from 17.1% in 1945 to 48.7% in 1965 (Schwartz, P. and González, M.J., 1978, 56).

In the 1940s it was in the field of electric power generation that INI investments were most successful. Suanzes attached great importance to the construction of new thermoelectric plants able to utilize poor quality coal which had no alternative use. Rapid growth in the generation of electricity was important to the INI because it needed reliable sources of electric power for its own industrial facilities and because its management understood that industrial expansion in Spain required the building of new electric power plants. In 1944 INI founded the E.N. de Electricidad, ENDESA, the 'national entity' responsible for the construction of new thermoelectric plants. A major project of ENDESA was the building of a power plant at Ponferrada, constructed on the basis of machinery imported from Belgium, Switzerland and the United States. In 1946, the E.N. Hidroélectrica de Ribagorzana, ENHER, was established to develop the power potential of the Noguera-Ribagorzana river in the Catalan Pyrenees. Both of these companies contributed in a significant way to reduce the excess demand for electric power in Spain and facilitated thereby the industrialization of the country.

The INI also participated in the development of shipbuilding companies such as the E.N. ELCANO and the E.N. BAZAN. It administered the airline company Iberia. It founded in 1943 the Sociedad de Aluminio, S.A., ENASA, which established production facilities in Valladolid and subsequently, in San Juan de Nieva.

In the decade 1949 to 1959, the INI organized three major industrial concerns: REPESA, ENSIDESA and SEAT. REPESA was founded in 1949 as a mixed company co-owned by the INI, the Compañía Española de Petroleos and Caltex. The goal of REPESA was to expand the supply of petroleum products in Spain, a goal rapidly achieved because of the American company participation in REPESA. The participation of foreign capital in REPESA announced the beginning of a change in the economic views of Spain's leadership.

In order to increase the domestic supply of steel, the INI created in 1950 the E.N. Siderúrgica, S.A., ENSIDESA, whose production facilities were located in Avilés in the province of Oviedo. The project called for an annual output of 3.1 million tons of steel, an ambitious goal in the early 1950s. It is noteworthy that concessions were granted to European and American firms to build the steelworks of Avilés and that the financing of these facilities was partly based on credits extended by foreign banks as well as on American financial aid.

In 1950, the Sociedad Española de Automóviles de Turismo, SEAT, was founded. Its plants were located in Barcelona. INI contributed 52% of its capital. SEAT was to produce automobiles under patents held by the Italian company FIAT. In terms of the value of its sales in the 1960s, SEAT was to become the leading industrial firm in Spain.

The INI also became active in exploration, research and engineering. It created in 1942 the E.N. ADARO whose task was to explore the potential mineral wealth of Spain. This company tried to discover, although without much success, new coal deposits near Palencia, Cuenca and León. It tried to find lead in the province of Jaén, iron in Asturias, oil in the region of Cádiz and in Morocco and phosphates in the Sahara.

Until 1959, the INI was financed by means of budgetary appropriations. A year earlier, the government had decided on a new method of financing the large public holding company. It forced savings banks to invest in bonds issued by the INI. This strategy forced Spanish savers to finance the INI and avoided the necessity of increasing taxes for that purpose.

The efforts of the government to achieve costly industrial goals in an economic environment marked by the presence of energy and raw materials scarcities strengthened inflationary pressures and forced the Spanish population to endure the heavy burden of consumer goods shortages and growing inflation.

During the 1940s and the 1950s, Spain's economy was subjected to persistent inflation, the Spanish rate of inflation in that period being one of the highest in Western Europe. Only four of the nineteen years in the period 1940 to 1959 showed rates of inflation measured in terms of the wholesale price index smaller than 5%; eleven of those years registered rates exceeding 9%. Furthermore, strong variations in such rates from year to year made planning by business firms quite difficult. During these nineteen years the trend in the rate of inflation based on the wholesale price index showed two distinct sub-periods. The first extended from 1940 to 1951 during which the annual rate of increase of wholesale prices averaged 14%. These were years of serious shortages imposed by both the Civil War and World War II, shortages exacerbated by the industrializing efforts of the government. As Graph 1 shows, the second subperiod 1951 to 1959 experienced a much more moderate inflation largely due to an increase in Spanish imports permitted by American aid.

During the years 1941, 1942 and 1943, years characterized by the urgency of reconstruction and the need for capital goods, and raw materials and foodstuff shortages, the wholesale price index climbed at an annual rate of 13.3%. This rate was surpassed in the period 1945 to 1947 when the rate of inflation attained 16.1%. The years 1948 and 1949 showed relative price stability but they were followed by a new outburst of inflation in 1950 and in 1951, when the wholesale price index increased at an annual rate of 23.1%. It should be noticed that during the 1940s the government failed to take any counter-inflationary measures and remained indifferent to the impact of inflation on the welfare of most Spaniards.

As shown by Graph 2, the high rate of inflation which characterized the first post-Civil War decade had no stimulating effects on Spanish production. Spain's Gross Domestic Product in this period stagnated. With a slowly expanding population and with the collapse of foreign demand for Spain's exports at the end of World War II, Spain's per capita income declined and unemployment increased.

The first decade of the Franco regime was thus marked by great governmental efforts to expand the country's industrial power. This was

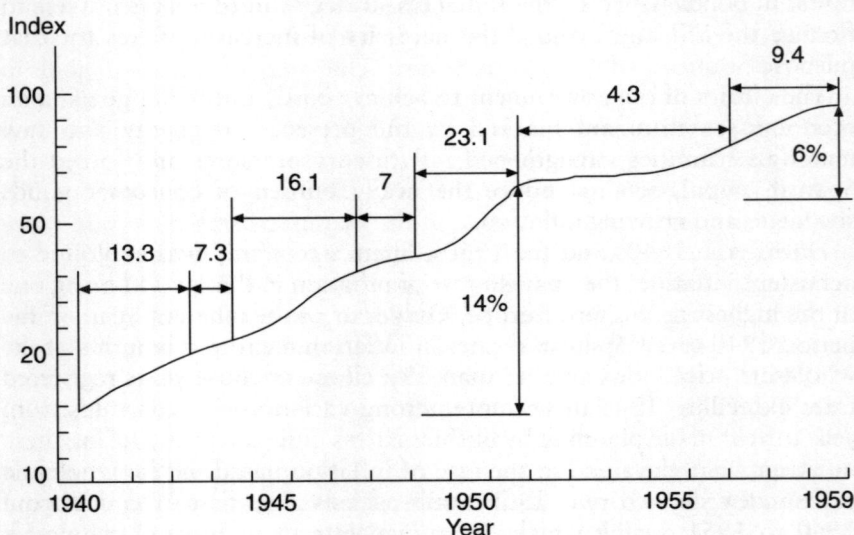

*Graph 1* Wholesale price index: 1940–59 (1958 = 100)

*Source*: González, M.J., 1979, p. 39

*Graph 2* Evolution of the Spanish GDP: 1940–58 (1958 pesetas)

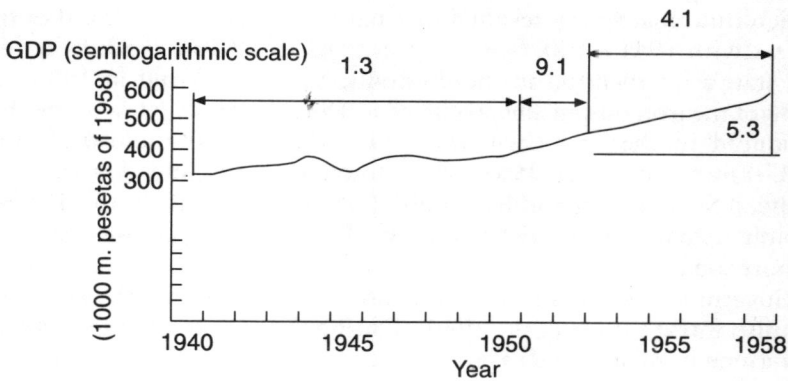

*Source:* Ibid., p. 45

done, as observed, by active participation of the state in the economy; in addition, the government embraced a policy of high protection to assure the exclusive exploitation of the domestic market to Spanish producers. Protection was strengthened by the imposition of quantitative import restrictions and by strict government control over foreign exchange transactions. Spanish foreign trade was subjected to bilateral commercial treaties specifying types and quantities of commodities Spain would exchange with countries with which it had entered into such arrangements. The efforts of the government to achieve costly industrial goals in an economic environment marked by the continuation of energy and raw materials scarcities strengthened inflationary pressures and maintained lengthy consumer goods shortages.

World War II brought some benefits to the Spanish economy. Spanish wolfram, an important alloy used in the manufacturing of certain types of steel, was coveted by both the United States and Germany. For its acquisition America was willing to pay Spain the $ 10,000-a-ton tax imposed by Franco's government in order to prevent the shipment of this metal to Germany. Spanish exports of wolfram increased from 800 tons in 1941 to 4,000 tons in 1943 while the value of these exports rose from US$ 700,000 in 1941 to US$ 60 million in 1943 (Shneidman, J.L., ed., 1973, 28).

The end of the war in Europe on 7 May 1945, put an end to the foreign demand for Spanish minerals. From that time on, and until the end of the decade, Spain found herself practically isolated from most of the world. If this isolation strengthened the resolve of Spanish leaders to become more autarky-oriented, it weakened considerably the Spanish economy, and in particular, the country's ability to import needed raw materials, processed goods and capital equipment. The lack of fertilizers and of agricultural machinery resulted in a fall in the total agricultural output index, with 1931 = 100, from 83.5 in 1943 to 79.4 in 1950. In spite of the state's intervention in the economy, Spain produced in 1950 only 84% of the iron output she produced in 1931, and only 71% of the ships produced in that pre-Civil War year. The pace of industrialization accelerated only after 1951 when foreign credits and American aid allowed Spain to expand her imports of capital goods. In the 1950s, a rapidly expanding tourist industry also strengthened the country's import capacity.

Government foreign exchange controls also restricted the growth of Spanish foreign trade in the 1940s. During the period 1939 to 1948, the government maintained a fixed exchange rate for the peseta. The exchange rate for Spanish exports was 10.95 pesetas for the US dollar, while the rate of exchange for imports was fixed at 11.22 pesetas to the US dollar. An exception was made in 1947 in order to encourage tourism in Spain, the rate of exchange for tourists being increased by 51.6% above the basic exchange rate (Donges, J.B., 1976, 48). Otherwise, the rate of exchange between the peseta and the US dollar or the British pound was maintained unaltered during this period. Because Spain's inflation rate was higher than that prevailing in the countries with which Spain traded, the peseta soon became overvalued in terms of most other currencies, a development which burdened Spanish exports and stimulated the growth of Spanish imports. To offset the effects of such overvaluation, the Spanish Institute of Foreign Currency established between 1945 and 1948 a system of 'special accounts'. Each Spanish firm engaged in foreign trade was given a 'special account' in which the foreign exchange it generated was deposited; the firm was entitled to obtain foreign exchange from that account to finance its imports, the amount of foreign exchange it could withdraw from its account being determined by the monetary authorities for each transaction. This amount depended on what the authorities felt was the importance of the particular import for the national economy. In certain cases, the firm was allowed to withdraw only part of the foreign exchange it had earned; in other cases, it was granted more foreign currency than it had received for its exports.

On 3 December 1948 a system of multiple exchange rates was introduced in order to narrow the gap between official and black market exchange rates. Different transactions were to command different exchange rates. Exports were classified into fifteen exchange rate groups for which the peseta–US dollar rate varied between 10.95 and 21.90 pesetas to the dollar. Imports were divided into nine rate groups for which the peseta–US dollar rate varied between 11.22 and 27.38 pesetas to the dollar (Ibid., 50). Because the most favourable export rate remained lower than the prevailing black market rate, the new exchange rate system failed to stimulate exports.

From 1951, the monetary authorities started reducing the number of export and import classifications commanding different exchange rates; exports were reduced to six different rate groups and imports to seven. At the same time, the operation of a 'free foreign exchange market' was permitted by the authorities; private banks were allowed to acquire up to 90% of the foreign exchange earned by Spanish exporters and could sell to Spanish importers in possession of an official import permit up to 100% of their foreign exchange needs as defined by their import permit. This multi-rate system remained operative until April 1957 (Lieberman, S., 1982, 176–8).

As Graph 2 indicates, in spite of the efforts of the government to expand and diversify Spanish industrial production in the 1940s, the economy as a whole stagnated. The main reasons for this lack of growth were, as noted, shortages of steel, fuels and electric power, as well as the scarcity of foreign exchange which limited the country's capacity to import. The government succeeded nevertheless in developing new lines of industrial activity such as a new automobile and truck manufacturing industry, a new petro-chemical industrial complex and important import-competing facilities which expanded the availability of cement, fertilizers, machine tools and electrical machinery. These new industries operated under the protection of a high tariff wall and governmental financial support and produced exclusively for the domestic market. As Table 5 shows, the percentage of domestically produced consumer goods in their total national supply, already high in 1941, i.e. 77.1%, increased to 94.4% in 1958. In the case of low technology manufactured products, such as glass, cement, paper products, fertilizers, iron and steel, etc., the corresponding percentage rose from 77.9% to 82.4% in the same period. The percentage for higher-technology capital equipment goods such as internal combustion engines, machine-tools, textile machinery, agricultural machinery, electric motors and transformers, etc., was only 32.7% in 1941 but increased to 70.6% in 1958 (Donges, J.B., 1976, 155). The rising participation of domestically produced capital equipment goods in their national supply undoubtedly helped to accelerate the process of national industrialization in the 1950s and was the foundation of the further development of Spanish industry in the following decade. The government's efforts to industrialize the country in the 1940s and 1950s centred however on the development of import-competing industrial facilities and neglected efforts to expand and modernize the country's export sector. A result of such one-sided public policy was that as late as 1958, the value of Spanish industrial exports as a percentage of the

Table 5 Import-substitution indicators: 1941–58 (percentages)

| Year | Participation of domestic production in aggregate domestic supply | | |
|---|---|---|---|
| | Consumer goods | Low technology manufactured products | High technology manufactured products |
| 1941 | 77.1 | 77.9 | 32.7 |
| 1951 | 79.7 | 81.4 | 47.3 |
| 1958 | 94.4 | 82.4 | 70.6 |

Source: Donges, J.B., 1976, p. 155

aggregate value of Spain's industrial output did not exceed 3% (Ibid., 157). The weakness of the country's export capacity at that time could not be attributed to a deficient foreign demand since world commerce boomed in the 1950s. The reasons for Spain's poor export performance centred on structural factors such as excessively small industrial enterprises producing goods on the basis of antiquated machinery and obsolete technology to sell exclusively in the highly protected national market.

## THE SPANISH ECONOMY IN THE 1950s

Josep Fontana and Jordi Nadal have called the period 1951 to 1959 the 'transition to economic liberalism' (Fontana, J. and Nadal, J., 1976, 512). Raymond Carr and Juan Pablo Fusi have described the Spanish economy in the 1950s as follows:

> Surrounded by high tariff walls, enclosed in a domestic market with limited power to consume industrial goods, and incapable of importing the raw materials and capital goods to supply and modernise its industry, the economy was starved. Physical controls and rigid price regulation from above distorted the market, favouring traditional entrenched sectors as opposed to the dynamic sectors of the economy.
> 
> Carr, R. and Fusi, J.P., 1979, p. 52

The Catalan strikes of January 1951 gave the government a clear signal that workers would no longer submit in silence to the rationing of foodstuffs which had remained in existence since 1938. Spaniards resented the chronic shortages of fuel, energy, raw materials and equipment they had to endure while the western European democracies showed an impressive recovery from the hardships inflicted on them by

World War II. It had become clear to everyone in Spain that the government's pursuit of extreme autarky had kept the country poor and economically backward and that any improvement in existing economic conditions required foreign aid.

Dark clouds did not cover the whole of Spain's economic horizon. From abroad shone sunny rays of economic and political hope. The outbreak of the Cold War between the United States and the Soviet Union, and more particularly, the beginning of the Korean War in June 1950, were significant events which General Franco turned to his advantage. General Franco had justified his rebellion against the government of the Second Republic as necessary patriotic action to save the country from 'godless communism'. During the late 1940s, the government of the United States as well as the political leadership of many western European democracies seriously apprehended the possibility that the Soviet Union was planning to annex, politically and even militarily, most of Western Europe. The anti-communist stance of General Franco pleased political leaders in Washington, London and Paris. Even though as late as 1947 exiled republican and socialist Spaniards still denounced Franco as a military ally of Hitler, the Franco-Spanish border was re-opened by France on 10 February 1948, and in the United States, President Truman made it known that he would allow American private banks to extend loans to the Franco government. In May of 1948, Spain signed commercial treaties with both France and England and received credits from those countries with which to purchase capital equipment (Tamames, R., 1979, 521).

Two events developing far away from Spain in 1948 further strengthened the international respectability of the Franco regime. These were the communist coup in Czechoslovakia in February 1948 and the Russian blockade of Berlin in June of the same year. It was not surprising that an American military mission appeared in Madrid in October and that it promptly concluded that it was in the interest of all anti-communist nations to help Spain acquire membership in the United Nations.

As early as February 1949 Spain received a loan of US$ 25 million from the American Chase National Bank. On 18 January 1950 Dean Acheson, then American Secretary of State, urged all member nations in the United Nations to send ambassadors to Madrid. In turn the Franco government declared shortly after the beginning of the war in Korea that Spain was ready and willing to help the United States contain the spread of communism in Asia by sending military units to Korea to fight side by side with American soldiers. Within weeks, the United States Senate authorized the Export-Import Bank to issue loans to Spain and an initial loan of US$ 62.5 million was quickly approved. In November of 1950, the General Assembly of the United Nations abandoned its earlier decision not to have ambassadors of member nations in Madrid. The government of General Franco had obtained world-wide acceptability.

It thus appeared that at the end of 1950 the regime of General Franco had overcome all potentially hostile foreign pressures. In Spain itself, the regime was strongly supported by both the military and the Church. The monarchists formed a 'loyal opposition' group which, though disagreeing with the ideologues of the Falangist movement, gave their support to the regime in the hope that the latter would eventually restore Don Juan de Borbón to the throne of Spain. Accepted abroad and secure at home, Franco's government presented the Caudillo as Spain's David ready to bring down the communist Goliath. In the words of Professor S.G. Payne:

> The regime continued to promote its bombastic rhetoric of triumphalism, claiming victory on every hand, with Franco the true leader of all western civilization and Spain the focus of world strategy because of its priority in opposing Communism and championing true spiritual values. It insisted on moral superiority over all the divided, multiparty regimes of western Europe, some of which struggled with sizable Communist opposition parties or were themselves led by Socialists.
>
> Payne, S.G., 1987, p. 414

The dictator decided to reshuffle his Cabinet on 18 July 1951, probably in response to the first significant manifestation of popular discontent which had started in Barcelona in March. What was initially a protest against an increase in public transport fares became a mass industrial strike which extended to the Basque region. The government in Madrid immediately replaced the conciliatory captain-general of Barcelona, Juan Bautista Sánchez, with a more militant officer, General Felipe Acedo Colunga.

General Franco changed the composition of his government in mid-July. The fourth Francoist government retained a number of ministers appointed six years earlier. The new Cabinet reflected more continuity than change. Among those retained were the Catholic Alberto Martín Artajo as Minister for Foreign Affairs, Blas Pérez González as Minister of the Interior, the Falangist José A. Girón as Minister of Labour and General Eduardo González Gallarza as Minister of the Air Force. The then Navy Captain Luis Carrero Blanco became Sub-Secretary of the Presidency, a position which had ministerial rank. The Falangist Raimundo Fernández Cuesta retired as Minister of Justice to become the Secretary General of the Falangist movement. A new Ministry of Information and Tourism was given to another Falangist, Gabriel Arias Salgado. The Ministry of Commerce and Industry, headed earlier by Franco's friend Juan Antonio Suances, was split into two agencies; a new

Ministry of Commerce was headed by the technocrat Manuel Arburúa while a distinct Ministry of Industry was entrusted to an army engineer and INI administrator, Col Joaquín Planell Riera. The Ministry of the Army went to Francoist Spain's most prominent officer, the former commander of the Spanish Blue Division which had joined the German *Wehrmacht* in Russia in 1942, General Agustín Muñoz Grandes.

The composition of this government clearly showed Franco's ability to form a Cabinet completely devoted to him, though constituted by men whose ideals and aims did not necessarily coincide. As in earlier years, Franco's Cabinet represented a delicate balance between military officers, non-religious Falangists and tradition-minded Catholics. It was this group of Ministers who during the period 1951 to 1957 succeeded in reducing, largely with the help of American economic aid, the country's rate of inflation and in boosting economic growth to an annual rate averaging 4.4%. It was this government which acquired United Nations membership for Spain in December 1955. These achievements could not have materialized without Spain's agreements with the United States specified in the Pact of Madrid which was signed on 26 September 1953.

Spain and the United States exchanged ambassadors early in 1951. José Felix de Lequerica, a supporter of the Falangist movement and a former ambassador to France, became Spain's representative in Washington. Admiral Forrest Sherman arrived in July in Madrid to initiate negotiations with General Franco; his mission was to incorporate Spain into the American defence network. Franco was counting on such possibility and the agreements reached by both men became the Pact of Madrid of September 1953. The Pact provided for American economic and military aid to be given to Spain in exchange for the use by American military forces of three new air bases and a new naval base to be constructed in Spain. One of the air bases was to be built at Torrejón de Ardoz near Madrid. A secret agreement allowed the United States to determine unilaterally when its forces could use such bases to counter 'evident Communist aggression' (Ibid., 419). The Pact allowed the United States to keep on such bases military aircraft armed with nuclear weapons.

In exchange for the American use of such bases, the United States was to provide direct economic and military aid to Spain. In addition, the Spanish government was to receive American credits which would allow Spain to buy American foodstuffs and raw materials at reduced prices. The value of aggregate American economic aid to Spain, including the credits, amounted to US$ 1.68 billion in the period 1953 to 1963. Furthermore, Spain received in the same period US$ 521 million in American military assistance (Ibid., 418).

Most important for General Franco, American economic and military aid strengthened his regime both in Spain and abroad. His Minister for

Foreign Affairs, Alberto Martín Artajo, lost no time in claiming that the Pact of Madrid was clear evidence that the United States had recognized that Franco's past policies had been correct from the start. Franco's political luck did not abandon him. American friendship allowed Spain to become a member of the World Health Organization in 1951, of UNESCO in 1952 and of the International Labour Organization in 1953. Even the leadership of the Soviet Union softened its relationship with the Franco government in 1956 by allowing the repatriation to their country of origin of about 4,000 Spaniards most of whom had left Spain as children in 1939, others being Blue Division soldiers who had survived Russian prisoner of war camps during the last fourteen years.

Franco's good relations with the United States suffered a shock after the Soviet Union launched its *Sputnik* satellite in 1957. The Caudillo realized that in a nuclear exchange between the two superpowers Madrid could be destroyed should the Soviets try to destroy the American nuclear base located at Torrejón. Franco's attempts to persuade the American military to withdraw nuclear weaponry from the Torrejón air base failed.

Professor R. Tamames has recognized that American aid played a significant role in reducing the rate of Spanish inflation in the first half of the 1950s and that it allowed the ending of food rationing in 1951. He feels however that American aid overemphasized the delivery of surplus foodstuffs stocked by the United States government and hardly provided Spain with badly needed capital equipment. One half of the value of such aid involved the delivery to Spain of cotton and soyabean oil (Tamames, R., 1979, 427). Nevertheless, given the serious foodstuffs and raw materials shortages existing at that time in Spain, the receipt of foodstuffs and of raw materials such as cotton, copper, scrap iron and aluminium from the United States was highly welcomed by the Spaniards. American aid facilitated the achievement of a larger Spanish production of electric power and the improvement of transportation and communications facilities; these in turn allowed an expansion in domestic manufacturing activity, a goal the Franco government had been unable to achieve in the 1940s in spite of its preferential treatment of industrial activity. American aid in the 1950s and expanding exports of agricultural products rendered the domestic economy more independent of the production rigidities of the 1940s.

Professor M.J. González, in his study titled *The Political Economy of Francoism, 1940–1970*, has pointed out that the years 1950 and 1951 constituted for Spain a watershed separating the stagnant 1940s from the period 1951 to 1956 during which the gross domestic product showed significant annual growth (González, M.J., 1979, 47). He indicated that there occurred marked discontinuities with past trends in the production of electric power and of manufacturing in 1950, in internal commerce in

1951, in banking in 1952 and in public works in 1953. Agriculture alone remained stagnant. Not only did Spanish production reveal growth in the years 1951 to 1956, but more significant, such growth was accompanied by a subsiding of the internal rate of inflation which in those years averaged an annual 4.3% (Ibid., 49).

Spain's economic performance during the 1950s was nevertheless handicapped by high-cost production and by the stagnation of the country's capacity to export. As Graph 3 shows, Spain's average propensity to export declined in the 1950s. The import-substitution policies of the government penalized exports and weakened the very sector which could have helped in a significant way to finance the process of industrialization. The country's deficient export capacity was largely due to the technological backwardness of Spanish production. Strong protection, foreign exchange controls and the high profits domestic sales brought to high-cost Spanish producers induced Spanish manufacturers to sell exclusively in the home market. The absence of foreign competition in the internal market kept production processes cost-inefficient; the smallness of this market encouraged the continued existence of small-scale firms operating on the basis of antiquated

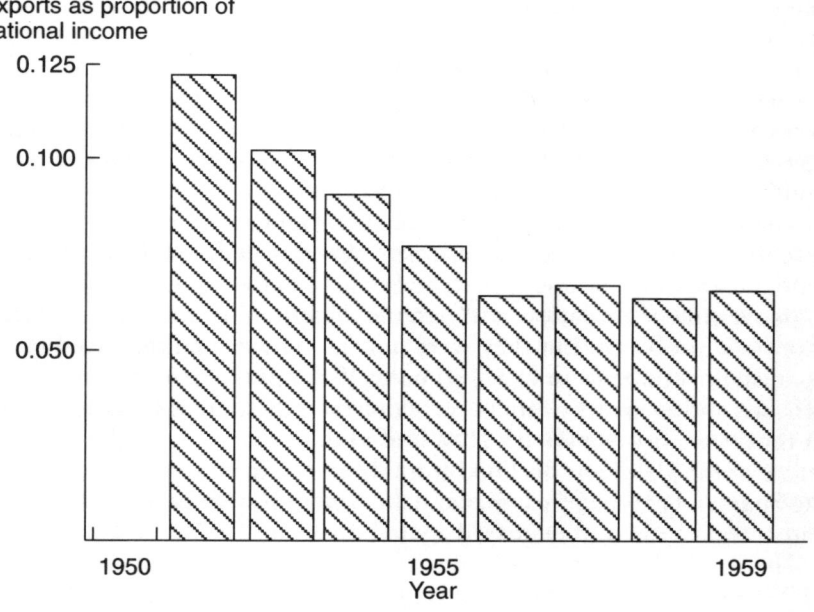

Graph 3  Relationship between Spanish exports and national income: 1950–9

Source: González, M.J., 1979, p. 85

technology. A vicious circle developed: protected Spanish firms earned large profits though they remained cost-inefficient from an international point of view; and the Spanish export sector, handicapped by high input costs, was unable to sell sufficient goods abroad to finance imports of new technology. Hence, technology in Spain remained backward and production costs continued to be high by international standards.

The failure of Spanish exports to act as a major agent of growth in the 1950s was evidenced by the fact that although the real Spanish Gross National Product increased at an annual average rate of 7.9% between 1951 and 1958, and although the dollar value of Spanish imports in this period doubled, the value and the quantity of Spanish exports stagnated. As a result there developed a foreign exchange crisis in 1957 and in 1958. J.B. Donges noticed that in those years two major Spanish exports, those of citrus fruit and olive oil, hardly increased at all at a time when the world trade volume of these products grew at an annual rate of 7.2% for citrus fruit and of 3.6% for olive oil (Ibid., 40).

The government's import-substitution policies did not alter the traditional structures in the industrial sector. As shown in Table 6, the various Spanish industries continued to be made up of small firms, the great majority of them operating on the basis of fewer than five employees. The percentage of firms with 500 employees or more in 1958 was only 2.4% in the important iron and steel sector, 0.3% in that of chemicals, textiles, paper and paper products and 0.05% in that of fabricated metal products.

In spite of the efforts of the government and of the INI to industrialize the nation, 45% of Spanish industry was still using pre-1920 equipment according to a 1958 UNESCO report. In that year, 65% of the Spanish merchant fleet was of pre-1939 construction and some of the ships were built before 1898 (Shneidman, J.L., 1973, 192).

The seriousness of the country's financial and economic problems was recognized by the Franco government when it petitioned the OEEC to send a team of economic experts to Spain to act as economic advisers to his government. Inflation and external disequilibrium were important economic problems, but they were not the only difficulties faced by the Spanish government. In 1956, students, Falangists, high-ranking church officials and even army officers revealed their discontent with the regime. In that year, prices rose by 20% and abroad the value of the peseta in terms of the US dollar declined from 43 to 50. In spite of American aid, the Spanish balance of payments deficit in 1956 was twice as large as it had been in 1955 and increased again by 10% in 1957.

The real value of wages and salaries in 1956 was probably 15% to 35% below the pre-Civil War level. Though nominal wages and salaries had increased by about six times since 1936, prices of meat had increased by ten times, those of bread by twelve times and those of potatoes by

*Table 6* Distribution of industrial plants according to persons employed: 1958

| Sector | Percentages | | | | | |
| --- | --- | --- | --- | --- | --- | --- |
| | 0–4 | 5–9 | 10–49 | 50–99 | 100–499 | 500 and more |
| Food | 87.7 | 7.2 | 4.4 | 0.4 | 0.2 | 0.04 |
| Beverages | 80.1 | 13.3 | 6.2 | 0.3 | 0.2 | 0.01 |
| Tobacco | 53.8 | 8.9 | 20.1 | 7.1 | 6.5 | 3.6 |
| Textiles | 75.3 | 7.7 | 10.4 | 2.9 | 3.4 | 0.3 |
| Clothing | 93.4 | 5.0 | 1.5 | 0.1 | 0.04 | 0.004 |
| Footwear | 95.1 | 2.5 | 2.0 | 0.2 | 0.1 | 0.002 |
| Wood and Cork products | 85.7 | 8.9 | 5.0 | 0.2 | 0.1 | 0.002 |
| Paper and Paper products | 52.4 | 14.3 | 24.7 | 3.5 | 4.8 | 0.3 |
| Leather and Leather products | 90.1 | 4.7 | 4.6 | 0.4 | 0.2 | 0.03 |
| Rubber products | 61.7 | 16.4 | 12.4 | 3.3 | 5.4 | 0.7 |
| Chemicals | 65.1 | 13.9 | 15.6 | 2.4 | 2.7 | 0.3 |
| Petroleum and Coal products | 69.8 | 9.7 | 11.1 | 4.2 | 4.2 | 1.0 |
| Non-metallic Mineral products | 71.5 | 14.7 | 12.1 | 1.0 | 0.7 | 0.03 |
| Glass and Glass products | 54.4 | 19.2 | 19.1 | 2.0 | 4.8 | 0.5 |
| Iron and Steel | 30.4 | 11.8 | 38.7 | 9.2 | 7.5 | 2.4 |
| Non-ferrous metals | 35.9 | 27.4 | 27.0 | 3.4 | 4.9 | 1.3 |
| Fabricated metals | 88.0 | 5.6 | 5.2 | 0.6 | 0.5 | 0.05 |

*Source*: Donges, J.B., 1971, p. 39

eighteen times. The Spanish per capita consumption of sugar, milk and meat in 1956 was lower than the corresponding consumption in the same year in a poor country such as Egypt (Ibid., 149). Industrial stagnation and decreed wage increases in April and October of 1956, coupled with an expansion of the currency in circulation by four million pesetas during the same year, fuelled an inflation which intensified the already serious economic inequalities of Spanish society and caused labour unrest. In April, workers in Navarra, Guipúzcoa, Vizcaya and Alava went on strike to protest price increases; in spite of many arrests, their example was followed by workers in Asturias and in Catalonia. J.L. Shneidman wrote:

> Northern Spain was rocked by a series of strikes, lock-outs and demonstrations from April 7, 1956, to the middle of May. Because of rigid censorship and because the government kept claiming, from April 14, that the strike was over, much of what transpired is unclear. The events are further beclouded by the fact that while

hundreds of people were arrested, few were brought to trial during the period of the strike. Many arrested were released immediately, only to be rearrested later; many arrested were kept in jail or detention camps without trial until late September...
Shneidman, J.L., 1973, p. 156

Concurrently, students at the University of Madrid circulated a manifesto calling for a general strike on 12 and 13 April, a call which was supported by a workers' declaration which asked for economic reforms such as a minimum hourly wage of 75 pesetas, equal pay for women for equal work, unemployment insurance and free labour unions. Students and workers united to protest existing economic conditions.

Student unrest had begun in the first days of February 1956. Students who were members of the *Falange*, the then only legal political party in Spain, and anti-*Falange* students became involved in street fights. When a young Falangist student was seriously wounded, the *Falange* published a list containing the names of one hundred Spanish intellectuals it threatened to murder should the wounded student die; among the names on the list were those of Dr Pedro Lain Entralgo, Rector of the University of Madrid, and of Gregorio Marañón, the son of the famous physician of the same name who had been a leading Spanish intellectual in the time of the Second Republic. On 10 February General Franco ordered the police to put an end to all demonstrations in Madrid; 57 persons were arrested for having been involved in the students' unrest and were charged with plotting against the state. Among them was a student named Ramón Tamames who became in later years a distinguished Spanish economic historian. Dr Pedro Lain Entralgo was dismissed from his position as Rector of the University of Madrid; a few days later, the government announced the dismissal of the 'too liberal' Minister of Education, Dr Joaquín Ruiz Giménez.

Other political and social problems in the same year distracted the interest of the government in improving the economy. Illegal political organizations, hostile to the regime, were formed in 1956. Among them were the leftist Christian-Democrat *Izquierda Demócrata Cristiana*, the monarchist and reformist *Partido Social de Acción Democrática*, and the revolutionary *Frente de Liberación Popular*, constituted by young militant communists. Church officials also attacked social and economic injustice in the country; the bishop of Málaga, Angel Herrera y Oria, denounced existing social inequities in a pastoral letter published on 2 January 1956 and condemned the 'collective unconsciousness' of the privileged classes. A Jesuit, Father José María Díaz Alegría, complained in a speech presented on 5 April that 'the Spanish worker is treated as an inferior being' (Ibid., 163).

The government was also aware of discontent in the army officer corps. General Franco had granted independence to Spanish Morocco on 7 April and many army officers were unhappy about the action taken by their supreme commander. Under the terms of the agreement concluded with Mohammed V, Spain retained only the Presidios of Melilla and Ceuta, as well as the enclave of Ifni. Morocco had had a special significance for many Spanish officers; a large number of them had started their careers or had been promoted in Spanish Africa and Franco's Moroccan policy in 1956 infuriated them. Army officers not only resented the loss of the Protectorate, they also opposed a greater assumption of power by the quasi-fascist *Falange*. On 10 February General Agustín Muñoz Grandes, Minister of the Army, informed General Franco that unless the government quietened Falangist extremists, the army would seize Madrid. In order to placate the military, the government ordered substantial increases in military salaries on 9 May. The salary of a first lieutenant was raised by 90%, that of a brigadier-general by 74% (Lieberman, S., 1982, 190).

At the same time, the government tried to turn the attention of Spaniards away from domestic economic problems. Newspapers carried long editorials cautioning them against the dangers of the ever-present 'Red peril' and lauded General Franco as the great champion of the West in the 'crusade' against international communism. When Juan Negrín, a former prime minister in the final days of the Second Republic, died on 15 November 1956 the Spanish press reminded its readers that, nearly two decades earlier, this man had transferred Spain's gold to the USSR. Great efforts were made by the government to relate the economic difficulties of 1956 to events that had occurred twenty years earlier.

Even the weather hindered the growth of the economy. During the same year, a cold spell and blizzards damaged the Spanish citrus crop to such an extent that the 1956 crop was only half that of 1955. As a result, the aggregate value of Spanish exports in 1956 was only 73% that of aggregate imports. Spain experienced major gold losses as well as losses of foreign exchange. Spaniards had reason to fear the future when on 18 December 1956 Manuel Arburúa, the Minister of Commerce, reported that the country's foreign reserves had fallen to US$ 40 million and that Spain was close to bankruptcy (Ibid., 188).

Public discontent with economic and social conditions continued in 1957 and in 1958. There were student riots in Madrid and in Seville at the start of 1957. Clerical opposition to the Franco regime continued in spite of the strong representation of *Opus Dei* in the new Cabinet formed in February of that year. The election of Pope John XXIII on 28 October 1958 encouraged a number of Spanish Archbishops and Bishops to join Bishop Angel Herrera in his demands for social reform.

In order to reduce the external deficit, the government decided to devalue the peseta so as to restrict imports and boost exports. On 9 April

1957 the peseta was devalued in terms of the US dollar, the official rate of exchange becoming 42 pesetas to the dollar. At that time, the black market exchange rate was 62 pesetas to the dollar; the government soon recognized that it had not devalued its currency sufficiently when it allowed a special exchange rate of 52 pesetas to the dollar for tourists and of 55 for American servicemen stationed in Spain. The devaluation was facilitated by the formation of Franco's fifth Cabinet on 25 February 1957.

General Franco, perhaps realizing that Spain's political and economic difficulties had to be faced by new, better trained men, replaced twelve of the eighteen ministers in his previous Cabinet. The key new figures were members of *Opus Dei*, a secret organization of prominent and successful Roman Catholics. At Cabinet level, *Opus Dei* was strongly represented by Alberto Ullastres, the new Minister of Commerce, and by Mariano Navarro Rubio, the new Minister of the Interior. Laureano López Rodó, head of the influential Office for Economic Coordination and Programming, and the general directors in the Ministries of Information and Tourism, Public Works and Education were also members of the organization.

Falangist representation in the Cabinet appeared to be weakened by the exit of José Antonio Girón as Minister of Labour and by the installation of the hard-line Falangist José Luis de Arrese as Minister of Housing, a position that was bound to weaken the political voice of the new appointee. The Catholics also lost weight in the new government, their only representative being Fernando María Castiella, the new Minister for Foreign Affairs. The new Cabinet finally included seven military officers with Admiral Luis Carrero Blanco still occupying the position of Sub-Secretary of the Presidency. It was clear that General Franco had entrusted to the men of *Opus Dei* the task of stabilizing and opening the Spanish economy. This Cabinet remained in power until 10 July 1962 when Franco changed the heads of a number of ministries and formed his sixth government, often referred to as the 'government of the first Development Plan'.

Five thousand Asturian miners went on strike in March 1958 to protest against their deteriorating purchasing power. The government broke up the strike by threatening to draft the striking miners into the army. There were strikes during the same month in San Sebastián and in Barcelona. Basque workers in Guipúzcoa stopped working on 1 April. The government responded by arresting 'communist agitators'; among those arrested was a young philosophy student, Miguel Nuñez González, who denied the government charges that he was a member of the Communist Party and that he had helped organize strike activity; he was nevertheless sentenced to fifteen years in jail. In order to discourage strikes, the government passed a new law on 22 March; it stipulated that in the case where strike leaders could not be identified by the police, 'the most outstanding members of the accused, or where all seemed equal, the oldest of them would be held responsible' (Gallo, M., 1974, 253). The law in effect allowed the authorities to seize hostages from among the striking workers and to punish them for the development of the strike. The government also instituted courts martial to prosecute people engaging in 'extremist activity', and participating in a strike was included in this. The government justified its action by claiming that it had the duty to protect Spain and Christianity against a sinister international communist conspiracy bent on destroying Spanish civilization. In the words of Max Gallo, 'A Spaniard's freedom hung constantly by a slender thread which the police, like Fate, could cut at will or leave dangling until the next arbitrary interruption' (Ibid., 255).

Inflation and the balance of payments deficit continued to plague the Spanish economy in the late 1950s. Taking 1940 as a price index base of 100, the index stood at 521.3 at the start of 1957, at 608.4 at the end of that year and at 668.2 at the end of 1958. An important cause of inflation was the liberal use of the printing press by the government to pay for its internal indebtedness. Inflation promoted capital flight. Wealthy Spaniards illegally converted domestic currency into foreign money which was deposited in Swiss banks. Inflation continued to erode the purchasing power of the masses of wage earners; this purchasing power was lower at the end of 1958 than it had been before the decreed 20% wage increase in 1956. Though industrial production expanded in 1957 and in 1958, industrial productivity remained low by international standards. Table 7 shows industrial productivity per inhabitant in a number of European countries in 1960.

Table 7 shows the gross value added per inhabitant in the various countries in 1960 for some basic industrial outputs such as electricity, steel and cement. In the cases of both these selected industrial outputs and aggregate industrial production, Spain appears at the bottom of the list. Writers have explained the country's low industrial productivity in terms of Spain's technological backwardness at the beginning of the century, the devastating effects the Civil War had on the economy, of Spain's political and economic isolation during the early post-World War II years and its exclusion from the Marshall Plan. Equally important reasons were the exaggerated pursuit of economic autarky by the Spanish government and the inefficient *dirigiste* policies of the authorities. In the 1950s, most industrial activity in Spain was carried out by small firms producing foodstuffs, beverages, textiles, clothing, shoes and other leather products whose productivity per worker remained comparatively low because of the continued use of antiquated equipment. Most of Spain's industrial sector continued to be tied to traditional methods of production.

Table 7  Industrial productivity in some European countries: 1960

|  | Gross value added by the industrial sector (US$ per inhabitant in 1960) | | Production per inhabitant 1960 | | |
|---|---|---|---|---|---|
|  | Sector total: Construction included | Construction excluded | Electricity (k/Wh) | Steel (kg) | Cement (kg) |
| German FR | 742 | 646 | 2,187 | 641 | 468 |
| Sweden | 725 | 581 | 4,652 | 425 | 375 |
| France | 648 | 544 | 1,584 | 379 | 315 |
| UK | 582 | 509 | 2,608 | 470 | 257 |
| Belgium | 454 | 387 | 1,656 | 785 | 479 |
| Norway | 432 | 350 | 868 | 137 | 321 |
| Austria | 401 | 334 | 2,255 | 447 | 400 |
| Netherlands | 381 | 320 | 1,438 | 169 | 157 |
| Italy | 239 | 192 | 1,138 | 167 | 324 |
| Spain | 111 | 98 | 609 | 63 | 171 |

Source: Velarde Fuertes, J. et al., 1973, p. 484

The industrial sector performed poorly in 1959. While economic activity was booming in the EC countries, Spain's industrial output was virtually the same as it had been in 1958. Taking 1958 as the base year of an industrial production index, the index stood at 100.1 in 1959. The economy faced serious problems: inflation continued uncontrolled; the balance-of-payments deficit threatened to bankrupt Spain before the end of the year; and no economic development plan guided the economic policies of the government. The annual report of the Banco de España reported that although the private sector of the economy showed a profit of 20.1 billion pesetas in 1959, the public sector registered in that year a deficit of 14 billion pesetas. In the spring of 1959, the economy approached catastrophe. As of 1 January 1959 the country's reserves amounted to only $ 57 million in gold and $ 4 million in convertible currency. The country could face bankruptcy by mid-year. On 14 May the OEEC issued a preliminary report on the Spanish economy in which it criticized among other things the artificially high exchange value of the peseta which contributed both to the external disequilibrium of the country and to its inflation.

The three *Opus Dei* Cabinet members, Alberto Ullastres Calvo, Mariano Navarro Rubio and Pedro Gual Villalví started advocating drastic economic reforms. They eventually proposed an economic 'stabilization plan' to General Franco who is reported to have acquiesced to the new programme by telling them, 'Do as you please!' (Shneidman, J.L., 1973, 215). The Economic Stabilization Plan of 1959 was then described in a twenty-two-page memorandum to the European Organization for Economic Cooperation, issued by the Spanish government on 30 June 1959. It announced the end of the unproductive period of autarky.

## THE NATIONAL STABILIZATION PLAN OF 1959

On 30 June 1959 the Spanish government presented to the International Monetary Fund and the OEEC a Memorandum in which it proposed that, in exchange for enumerated economic reforms the Franco government was willing to adopt, Spain should have the right to obtain financial assistance from the two organizations. Explaining Spain's economic problems, the authors of the document set aside in its preamble the much used Francoist propaganda which claimed that Spain's economic difficulties were largely due to 'evil foreign conspiracies'. In lieu of attributing the country's economic hardships to boycotts by third countries or to an attempt by an 'international Jewish plot' to sabotage 'Christian Spain', the writers of the Memorandum briefly noted that the economy suffered from 'the heavy burden of reconstruction' and from the impact of 'factors of a structural character, inadequate resources and low levels of income and savings' (M.J. González, 1979, 199). Spanish inflation was explained in terms of pressures generated by public investment and was presented as the main reason for the government's use of multiple exchange rates. The authors acknowledged that their government intended to abandon its earlier commitment to a policy of economic autarky. 'The Spanish government feels that the time has arrived to formulate economic policy so as to direct the Spanish economy in conformity with the policies of the nations of the western world and to liberate it from public interventions, inherited from the past, which no longer support the needs of the present situation' (Ibid., 200).

The Memorandum itself was divided into four parts. The first dealt with the public sector, the second with monetary policy, while the remaining parts addressed themselves to greater flexibility in the economy and to its opening to the outside world. In its first section, the Memorandum contemplated the imposition of a ceiling on aggregate public spending in order to reduce the country's high rate of inflation. Aggregate public spending was not to exceed 80 billion pesetas per year. It was proposed that the government would reduce the spending of the INI and would integrate the investments of that organization into a general development plan. The country's fiscal system was to be improved in order to allow the government to receive increased revenues; certain taxes were to be raised, the document referring to an excise tax on sales of gasoline, to import duties and to 'other', non-specified taxes.

The government's past ability to borrow at will from the Bank of Spain was to be sharply curtailed.

Proposed monetary policy changes stressed the implementation of a number of measures designed to limit the government's power to finance the public sector. The government indicated its willingness to stop selling securities which were immediately redeemable at the Bank of Spain. The rate of annual growth of bank credits to the private sector had to be reduced and it was proposed that it would be reduced from 16% in 1958 to about 7%. Finally, in order to restrict Spanish imports, importers would be required to deposit with the Bank of Spain prior to actual importating 25% of the value of the imported goods.

In the third section, the document indicated that the government would authorize salary increases only when the latter were justified by increases in productivity. The document further assured its readers that 'There will also be a tendency to eliminate the rigidities imposed by labour legislation, as well as those originating in restrictions of competition' (Ibid., 203). The last part of the Memorandum dealt with proposed changes in Spain's external trade and financial policies. These covered the country's foreign exchange system, the liberalization of Spain's commercial policy, the softening of restrictions on foreign investment in Spain and those affecting the repatriation of capital held abroad by Spaniards.

After condemning the existing system of foreign exchange controls and announcing its abrogation, the document stated that 'a parity of the peseta will be established in conformity with the rules of the International Monetary Fund' (Ibid.). A new commercial policy was to liberalize Spain's foreign trade. The new policy would however apply only to those nations which would allow the convertibility of Spain's net earnings originating in commercial exchange with them. Nations disallowing such convertibility would have to trade with Spain under the existing regime of bilateral exchange. Furthermore, the liberalization of Spanish imports was to be initially limited to foodstuffs, raw materials which were not part of state trading, replacement parts and a limited number of capital goods. All other Spanish imports were to remain subject to the prior release of government-issued import permits. Finally, the document briefly specified that existing restrictions on the participation of foreign capital in Spanish firms would be eased and that impediments to the repatriation of capital held abroad by Spaniards would be eliminated (Ibid., 205).

At the end of the Memorandum its authors reaffirmed the government's commitment to a programme of economic reform and promised that it would take further measures in that direction in 1960. They also indicated that Spain needed financial aid from international organizations and from foreign governments to be able to implement the reform programme. The latter acquired the force of law through the Decree/Law 10/1959 of 21 July 1959. The Decree fixed the value of the peseta in terms of gold and established its convertibility. The gold parity of the peseta was defined as 0.0148112 grams of fine gold. Such parity amounted to a devaluation of the peseta in terms of the US dollar from 42 to 60 pesetas per dollar. Furthermore, by adopting a gold-exchange standard, the Spanish government in effect announced its intention to join the International Monetary Fund.

The proposals of the Memorandum of June 1959 and the reform measures specified by the Decree/Law enacted one month later to give the force of law to the June proposals clearly showed that the Spanish authorities were not eager to transform Spain's economy into a relatively free market system. Although a condition of Spain's entry into the OEEC was a commitment on the part of the Spanish government to liberalize 50% of the country's imports, the Decree/Law 10/1959 maintained a regime of individual import licences on non-liberalized Spanish imports and placed a ceiling on their allowed aggregate value. The law maintained a discriminatory treatment of a good part of the country's private foreign trade. Furthermore, the possible consequences of import liberalization were immediately neutralized by the provisions of a Decree of 24 July 1959 which burdened a large number of Spanish imports with higher import duties. Another Decree of 27 July mandated Spanish importers to deposit in the Bank of Spain prior to any import an amount equivalent to 25% of the value of the goods covered by such import. This additional burden on imports was abolished one year later.

The acquisition and use of foreign exchange by Spaniards and by Spanish firms was still closely controlled by the government. A major change contained in the Decree/Law 10/1959 allowed foreign capital to participate without prior official permission in the capitalization of a Spanish firm as long as it did not exceed 50% of the total capital and as long as other laws did not prohibit such foreign investment. Previous authorization by the Council of Ministers was required in the case when foreign interests were to contribute more than 50% of the capital of a Spanish firm. The Law imposed greater restrictions on foreign contributions to the capital of a Spanish firm in a number of commercial and industrial sectors; foreign investment was limited in mining, banking, shipbuilding, real estate investment, hydrocarbons and cinema. The treatment of foreign investment was also to differ depending upon whether the Spanish recipient enterprise was classified as a 'firm of preferential economic and social interest' or was not designated as such (Ibid., 219). Foreign interests investing in the first group of firms were given the right to repatriate their profits, as generated by the particular firm, in terms of foreign exchange, and were also able to repatriate their investment in the firm's capital within two years, such repatriation of capital having to occur within a time span of two years. Foreign investors in the latter group of Spanish firms were allowed to repatriate their profits up to a maximum representing 6% of their investment in the firm's capital; they were also allowed to repatriate their investment in the firm's capital but were not allowed to complete such repatriation in less than four years. The Law allowed 'foreign investment' to take various forms such as technical assistance, grants of patents or licences, transfers of capital equipment, as well as investments in the form of foreign exchange or of convertible pesetas.

In spite of its various restrictions on foreign investment in Spain, the new legislation allowed in effect the taking of control of large Spanish concerns by foreign interests. Even though the participation of foreign capital in a given Spanish firm was on a minority basis, agreements between that firm and foreign enterprises regarding technical and commercial assistance by the latter allowed foreign investors in the firm to obtain effective control over the latter. Though the principal aim of the Spanish legislation of 1959 was to attract foreign capital and technology to Spain, it also facilitated during later decades the acquisition of foreign dominance in Spain's expanding industrial sector. Foreign control of Spanish industry was further eased by provisions in the Decree/Law 10/1959 which allowed foreign concerns to establish their own branches in Spain.

The opening of the Spanish market to foreign investment and to foreign competition in 1959 filled Spanish entrepreneurs with such misgivings about their future that they suspended their own investment projects, a development which strongly contributed to the development of recession in the country during the second half of 1959 and during the entirety of 1960. A stronger reason for the sharp drop in private investment in 1959 was the government's decision to curtail credits to the private sector of the economy; worsening entrepreneurial expectations led to a decline in the rate of gross capital formation during the second half of 1959. As firms stopped using workers on an overtime basis, consumption demand weakened. The fall in private consumption demand continued throughout 1960 and sharply reduced sales of durable consumer goods. Public consumption spending fell with private consumer demand in 1960 and intensified the recession.

The recession came to an end at the start of 1961 when entrepreneurial expectations improved in response to the enactment of the protectionist tariff of 1960. The rate of economic growth was also strengthened by a surge in liberalized imports of capital equipment needed to renovate the industrial sector; the growth in such imports was facilitated by a more realistic exchange rate, by international aid, by earnings from expanding tourism and by remittances from Spaniards working abroad. The 1950s thus ended in Spain with an economic crisis which affected mostly the service industries such as banking, commerce, transport and sales of real estate. Manufacturing and energy industries also experienced a temporary decline. The production of electric power fell between April and October 1959 but expanded again at the start of 1960. Steel output experienced a drastic fall as of May 1959 and bottomed in November but recovered its initial level at the end of 1960. The production of cement started declining in October 1959, reached a low point in January 1960 then slowly began recovery in February. The structurally inefficient textile industry experienced serious difficulties during the second half of 1959 and started recovering slowly only in May 1960.

The Stabilization Plan had an immediate adverse effect on the real income of industrial workers; their income declined by about 23% in 1959. During the second half of the latter year, industrial workers' real income fell mostly because of a shortening of their working week. The growing 'unemployment' at that time was basically a growth in partial unemployment. Firms reacted to the publication of the Stabilization Plan by reducing the weekly work hours of their uncharged labour force. They produced less on the basis of the same number of workers. 1960 brought an increase in the number of job losses. According to the Spanish authorities, 58% of the country's unemployment in that year was explained by job losses. An important reason for such development was the initiation in that year of a programme of government subsidies to firms to help the latter modernize their production techniques. Most of the firms favoured the adoption of labour-saving methods of production and started laying off workers; this trend continued in 1961 when 76% of the unemployed were persons whose job had been terminated by their former employer.

## REFERENCES

Carr, R. and Fusi, J.P., *Spain: Dictatorship to Democracy*, London, George Allen & Unwin, 1979.

Carreras, A., 'La producción industrial española, 1842–1981: construcción de un índice anual', *Revista de Historia Económica*, Nr. 1, 1984, pp. 127–57.

Donges, J.B., *La Industrialización de España*, Barcelona, Oikos-Tau Ediciones, 1976.

Fontana, J. and Nadal, J., 'Spain, 1914–1970', in Cipolla, C.M., ed., *The Fontana Economic History of Europe, Contemporary Economies*, Glasgow, Collins/Fontana Books, 1976, pp. 460–529.

Gallo, M., *Spain under Franco, A History*, New York, E.P. Dutton & Co., 1974.

García Delgado, J.L., 'Estancamiento Industrial e Intervencionismo Económico Durante el Primer Franquismo', in Fontana, J., ed., *España Bajo el Franquismo*, Barcelona, Editorial Crítica, 1986, pp. 170–91.

González, M.J., *La Economía Política del Franquismo, 1940–1970*, Madrid, Editorial Tecnos, 1979.

Lieberman, S., *The Contemporary Spanish Economy, A Historical Perspective*, London, George Allen & Unwin, 1982.

Payne, S.G., *The Franco Regime, 1936–1975*, Madison, Wisconsin, The University of Wisconsin Press, 1987.

Prados de la Escosura, L., 'El Crecimiento Económico Moderno en España, 1830–1973: Una Comparación Internacional', *Papeles de Economía Española*, Nr. 20, 1984.

Schwartz, P. and González, M.J., *Una Historia del Instituto Nacional de Industria, 1941–1976*, Madrid, Editorial Tecnos, 1978.

Shneidman, J.L., ed., *Spain and Franco, 1949–1959*, New York, Facts on File, 1973.

Tamames, R., *Historia de España, La República, La Era de Franco*, Madrid, Alianza Universidad, Alfaguara, 1979.

Velarde Fuertes, J. et al., *La España de los Años Setenta*, Madrid, Editorial Moneda y Crédito, 1973.

# 2

# STIMULANTS AND IMPEDIMENTS IN THE ECONOMIC BOOM OF THE 1960s

J. Fontana and J. Nadal clearly summarized the characteristics of Spain's politico-economic developments in the decade of the 1960s.

> The change of policy which began in 1957 and was consolidated from 1959 onwards took place within the framework of a new, large-scale and long-lasting expansion of international capitalism, caused by the economic integration of large areas (The Treaty of Rome, 1957, creating the Common Market), the convertibility of currencies with the consequent ending of the European Payments Union (at the end of 1958), and the progressive liberalisation of all forms of interchange between countries. In order to survive, the Franco regime had to bring itself to write off twenty years of aggressive nationalism, acute protectionism and arbitrary interventionism; on the other hand, for obvious reasons, it felt unable to abandon the system of a strong executive, of a public order maintained by strong-arm methods, of a reactionary fiscal policy and of a tough wage control. Undoubtedly, the new era was one of a novel economic line within the old political framework. No analysis of the period of growth in the sixties can ignore the contradictions and the limitations inherent in such a situation.
> 
> This blueprint for economic growth which emerged with 'Stabilisation' worked successfully until the energy crisis of 1973. In this success the contributions from Europe, and to a lesser extent, that from the United States, were decisive. For fifteen years, Spain's connection with the most prosperous Western countries opened up the channels through which flowed Spain's surplus manpower in one direction and in the other the surplus capital, plus the tourists, of the rich countries. In financial terms, the inflow and outflow were converted into a single flow of currency in Spain's direction.

This money was the lubricant which allowed industry and the services to take off, and brought about at last a crisis of traditional agriculture.

Fontana, J. and Nadal, J., 1976, pp. 517–18

As noted, the reform measures taken by the Spanish government in 1959 were followed immediately by a stagnation of demand and of production. Economic recovery in 1960 was very weak and it was only in the last months of 1961 that economic activity started a true expansion. It was thus only at the end of 1961 that a new process of economic growth brought significant transformations both to Spain's economy and to her society. Professor Enrique Fuentes Quintana pointed to seven developments as constituting the principal explanatory variables of Spain's surge of economic activity which began in the last months of 1961 (Fuentes Quintana, E., 1988, 12–14). The Spanish economist placed great weight on the 'demonstration effect' booming Western European economies had on Spanish minds; Spaniards in the 1960s became determined to have their own 'economic miracle', to improve their standard of living forthwith by seeking new economic opportunities either in the country's large cities or in other European nations. Ironically, economic advance at that time in Spain was facilitated by the country's enormous technological backwardness. In 1961 Spain fitted too well Alexander Gerschenkron's model of relative economic backwardness in Western Europe. Gerschenkron could have had Spain in mind when he wrote,

> Industrialization always seemed the more promising the greater the backlog of technological innovations which the backward country could take over from the more advanced country. Borrowed technology, so much and so rightly stressed by Veblen, was one of the primary factors assuring a high speed of development in a backward country ... the contingency of large imports of foreign machinery and of foreign know-how ... increasingly widened the gulf between economic potentialities and economic actualities in backward countries.

Gerschenkron, A., 1965, p. 8

A reduction of the differential between the state of development attained by a number of Western European economies and by Spain was an important goal Spaniards wanted to bring about, a general aspiration of the Spanish people which generated Gerschenkron-like 'tensions' propitious to economic growth.

The principal vehicle of economic growth in the 1960s was Spain's liberalization of her imports as provided by the Stabilization Plan of 1959. As of 1961, massive imports of foreign capital goods facilitated a significant increase of Spain's output and national income; higher real incomes were in turn translated into a rapid expansion of the various components of the country's aggregate demand. Not only did private and public consumption increase during the decade, but more significantly, private investment spending expanded, fuelled by the eagerness of the country's entrepreneurs to modernize their methods of production and to innovate. The spectacular increase in the aggregate demand for Spanish products and for Spanish services included the foreign demand for such goods and services. Spain's performance as an exporter of services remained superior to her role as an exporter of goods. Spain's sales of services to foreign tourists and the remittances to the home country by Spaniards working abroad played a vital role in permitting Spain to finance a growing balance of visible trade deficit.

Spain's 'industrial take-off' in the 1960s was finally also eased by the country's large reserves of agricultural surplus labour. The country's traditional agriculture had been based until then upon the continuing existence of abundant agricultural labour, on an inelastic demand for foodstuffs centring on cereals and on relatively high prices established by government, as well as on strongly protectionist measures. Industrialization and emigration to other countries sounded the death knell of traditional agriculture in Spain. We should notice, however, that as late as 1964, Spain's active agrarian population still represented 35.7% of the country's total active population. This figure declined to 16.3% twenty years later. Spain's large reserves of low productivity agricultural labour at the start of the 1960s, and the migration to the country's industrial centres or to industrial employment outside the country appear to be a marked example of the model of industrial development presented by W. Arthur Lewis in his classical article of 1954 (Lewis, W.A., 1954, 139–91). Enrique Fuentes Quintana noticed that the process of industrialization was further helped in Spain by the slow and gradual incorporation of a female labour force into the aggregate labour force of the country; he estimated that in the course of the 1960s, female employment in Spain increased by about one million (Ibid., 14).

An interesting question raised by Professor Everett E. Hagen is whether a significant increase in aggregate demand in a low-income country, or a steadily rising demand, can be the initiating force launching a process of accelerated growth. More specifically, the question deals with the relationship between an increase in aggregate demand in the relatively poor country and the adoption in that country of productivity-increasing production and distribution techniques which will facilitate the development of industrial activity in that country and which will raise its real national income (Hagen, E.E., 1975, 176–80). This question is very relevant to the study of Spain's economy in the 1960s because, as noted above, the beginning of modern Spanish industrialization during that decade coincided in time with a steady expansion of aggregate domestic demand and with a noticeable increase of foreign demand for Spain's exports, particularly exports of tourism-related services. As observed earlier, the growth of Spanish domestic demand at that time was made possible by rapidly rising consumption spending and private investment based on dissaving, expanding bank credit to the private sector as well as on the effects of rising foreign investment in Spain.

Professor Hagen observed after a careful review of the literature that the role of increasing foreign demand in the growth process of a low-income country appears to be uncertain. Professor Douglas North explained economic growth in the United States between 1790 and 1860 in terms of the expansion of American exports in that period (North, D.C., 1961). North's conclusion was supported by Ragnar Nurkse who asserted in the same year that expanding exports were the 'engine of growth' for Argentina, Australia, Canada, New Zealand, South Africa and for the United States (Nurkse, R., 1961). And yet, a study by Irving Kravis showed that in other cases a growing foreign demand for the developing country's exports had little effect on the latter's growth process. Kravis's article concluded that in the nineteenth century, exports to the industrial 'center' countries by the newly-developing countries of the 'periphery' failed to activate any 'engine of growth' in the latter countries (Kravis, I.B., 1970, 850–72).

Equally important is the question whether improved production technology and resulting increases in output in the low-income country can generate a process of accelerated economic growth. The use of improved technology means that a given output can be produced with fewer inputs, or, meaning the same thing, that a larger output or a qualitatively better output can be produced with an unchanged amount of inputs. Professor Hagen observes that improved methods of production are usually based on labour saving and more capital-intensive technology. The new methods of production are adopted by innovators because the consequent increase in capital cost is less than the resulting decrease in labour cost. This writer noticed that the adoption of more advanced, capital-intensive technology does not necessarily bring about increases in per capita and in aggregate incomes (Hagen, E.E., supra, 181).

Spain's import liberalization of 1959 and increased foreign investment in that country during the 1960s allowed Spain to increase her imports of capital goods and of advanced foreign technology in that decade. Were such imports at the base of the Spanish economic miracle of the 1960s? As noticed, the use of improved techniques of production allow the manufacture of goods with fewer inputs per unit of output than before the adoption of such techniques. If the innovator sells the more efficiently produced goods at the same price they commanded when they were less efficiently produced, he (or she) will be able to keep the entire reduction in cost per unit of output in the form of a larger profit margin. If he sells the more efficiently produced good at a reduced price in order to expand his sales, he will still benefit from a larger profit margin. Consumers of the more efficiently produced good will be 'buying less inputs' than before the adoption of the improved technique of production, most of the latter being probably labour inputs. The innovator will lay off workers if he sells at an unchanged price; competitors in the industry will lay off workers if the innovator sells at a reduced price. For the economy as a whole, the new techniques of production will bring about net disemployment.

The reduced spending of workers laid off will trigger a Keynesian downward multiplier effect unless the innovator increases his spending by at least as much as an amount equivalent to the decrease in spending by laid off workers. Even though the innovator increases his spending by such an amount, such increase will not assure the re-employment of laid off workers, but will simply prevent the further growth of unemployment which could have been generated by the downward multiplier effect. This 'technological unemployment' may in turn cause a fall in Gross National Product.

On the other hand, the adoption of new capital-intensive technology usually requires the building of new plant and equipment. Such building will bring about a temporary increase in employment, an increase which will end once the construction of these capital goods is completed. If the economy experiences a Schumpeterian 'cluster' of innovations, it will benefit from a continuing flow of capital formation financed either by past savings or by bank credit. This flow, as well as the multiplier effect it produces, will boost employment in the economy. If the flow of capital formation expands over time, income and employment creation will also increase. Rising incomes will be translated into increased consumer spending; such increased spending, together with the growing demand for capital formation will encourage domestic producers other than innovators to increase in turn their productive capacity. An accelerator effect enters into play and the resulting multiplier effects will further boost employment and incomes.

Professor Hagen relies on United Nations data to show that both disemployment and re-employment occurred in the less developed countries between 1955 and 1970. In such countries, manufacturing output rose at an annual rate of 7% while employment in manufacturing increased at an annual 4% rate (Ibid., 183). The fact that output increased faster than employment indicates that disemployment took place while a positive rate of employment growth shows that employment-inducing effects overcompensated disemployment effects. The important point, as mentioned by the writer, is that there is no economic law that will assure that output growth based on the use of improved technology will bring about a re-employment of all the disemployed. Continuing unemployment may accompany economic growth.

Professor Luigi L. Pasinetti has presented an interesting model of the structural dynamics of output, prices and employment in any type of economy. The principal key explanatory variables in this model are population and productivity changes, as well as changes in the structure of demand for the goods and services produced in that economy (Pasinetti, L. and Lloyd, P., eds, 1987, 7–12). Pasinetti distinguishes three main sources of economic change: changes in population and in the ratio of active to total population; changes in the application of scientific knowledge to production methods; and changes in the growth of demand for the various goods and services produced in the economy.

The second type of change refers to changes in quantities of output per unit of 'factors' employed, the latter being considered to be proportional to the factor 'labour' used. Technological change will differ from one production sector in the economy to another. The rate of annual productivity increase in sector i is denoted as $p_i$. The rate will be $p_1$ for sector 1, $p_2$ for sector 2 ..., $p_n$ for sector n. The model assumes that each sector produces a single good or service, i.e., sector 1 produces good or service 1. The writer also assumes that technological progress translates into a continuous growth of average real per capita incomes, meaning a continuous growth in the demand for the various goods and services. He points out that for each productive sector there is a relation which links the rate of growth of sectoral demand, the capital/output ratio in that sector and the direction of employment growth in that sector.

For each sector i, (i = 1, 2, ..., n), physical output will grow at a percentage rate $(g + r_i)$ per year, where $g$ is the annual percentage rate of population growth and $r_i$ is the annual per capita percentage rate of growth of demand for the ith good or service. All $r$'s are different from each other. This relation between the annual rate of growth of output and the annual rate of population and demand growths in each production sector establishes the structural dynamics of production.

For each sector, the annual percentage rate of growth of productivity, i.e. $p_i$, translates into a decrease in the per unit cost of sectoral output which will tend to bring about an equivalent decrease in the equilibrium price of output, or, if the latter remains unchanged, increased rewards to the factors of production. In the latter case, wages and salaries will increase at differing rates in the various sectors. This relation between productivity growth and changes in wages, salaries and prices defines a structural dynamics of prices.

Over time, the various sectors in the economy experience their own production and price dynamics. Such structural dynamics produce for each sector a structural dynamics for the demand of factors of production, particularly for labour. If in sector i labour productivity grows at a percentage rate $p_i$ and at the same time demand for good i grows at the percentage rate $r_i$, only in the unlikely event where $p_i = r_i$ will the sectoral demand for labour remain unchanged.

If $r_i > p_i$, the demand for labour in sector i will increase. If $r_i < p_i$, the demand for labour in sector i will decline. These relations define a structural dynamics of employment. Given these observations, how should the structural dynamics of production, prices and employment of Spain in the 1960s be interpreted?

## THE BEGINNING OF ECONOMIC RECOVERY AT THE END OF 1961

The economic reform measures mandated by the Stabilization Plan of 1959 produced demand and output stagnation in 1960; it was only during the last months of 1961 that appreciable economic expansion began. A major reason for the country's poor economic performance in 1960 and during most of 1961 was the Franco government's reluctance to embrace a true market economy. Although many Spanish imports were liberalized following the enactment of the Stabilization Plan, the government continued to practise a strong *dirigiste* policy which was not consistent with its 1959 commitment to give Spain a market-oriented, open economy.

Internal demand strengthened in the autumn of 1961 and became the principal mover of economic growth. External demand for most Spanish goods stagnated however in that year and Spanish exports failed to act as an 'engine of growth'. Aggregate internal demand became the principal force initiating economic recovery at the end of the year because of a number of developments. The rise of domestic demand was largely based on an expansion of bank credit to the private sector and this credit allowed Spanish firms to increase their fixed investment and to expand their imports of raw materials and capital goods. It also allowed these firms to rebuild their stocks whose level had sharply declined since the summer of 1959. A second factor in the process of economic recovery was an increase in private consumption expenditure made possible by partial wage increases allowed by the authorities and by a longer work week in some industrial sectors. Domestic demand was further boosted by rising remittances sent to their families in the country by Spanish workers residing abroad. The public sector did not play a significant role in the expansion of internal demand in 1961.

While in a few industries the level of output attained in 1961 remained lower than that of 1958, other industries registered significant production gains. Compared to the production index in 1958, steel output in 1961 showed a gain of 21%. The corresponding index for the production of electric power registered an increase of 30.4%. Gains in industrial productivity in a number of sectors were very strong, a probable result of the effects of increased imports of improved capital equipment (OECD, 1962, 8). It appears that for Spain's secondary sector as a whole, and in terms of Pasinetti's above-mentioned notation, $p_i \geqslant r_i$ in 1961.

Official Spanish sources reporting the numbers of registered unemployed in 1960 and in 1961 calculate the latter as 114,000 and 125,000 (Ibid.). To these numbers should be added those of Spanish workers who left the country in search of jobs abroad. Regardless of their doubtful accuracy, the official estimates of the trend in Spanish unemployment from 1960 to 1961 appear to support Pasinetti's prediction.

Table 8 below shows industrial production indices in 1960 and 1961. Table 9 shows industrial employment indices, as well as the numbers of registered unemployed in Spain in those years. Table 8 shows that industries such as minerals-mining, basic metals, machinery and appliances, transport equipment, cement and electricity recorded significant expansion in 1961. Even an old industry such as textile production registered a production gain of 9%.

The strengthening of internal aggregate demand in 1961 was also favoured by the continuation of a balance-of-payments surplus.

*Table 8* Indices of industrial production: 1960 and 1961 (1958 = 100)

| Sector | 1960 | 1961 |
|---|---|---|
| Food | 116.2 | 117.5 |
| Drink | 103.0 | 121.2 |
| Tobacco | 102.9 | 107.3 |
| Wood and cork | 86.0 | 101.5 |
| Pulp and paper | 107.8 | 114.0 |
| Leather and footwear | 101.0 | 104.5 |
| Textiles | 99.1 | 108.2 |
| Coal-mining | 91.0 | 93.1 |
| Minerals-mining | 99.2 | 119.9 |
| Basic metals | 113.4 | 127.6 |
| Machinery and appliances | 75.9 | 91.0 |
| Transport equipment | 128.9 | 164.7 |
| Chemical products | 118.0 | 123.3 |
| Coal and Petroleum products | 107.9 | 109.1 |
| Cement | 108.3 | 123.1 |
| Electricity | 117.7 | 130.4 |

*Source*: OECD, *Economic Surveys, Spain*, Paris, 1962, p. 7

Table 9 Indices of industrial employment and numbers of registered unemployed: 1960 and 1961 (1958 = 100)

| Sector | Employment index | | Numbers of unemployed (in thousands) | |
|---|---|---|---|---|
| | 1960 | 1961 | 1960 | 1961 |
| Agriculture and fishing | – | – | 35.0 | 42.6 |
| Construction | – | – | 28.8 | 30.3 |
| Industry and services | – | – | 50.6 | 51.7 |
| Food processing | 98 | 94 | – | – |
| Textiles | 94 | 92 | – | – |
| Leather and footwear | 92 | 91 | – | – |
| Pulp and paper | 89 | 89 | – | – |
| Coal-mining | 91 | 89 | – | – |
| Basic metals | 112 | 112 | – | – |
| Machinery and appliances | 84 | 83 | – | – |
| Chemicals | 103 | 103 | – | – |
| Cement | 88 | 85 | – | – |

Source: OECD, *Economic Surveys, Spain*, Paris, 1962, p. 9

Although Spain's balance of trade deteriorated by about US$ 331 million in 1961, increases in Spanish invisible earnings and in private long-term capital inflows in that year more than offset the country's trade deficit and Spain was able to record an overall external surplus of about US$ 370 million in 1961.

The dramatic increase in the country's 1961 balance of trade deficit was due to the value of total imports increasing from US$ 721 million in 1960 to US$ 1.09 billion in 1961, while the value of total Spanish exports declined from US$ 726 million in 1960 to US$ 710 million in 1961 (OECD, 1962, 18). The sharp increase in Spanish imports in 1961 was partially financed by a new inflow of private capital which expanded from US$ 106 million in 1960 to US$ 191 million in 1961, as well as by a significant increase in credits extended to the private sector by Spanish commercial banks. These credits increased by 24% between 1960 and 1961. The rapid rise of bank credit to the private sector is shown by Graph 4.

One additional factor which contributed positively to Spain's economic recovery at the end of 1961 was the relative labour peace which prevailed in that year. Isolated strikes were easily dealt with by the government. The outcome of these conflicts was invariably uniform: some workers were arrested; local authorities were often blamed for the occurrence of a strike; and a few minor government officials were dismissed and in some cases the government promised to extend some concessions to the workers. In general, the official 'syndicates' abstained

*Graph 4* Bank credit and the money supply: 1956–61 (billion pesetas)

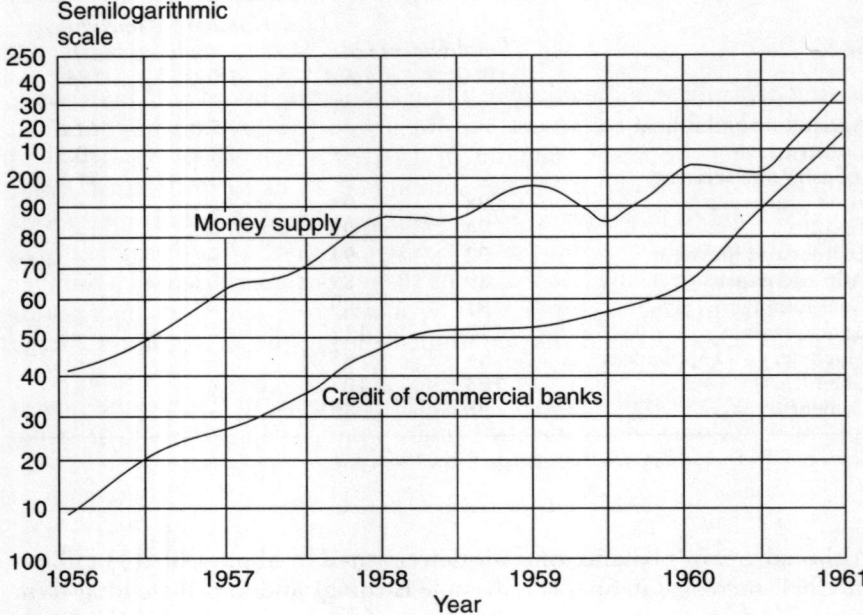

Source: OECD, *Economic Surveys, Spain*, 1962, p. 13

from supporting workers' demands. These syndicates incorporated both workers and their employers and were led by government officials, very often Falangists, whose task was to serve the interests of the state, not necessarily the same as the interests of the workers. Deprived of their historical trade unions, facing harsh government punishment for participating in outlawed strikes and forced to be members of official syndicates whose principal mission was to preserve 'social discipline', workers, concerned above all with their own survival, appeared to have abandoned for the time being all interest in collective action. They had not been cowed however into complete submission to the will of the authorities. The renewal of mass strike activity in Asturias, in Catalonia and in the Basque region in 1962 proved that Spanish workers had not lost their 'class consciousness'. And though no major strikes occurred in Spain in 1961, 32,000 Spaniards left their country in that year, 27,000 of them migrating to the German Federal Republic.

# THE ECONOMIC BOOM OF THE 1960s
## CONTINUED ECONOMIC GROWTH AND THE RENEWAL OF STATE *DIRIGISME*

### 1962

Rising consumers' expenditures, a house-building boom and an expanding private demand for stocks and for productive investment continued to strengthen domestic demand in 1962. Prices, whose increase had remained very limited from the summer of 1959 to the end of 1961, showed marked increases in 1962. Both wholesale and consumer goods price indices registered sharp increases in that year. The government was not successful in trying to contain the rising consumer prices of a number of key food products. Graph 5 below shows the rise in consumer goods prices in 1962, a trend that continued during the first quarter of the following year.

Facing unexpected workers' unrest in Asturias, in the Basque region and in Catalonia and eager to bring an end to an outbreak of strike

*Graph 5* Bank credit and prices: 1956–63

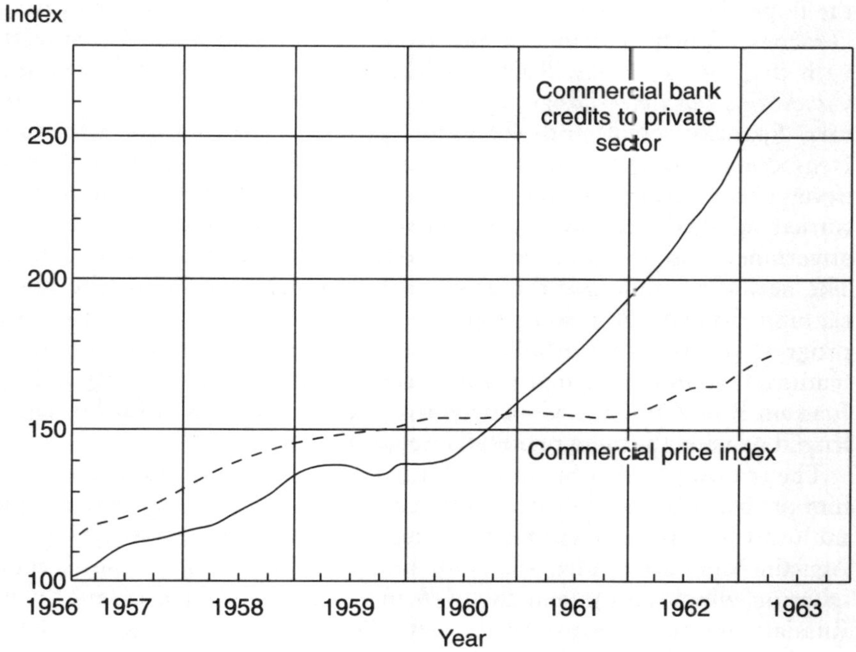

*Source*: Ibid., 1963, p. 12

activity which endangered 'Franco's Peace' and which could weaken the process of domestic economic expansion, the government gave its blessing to a large number of wage rises provided by the then legalized agreements between employers and their workers. At the end of 1962 the government established a minimum daily wage of 60 pesetas. These concessions to labour came too late to prevent an outburst of illegal strikes in the course of 1962 in which 45,000 Asturian miners, 50,000 Basque and 70,000 Catalan workers took part (Carr, R. and Fusi, J.P., 1979, 139).

It should be noticed that in the same year, demonstrations by students against the Franco regime informed the world that the Caudillo was not an idol for all Spaniards. Students joined small opposition groups led by Christian Democrats, 'Revolutionary Socialists' and communists. The cause of Christian Democracy in Spain at that time was strongly supported by the Vatican. Pope John XXIII defended ideological pluralism and the defence of human rights. Not only did he advocate freedom of religious expression and freedom of association, but he also encouraged the beginning of a dialogue between conservatives and communists. The proposals of Pope John XXIII became so disturbing to the Franco government that the latter started censoring the encyclicals of the Pope. The Pope asked a Spanish Christian Democrat, Joaquín Ruiz Giménez, to help disseminate the Vatican's views in Spain. Complying with the Pope's wishes, Ruiz Giménez founded a monthly review, the *Cuadernos para el Diálogo*, a journal containing studies of contemporary Spanish social and economic problems written by Christian Democrats, Social Democrats and even by Marxists. General Franco never understood why the head of the Roman Catholic Church had turned against him. Relations between the Vatican and the Franco government did not improve when Pope Paul VI succeeded John XXIII. The new Pope endorsed the views of his predecessor. While the high-ranking officials of Spain's Church remained loyal to Franco's rule, progressive Spanish Catholics started disagreeing with the country's 'national Church' and many joined the 'Democratic Left' party led by Joaquín Ruiz Giménez. Concurrently, Franco's Peace was further challenged by newly formed regionalist separatist movements.

The realization that Spain was far from being strongly united around him probably induced General Franco to form his sixth government on 10 July 1962. This government was headed by a Vice-President, General Agustín Muñoz Grandes, the commander of the wartime Spanish Blue Division which had joined the *Wehrmacht* in its ill-fated campaign in Russia. The main feature of the new 'Development Plan' government was however the strong representation of *Opus Dei* in it. Two former ministers, both *Opus Dei* members, retained their earlier positions. They were Alberto Ullastres, the Minister of Commerce in the previous government, and Mariano Navarro Rubio, the head of the Treasury in that government. In addition, members or supporters of *Opus Dei* became the new heads of a number of ministries. Jesús Romeo Gorría became the new Minister of Labour. Gregorio López Bravo was the new Minister of Industry and Manuel Lora Tamayo received the Ministry of Education. All these men were members of *Opus Dei*. So was Laureano López Rodó, the head of the Commissariat for the Development Plan.

The new government lost no time in giving publicity to its intended preparation of an Economic Development Plan for the period 1964 to 1967, a Plan that was advertised as being the key to the modernization and expansion of Spanish industry and a major stepping stone leading to a higher standard of living for all Spaniards.

The acceleration of the rate of Spanish economic growth in the early 1960s was largely the product of the rapid economic advance experienced in many Western European countries during the 1950s. Until about 1950, economic growth in those countries had mostly been due to the process of post-war reconstruction and to the effects of a large unsatisfied demand for consumer goods. After that year, other explanatory factors played an important role in the rapid growth process which developed in those countries in the 1950s and in the 1960s. A significant increase in the population of the OEEC countries in the 1950s, the expansion of credit available to consumers and the continuation of a post-war pent-up demand for old and new consumption goods made for an expanding internal demand for both domestically produced and for imported goods and services. Aggregate demand was further strengthened by the expanded role of government in the countries' economic activity. Government was given greater responsibility for the creation and maintenance of social fixed capital. It participated more directly and more actively in the process of industrial expansion and modernization and provided more extensive educational, health and welfare services to the people. Public consumption spending as a percentage of the Gross National Product rapidly increased in the countries of Western Europe. Another major cause of growth in that area was the sustained growth of intra-European trade, facilitated by a general reduction of national tariffs and by the removal of quantitative restrictions on imports. The OEEC succeeded in providing Western Europe with freer intra-European trade by establishing a European Payments Union in 1950, an international payments system which rendered obsolete earlier bilateral trade agreements and ended their adverse economic effects. The creation of a supranational European Economic Community in 1957 had important trade-creation effects within the EC area and gave rise to a rapid expansion of intra-EC trade in the 1960s. During that decade, intra-Community trade increased much faster than world trade. Between 1959 and 1971, intra-Community trade grew at an annual average of 15%, whereas the yearly average rate of growth of world trade was 8%. For each of the EC member countries, intra-Community trade increased faster in that period than trade with countries outside the Community. The European Free Trade Association, EFTA, formed in 1960 by Austria, Denmark, Norway, Portugal, Sweden, Switzerland and the United Kingdom, the 'Outer Seven', further boosted intra-European trade.

An equally important factor in the accelerating pace of Western European economic growth in this period was rapid capital accumulation made possible by high investment/GNP ratios. During the period 1959 to 1964, the Netherlands invested every year about 20.9% of her GNP; the corresponding figure for France was 15.1%. This pattern of investment explains an average yearly rate of industrial growth in Western Europe of 5.4% for the years 1958 to 1967 and of 5.5% for the period 1967 to 1971. (González, M.J., 1979, 279). A high rate of investment in most Western European countries produced in turn an increasing demand for labour, a demand which allowed Spanish surplus labour to be syphoned-off to nearby countries.

Rapid capital accumulation in Western Europe in the 1950s and high rates of economic growth in that region constituted the foundation of Spanish economic prosperity in the 1960s. It was the strong economic advance outside Spain in the 1960s, and not the Spanish economic planners of that decade, which made it possible for millions of Europeans to enjoy for a few weeks in the year the Spanish beaches and the Spanish sun. It was Western European economic prosperity which allowed hundreds of thousands of underemployed or unemployed Spaniards to receive training and employment in the factories of France or of West Germany; it was that prosperity which induced Western European entrepreneurs to invest in Spain. Indeed, during the 1960s, the spending of foreign tourists visiting Spain, the remittances of part of the earnings of Spaniards working abroad and foreign investment allowed Spain to finance the spectacular increase of her imports developing after 1959. Given the country's weak commodity export performance, these earnings of foreign exchange allowed Spain to finance increasing balance-of-trade deficits while maintaining at the same time a favourable balance of trade. Indeed, as of 1961, Spain's foreign trade balance started recording growing deficits. The deficit on physical trade amounted to US$ 278.7 million in 1961, to US$ 705 million in 1962 and to US$ 1,013 million in 1963. These expanding deficits reflected not only the expansion of Spanish internal demand which resulted in a surge of imports, but also the fact that the rising internal demand limited Spanish exports.

The expanding commodity trade deficits were however more than offset by Spain's earnings from tourism, by her receipts of funds sent to

Table 10  Tourism in Spain: 1955–64

| Year | Number of foreign visitors (millions) | Average spending per tourist (pesetas) | Earnings from tourism (millions US$) |
|---|---|---|---|
| 1955 | 2.5 | 4,680 | 90.7 |
| 1956 | 2.7 | 4,428 | 94.8 |
| 1957 | 3.2 | 4,304 | 76.9 |
| 1958 | 3.6 | 3,158 | 71.6 |
| 1959 | 4.2 | 4,649 | 128.6 |
| 1960 | 6.1 | 6,615 | 297.0 |
| 1961 | 7.4 | 6,743 | 384.6 |
| 1962 | 8.7 | 6,743 | 512.6 |
| 1963 | 10.9 | 6,596 | 679.3 |
| 1964 | 14.1 | 6,316 | 918.6 |

Source: González, M.J., *La Economía Política del Franquismo*, 1979, p. 286

their relatives in Spain by Spaniards working abroad and by foreign investment in Spain. The millions of foreign tourists who started visiting Spain after 1959 played a key role in the revival of Spanish economic activity in the 1960s. They not only provided Spain with an important net inflow of foreign exchange, but they also induced Spaniards to emulate their consumption patterns and encouraged Spanish manufacturers to supply the tourist trade with the new goods foreigners demanded. The growing surpluses recorded by the country's balance of services in the period 1959 to 1964 were due to net earnings from tourism. The numbers of foreign tourists as well as their average spending in Spain rapidly increased after 1959 as shown by Table 10. The number of foreign visitors rose from about 3.5 million in 1958 to over 14 million in 1964. Average spending in the country per tourist increased from 3,158 pesetas in 1958 to 6,316 pesetas in 1964 (Ibid., 286). The combination of rising real per capita incomes in their countries and Spain's devalued peseta turned Spain into Western Europe's favoured 'vacation land'.

The rapid increase in the number of foreign tourists visiting Spain in the early 1960s and the surge of their spending in the country had two important consequences for the Spanish economy. First, earnings from tourism gave greater vigor to the construction industry; second, they allowed Spain to finance with greater ease imports needed by the country for her economic development.

The large numbers of Spaniards migrating to Western European countries after 1960 also contributed to the maintenance in this period of a favourable Spanish balance of payments. Table 11 shows that the quantum of the remittances sent by Spaniards working abroad to their home country doubled in the period 1961 to 1964.

Table 11  Spanish emigration to Europe and emigrants' remittances

| Year | Net emigration to Europe | Remittances (millions US$) |
| --- | --- | --- |
| 1960 | 26,588 | 55 |
| 1961 | 107,557 | 116 |
| 1962 | 96,661 | 148 |
| 1963 | 82,311 | 201 |
| 1964 | 80,128 | 239 |

Source: Ibid., p. 289

Table 12  Foreign capital investment in Spain 1959–64 (million pesetas)

| Year | Direct investment | Portfolio investment | Real estate investment |
| --- | --- | --- | --- |
| 1959 | 964.2 | 95.4 | 5.4 |
| 1960 | 2,165.4 | 652.2 | 19.2 |
| 1961 | 2,247.6 | 1,096.8 | 90.6 |
| 1962 | 1,377.6 | 2,892.0 | 969.6 |
| 1963 | 2,478.0 | 5,228.4 | 1,557.6 |
| 1964 | 4,687.8 | 4,288.8 | 2,281.2 |

Source: Ibid., p. 290

The liberalization of Spanish restrictions regarding foreign investment in the country also helped in the balancing of Spain's external accounts. Foreign investment in Spain started expanding in 1960. Table 12 shows that this was true of direct foreign investment, portfolio foreign investment and foreign investment in Spanish real estate. The growth of the money quantum of such investments was not their only benefit to the Spanish economy. Foreign investment also brought to Spain new industrial technology and modern managerial techniques. On the other hand, expanding foreign investment in Spain also signified a growing control of Spain's economy by foreign interests.

A striking feature of the Spanish economy in 1962 was the continuing increase of aggregate internal demand. Consumers' expenditures continued to rise in response to widespread increases in money wages and in agricultural incomes boosted by sharp increases in the prices of foodstuffs and by good harvests. The most expansionist factor of demand was, however, private investment in the form of either housebuilding or productive fixed investment. The latter was in turn boosted by large imports of producers' goods, made possible by a still favourable balance of payments. The Spanish Institute of Statistics reported that in 1962, the value of the domestic industrial output at constant prices exceeded by almost 11% that of the previous year (OECD, 1963, 7). The output of a number of Spanish industries showed remarkable growth. This was the case in the chemical, transport equipment and machinery and appliances industries.

In spite of the surge in house-building and in productive investment, the Spanish Ministry of Labour estimated that 65,000 Spaniards migrated in 1962 to European countries in search of work. Statistics of the Syndical Organization reported a small fall in employment in 1962 from the level attained in 1961 (Ibid., 10). It is possible that in spite of substantial wage increases granted under the collective agreements between workers and employers in 1962, rising consumption goods prices in that year acted to restrict the growth of the $r_i$ as defined above in the Pasinetti model. For most sectors of the economy, an accelerated growth of the money supply in 1962, made possible by an expansion of bank credit to the private sector, translated into a continuing expansion of imports. Imports of equipment goods increased by 60% over their 1961 value level, while imports of semi-manufactured goods in 1962 attained twice their 1961 value. This dramatic expansion of imports permitted significant increases in production efficiency. $p_i$ in the Pasinetti notation. The other side of the coin showed that Spanish industrialists, facing a strongly expanding internal demand for their products, showed little interest in strengthening their exports.

Net receipts from tourism and remittances by Spaniards working abroad continued to expand in 1962 and were able to cover the largest part of the balance-of-trade deficit. The first rose by 40% above their value in 1961, the second increased by 25% (Ibid., 25). Concurrently, the net inflow of foreign capital in 1962 was much higher than the deficit on current account.

## 1963

The Spanish economy continued to expand in 1963. Spurred by an increase in the various components of domestic demand and by rapidly rising imports, national production went on increasing. Spain's import boom aggravated the country's trade deficit, but rapidly rising receipts from tourism and a larger volume of remittances from Spaniards working abroad, together with an expanding inflow of foreign private capital allowed Spain not only to cover her growing trade deficit, but also to increase her foreign reserves which attained US$ 1.1 billion in May 1964 (OECD, 1964, 5). According to official data, Spain's domestic product increased by 7% in real terms in 1963. This increase was largely due to the expansions of the secondary and tertiary sectors of the economy, such growth being stimulated by higher agricultural incomes, rises in industrial wages, increased governmental expenditures, sharp increases in domestic private investment, a boom in house-building, as well as by larger workers' remittances from abroad. Generally good harvests in 1963 and improvements in the marketing of agricultural commodities allowed farmers' incomes to rise. The country's industrial production index in 1963 rose by 7.9% above its 1962 level, with the production of chemicals, construction materials, means of transport, machinery and appliances showing the strongest gains.

The OECD Survey noted that Spanish statistics on employment at that time were not very reliable, but estimated that aggregate industrial employment probably increased by 2.5% in 1963, with employment also increasing in that year in the construction and service industries (Ibid., 11). A net emigration of 180,000 Spaniards to Western Europe in the same year probably reduced the numbers of unemployed in Spain. Official data reported however an increase in industrial unemployment in 1963; this apparent paradox is explained by the fact that increasing numbers of former underemployed or unemployed rural workers who had never registered as unemployed in the primary sector, registered as such after moving to urban-industrial centres either to survive as jobless in the secondary sector or to facilitate the process of official emigration.

In December 1963, the Spanish Parliament, the *Cortes*, approved a Four Year Development Plan which became operative on 1 January 1964. This so-called First Development Plan enumerated a number of goals its framers intended to achieve. It aimed to achieve a 6% annual rate of increase of the country's gross national product, to raise overall productivity by 5% per year and to boost the country's average per capita income from US$ 360 in 1962 to US$ 470 in 1967. Investment and other development expenditures were to be financed by increases in domestic savings, expanding exports and inflows of foreign capital. The Plan was 'indicative' for the private sector of the economy, mandatory for the public sector.

It is interesting to notice the reasons which led the Spanish government to formulate this Plan. The main objectives of the Stabilization Plan of 1959 had been to raise rapidly the productivity of Spanish firms in order to obtain an outward displacement of the economy's production possibility frontier. Spain's output had to increase and to diversify along lines of comparative advantage and had to improve qualitatively. The drafters of the Plan of 1959 believed that greater economic efficiency could be obtained by transforming the Spanish economy into a relatively free market system. The economic reformers of 1959 felt that the government's past *dirigisme* had unwisely distorted the economy because public decision-makers had minimized the importance of economic efficiency in production. They reacted to the effects of the pervasive government regulations of the 1940s and of the 1950s much in the same way Adam Smith had reacted to the mercantilist controls of his time.

The transformation of the Spanish economy into a free market system and the repeal of many governmental economic controls were also advocated by experts of the International Bank for Reconstruction and Development (IBRD) who published in 1962 a report asked for by the then Minister of the Interior, Mariano Navarro Rubio. The report proposed a growth model for the Spanish economy which assumed a free market system in Spain; it urged the discarding of the extensive network of public economic regulations which the Bank's experts considered to be a major obstacle hampering the development of the economy (IBRD, 1963).

Many Spaniards believed in the 1960s that the remarkable performance of their economy at that time was largely the result of indicative economic planning and that this type of planning supported the economic policies advocated by the framers of the Stabilization Plan of 1959 and by the experts of the IBRD. Nothing could be further from the truth. It was Mariano Navarro Rubio who had solicited the IBRD study; it was the head of Spain's planning agency, Laureano López Rodó, who revised the Bank's report before its official version was presented to Spain's political leadership (Schwartz, P. and González, M.J., 1978, 93). Men such as Laureano López Rodó and Gregorio López Bravo, the new young Minister of Industry, had no intention of abandoning *dirigisme* and the power it gave to those in charge of the management of the economy. These men clearly realized that the installation at short notice of a relatively free market system could have had disastrous political and economic consequences for them. In the end the Spanish government opted neither for a free market economy nor for a rationally planned economy in the sense that indicative planning represented an attempt to obtain greater economic efficiency. The government favoured instead the establishment of a partnership between its economic managers and the representatives of selected sectors in the private economy. The adopted strategy was to allow high-ranking government officials to act with sufficient discretion to favour the interests of selected private entrepreneurs, particularly those commanding political influence.

In the words of M.J. González:

> Spanish industry was conceived by López Bravo and by López Rodó as a large enterprise in which they were the managers. If one [industry] was benefited by means of an *acción concertada*, others were given a bonus in the form of a special line of credit, etc. Competition existed as long as there was conflict. And it is evident that entrepreneurs competed, at times in terms of prices and quality; but in general, they competed to obtain official rewards. And in this race, the most powerful and the best connected tended to have the advantage. The men of development tended to replace

competition with discretion. As was expected, they were not able to suppress the former even though they noticeably produced a discretionary economy. It is therefore not amazing that the result was a production strategy based on the supported growth of some large sectors ...

González, M.J., 1979, p. 321

The official version of the IBRD report of 1962 had extolled the economic benefits flowing from a free market system. The document was critical of the high level of government intervention which had burdened the Spanish economy and found undesirable the preferential treatment given by the government to all public enterprises. The report deplored the effects of a Law of 24 October 1939 which extended generous privileges to national interest enterprises. It noted that the automatic inclusion of all national enterprises in the category national interest enterprises was completely unjustified.

The Spanish government reacted to this criticism by passing a new law, Law 152/1963, which substituted the concept of 'preferential interest' for that of national interest. The advantages extended by the government to economic activities it considered to be of preferential interest were not to be granted to individual firms, private or public, but were to be bestowed upon selected sectors or subsectors of the economy or upon chosen geographical areas. Once a firm located in these sectors or areas was deemed to perform activities of preferential interest it was granted important financial, fiscal and other privileges. Compared to the law of 1939, the new law narrowed but did not eliminate administrative discretion in the choice of favoured firms. Subsequent regulations, issued in the form of decrees, gradually enlarged the scope of administrative discretion and gave evidence that the government was once again rejecting the implementation of a free market system. For instance, the Decree 1775/1967 brought back prior government permission as a requirement for the installation, enlargement or movement of certain industrial plants; industrial facilities not subjected to such authorization were required to comply with official mandates regarding size of plant and technology used. Firms which remained free of these various requirements were requested to file reports about their activities with an Industrial Registry; the process was cumbersome and forced firms to detail the scope of their activities; a Provincial Chief of Industry had the power to bar any firm from pursuing an activity that was not listed in the report it had filed. The net effect of these measures was to restrict free competition and to give larger discretionary powers to government administrators.

A new form of state intervention was the *acción concertada*. The concept was borrowed from the French 'quasi contracts' arranged between private firms and the government. In France, the principal objectives of such contracts were to facilitate structural changes in given sectors of the economy, to modernize methods of production, to achieve optimum scale of plant, to raise productivity and to attain better working conditions for workers. The idea of 'concerted action' between a firm and the government was incorporated into Spain's First Development Plan. A firm was allowed to enter into negotiations with the Ministry of the Interior, the Ministry of Industry or the Ministry of Agriculture in order to form an *acción concertada*. In return for the firm's promise to attain certain production and productivity levels, or other specified goals, the government agreed to extend financial, fiscal or other types of aid to that firm in conformity with the arrangement agreed to by the parties. This arrangement was to have a limited duration, usually a period between four and eight years. State financial aid mostly took the form of low-interest government credit which could cover as much as 70% of the cost of building new plants or of the cost of expanding and modernizing existing ones. The underlying rationale was that this arrangement would facilitate the attainment of the targets of the Development Plan. Fiscal benefits consisted of reduced tax liability or tax exemption, as well as of avoidance of import duties. Other benefits granted by the government to the firm operating in concerted action related to freedom in the accounting of depreciation and the privilege of being able to acquire land by means of the power of eminent domain. Benefits could vary among firms doing business in the form of *acción concertada* and operating in the same sector, subsector or area.

Article 6 of the law which made effective the First Plan of Economic and Social Development, Law 194/1963, stipulated that

> The state's action programme for improving the standard of living of the economic zones or regions of low income per inhabitant will be achieved by promoting industrialization, improving agriculture and modernizing the services ... and the furtherance of industrialization will be effected by the creation of development poles, growth poles and industrial estates.
>
> Comisaría del Plan, 1963, p. 150

This new policy of regional development was another step in the direction of economic *dirigisme* and enhanced the discretionary powers of government administrators. The new legislation aimed above all to achieve a spatial distribution of industrial activity that would appear satisfactory to the government leadership. It sanctioned the public grant of a number of benefits to approved firms operating in designated 'economic poles'. The law established two principal types of poles. Development Poles were to be developed in areas which had already experienced some industrialization. Industrial Promotion Poles were to be created in areas which were practically devoid of any industrial activity. Five Development Poles were announced in 1964; these were Vigo, La Coruña, Valladolid, Zaragoza and Sevilla. Burgos and Huelva were designated as Industrial Promotion Poles. Five new Development Poles were added to the official list at the start of the 1970s: Oviedo, Logroño, Villagarcía de Arosa, Córdoba and Granada.

The First Plan also provided for the development of 'deglomeration poles', *polígonos de descongestión industrial*, designed to reduce demographic pressures in the cities of Madrid and Barcelona, as well as for 'zones of preferential industrial location' in economically depressed areas. Both of the latter areas were to receive the same favoured treatment as the poles. The law designated as deglomeration poles Aranda del Duero, Alcázar de San Juan, Guadalajara, Manzanares and Toledo. Mieres, Langreo, Cáceres and Valle del Cinca became zones of preferential industrial location.

The benefits granted by the government to firms settling or expanding in the various poles included favoured tax and customs treatment, direct monetary subsidies and the extension of cheap government credit. The government retained the discretion of awarding differing benefits to eligible firms. The law did not specify what explicit criteria should be observed by administrators in their formulation of benefits granted to private and to public enterprises operating in the poles.

The authorities' strategy in the planning of growth poles consisted in first selecting the region in which the pole would be located, the apparent choice guideline being the equalization of per capita income differences existing regionally in the economy. Looking, however, at Table 13 it appears that two or even three of the seven selected poles in 1964 were not located in relatively poor provinces in terms of per capita income. The other selected poles did not appear to have a per capita income low enough to be ranked as 'poor' under the regional inequality criterion of

*Table 13* Per capita income of selected pole provinces in 1964 (1964 pesetas)

| Province | Per capita income |
|---|---|
| Burgos | 30,702 |
| Huelva | 21,180 |
| La Coruña | 21,358 |
| Sevilla | 22,683 |
| Valladolid | 31,634 |
| Vigo | 25,563 |
| Zaragoza | 32,392 |
| Spain | 31,036 |

Source: Banco de Bilbao, *Renta nacional de España y su distribución provincial, 1964*, Bilbao, 1967, p. 20

the United Nations Commission for Europe, a criterion apparently taken into account by the Spanish Planning Commission. According to this criterion, there is regional inequality in income when parts of the population of a region have per capita incomes which are less than two-thirds of the national average. Although this criterion would have applied to eight Spanish provinces in 1964, none of these were selected to become pole provinces.

Spanish administrators may have looked at other criteria in the selection of poles. One criterion may have been the development of an 'economic axis' between two regional centres; the planners may have given importance to the selection of locations representing natural economic growth areas for large regions. Sevilla, Burgos, La Coruña and Zaragoza were probably chosen as poles for being natural centres for areas which included a number of provinces. Poles could have been selected because they were located in areas outside the rapidly developing northeastern quadrant of Spain, the quadrant including Madrid, Barcelona, Valencia and the Basque region. Provinces such as La Coruña, Vigo and Sevilla may have been selected to become 'counterpart' areas of economic growth. It was reported that political considerations played a dominant role in the selection of pole centres; M.J. González reported that the head of the Regional Action department of the Planning Commission was first informed of the creation of the pole of Villagarcía de Arosa by reading the newspaper. The selection of pole locations resulted in the end from a combination of economic research and arbitrary decisions reflecting more political than economic considerations.

The First Plan of Development was followed by a Second Plan, and, at the beginning of the 1970s, by a Third Plan. The Second Plan gave emphasis to the creation of development axes, such as an axis linking Madrid to the north via the Burgos and the Valladolid poles, as well as development axes running along the coasts and along the Ebro and the Guadalquivir valleys. The Third Plan integrated development pole and urbanization strategies. By 1970 it had become evident that the development pole programmes had not been successful. In most poles investment targets had not been attained. In spite of the various benefits offered by the government to firms settling or expanding in the pole centres, deficient infrastructure and the relative absence of qualified labour discouraged private investment in the pole areas. Investment targets were almost achieved in Vigo by 1970, but in other pole centres the achieved investment level in that year varied between 46% and 50% of the targeted amount. The First Development Plan estimated that the development pole programme would create about 73,000 new jobs in the period 1964 and 1967; in fact, only 27,900 new jobs were created by the programme in those years; as late as 1971, the development pole policy had generated only 41,000 new jobs and the programme benefited only 350 firms (González, M.J., 1979, 341).

By the end of the decade of the 1960s, Spain's political leaders appeared to interpret the concept of a market economy as an economy in which government took an active role in extending aid to a select group of private entrepreneurs.

## 1964

The First Development Plan became operative on the first day of 1964. During that year, aggregate demand and output continued to rise; the Spanish gross domestic product increased by about 7% in 1964. The rapid growth of private consumption and private investment stimulated the modernization of Spanish industry and the latter in turn produced great advances in industrial productivity.

Although in 1964 the cost of living increased at a rate of about 7.7%, inflationary pressures did not hinder the growth of domestic output and 1964 recorded output gains in nearly all manufacturing activities. Table 14 compares Spanish industrial growth in 1964 with the corresponding situation one year earlier. While the production index for mining declined in the former year, all of the other listed industrial production indices showed increases.

An important explanatory factor in the surge of price inflation in 1964 was the government's large increases of guaranteed prices at the wholesale level in a year in which harvests were not as good as in 1963 and in which imports of foodstuffs did not expand sufficiently to stabilize food prices in the country. In 1964 the government increased the guaranteed price of milk by 21.4%; that of maize was raised by 23.2% and that of sugar by 19.2% (OECD, 1965, 13).

*Table 14* Industrial production indices: 1963 and 1964 (1960 = 100)

| Sector | 1963 | 1964 |
|---|---|---|
| Food, drink and tobacco | 116.2 | 130.1 |
| Textiles | 125.8 | 131.7 |
| Basic metals | 151.2 | 172.5 |
| Engineering and transport equipment | 172.2 | 223.2 |
| Chemical and petroleum products | 151.7 | 169.1 |
| Other manufacturing | 150.3 | 170.1 |
| Total manufacturing | 144.1 | 166.4 |
| Mining | 97.1 | 94.7 |
| Electricity and gas | 137.5 | 155.7 |

*Source*: OECD, *National Surveys, Spain*, Paris, 1965, p. 8

Hourly wages in manufacturing in turn rose by 15%. In the same year, the money supply grew by 19%, compared to a growth rate of 15% in 1963. National liquidity expanded, fed by a rapid accumulation of reserves and by expanding bank credit to the private sector. Increased public spending completed the financial picture of the economy.

Spain's balance of payments continued to show a surplus and foreign reserves attained US$ 1.4 billion at the end of 1964. The favourable trend in Spain's external accounts was due to a number of reasons. Though they had remained relatively stagnant in earlier years, the country's commodity exports increased by 26% in 1964, the increase affecting non-agricultural as well as agricultural exports. Spanish imports in the same year increased by only 16%, their rate of growth having been 25% one year earlier (Ibid., 19). Invisible receipts continued to surge. Net earnings from tourism were 40% larger in 1964 compared with 1963 and remittances by Spaniards working abroad increased by over 20%. These developments allowed Spain to record a small current account surplus in 1964. Concurrently, the net inflow of private capital increased to nearly US$ 300 million. All this allowed the country's balance of payments to show a surplus of about US$ 326 million at the end of 1964.

The major flaw in the Spanish mechanism of economic expansion was the intensification of inflationary pressures. Inflation threatened to worsen as both private and public consumption, as well as private and public investment went on climbing. The government, fearful of weakening private investment, refused to mandate ceilings on the growth of bank credit. Instead, it announced in November 1964 a number of counter-inflationary measures whose effectiveness was soon questioned. The list of liberalized imports was expanded and import quotas were enlarged for commodities whose domestic prices had shown strong increases. Certain import duties were reduced by about 5%. In the spring of 1965, the government increased its imports of food and of animal feed and suspended the issue of new authorizations for state-supported house-building. As shown by Graph 6, most prices continued rising.

Since the end of 1961, a rapidly expanding domestic demand had been accompanied by strong gains in industrial output. The growth in such output was made possible by the partial liberalization of the country's imports and by the rapid accumulation of foreign exchange reserves. The relaxation of administrative controls over industrial activity in Spain and foreign investment in the country played a significant role in the expansion of the country's industrial production. Such expansion prevented the development of financial disequilibria in the early 1960s. As internal demand continued to increase,

*Graph 6* Price indices: 1962–7

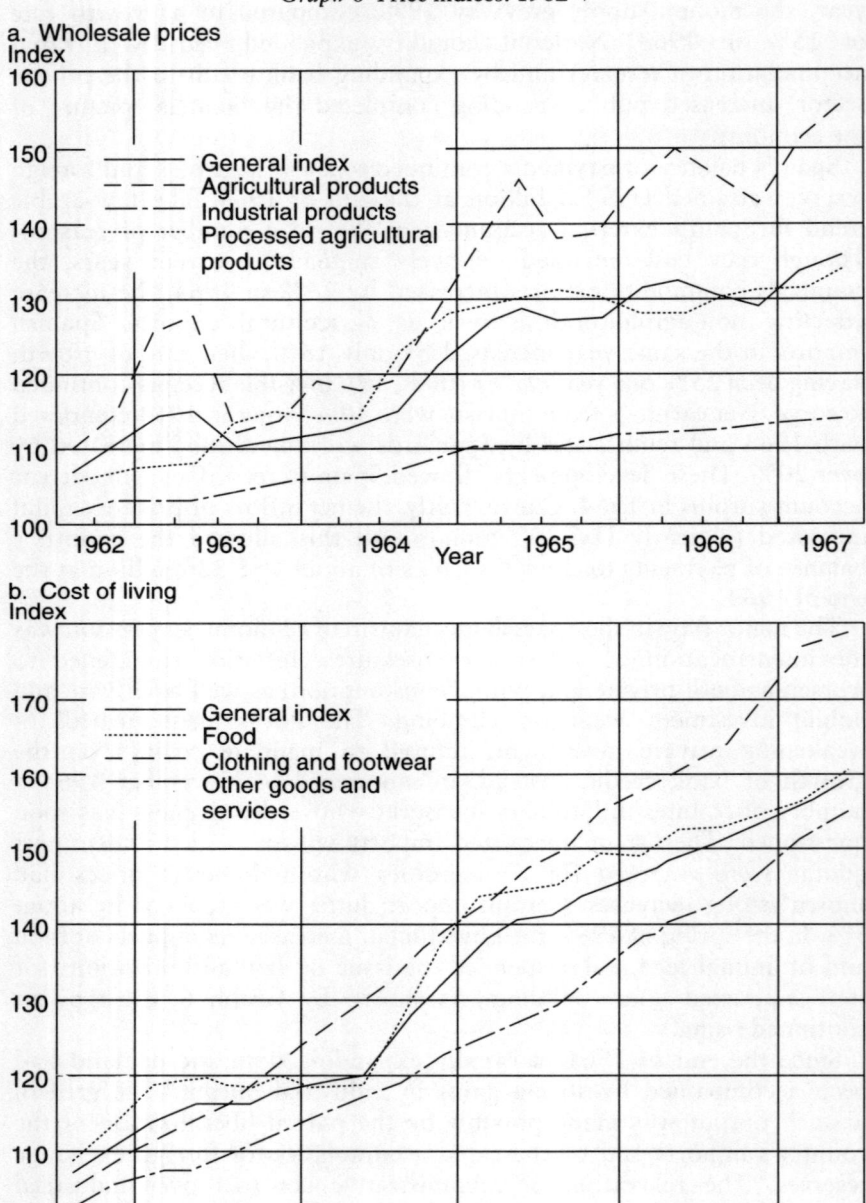

Source: OECD, *National Survey, Spain*, Paris, 1967, p. 13

inflationary pressures gained strength in 1964, to a large extent because government, in order to benefit agricultural incomes, decided to raise guaranteed agricultural prices and to diminish governmental imports of foodstuffs. Internal demand continued to grow at an accelerated pace in 1965. In spite of expanding production, the wholesale price index as well as that of the cost of living rose, the increase of the gross national product general price deflator being in the order of 12% (OECD, 1966, 12).

## 1965

The threat of inflation and stagnating commodity exports constituted the main weaknesses of an otherwise strong Spanish economy. Inflationary pressures were strengthened in 1965 by rapidly rising public expenditures which became twice as large as they had been four years earlier. Public spending was much higher in 1965 than it had been in 1964. Budget expenditures in the former year were 20% higher than in the latter; concurrently, lending to the private sector by public credit institutions increased by 30% (Ibid., 24). Gross fixed investment rose by nearly 20% in volume, spurred by an increase of 34% in Spanish imports.

The only factor restraining the growth of domestic liquidity was the development of a deficit in the country's balance of payments caused by a substantial trade deficit. A decline in agricultural exports caused aggregate exports to remain practically stationary in 1965. As noticed, imports expanded by 34%. Although net receipts from tourism and remittances by Spaniards working abroad continued to increase, Spain registered in 1965 a current account deficit of about US$ 500 million. Inflows of foreign capital limited the decline in official foreign reserves to US$ 105 million (Ibid., 34). Graphs 7 and 8 show the trend of Spanish foreign trade during this period.

The principal costs of Spain's continuing rapid economic growth in 1965 were the appearance of an external deficit on current account and mounting inflationary pressures. In order to counteract inflation, the authorities further liberalized imports and decided to maintain large public imports of foodstuffs. In December the government took measures to limit the growth of total credit extended to boost public and private consumption, house-building and stock accumulation; credit for exports and for investment was to be encouraged. The problem faced by the government was how to maintain financial equilibrium without damaging the process of economic growth. Possible solutions to this problem did not strongly appeal to a government which counted on a rising standard of living to bolster its political strength. It could reduce public expenditure by limiting subsidies and transfers to various public

*Graph 7* Imports: 1963–6

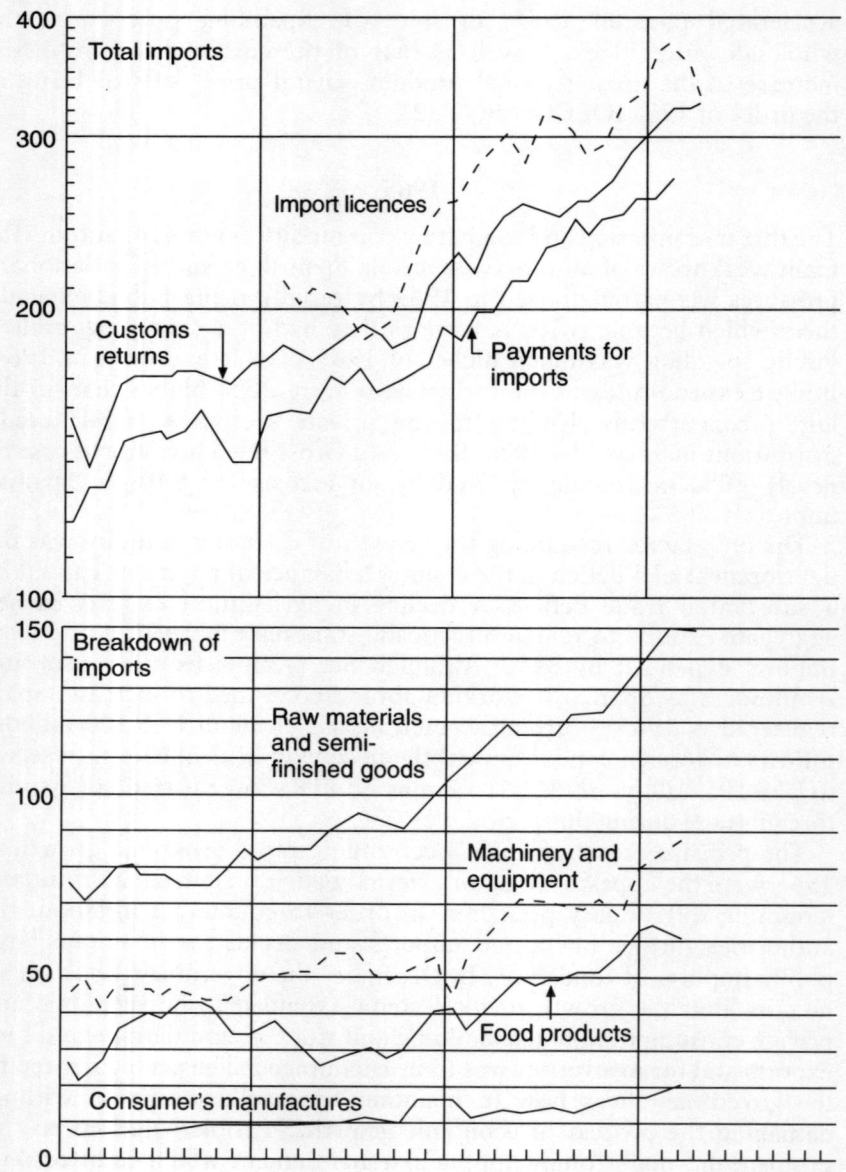

Source: Ibid., 1966, p. 35

Graph 8 Exports: 1963–6

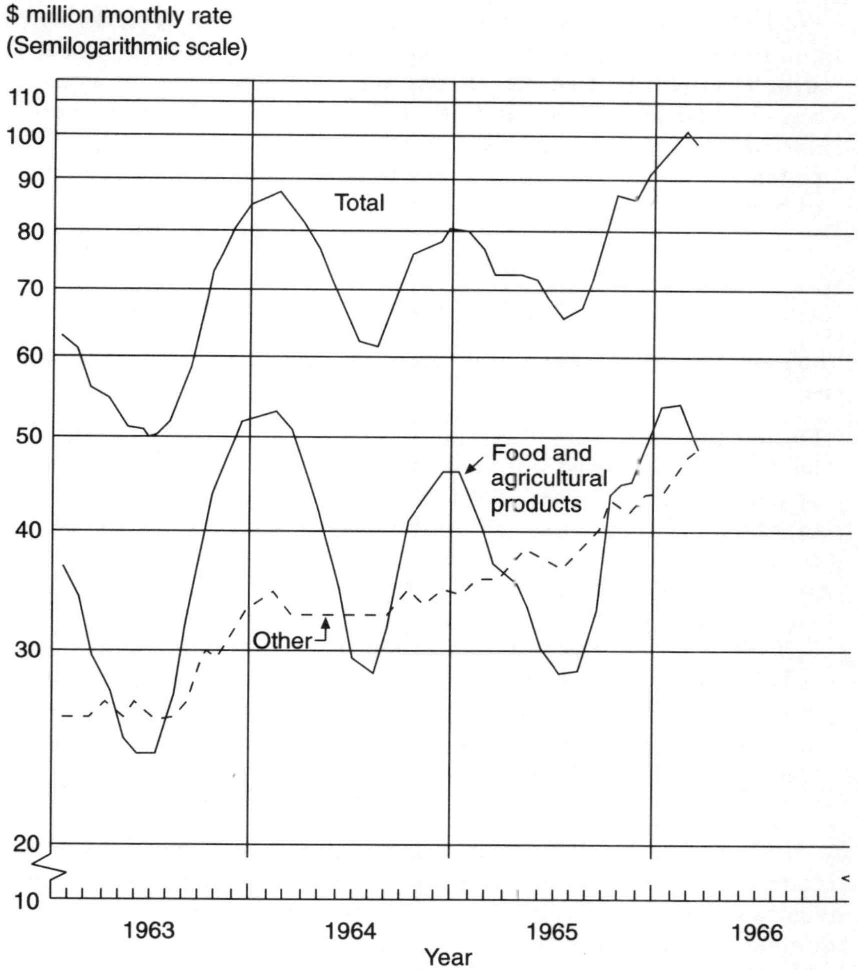

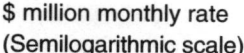

*Source*: Ibid., p. 36

service agencies which were selling their products at relatively low and stable prices. The government could also rely on increased restrictions of bank credit to the private sector, restrictions which would not only weaken the growth of private consumption, but also that of private investment. Finally, an increasing external deficit could also be used as a counterinflationary device. Observing the Spanish economy in 1965, OECD experts concluded:

## GROWTH AND CRISIS IN THE SPANISH ECONOMY

The progress of the Spanish economy since the general re-orientation of economic policy in 1959 has been considerable. Productive capacity and living standards have risen remarkably, and the underlying situation of the balance of payments contrasts strikingly with that of the 1950s. But these achievements would seriously be jeopardized if further drift into inflation were permitted ... failure to apply appropriate measures in time will certainly reduce Spain's ability to maintain a high but balanced rate of growth in the years ahead.

OECD, 1966, p. 43

## THE FRANCO REGIME IN THE MID-1960s

Professor Stanley G. Payne, an eminent expert on Spanish history, wrote:

During the mid-1960s the regime weathered the rise in student, labor, and regionalist unrest with little loss in stability, and few Spaniards really expected its collapse or overthrow before the death of Franco. General expectation tended to accept Franco's own conclusion that he had prepared the institutions to succeed himself, and so hostile an observer as the American historian Gabriel Jackson, long a foe of the regime, published an article on October 7, 1968, entitled 'Fascism for the Future.' He prognosticated that 'a Franquist type of dictatorship may continue for decades in Spain and by so doing may provide a "model" for other nations that achieve a minimum of economic prosperity in the absence of strong traditions of political liberty'.

Payne, S., 1987, p. 536

By 1965, the Franco regime had survived the beginning of its third decade. It was still based on an authoritarian, bureaucratic system, invigorated since 1959 by a new economic policy. An economically booming Western Europe was bringing to Spain endless waves of tourists and badly needed capital. As noticed by Professor Payne, the standard of living of most Spaniards was rising, and in the absence of a strong political opposition, the dictator appeared justified in claiming that his 'organic democracy', based on the values, principles and institutions he had imposed on Spain, would not only remain unchallenged during the rest of Franco's lifetime, but would survive the Caudillo and remain in place in the post-Franco era.

Nevertheless, not everything was quiet on the Francoist front during the first half of the 1960s. As noted above, Asturian coal miners defied the law and went on strike for higher wages in the spring of 1962; similar strikes occurred later in other industrial areas of Spain. In Asturias, the miners were represented in negotiations with employers by *ad hoc* committees constituted most often by communist workers and by progressive Catholic militants. These *comisiones obreras* were dissolved as soon as workers and employers reached an agreement. Although in May 1962 the government declared a 'state of exception' in three northern provinces, and although striking workers were arrested, the action taken by the authorities was restrained. The government raised minimum wages and in July, the *Cortes* approved a law providing for workers' representation in the councils of industrial enterprises. Strikes remained unlawful.

The regime also came under attack by large numbers of young priests and by young Catholic activists, most of whom were members of the *Hermandades Obreras de Acción Católica*, Workers' Brotherhoods of Catholic Action. These men, inspired by the Pope's stand in favour of progressive social policies, protested the government's repression of industrial strikes.

Strong opposition to the Franco regime was also voiced at a European Movement Congress held at Munich on 7 and 8 June 1962. This Congress met only a few months after Franco's government had officially petitioned Spain's membership in the European Economic Community. At Munich, the Spanish delegation urged that Spain's petition should not be acted upon by the EC as long as Spain maintained her existing political system. Furious about such recommendation, the Caudillo ordered that delegates to the Munich meeting who lived in Spain would be given the choice of either leaving the country or of being exiled for at least two years to the island of Lanzarote in the Canaries.

The Franco regime came under attack in many countries in 1963 following the execution in Spain of an alleged communist named Julián Grimau who had been found guilty of having tortured and murdered nationalists in his capacity as Republican police officer at the time of the Civil War. Grimau's execution on 20 April 1963 brought widespread foreign criticism of the judicial system in Franco's Spain. Reacting to such charges, the Spanish government established at the end of 1963 a Tribunal of Public Order constituted by civil judges who were to hear cases involving political crimes and subversion. Such cases had been adjudicated until then by either military courts or by the Special Tribunal for the Repression of Masonry and Communism.

Moved probably by the labour unrest starting in May of 1962, General Franco reshuffled his Cabinet and formed a new government on 10 July of that year. A new Vice-Presidency of the Government was established which Franco gave to the ageing General Muñoz Grandes. *Opus Dei* gained a stronger representation at the highest levels of government. Professor Payne has noticed that different lines of thought placed the various Cabinet members in rival groups. According to him, a number of 'Technocrat-monarchists' sought a 'symbiosis between Catholic values, an authoritarian political system and the American way of life' (Ibid., 506). These men were not interested in immediate political reform and hoped that rapid economic growth and an eventual monarch would make Spain politically more acceptable to the Western democracies. They favoured the designation of Prince Juan Carlos de Borbón as Franco's successor. The most important figures in this group were Admiral Luis Carrero Blanco, the Subsecretary of the Presidency, and Laureano López Rodó, the man in charge of the First Development Plan. The 'Regentialists', led by General Muñoz Grandes and by the Secretary General of the Movement, José Solís Ruiz, minimized the importance of having a new king designated in the lifetime of the Caudillo.

The new political leadership also disagreed about the need for internal political reform. Fernando Ma. Castiella, the Foreign Affairs Minister, Manuel Fraga Iribarne, the new Information and Tourism Minister and José Solís Ruiz favoured changes in the country's political institutions. They were supported by Jesús Romeo Gorría, the new Minister of Labour, by Pedro Nieto Antúnez, the Minister of the Navy, and by Gregorio López Bravo, the Minister of Industry. Luis Carrero Blanco, General Jorge Vigón, Minister of Public Works, General Pablo Martín Alonso and Laureano López Rodó gave greater emphasis to economic development and to the question of who would succeed Franco than to internal political reform.

General Franco remained antagonistic to political reform. While Castiella, Solís and Fraga worked on their own reformist proposals, Carrero Blanco and López Rodó drafted a new Organic Law which they presented to the Caudillo. Franco did not accept it. Disagreement within the Cabinet about the necessity of political reform probably induced the dictator to reorganize his Cabinet on 7 July 1965. Six ministers were replaced, including Alberto Ullastres at the Ministry of Commerce and Mariano Navarro Rubio at the Ministry of Finance. Laureano López Rodó, the influential Commissar of the Development Plan, was added to the Cabinet as minister without portfolio. Another interesting addition was Federico Silva Muñoz, later known as 'Minister Efficiency', who became the new Minister of Public Works. Silva Muñoz lost no time in trying to implement as rapidly as possible a National Plan for Spanish Motorways, PANE, and in giving a start to a Plan for a Network of Asphalt Roads, the Plan REDIA. The quality of the new highways and major roads built under the guidance of Silva Muñoz was sacrificed for the sake of rapidity in construction and proved soon to be deficient. A railway line connecting Madrid and Burgos, built under the direction of Silva Muñoz, soon proved unable to support high speed traffic. However, 'Minister Efficiency' retained his ministry for five years.

*Opus Dei* continued to control top level positions in the government of July 1965. Men connected with *Opus Dei* were in charge of the ministries of Commerce, Education, Finance, Governance and Education. Once again, the Cabinet was constituted by activist Catholics, generals and men of *Opus Dei*; though they were all completely loyal to Franco, their views on economic and political policy differed and the Caudillo went on supporting those who shared his own views.

## THE CRISIS OF 1967 AND THE BALANCE OF THE 1960s

### The economy in 1966

The expansion of internal demand which characterized Spain's economy during the early 1960s continued in 1966. Real gross national product grew at a rate of about 8% in that year. In spite of such growth, inflationary pressures were translated into both price increases and a rising external deficit. The general price level rose by over 6%. In order to counteract intensifying inflation, the authorities adopted restrictive monetary measures during the winter 1965–6 which succeeded in weakening the surge of domestic demand during the second half of 1966; speculative stockbuilding came to an end and the rate of growth of imports declined. Employment increased in both manufacturing and service sectors.

Demand was strengthened by significant wage increases in both the private and the public sectors of the economy, while excellent harvests boosted farm incomes. Both private and public consumption expenditures expanded, higher consumption spending representing about 75% of the total increase in internal demand; another 15% of such increase was due to growing fixed investment (OECD, 1967, 6).

Spain went on industrializing. Although for most manufacturing subsectors annual percentage industrial output indices increases were lower than they had been in 1965, the general industrial production index rose by about 12%, as shown in Table 15. The growth of industrial output was in turn accompanied, as noticed, by rising employment in the secondary and tertiary sectors of the economy. Although different Spanish ministries reported different employment growth figures, they all concluded that industrial employment had risen in 1966. The Ministry of Labour estimated that in 1966 industrial employment grew by about 3% with the creation of 128,000 new jobs, including construction jobs. The Ministry of Industry calculated that such employment had risen by 5.4%, with the creation of 200,000 new jobs. Concurrently, the emigration of Spaniards to the rest of Europe declined from 180,000 in 1965 to 130,000 in 1966; given the new immigration of former Spanish emigrants who started returning to their home country

Spain, for the first time since 1960, did not record a net emigration in 1966 (Ibid., 11).

Although substantial imports of foodstuffs during the early part of the year and excellent harvests restrained the pace of inflation in 1966, considerable wage increases, as well as salary increases for members of the military and of the civil service achieved the opposite effect. The increase in total public spending in 1966 further strengthened the inflationary process. Though the rate of annual increase of budgetary expenditure in 1966 was lower than that recorded one year earlier, it still attained 17% in the former year (Ibid., 14).

Measures were taken in late 1965 and early 1966 to restrict the growth of bank credit to the private sector; the latter still expanded by 14.4% in 1966.

Spain's external trade deficit expanded in 1966. In spite of larger capital inflows, official reserves in that year decreased by US$ 200 million. The larger trade deficit was largely due to the acceleration in the growth of imports which occurred in 1965 and during the early months of 1966. During the first quarter of 1966, the value of Spanish imports was 50% higher than the value attained one year earlier (OECD, 1967, 23). This import expansion reflected in turn the strong investment boom and the growth of consumption spending prevailing in the economy in 1965. The government supported large imports of foodstuffs in order to restrain the rise of food prices and the high level of internal investment produced large increases in imports of raw materials and of semi-manufactures.

Following the imposition of special import taxes in the spring of 1966,

*Table 15* Industrial production indices: 1964–6 (1960 = 100)

| Sector | Annual percentage increases | | |
|---|---|---|---|
| | 1964 | 1965 | 1966 |
| Food, drink and tobacco | 15.9 | 7.4 | 4.4 |
| Textiles | 4.8 | 0.5 | 9.0 |
| Basic metals | 12.7 | 19.8 | 8.2 |
| Engineering and transport equipment | 19.9 | 20.2 | 15.9 |
| Chemical and petroleum products | 13.9 | 14.7 | 14.2 |
| Other manufacturing | 10.1 | 15.0 | 15.5 |
| Manufacturing total | 13.7 | 13.3 | 12.2 |
| Mining | −2.9 | 6.0 | −0.4 |
| Electricity and gas | 13.7 | 7.2 | 18.6 |
| General Index | 12.9 | 12.5 | 12.1 |

*Source*: OECD, *National Surveys, Spain*, Paris, 1967, p. 9

the value of imports declined by about 11% during the second quarter of 1966. During the same year, Spanish exports expanded by about 23% in value, and, of major significance, the growth of non-agricultural exports registered an even higher rate of growth. For the first time, the value of non-agricultural exports exceeded that of exports of agricultural goods (Ibid., 25).

Concurrently, Spain's net invisible receipts surpassed US$ 1.3 billion. This development was largely due to two main causes. As Spaniards who had worked abroad started returning to their home country, they brought with them their savings, and this repatriation of savings boosted the inflows of transfers from abroad. Further, the net inflow of foreign capital attained the record total of US$ 390 million.

The dark cloud in Spain's economic sky in 1966 was a weakening of internal industrial investment. This trend reflected mostly the impact on industrial profit margins of rapidly increasing wages and salaries. Another threat to prospective Spanish economic growth was the continuing growth of the country's external trade deficit which caused official reserves to decline by some US$ 200 million in spite of record capital inflows.

It may be useful at this point to review the comparative performance of the Spanish economy in the period 1960 to 1966. As observed, this economy started experiencing steady and pronounced growth as of the end of 1961. Until the end of 1966, real output grew at an average annual rate of 7.5%, industrial production rising at the average rate of 11%. During this period, the average rate of fixed capital formation attained 15%. The rise in investment spending was at the base of expanding merchandise imports whose average annual rate of growth reached 30%. But while Spain's merchandise imports boomed, Spanish merchandise exports increased on the average by only 7% per year. Even in 1966, a year of strong export growth, the value of Spain's exports amounted to only one-third of the value of the country's imports. To prevent a further deterioration of Spain's external trade deficit, exports would have to rise three times faster than imports; Spain's export industries were unable to achieve this economic miracle. Not only was the share of merchandise exports in the country's GNP one of the lowest among the European OECD countries but, worse, this share declined from 7.5% in 1960 to 5.3% in 1966 (OECD, 1969, 6).

Because Spanish imports grew much faster than Spanish exports during the period reviewed, the country's balance of payments on current account had to deteriorate. Until 1964, this deterioration was hidden by the annual inflows of transfers and of capital from abroad. Starting in 1965, Spain's balance of payments registered its first overall deficit in the 1960s and for the first time in this period, the country lost foreign reserves.

In addition, the general equilibrium of the economy was increasingly disturbed by stronger inflation. Between 1960 and 1965, the country's GNP price deflator increased at a yearly average rate of 6.5%, while the corresponding rate for most other European OECD countries averaged 4.5% (Ibid., 7). In spite of the 1959 devaluation, Spain's competitiveness in the world weakened. Repeated increases of the guaranteed prices of agricultural products strengthened Spain's inflationary pressures. For the period 1960 to 1966, OECD food prices rose at an average yearly rate of 3.5%; this rate was 7% for Spain. Concurrently, the total Spanish wage bill increased during this period by about 16.5% per year; rising labour costs explained to a large extent the slowdown in investment spending taking place in 1966 (Ibid., 8).

## 1967

The pace of growth of the Spanish economy fell drastically at the beginning of 1967. Whereas the rate of growth of GDP in real terms had attained about 8% in 1966, it fell to 3.5% in the following year. Compared with 1966, investment in machinery and equipment declined in 1967 by 5% in real terms and investment in residential construction fell by over 10%. In the latter year, consumer spending constituted the most vigorous component of domestic demand; consumers' expenditures rose by 6.4%, an increase which was based on wage and salary increases and on a fall in the saving ratio. The rise in consumer spending accounted for practically the entire increase in domestic demand in 1967.

Spain's foreign trade decreased considerably. Commodity exports registered an increase of only 3.5% in value and gross receipts from tourism declined by 6% from their 1966 quantum. The percentage increase in the value of imports of goods and services was only 1.4% (Ibid., 10). For 1967, the annual rate of growth of industrial production was less than 3% and employment in manufacturing and mining at the end of the year was 1.5% below the level attained at the end of 1966 (Ibid., 13). And yet the general price index showed an increase of 6.4% for the year as a whole. Spain's external accounts continued to deteriorate in 1967. A net outflow of short-term capital caused an overall balance-of-payments deficit of US$ 140 million, while the external deficit on current account reached US$ 460 million. The trade deficit climbed to US$ 1.8 billion.

1967 thus brought to the Spanish economy a situation of near-stagnation, of rapidly weakening foreign trade and of rising unemployment. In spite of such trends, the price level continued to rise. The country lost convertible foreign reserves in the amount of US$ 154 million and devaluation by other countries threatened the survival of

Spanish exports. The Spanish government decided to duplicate Britain's devaluation decision in order to encourage an internal shift of resources from private and public consumption to fixed investment and exports. On 9 November 1967, the peseta was devalued by 14.3%. The new rate of exchange for one US dollar increased from 60 to 70 pesetas.

At the same time, the government adopted a number of fiscal and monetary measures in order to boost investment. Private consumption spending was to be restrained by freezing personal wage and salary incomes until the end of 1968. Extensive price controls were introduced. The Bank of Spain's re-discount rate for commercial paper was raised, and in order to encourage personal saving the interest rate earned by bank time deposits was increased. To stimulate investment the depreciation allowances that firms could take for tax purposes were increased. An increase in Social Security contributions paid by employers which had been announced earlier was postponed until July 1968. The programme for the construction of state subsidized residential housing was enlarged while customs duties were reduced for specified groups of imports.

## 1968

Following the decline of the rate of economic growth in 1967 and the devaluation in November of that year, the economy experienced a slow recovery in 1968. Reduced demand pressures were translated in that year into relatively stable domestic prices and into an improvement in the country's external accounts. As in 1967, the dynamic element in the growth of aggregate internal demand was not productive investment, but rising private and public consumption.

Industrial employment and prices remained practically unchanged in 1968, while agricultural prices showed a rising trend. A decline of the rate of growth of the money supply measured in terms of currency in circulation and sight deposits undoubtedly helped in the maintenance of relative price stability. Given the weak growth of domestic demand, the effects of the devaluation of the peseta in 1967 and the strength of world trade, Spain's external accounts improved in 1968. While imports of machinery, equipment, foodstuffs and agricultural products declined below their 1967 value levels, the value of exports rose above those of 1967 (Ibid., 32). Gross receipts from tourism exceeded by 7% those obtained one year earlier. Spain's current account deficit fell to US$ 200 million by September 1968 and at the end of that year, the country's balance of payments recorded an overall surplus of about US$ 100 million.

A Second Development Plan was submitted to the *Cortes* at the end of 1968. This Plan, prepared in 1967, was intended to cover the period

1968 to 1971. Because it had to be revised to take account of the foreseeable effects of the devaluation of November 1967, it could not be presented to the Spanish Parliament before December 1968. This Second Plan, compared with the First, involved a more sophisticated study of the economy and extended the scope of recommended prescriptions. Not only did it contain an evaluation of the economy's performance in the years 1964 to 1967, but, unlike the First Plan, besides estimating future trends of industrial activity, it also presented guidelines for the future of agriculture and education. It included 'warning signals' about excessive deviations of actual trends in the economy from planned trends.

The Second Plan aimed to achieve an annual rate of growth of GNP of 5.5% in real terms for the period 1968 to 1971 which could be accompanied by a rate of inflation not exceeding 2.7% per year. The output growth target was to be obtained by means of an annual increase in output per employed person of 3.9%. The Plan contemplated an annual increase in total employment of 1.25% and an average unemployment rate of 2%. It predicted the creation during the life of the Plan of one million new non-agricultural jobs while it also estimated that 420,000 persons would leave the primary sector of the economy (Ibid., 45).

The principal aims of the Plan involved the removal of existing obstacles to the growth of the economy. Among these were low labour productivity, inadequate availability of capital equipment in many industries, an excessive number of small enterprises, insufficient investment in agriculture, an inefficient financial system and a growing foreign trade deficit. To increase the international competitiveness of Spanish production, the planners called for a more efficient allocation of resources and for improvements in the country's infrastructure. The Plan also contained detailed guidelines for the improvement of the national system of education. The planners intended to double the number of students in the 11 to 14 years age groups, to increase the number of centres of higher education and of technical schools, and to raise the ratio of public investment devoted to education. They also gave emphasis to the re-organization and the modernization of the industrial sector, as well as to the expansion of the country's agricultural output and its change in composition so that the latter would better satisfy the contemporary demands of Spanish consumers and would help stabilize imports of foodstuffs at their 1967 level.

## 1969

Given the weak performance of the economy in 1968, the Plan's revised projections for the years 1969 to 1971 contemplated an annual average rate of growth of GNP in real terms of about 6%. The planners called

## THE ECONOMIC BOOM OF THE 1960s

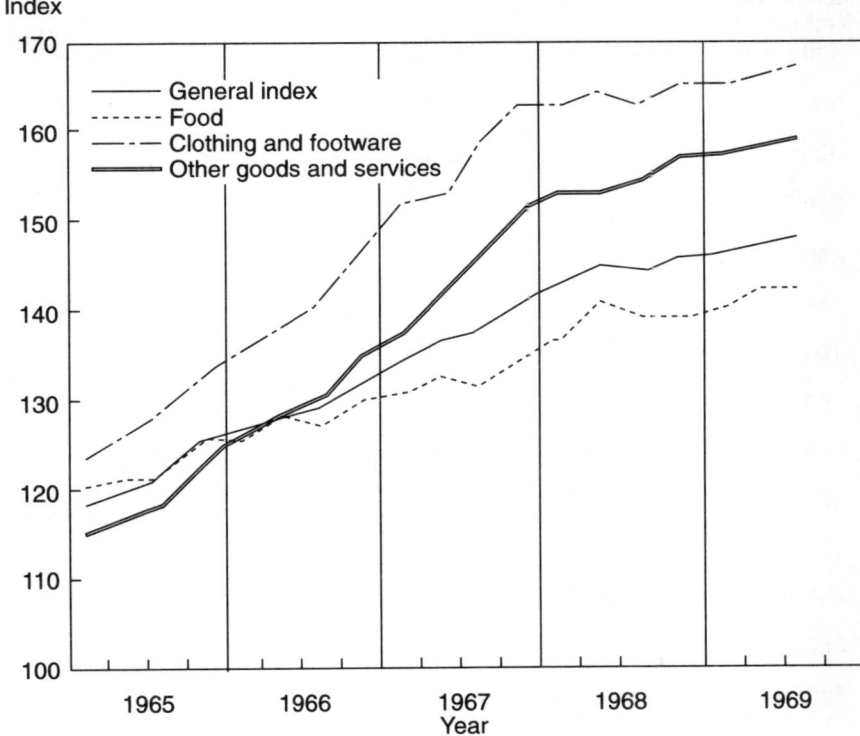

Graph 9 Cost of living: 1965–9

Source: Ibid., 1970, p. 18

for an annual increase in the value of exports of 9% to 10% and for a comparable rate of growth of the value of imports.

The pace of economic recovery accelerated in 1969. Largely because of an increase in investment spending in that year, domestic demand strengthened. Business fixed investment rose over 10% above the level of 1968 and public fixed investment continued to expand. Rising employment and increasing labour earnings stimulated the growth of consumption spending. The increase in consumption demand was largely satisfied by the increase in the output of manufactured goods and consumer prices stayed stable during the first half of 1969. As shown by Graph 9, the cost-of-living index rose by 2.6% during the latter half of the year mostly because of increasing food and public utility prices (OECD, 1970, 16).

A strong recovery of imports increased the foreign trade deficit for 1969. Spain's exports also increased in that year, and it should be noted that Spanish exports of manufactured goods to the OECD countries

# GROWTH AND CRISIS IN THE SPANISH ECONOMY

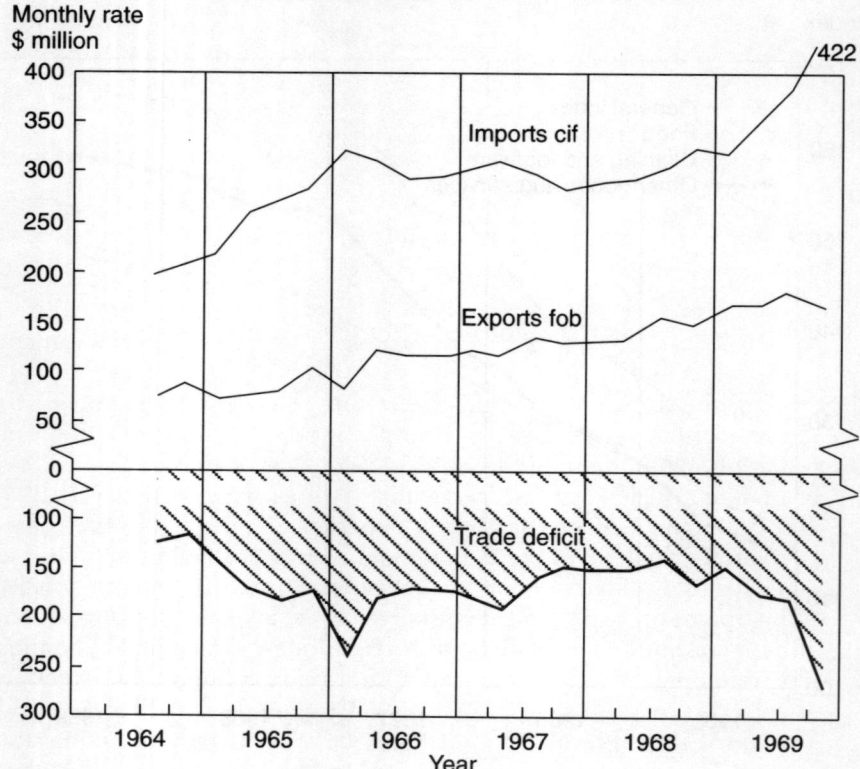

*Graph 10* Spain's foreign trade: 1964–9

*Source*: Ibid., p. 21

were 34% larger than in 1968. By the end of 1969, the current account deficit had attained US$ 500 million even though the country's net invisible earnings in 1969 were 10% higher than in the previous year. Given the net long-term capital inflow and a short-term capital outflow, the country's balance of payments in 1969 recorded an overall deficit of US$ 200 million. Graph 10 shows the trends of Spanish foreign trade for the period 1964 to 1969, as well as the evolution of the country's foreign trade deficit in the same period.

## AN EVALUATION OF SPAIN'S ECONOMIC GROWTH IN THE 1960s

Spain's economic miracle was still ongoing by the end of the 1960s. The country's industrialization efforts in that decade, when compared to the

## THE ECONOMIC BOOM OF THE 1960s

*Table 16* Annual rates of growth of real GNP, selected countries (average 1959–71)

| Country | Percentage rate of growth of GNP |
|---|---|
| Spain | 7.3 |
| France (GDP) | 5.8 |
| Italy | 5.5 |
| German FR | 4.9 |
| USA | 4.1 |

Source: Hudson Institute for Europe, *El resurgir económico de España*, Madrid, 1975, p. 51

industrialization experience of the advanced countries of Western Europe during the same period, produced remarkable achievements indeed.

During the 1950s, the Spanish economy had still been one of the poorest economies in Western Europe. In 1953, the gross domestic product of Spain amounted to only 14% of that of France and 23% of that of Italy. By 1965, these percentage figures were respectively 22% and 39%. Spain's economic growth experience in the 1960s was based on a relatively high investment–national income ratio, on rapid increases in industrial productivity, on rising expenditures by foreign tourists visiting Spain, on expanding remittances by Spaniards working abroad and by a continuous net inflow of foreign long-term capital. The most visible outcome of such trends was a continuously improving standard of living.

Evaluated in real terms, Spain's GNP grew at an average annual rate of about 7% in the period 1959 to 1971. This was one of the highest growth rates recorded by advanced countries of that time. Only Japan recorded a higher rate of economic growth in that period. Even though in 1972 Spain's GNP was still relatively small when compared to that of the major industrial nations of Western Europe, it doubled in value in the 1960s. Table 16 shows the average annual rates of growth of real GNP for selected countries in the period 1959 to 1971. Graph 11 shows the growth of GNP for a number of countries in the period 1955 to 1980. Graph 12 shows industrial production trends in the same countries in the same period.

Not only did the Spanish gross industrial product expand rapidly during the 1960s, but its composition also changed. The products of the capital goods industries acquired a larger share in the totality of industrial production. Industries such as metallurgy, construction materials, chemicals, rubber and means of transport increased their participation in the aggregate domestic industrial output, expanding the supply of industrial raw materials and of capital equipment and facilitating thereby the continuation of a self-sustaining process of industrialization.

*Graph 11* Evolution of the GNP for selected countries: 1955–79

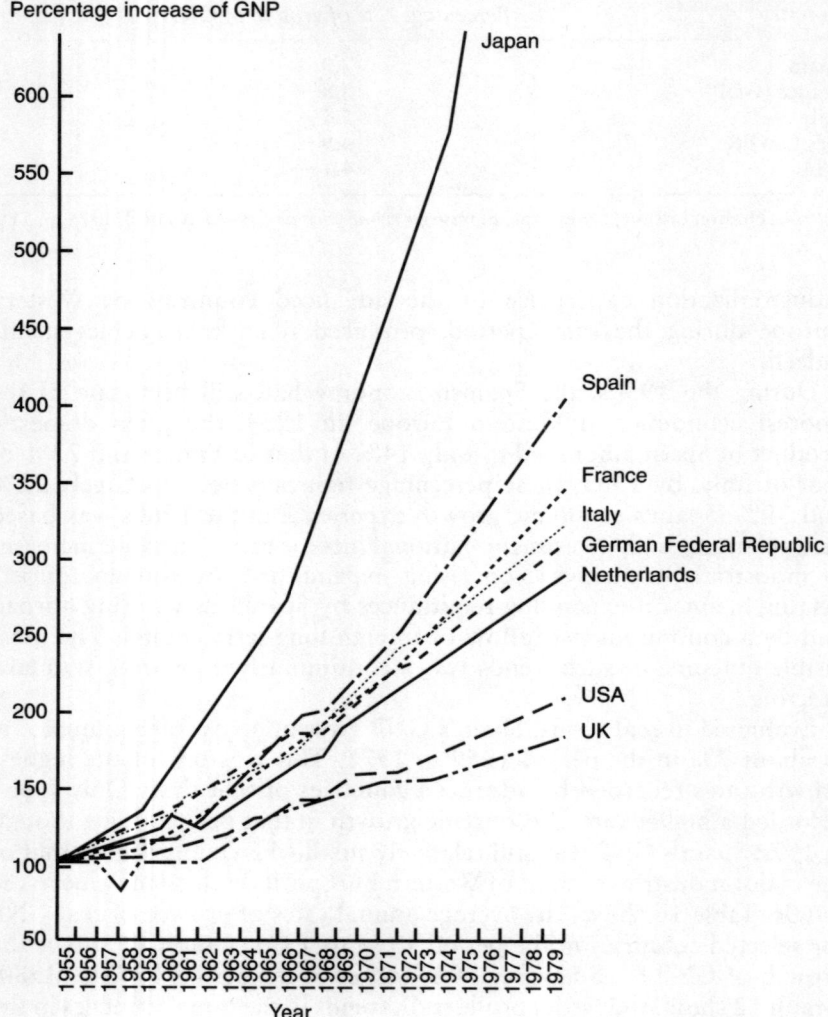

*Source*: Hudson Institute for Europe, supra, 1975, p. 52

Traditional industries such as foodstuffs, beverages, tobacco, textiles and wood products diminished in relative importance. The changing relative weight of various Spanish industries in the course of the period 1960 to 1972 is shown by Table 17.

The expansion of industrial production in the 1960s was accompanied by a significant increase in industrial employment; its relative share in

*Graph 12* Industrial production trends in selected countries: 1960–80

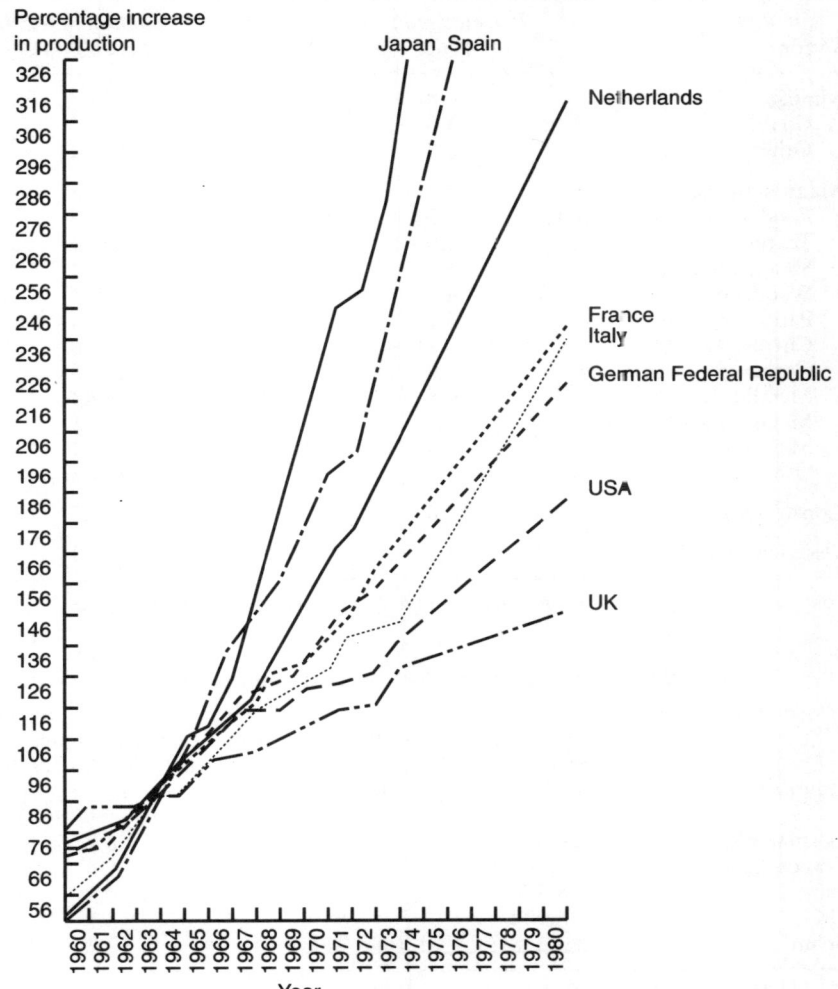

*Source*: Ibid., p. 53

total employment expanded from 31.5% in 1960 to 37.8% in 1972. By 1972 the manufacturing and extractive industries provided the major source of employment in the Spanish economy. While employment grew fastest in industries such as metallurgy, means of transport, electrical machinery, paper and printing, it fell in the extractive industries.

In spite of the growth of industrial employment, the industrial sector experienced significant increases in average productivity. The value of

Table 17  Spain, composition of the gross industrial product in 1960 and 1972

| Sector | Percentage in 1960 | Percentage in 1972 | Production index in 1972 (1960 = 100) |
|---|---|---|---|
| Mining | 6.8 | 3.0 | 120.7 |
| Coal | 3.0 | 1.2 | 102.3 |
| Other | 3.8 | 1.8 | 137.2 |
| Manufacturing | 70.2 | 75.9 | 312.5 |
| Food, beverages, tobacco | 14.7 | 11.0 | 216.5 |
| Textiles | 6.9 | 4.6 | 193.3 |
| Shoes, apparel, leather | 9.2 | 9.5 | 297.3 |
| Wood, cork | 4.3 | 3.8 | 259.1 |
| Paper, printing | 3.3 | 3.9 | 334.8 |
| Chemicals, rubber | 7.1 | 8.6 | 352.6 |
| Construction materials | 3.0 | 4.7 | 445.6 |
| Metallurgy | 4.8 | 6.1 | 369.3 |
| Metal transformation | 9.8 | 10.4 | 309.5 |
| Means of transport | 5.3 | 10.2 | 553.3 |
| Other | 1.8 | 3.1 | 489.7 |
| Construction | 17.8 | 15.9 | 264.5 |
| Electricity, gas, water | 5.2 | 5.2 | 292.3 |

Source: Banco Urquijo, *El Crecimiento de la Industria Española*, Madrid, 1974, p. 18

Table 18  Productivity indices, selected countries: 1969

| Country | Total non-military employment in 1969 (millions) | GDP at factor costs (current prices in US$ billions) | GDP per employed person (US$ 1,000 1969) |
|---|---|---|---|
| German FR | 26,337 | 162.98 | 6.2 |
| France | 19,967 | 112.40 | 5.6 |
| Italy | 18,678 | 72.80 | 3.9 |
| UK | 24,904 | 91.60 | 3.7 |
| Spain | 12,243 | 26.60 | 2.2 |

Source: Hudson Institute for Europe, supra, Madrid, 1975, p. 54

industrial output per person employed in that sector, measured in terms of constant pesetas of 1972, increased from 85,800 pesetas in 1960 to 202,000 in 1973, an increase of 135.4%. This meant that in real terms, productivity in industry increased at the annual rate of 6.8%. Among the industries registering the highest productivity gains were those producing construction materials, means of transport, chemical products, rubber and various types of manufactured goods.

It should be noticed however that compared to overall productivity

Table 19  Indices of industrial productivity, net production per employed person: 1963–70 (1963 = 100)

| Country | 1963 | 1964 | 1965 | 1966 | 1967 | 1968 | 1969 | 1970 |
|---|---|---|---|---|---|---|---|---|
| Spain | 100 | 109 | 122 | 138 | 146 | 156 | 176 | 186 |
| German FR | 100 | 108 | 112 | 114 | 119 | 133 | 143 | 146 |
| Italy | 100 | 102 | 110 | 121 | 129 | 139 | 146 | 153 |
| Netherlands | 100 | 109 | 114 | 121 | 131 | 149 | 165 | 181 |
| Portugal | 100 | 112 | 120 | 126 | 134 | 139 | 147 | 155 |
| Sweden | 100 | 111 | 120 | 126 | 135 | 148 | 155 | 163 |
| UK | 100 | 106 | 109 | 111 | 114 | 122 | 125 | 129 |

Source: Hudson Institute for Europe, supra, 1975, p. 55

levels attained in most of the European Community countries, the 1969 level of productivity in Spain remained quite low. Taking as a measure of productivity the GDP per non-military person employed, at factor costs and in terms of 1969 US dollars, Table 18 shows that among the selected countries, Spain ranked last in 1969.

A comparison of industrial productivity growth trends in a number of Western European countries indicates however that Spain was one of the countries experiencing the most rapid rate of productivity increase in the 1960s. Industrial productivity in Spain almost doubled between 1960 and 1971 and rose faster in that period than in the German Federal Republic or Sweden. Industrial productivity in Spain in the period 1963 to 1972 increased at an annual rate that was twice the rate of the German Federal Republic and 2.3 times that of the United Kingdom. Indices of net industrial output per employed person for a number of European countries in the period 1963 to 1970 are shown in Table 19.

Spain's productivity growth performance is explained to a large extent by the country's comparatively low productivity level at the start of the 1960s. It is also explained however by the country's relatively high investment rate. Labour productivity is directly linked to the quantum of investment in productive capital. The annual flow of investment determines the degree of capitalization in any economy and hence the efficiency and costs of production. In Spain, the investment rate reached 23% of the GDP in 1965, a rate which was higher than those attained in that year by Italy, the United Kingdom and the United States. Graph 13 shows investment levels, expressed as a percentage of the GDP measured in current prices, for a number of selected countries in 1955, 1965 and 1972.

The major cause of the great advance in labour productivity in the 1960s was the remarkable Spanish investment effort which generated a rapid rise in the value of capital per person employed. Estimated in

*Graph 13* Investment as a percentage of GDP, selected countries: 1955, 1965, 1972

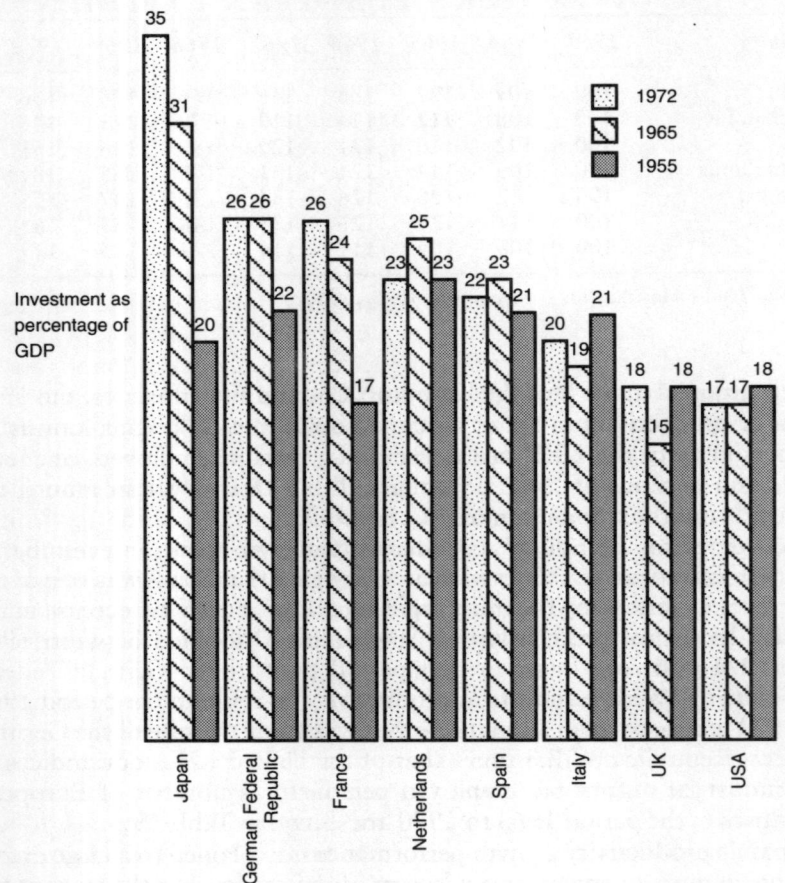

Source: Ibid., p. 57

constant pesetas, the value of capital per worker rose from 353,050 pesetas in 1963 to 565,650 in 1973, an increase of 60.2%. Even so the secondary sector of the Spanish economy provided only 35% of the country's GDP in 1972, a relatively small contribution when compared to the secondary sector's contribution to GDP in other Western European countries.

# THE ECONOMIC BOOM OF THE 1960s

## WAS SPAIN'S INDUSTRIALIZATION HISTORY TYPICAL OF WESTERN EUROPEAN EXPERIENCE?

Professor Albert Carreras has rejected what he called 'particularist' explanations of Spain's historical position of relative industrial backwardness in Western Europe. He has belittled the arguments of non-Spanish economic historians who have, according to Carreras, placed undue emphasis on the effects of Spanish political, religious and social institutions as major causes of the country's industrial weakness (Carreras, A., 1988, 82).

Carreras compared rates of growth of industrial output estimated for a number of periods in both the nineteenth and twentieth centuries in selected countries. He noted that following the Napoleonic Wars, the United Kingdom and France experienced an average annual rate of industrial growth of between 2% and 3%, and that this rate remained quite stable until the early 1860s. According to the calculations of Leandro Prados de la Escosura, industrial growth in Spain between 1831 and 1861 attained an annual rate of 2.6%, a rate very similar to those achieved in the same period by France, Germany and the United Kingdom (Prados, L., 1988). Other estimates point to an even higher Spanish rate of industrial growth in this period. Carreras thus concludes that during this period Spain cannot be classified as an economically backward country in comparison to the most developed countries of Western Europe.

Though the rate of industrial growth in Spain diminished during the decades 1861 to 1913, Spain's industrialization performance in this period was similar to that in France and in the United Kingdom but was inferior to the pace of industrialization in Germany, Sweden, Russia and the United States. Carreras explains the deceleration of Spanish industrialization during these five decades in terms of weak Spanish international competitiveness and in terms of the smallness of the country's domestic market. He believes however that on the whole, Spain's pace and pattern of industrial growth in the nineteenth century conformed to the Anglo-French model of industrialization in that century. The writer observed that the relative weakness of Spanish industrialization efforts in the past 'were perhaps related, since the last third of the nineteenth century, to [Spain's] physical and economic remoteness from countries who experienced the most intensive industrialization, Germany and the United States' (Carreras, A., 1988, 95). The Spanish economic historian concludes however that Spain's nineteenth- and twentieth-century patterns of industrialization were very similar to those of other industrializing European nations.

Probably because of the twentieth century's large wars, civil wars and depressions, industrial growth in the current century was much more

## GROWTH AND CRISIS IN THE SPANISH ECONOMY

*Table 20* Rates of growth of industrial output: 1913–73 (percentage per annum)

| Country | 1913–22 | 1922–35 | 1935–50 | 1950–60 | 1960–73 |
|---|---|---|---|---|---|
| German FR | 0.2 | 1.5 | 2.5 | 9.5 | 5.2 |
| Spain | 0.9 | 2.8 | 0.6 | 6.7 | 9.9 |
| USA | 2.3 | 1.4 | 6.0 | 3.4 | 5.1 |
| France | 0.1 | 1.8 | 2.4 | 5.4 | 6.9 |
| UK | –0.9 | 3.3 | 2.8 | 3.1 | 2.8 |
| Italy | 0.8 | 2.7 | 2.6 | 8.7 | 6.3 |
| Russia/USSR | –10.9 | 16.0 | 4.4 | 9.2 | 8.2 |
| Sweden | –1.5 | 5.6 | 4.7 | 3.8 | 5.3 |
| Western Europe | –0.5 | 2.6 | 2.7 | 5.9 | 4.9 |

*Source*: Carreras, A., 'La Industrialización Española ...', 1988, p. 99

irregular than in the preceding one. France, Italy, Spain and the Soviet Union increased their pace of industrialization in the period 1913 to 1984, while such pace declined in Germany, Sweden, the United States and to a lesser extent, in the United Kingdom. Table 20 indicates that Spain's industrial output expanded at a rate which was comparable to that prevailing in other leading industrial nations.

During the period 1922 to 1935, Spain's rate of industrial growth surpassed corresponding rates in France, Germany and Western Europe in general. Spain's industrial expansion during that period was apparently based on the stimulus given by World War I to the Spanish economy. The Spanish rate deteriorated dramatically in the period 1935 to 1950. Carreras explains this trend in terms of the effects of the country's civil war, as well as in terms of the impact of the autarkic policies of the Franco regime and that of its political alliance with the Axis Powers during World War II. Spain's rate of industrial growth recuperated in the 1950s and became the highest in Western Europe in the 1960s. The writer noted that from 1974 on, the Spanish and the OECD indices of industrial production followed the same trend. Carreras concludes that Spain's industrialization experience in the twentieth century remained very similar to that of her European neighbours and that wars and external economic change explain most of the country's relative economic position in Western Europe.

The most salient and lasting characteristic of Spain's industrialization pattern, whether we observe it in its beginnings during the second half of the nineteenth century, or during the years of economic miracles in the 1960s, or more recently in the late 1980s, is that industrial achievement in that country was from its start, and still remains, foreign-financed, foreign-controlled and highly dependent on the use of foreign technology. To the extent that an 'industrial revolution' refers to an accelerated industrialization effort largely based on industrial investment by native entrepreneurs and on the utilization of domestically developed technology, Spain never had an industrial revolution. The process of Spanish industrialization was simply an extension of industrial revolutions which had occurred in other countries. In this regard, the Spanish industrialization experience has differed in a 'particular' way from the industrialization pattern followed by France and the United Kingdom. Given the central role played by foreign enterprise, by foreign capital and by foreign technology in the development of Spanish industry, Spanish industrialization recalls the pre-Soviet Russian experience.

The Spanish economy of the 1850s was essentially an agrarian economy, an economy which lacked, with the exception of the Catalan textile industry, a significant industrial sector and which was characterized by poor means of inland transport. In 1855, Spain possessed only 434 kilometres of railroad track. The country's economic policies protected the traditional interests of the landowning oligarchy. The slow transformation of the economy after mid-century was engineered by foreign entrepreneurs and by foreign capital whose entry into Spain became significant only during the latter half of the nineteenth century. Although at that time Spain's aristocracy had attempted to impede the growth of middle-class political and economic powers, it did not oppose the penetration of the economy by 'international capitalism'. Spain's wealthy oligarchy did not see the entry of foreign enterprise and of foreign capital into Spain as a threat to its economic position; it correctly perceived that foreign business interests would have to depend on it for the passage by the *Cortes* of laws favourable to foreign investment. For the financial aristocracy, the founding of commercial and industrial enterprises by foreign capital meant above all a greater number of lucrative positions its members could hold, positions which enhanced rather than diminished their economic power. In its assessment of the impact of foreign investment on its own politico-economic interests, Spain's financial élite did not err. It welcomed the import of foreign capital and foreign technology as long as the latter did not seem inconsistent with the maintenance of its political and economic powers.

Three basic laws were approved by the *Cortes* after 1850 to encourage the entry of foreign talent and of foreign capital into Spain. The first was the Royal Decree of 17 November 1852 which provided in its Article 18 that 'foreigners are allowed to acquire and to possess real assets, to develop industries and to participate in all those enterprises which are not exclusively reserved by laws and existing regulations to Spanish citizens'. The second was the Law of 4 December 1855 which stated in its first article that 'the extradition of foreigners, indicted and prosecuted for political actions and offences, will not be stipulated in any diplomatic agreement or treaty' and that 'the properties of foreigners will not be confiscated, even in the case of Spain being in a state of war with the nation to which they belong'. The third was the Law of 9 September 1857 which allowed foreign professionals to practise in Spain provided they gave evidence that they had exercised their profession for at least three years prior to their arrival in Spain and provided they were willing to pay the same dues and taxes their Spanish colleagues had to pay (Sainz Moreno, 1965, 378).

Foreign investment in Spain was further encouraged by the enactment of the Law of Railroad Companies of 3 July 1855, the Law of Credit Societies of 28 January 1856, and the Law of Mining Companies of 6 July 1859. The Law of Credit Societies allowed the establishment in Spain of three new industrial investment banks, controlled and funded by French interests. These played a key role in the development of public works, mining activities and railroad construction in the country.

1 *La Sociedad de Crédito Mobiliario Español*, established on 6 May 1856, had been promoted by the Péreire brothers of Paris who had originally entertained the hope that Spain would become their exclusive investment preserve.
2 *La Sociedad Española Mercantil e Industrial*, also established in May of 1856, remained throughout its life a branch of the Rothschild Bank of Paris. The business of this company centred on the building of railroad lines; the Madrid–Zaragoza line was completed in 1858 and a Madrid–Alicante line was terminated in 1863.
3 *La Compañía General de Crédito en España*. G. Tortella Casares reports that 'its board was a mixture of French and Spanish bankers, noblemen and politicians ... Its president was initially the Duke of Abrantes, a member of the *Cortes* who soon resigned and was replaced by the hardly less aristocratic Marquis of Alcañices, grandee and Royal Master of the Horse of the Princess of Asturias ...' (Tortella Casares, G., 1977, 121). This company participated in the building of the Lérida–Reus–Tarragona railroad line; it was however most active in the promotion and financing of mining enterprises, banks and insurance companies as well as public utilities. It founded in 1857 *La Compañía General de Minas de España* which acquired copper, lead and coal mines throughout the country.

The Spanish historian G. Tortella Casares estimated that 'by the end of 1858 the three French companies in Madrid had the largest proportion of their investment assets sunk in railway construction' (Ibid., 125).

The General Railroad Law of 3 June 1855 stimulated railway construction by introducing a system of operating concessions of a duration of 99 years and by guaranteeing a minimum profit to foreign capital invested in domestic railroad construction. Within a decade, the main arteries of the Spanish railway network had been completed. Foreign capital, mostly French, had founded by 1861 a number of new railroad companies whose lines linked Pamplona to Zaragoza, Barcelona to Zaragoza, Montblanch to Reus, Grao de Valencia to Almansa, etc. Because these lines were built on the basis of imported materials, they had on the whole a weak stimulating effect on the development of domestic industry. Unlike the case in other countries, railroad construction in Spain failed to induce the development of domestic metallurgy and of allied industries (Sainz Moreno, 1965, 383).

Mining occupied second place as a foreign investment outlet in Spain. The mining operations of foreign companies failed, however, to stimulate economic development in Spain though they facilitated industrialization in their countries of origin. Mining operations in Spain were highly profitable for foreign firms but their profits were not invested in the country and their extraction and export of Spanish ores remained 'enclave activities' with little benefit for the domestic economy. A law of 4 March 1868 allowed Spanish citizens and foreigners to obtain mining rights as perpetual concessionaires by paying royalties to the Spanish government. This law placed at the disposal of foreign capital the best mines in the country. The elimination in 1870 of a duty on exports of minerals expanded foreign mining in Spain (Sánchez Albornoz, N., 1969, 139). Low taxes and the easy avoidance of their payment, the right of foreign investors to transfer capital and profits out of the country, the absence of restrictions on the import of raw materials and of equipment and Spain's wealth in minerals were all factors which attracted foreign capital into the country's mines (Sardá, J., 1948, 146).

Even though the Spanish government embraced protectionism from 1891, the role of foreign enterprise was still of major importance at the beginning of World War I. Most railroads, urban streetcar transport, the utilities, mining and an incipient chemical industry were controlled by foreign interests. The Basque metallurgical industry, shipbuilding, the Catalan textile industry and small manufacturing firms escaped foreign control. Most capital goods were however imported and foreign capital alone was able to finance these imports. This was the situation in Spain during the first and the sixth decades of this century.

World War I brought an end to the large inflows of foreign capital which had in the past financed the construction of railroad lines, hydroelectric plants and mining facilities. The war made it difficult, if not impossible, to continue importing manufactured goods from abroad in the traditional way. Spurred by the strongly protectionist middle class, the Spanish authorities decided to follow policies of import substitution and of national self-sufficiency. From 1914 until 1959, the policy of import substitution formed the core of Spain's economic policy. The closing of the Spanish market to foreign goods, initially through high tariff barriers and later through quantitative import and foreign exchange controls, encouraged the development of a domestic industry which from its very beginning remained free of foreign competition. The strong protection they received from their government allowed them to survive even though their costs of production were much higher than those of foreign rival firms. Protected from foreign competition, domestic firms had little inducement to become more cost-efficient and to seek economies of scale. High production costs and low product quality adversely affected Spanish exports and weak export performance limited in turn the country's ability to import capital goods. Since the quantum of imports of capital goods determined the pace of domestic industrialization, the protectionist and autarkic policies that were maintained between 1914 and 1959 acted as a brake on Spain's economic growth.

A mere inter-countries comparison of industrial production indices over time cannot shed much light on an adequate understanding of Spain's industrial performance. A quantitative study of the country's past industrial achievements cannot explain *per se* the persistent high dependence of Spain's industrial sector on foreign capital and on foreign technology. The motto 'Que inventen ellos!' characterized too well that sector in the 1870s as well as in the 1960s. The traditional absence of a developing, truly Spanish industrial technology must be explained in terms of Spain's typical aristocratic society. A historical note on the characteristics and values of that society is in order.

At the end of the eighteenth century, Spain counted ten and a half million inhabitants. Of these, 400,000 possessed a title of nobility. On the average, there was one nobleman for every twenty-seven Spaniards. All of the inhabitants of Guipúzcoa were *hidalgos*, low-ranking aristocrats. Over ten per cent of the population of Navarre, Alava, Burgos and León had noble status (La Rosa, T., 1971, 60). Spain's society at that time could be described as an aristocratic society which depended on a poor agrarian economy. The lifestyle and ideals of the great majority of the people were strongly influenced by aristocratic values and attitudes. The nascent wealthy urban middle class, small landowners, craftsmen, intellectuals, bullfighters and beggars, all Spaniards adopted in some measure the aristocratic concepts of hierarchy and honour.

A major tenet of the aristocratic lifestyle was that a nobleman could not engage in 'dishonourable work'. The nobles considered any type of manual work to be dishonourable and despised the manual worker. The 'mechanical arts' were considered to be 'vile professions' that brought dishonour to those engaged in them. A nobleman, regardless of his poverty, did not engage in what society at large considered to be a vile occupation (Palacio Atard, V., 1964, 51). This public disdain for the mechanical arts impeded economic and technological development in the country to such an extent that King Carlos III felt it necessary in 1783 to enact a Royal Decree which established 'legal honour' for all occupations without exception. Spain's nobility continued however to reject as improper its participation in commercial and industrial enterprise for a long time and continued to look at the masses of workers as inferior creatures who should be barred from any political role in the country. It was only very gradually that a few noblemen became willing to invest in industrial and mercantile ventures. The positive economic effects of such behaviour were, however, limited by the attempts of the wealthy bourgeoisie to duplicate the lifestyle of the nobles.

Wealthy noblemen sought high positions in government or in the armed forces. As an alternative, they preferred a life of leisure. Impoverished aristocrats also abounded in the country. Gaspar Melchor de Jovellanos saw the latter as 'lost to the useful professions, which they despised, as well as to illustrious careers which they were unable to follow' (Jovellanos, G.M. de, 1955, 46). Indeed, and with very few exceptions, most Spanish noblemen lacked the learning and the training required by any useful public or private career. Most noblemen centred their interests on court politics, festivities, bullfights and mistresses (Sarrailh, J., 1957, 87). Jovellanos has left us his description of noblemen he knew. In his words, the Count of Lerena, a Cabinet Minister, was 'not only an illiterate man, but lacked any type of learning and knowledge in all fields, a man without manners ...' (Jovellanos, G.M. de, 1953, 245). He described the Count of La Vega as a 'blessed man; he talks about everything without understanding anything' (Ibid., 475). Although many noblemen attended one of the twenty-three Spanish universities in their youth, they left these institutions in the same state of high ignorance in which they had started their 'studies'. In the great colleges, the *Colegios Mayores*, they acquired a great disdain for scientific knowledge and, whatever reading they engaged in, never developed a talent for observation and the ability to experiment and reason.

The mentality of the nobles spread to other favoured social groups through the incorporation into the aristocratic class of military officers with a distinguished service record or who had become favourites of the crown, of wealthy merchants and of leading politicians. Titles of nobility were generously granted by Carlos IV. The 'new nobles' soon adopted the values of the 'old aristocracy'. The ennoblement of military officers and of wealthy commoners led to an alliance between the former and the old nobility. A similarity of interests and of goals fused these initially different social groups into a unique and well-defined oligarchy, a closed privileged class who strove above all to maintain the economic and social status quo in Spain.

To preserve and to perpetuate its privileges, the Spanish oligarchy did not hesitate to do its utmost to isolate the masses of poor Spanish workers economically, socially and politically and to keep them as a separate pariah class. When in 1855 workers in Barcelona took spontaneous action to protest rising food prices and growing unemployment and demanded the right to form trade unions, the oligarchy quickly took harsh measures to silence the workers. General Juan Zapatero, Captain General for the Catalan region, issued orders prohibiting any trade union activity and his soldiers treated the striking workers as dangerous enemies. When workers' insurrections extended two years later to Burgos, Palencia and Valladolid, a fearful oligarchy developed such hostility toward organized labour that it persisted during the following one hundred years. This fear culminated in the 1930s and became a major cause of the cruel Spanish Civil War of 1936–9.

Another bastion of conservatism in Spain was the country's Roman Catholic Church. During the last decades of the eighteenth century, the Church owned about one-seventh of all the land in the country. A.H. Hull has estimated that although the Church's income from the lands it owned exceeded one billion *reales* per year, barely one-fortieth of such income reached the national treasury (Hull, A.H., 1980, 157). As one of the most important landowners in Spain, the Church acted as a strong defending champion of the country's traditional feudal society. In its eagerness to protect at all costs its privileges and wealth, the Church joined the socio-economic oligarchy and ignored the plight of the rural and urban workers. During the second half of the eighteenth century, the Church's opposition to any type of social and political reform hardened as the ideas of the French Enlightenment started reaching large numbers of educated Spaniards. Concurrently, the Church also opposed the reformist ideas of Carlos III. With some exceptions, ecclesiastics feared any change an enlightened king could force on existing social and political institutions.

During the first half of the eighteenth century, at a time when the views of the French philosophers were known by only a few Spaniards, a small number of Spanish clergymen supported the reform of university curricula and favoured the advance of scientific knowledge and the abandonment of superstitious beliefs and practices. One of these men was the Benedictine monk Benito Gerónimo Feijóo who attacked the scholasticism of Spanish universities and who deplored the backwardness of scientific knowledge in the country. In 1768, Carlos III limited the power of the Inquisition to condemn books, but the latter continued to prohibit the dissemination in Spain of translations of the works of foreign philosophers. The Church remained the strongest enemy of the Enlightenment. It was the strongest advocate of traditionalist, reactionary thought in Spain.

The Church successfully convinced the Spanish masses that the thoughts of the French philosophers originated in a conspiracy of the forces of Evil which aimed to destroy the Church and the Spanish monarchy. It argued that the new French ideas were inconsistent with the Catholic, hierarchical society established by God. Priests and monks asserted that Voltaire and Rousseau were agents of the Anti-Christ whose mission was to destroy Spanish civilization. At the end of the century, the Spanish apologists of the Old Regime claimed that their assertions had been vindicated by the horrors of the French Revolution. They warned their countrymen that the French philosophers' insistence on the free exercise of human reasoning necessarily brought about a society ruled by brutal carnal passions and by the absence of God-given morality. For the Spanish Church, the most dangerous tenet of the Enlightenment was its support of religious tolerance. Its representatives endlessly claimed that intellectual freedom and religious tolerance were the weapons used by the Enlightenment philosophers to destroy the foundations of traditional Spanish society.

The French Revolution, the war between Spain and the French revolutionary government of 1793 to 1795 and the later invasion of Spain by the troops of Napoleon Bonaparte were offered as proofs of the arguments advanced by the Spanish clergy to give greater credence to the reactionary myth it preached. The French Revolution was interpreted as the inevitable result of the impiety disseminated earlier in France by the leaders of the Enlightenment. The war between France and Spain was held out as proof of Satan's success in the former country. Together with these claims, Spanish ecclesiastics denounced the expulsion of the Jesuits from the Spanish empire, the changes imposed on Spanish universities, economic reforms and the crown's appointments to high office of men of humble social origin. Looking at the beheading of Louis XVI and at the bloodbath of the Terror in Paris, the Spanish voice of reaction warned that emphasis on reason leads to anarchy and that religious tolerance promotes atheism. What Spanish conservatives wanted was a politico-social system in which the Church would have complete authority over the intellectual and social life of the country. The Church strove for such a goal in the late eighteenth century; it was still striving for the same goal throughout the era of General Franco's regime. In the eighteenth century, just as in the 1940s, the champions of the Church preached political and religious absolutism, and a social climate that necessarily inhibited free scientific inquiry and discouraged economic and technological change.

Between 1810 and 1975, a traditionalist, conservative Spain coexisted with and opposed a weaker and smaller liberal Spain. There was a Spain belonging to the nobility, to high-ranking ecclesiastics and to a wealthy middle class. That Spain feared and opposed economic, social and political change and clung to often non-rational, traditional institutions which a weaker and smaller liberal Spain was unable to set aside. That smaller Spain was constituted by lawyers, university professors and intellectuals, as well as by multitudes of propertyless rural and urban workers anxious for change in the politico-economic system under which they suffered. Both Spains clashed in 1936.

Paradoxically, the birth of a new wealthy middle class in Spain in the eighteenth century did little to change the aristocratic values which permeated Spanish society. From its very beginning, this upper-bourgeoisie embraced the values and the ideals of the nobility. Just like the nobleman, the wealthy merchant felt that he lived in a world that was entirely apart from that of the manual worker, and whether the latter was a landless, destitute rural day worker from Andalusia or an urban factory worker from Catalonia, his employer did not see any meaningful difference between such worker and the mules he owned. Too many members of the wealthy Spanish middle class became eager to acquire blue-blood status and to adopt an aristocratic lifestyle. Many of them abandoned their commercial or manufacturing activities to play the role of Molière's *Bourgeois Gentilhomme*.

The high living standard of the wealthy middle class induced some aristocrats to cast aside their traditional disdain for business. A few noblemen started investing in commercial and in industrial enterprises. But this *embourgeoisement* of part of the aristocracy and its positive effects on the economy were at least partly offset by the ennoblement of the upper strata of the Spanish middle class. At the end of the eighteenth century, Spanish society was still aristocratic in nature and its leaders continued to disdain and ignore the benefits of technological advance.

For a long time, the Church viewed with concern the appearance of a wealthy middle class in traditionalist Spanish society, even though the members of the new social group claimed to be devout Catholics and did not contest the Church's power and privileges. The new class strove however to subject human life to a rational order guided by economic criteria. It accepted Catholic morality, but tried to have the Church clarify the tenets of this morality as they related to economic activities. Initially, the Church took a strong anti-bourgeois stance; churchmen denounced interest-bearing loans as repugnant to the Roman Catholic dogma. Friars such as Diego de Cádiz and José Jerónimo de Cabra condemned in their sermons the taking of any type of interest (Palacio Atard, V., 1964, 104).

The aristocratic, conservative and traditionalist character of Spanish society did not disappear in the nineteenth, nor in the twentieth centuries. Male members of Spain's élite social groups were willing to assume leading, though generally merely honorific positions in commercial and industrial enterprises controlled by foreign interests; they were seldom technically proficient to understand, let alone improve, the operations of their firms. They generally brought to the latter a name instead of desirable business or technical training.

These aspects of Spanish society were, and still are, key factors in the explanation of Spain's continued high dependence on foreign capital and on foreign technology. They turned the country into a 'European colony' used by foreign enterprises for their own benefit. This was Spain's 'particular' economic weakness. It still persists today.

## DID THE SPANISH ECONOMY MOVE TOWARD A FREE MARKET SYSTEM IN THE 1960s?

The new Minister of Industry in the government formed in July 1962 was the young naval engineer Gregorio López Bravo, a man who had previously served as Director of Foreign Commerce and as Director of the Spanish Institute of Foreign Currency under Alberto Ullastres. Some economic historians appear to believe that the remarkable performance of the Spanish economy in the 1960s was due either to Spain's gradual adoption of a free market system, and/or to the indicative economic planning put into effect by the government of 1962. Nothing could be further from the truth. Men such as Gregorio López Bravo and Laureano López Rodó, the head of the Planning Commission, had no intention of abandoning *dirigisme* and the power it gave to those in charge of the management of the economy. They clearly realized that rapid progress to a relatively free market system could bring disastrous political consequences for them. In the end, they opted neither for a free market economy nor for a rationally planned economy in the sense that indicative planning should be used to achieve greater economic and technological efficiency. They favoured instead the establishment of a partnership between the managers of large private firms and themselves. The philosophy adopted was to work out a 'marriage' between a group of select private entrepreneurs and high-ranking government officials. In the words of M.J. González, 'The men of development tended to replace competition with discretion. As was expected, they were not able to suppress the former, even though they noticeably produced a discretionary economy' (González, M.J., 1979, 321). Institutions remained stronger than the challenge of reform, and true to old traditions, the 'men of development' centred their efforts on protecting the interests of élite groups in Spanish society.

From the very start of his term as Minister of Industry, Gregorio López Bravo embraced a policy that was highly favourable to large private industry. On 26 January 1963 a new decree abolished some of the restrictions imposed earlier by the government on the installation, relocation and enlargement of industrial enterprises in the country. The new law became a means to protect pre-existing large industrial firms facing financial difficulties such as Barreiros-Chrysler (Tamames, R., 1979, 481). Private companies burdened by financial problems started receiving government credits; other forms of public assistance were extended by the government to private enterprises which negotiated 'concerted action' contracts with the authorities.

López Bravo let it be known that he favoured an increased privatization of the economy and increased limitations on the activities of the INI. The latter, according to the Minister's views, should only engage in economic activities deemed necessary by the government and in which private enterprise showed no interest. Otherwise, most economic activities should be performed by private enterprise. For López Bravo, INI's investments should be determined by two main criteria: the INI should finance activities of questionable long-run viability which government wanted to preserve, perhaps because of political interest; and it should also assist private enterprises facing financial problems. He cautioned however that INI's aid to private firms should be temporary and should cease once the firms INI supported were in a position to compete without public aid. The INI was also to protect 'infant industries' until the latter became able to compete with foreign rivals. What López Bravo wanted was an INI playing a subordinate role to that of private enterprise. This view was shared by the head of the Planning Commission, Laureano López Rodó, and received increasing support from General Franco. It was however opposed by the then President of the INI, Juan Antonio Suanzes Fernández, an old friend of the Caudillo. Disagreements between Suanzes and López Bravo soon multiplied. Suanzes was dismissed from his position in October of 1963. He was succeeded by the Secretary General of the INI, José Sirvent Dargent, an engineer educated at the Artillery Academy, who remained the INI's President until May 1969.

During the Suanzes presidency, all major decisions regarding the INI had been made by Suanzes with the approval of General Franco. Sirvent, on the other hand, submitted all of the INI's proposed investments to the scrutiny of Admiral Luis Carrero Blanco who consulted in turn with Gregorio López Bravo before making a final decision. Thus, under Sirvent's presidency, López Bravo acquired a dominant voice in the formulation of INI's policies even before the formal transfer of the INI to the Ministry of Industry.

Although Gregorio López Bravo advocated an increase in the relative importance of the private sector in the economy, he was not a champion of the free market system. He wanted a managed economy and supported the discretionary powers of public administrators. His views were well expressed by the language of Point 2 of Article 4 of the Law 194/1963 which provided that 'Government will evaluate the insufficiency of private initiative and the opportunity to supplement it with public activity, among other instances when the former will not achieve in a determined sector the objectives defined for it, in an indicative way, by the Plan of Economic and Social Development'. The scope of administrative discretion was widened by the assertion that 'government will evaluate the insufficiency of private initiative'. This provision allowed government officials to create public enterprises for reasons of their own since the language of the law did not specify the exact meaning of the word insufficiency. The government claimed to have enacted an indicative Plan, yet the law contained the threat of exposing private firms to public competition if the former did not achieve the goals set in the indicative Plan.

It must be noted that INI investments continued to expand during the presidency of José Sirvent. The INI acquired a 40% participation in HISPANOIL, a new company whose aim was to acquire petroleum sources located outside Spain. Of greater significance were INI's investments in the Asturian steel complex UNINSA and in the coal mining enterprise Hulleras del Norte, S.A., better known as HUNOSA. The creation of UNINSA reflected the government's realization that concerted action in ferrous metallurgy had not achieved any significant transformation of that industry. The modernization and the concentration of the steel industry had failed, particularly in the light of the resources which had been generously placed by the government at the disposal of concerted action enterprises. At the request of three private steel producers, the INI agreed to participate in their fusion and to contribute 60% of the capital of the resulting new nationalized enterprise, UNINSA. The latter was founded in 1966 and was to be acquired by ENSIDESA in 1971. HUNOSA was created to reduce the operational fragmentation and the production backwardness of the coal mining industry. The INI obtained complete ownership of HUNOSA in 1970.

Government *dirigisme* grew stronger in the latter part of the 1960s. Critics denounced the expanding governmental interventionism as being inconsistent with the major goals of the economic reformers of 1959 and incompatible with the 1962 recommendations of the IBRD. The Minister of Industry remained indifferent to these assertions. In order to control inflation, the government pursued a 'stop-go' type of monetary policy; the resulting erratic contractions of short-term bank credit made the availability of credit to small- and medium-size firms uncertain; since most firms in Spain financed themselves principally by means of such credit, the monetary *dirigisme* discouraged aggressive private investment and made for an actual rate of economic growth which remained below the potential growth ceiling (Lluch, C., 1974, 57).

As noted, the 1960s witnessed remarkable industrial growth in Spain. This growth was largely the result of the liberalization of foreign trade and of the removal of impediments to foreign investment in the country. The possibility of importing sufficient industrial raw materials, much needed capital goods, foreign capital and foreign technology, coupled with the presence of a strong domestic demand for new and better quality products, created a climate propitious to private investment and to industrial innovation.

In an economy in which most firms could not expand and modernize on the basis of self-finance, it was usually the large firm which was able to obtain on reasonable terms the private, public and foreign credit it needed to increase its productive efficiency. Credit was not equally available to all industrial firms. Those that could obtain it were able to raise their productivity and their output. The others continued to produce exclusively for a small, highly protected domestic market on the basis of antiquated methods of production.

## REFERENCES

Carr, R. and Fusi, J.P., *Spain, Dictatorship to Democracy*, London, George Allen & Unwin, 1979.

Carreras, A., 'La Industrialización Española en el Marco de la Historia Económica Europea: Ritmos y Carácteres Comparados' in García Delgado, J.L., ed., *España, Economía*, Madrid, Espasa Calpe, 1988, pp. 79–115.

Comisaría del Plan de Desarrollo, *I Plan de Desarrollo Económico y Social*, Madrid, 1963.

Fontana, J. and Nadal, J., 'Spain 1914–1970', in Cipolla, C.M., ed., *The Fontana Economic History of Europe, Contemporary Economies*, Glasgow, Collins/Fontana Books, 1976, pp. 460–529.

Fuentes Quintana, E., 'Tres Decenios de la Economía Española en Perspectiva', in García Delgado, J.L., ed., *España, Economía*, Madrid, Espasa Calpe, 1988, pp. 1–78.

Gerschenkron, A., *Economic Backwardness in Historical Perspective*, New York, F.A. Praeger Publishers, 1965.

González, M.J., *La Economía Política del Franquismo, 1940–1970*, Madrid, Editorial Tecnos, 1979.

Hagen, E.E., *The Economics of Development*, Homewood, Ill., Richard D. Irwin, Inc., 1975.

Hudson Institute for Europe, *El Resurgir Económico de España*, Madrid, Instituto de Estudios de Planificación, 1975.

Hull, A.H., *Charles III and the Revival of Spain*, Washington, D.C., University Press of America, 1980.

IBRD, *The Economic Development of Spain*, Baltimore, The Johns Hopkins Press, 1967.

Jovellanos, G.M. de, *Informe Sobre la Ley Agraria*, Madrid, Instituto de Estudios Políticos, 1955.

―――― *Diarios*, Oviedo, Instituto de Estudios Asturianos, vol. I, 1953.

Kravis, I.B., 'Trade as a Handmaiden of Growth: Similarities between the Nineteenth and the Twentieth Centuries', *Economic Journal*, vol. 80, 1970, pp. 850–72.

La Rosa, T., *España Contemporanea, Siglo XIX*, Madrid, Ediciones Destino, 1971.
Lewis, W.A., 'Economic Development with Unlimited Supplies of Labour', *The Manchester School*, vol. 22, 1954, pp. 139–91.
Lluch, C., *La Industria Española del Futuro*, Madrid, Guadiana de Publicaciones, 1974.
North, D.C., *The Economic Growth of the United States, 1790–1860*, Englewood Cliffs, N.J., Prentice Hall, Inc., 1961.
Nurkse, R., *Equilibrium and Growth in the World Economy*, Cambridge, Mass., Harvard University Press, 1961.
OECD, *Economic Surveys, Spain*, Paris, (various issues).
Palacio Atard, V., *Los Españoles de la Illustración*, Madrid, Ediciones Guadarrama, 1964.
Pasinetti, L. and Lloyd, P., eds, *Economic Interdependence and World Development*, vol. 3, New York, St. Martin's Press, 1987.
Payne, S.G., *The Franco Regime, 1936–1975*, Madison, The University of Wisconsin Press, 1987.
Prados de la Escosura, L., *De Imperio a Nación, Crecimiento y Atraso Económico en España, 1780–1930*, Madrid, Alianza Editorial, 1988.
Sainz Moreno, F., 'Historia de las Inversiones Extranjeras en España', *Boletín de Estudios Económicos*, no. 65, Bilbao, 1965.
Sánchez Albornoz, N., *España Hace Un Siglo, Una Economía Dual*, Barcelona, Ediciones Península, 1969.
Sardá, J., *La Política Monetaria y las Fluctuaciones de la Economía Española en el Siglo XIX*, Madrid, Instituto Sancho de Moncada, 1948.
Sarrailh, J., *La España Ilustrada de la Segunda Mitad del Siglo XVIII*, México, Fondo de Cultura Económica, 1957.
Schwartz, P. and González, M.J., *Una Historia del Instituto Nacional de Industria, 1941–1976*, Madrid, Editorial Tecnos, 1978.
Tamames, R., *Historia de España, La República, La Era de Franco*, Madrid, Alianza Universidad, 1979.
Tortella Casares, G., *Banking, Railroads and Industry in Spain, 1829–1874*, New York, Arno Press, 1977.

# 3

# THE 1970s

## The ending of Spain's economic miracle years and that of the Franco era

On 29 October 1969 General Franco formed the last government over which he presided in person. This government remained in power until 8 June 1973. It was known as the 'monocolour government' because eleven out of the nineteen appointed ministers were members of *Opus Dei* or closely connected with that organization. The Vice-Presidency remained in the hands of Admiral Luis Carrero Blanco. Gregorio López Bravo was transferred from the Ministry of Industry to that of Foreign Affairs; the new Minister of Industry was José María López de Letona, the man who succeeded in bringing the Ford Motor Company to Spain.

López Bravo probably saw in his new appointment a stepping stone that would allow him to reach in time the position of President of the Government. He proceeded without delay to enhance his fame at home and abroad by strengthening Spain's diplomatic and commercial relations with Eastern European and with North African nations. Treaties were signed with Czechoslovakia, Hungary, Poland and Rumania which allowed those countries to open offices in Madrid which functioned very much as regular embassies. In 1973, Spain established full diplomatic relations with the People's Republic of China and with the German Democratic Republic. In the same year, López Bravo signed a commercial agreement with the USSR and the latter country was allowed to establish a 'diplomatic delegation' in Madrid. Spain also renewed her military alliance with the United States and American armed forces were allowed to continue to operate their military bases in the country.

López Bravo also succeeded in concluding a preferential trade agreement with the European Community under which the latter extended to Spain the trade benefits it had granted to countries of the Mediterranean Basin; it must be noted that in 1970 the Community did not consider Spain as a European country entitled to consideration for full membership in the Community. López Bravo's diplomatic achievements brought only limited economic benefits to Spain. His advocacy of an extension of national sovereignty over bordering sea waters to a distance of 200 miles was contrary to the interests of Spain's fishing industry. In matters of domestic economic policy, the new government took monetary and fiscal measures to contain the growth of domestic demand.

## THE LAST YEARS OF GENERAL FRANCO'S LIFE: 1970–5

### 1970

The rate of growth of the world economy decelerated in 1970. While the rate averaged 5% in 1969, it averaged only 3% in 1970. In spite of a general tendency for national rates of growth to decline, inflation appeared to be the major economic problem in most countries. While the rate of inflation in developed countries had averaged 2.8% per year in the period 1958–68, the global rate of inflation in 1970 attained 5.5% (Banco de Bilbao, 1971, 10–12). Table 21 shows annual percentage changes in real GNP and in price indices in seven developed nations for the period 1958 to 1968, as well as for 1969 and 1970.

In Spain, the government established in 1969 decided to follow restrictive economic policies in order to weaken the strong growth of internal demand and to reduce the rate of increase of Spanish imports. Rapidly rising imports had reduced Spanish foreign reserves to only US$ 834 million at the end of 1969, their lowest level since 1962. Given the fact that Spanish imports were highly demand-elastic, and being reluctant to diminish import growth by drastically reducing consumption spending and investment, the government decided to impose on Spanish importers a mandatory charge payable prior to the actual entry into Spain of the imported goods.

Another major goal of the government was to maintain the rate of domestic inflation at a level which would not exceed the global rate. It thus took measures to postpone the spending of about 10% of the approved national budget, proceeded to limit bank credits to the private sector and raised interest rates. The government increased interest rates for two reasons: first, this measure was to help contain the growth of inflation; and second, the government tried to bring Spanish interest rates more in line with those prevailing in the international market. The measure resulted in a significant improvement in Spain's balance of payments, particularly because it discouraged movements of capital out of the country and acted as a stimulus to the entry into Spain of foreign capital.

An equally important measure taken by the government was the postponement of the spending of 10% of the national budget. The government's intention to reduce the growth of public spending was not fully carried out because only three months after such resolution exceptions to the public spending freeze were accepted by the authorities.

Table 21 Annual percentage changes in real GNP and in prices

| Country | Average 1958–68 | 1969 | 1970 |
|---|---|---|---|
| USA | | | |
| GNP | 4.7 | 2.8 | –0.25 |
| Price index | 2.1 | 4.7 | 5.25 |
| Canada | | | |
| GNP | 4.8 | 5.0 | 2.75 |
| Price index | 2.5 | 4.7 | 4.0 |
| Japan | | | |
| GNP | 11.1 | 12.3 | 11.5 |
| Price index | 4.5 | 4.5 | 5.75 |
| France | | | |
| GNP | 5.4 | 7.9 | 5.75 |
| Price index | 4.0 | 6.9 | 5.5 |
| German FR | | | |
| GNP | 5.0 | 8.0 | 4.5 |
| Price index | 2.8 | 3.5 | 7.0 |
| Italy | | | |
| GNP | 5.7 | 4.8 | 6.5 |
| Price index | 3.5 | 4.1 | 6.25 |
| UK | | | |
| GNP | 3.2 | 1.9 | 1.75 |
| Price index | 3.1 | 5.1 | 6.0 |
| Average for the G-7 countries | | | |
| GNP | 5.4 | 4.8 | 2.5 |
| Price index | 3.5 | 4.8 | 5.5 |

Source: Banco de Bilbao, Informe Económico 1970, Bilbao, 1971, p. 12

Private banks responded to the government's restrictive monetary policy by reducing their real liquidity as much as possible in order to maintain the previously existing rate of expansion of credit to the private sector. By May of 1970, the banks' liquidity reached such low levels that the banks suddenly reversed their credit policy and drastically reduced their lending. Such action brought a sharp deterioration of entrepreneurial expectations and a marked slowdown in domestic economic growth. During the third quarter of 1970, consumers' and investment demands had weakened to a point which induced Spanish entrepreneurs to claim that the economy was in a state of recession. Alarmed by such developments, the government decided at the start of 1971 to reactivate the economy and in January of that year reduced interest rates by 0.25% (J. Muñoz et al., 1974, 19–25).

The government's economic policies for 1970 were quite successful. In that year, Spain's GNP increased by 6.5% in real terms and by 12.4% in terms of current prices. More important, these policies contained the pace of inflation growth and kept its rate equal to the world rate. The country's foreign reserves expanded by US$ 958 million. The improvement in the country's external accounts was largely due to the spectacular performance of Spain's exports in 1970. While Spanish imports in that year increased by 12% in terms of current prices, the country's exports rose by 26.5%. The growth of exports in 1970 surpassed all predictions (Banco de Bilbao, 1971, 85).

However, domestic economic growth experienced a slowdown. The year 1970 witnessed decelerations in the growth rates of investment both in fixed capital and in industrial production. While stocks of finished goods expanded, stocks of agricultural commodities and of industrial raw materials diminished. In spite of the deceleration in the rate of growth of industrial production, total employment in 1970 remained relatively stable. Emigration allowed the overall rate of unemployment to remain at 1.5%. According to official data, the active populations of the secondary and tertiary sectors of the economy actually increased by 2.1% and 2.3%, while that of the primary sector declined by 1.3% (Ibid., 88). Concurrently, and in spite of a 5.5% rate of inflation, real per capita incomes in 1970 rose by 5%. By the end of that year, Spain's average per capita real income stood at US$ 824. This was a remarkable achievement for an economy whose average per capita income in 1959 amounted to only US$ 325. These dollar figures were of course affected by global price changes, as well as by the peseta–dollar rate of exchange. Spain's economists proudly predicted in 1970 that Spain's real per capita income would attain US$ 1,000 in 1972. This figure was still relatively low when compared to a real per capita income of US$ 2,000 prevailing in 1970 in most EC countries (Ibid., 94).

Spaniards also pointed with pride at the rate of growth of their Gross Industrial Product in the 1960s. Indeed, the annual rates of Spanish

*Table 22* Comparative rates of growth of the industrial GDP: 1960–6, Spain, EC and Japan

| Year | Spain | GFR | France | Italy | Netherlands | Belgium | EC | Japan |
|---|---|---|---|---|---|---|---|---|
| 1960 | 2.7 | 8.8 | 7.1 | 6.3 | 8.4 | 5.5 | 7.6 | 14.1 |
| 1961 | 13.6 | 5.7 | 5.4 | 8.3 | 3.4 | 4.9 | 5.9 | 15.6 |
| 1962 | 11.3 | 4.4 | 6.8 | 6.3 | 3.8 | 5.6 | 5.5 | 6.4 |
| 1963 | 12.2 | 3.4 | 5.8 | 5.4 | 3.7 | 4.7 | 4.6 | 10.6 |
| 1964 | 13.3 | 6.8 | 6.6 | 2.9 | 8.9 | 6.9 | 6.1 | 13.4 |
| 1965 | 9.4 | 5.8 | 4.7 | 3.6 | 5.4 | 3.9 | 4.9 | 4.5 |
| 1966 | 9.3 | 2.5 | 5.5 | 5.9 | 2.6 | 2.8 | 4.1 | 10.0 |

*Source*: Ardura Calleja, M.L., 1973, p. 330

industrial growth in that decade exceeded corresponding rates in the industrially advanced countries with the exception of Japan. Table 22 shows that between 1961 and 1966 the annual rate of growth of the GDP of Spain's industrial sector was more than twice the corresponding rates in both the German Federal Republic and the EC-6 as a whole.

Growth was not uniform for Spain's various industries. During the 1960s, the industrial subsectors showing the highest rates of growth were those experiencing the most rapid technological advances. Foremost among these were the capital goods industries such as those producing mechanical and electrical equipment, transport materials, as well as chemicals. In the period 1954 to 1970, extractive industries reduced their share in gross domestic industrial output while the share of manufacturing activity expanded. Looking at the percentage contribution to aggregate industrial value added, OECD data indicate that such percentage contribution declined for traditional manufacturing activities such as the production of processed foodstuffs, beverages, tobacco and textiles while it increased in the case of those capital goods industries whose output played an important role in the country's

Table 23  Relative contributions by Spanish industries to the aggregate industrial value added: 1954, 1960, 1970 (in constant 1964 pesetas)

| Sector | Percentages of the aggregate | | |
|---|---|---|---|
| | 1954 | 1960 | 1970 |
| Extractive industries | 6.65 | 5.54 | 2.67 |
| Manufacturing industries of which: | 72.20 | 75.42 | 76.91 |
|    Foodstuffs, beverages, tobacco | 17.34 | 15.36 | 11.65 |
|    Textiles | 10.80 | 9.56 | 5.78 |
|    Clothing and footwear | 4.83 | 5.80 | 5.81 |
|    Wood, cork and furniture | 5.12 | 4.74 | 3.83 |
|    Paper and printing | 2.84 | 3.09 | 3.63 |
|    Chemicals | 6.48 | 7.87 | 9.66 |
|    Cement, glass and stone | 3.81 | 3.85 | 4.80 |
|    Metallurgy | 4.78 | 5.33 | 6.40 |
|    Mechanical and electrical equipment | 9.04 | 11.17 | 11.33 |
|    Transport materials | 3.92 | 6.01 | 10.30 |
|    Other industries | 3.24 | 2.92 | 3.67 |
| Electricity, gas, water | 4.66 | 6.01 | 6.61 |
| Construction | 16.49 | 13.03 | 13.81 |
| Total | 100.00 | 100.00 | 100.00 |

Source: Ardura Calleja, M.L., 1973, p. 332

economic development. Table 23 shows the relative contributions to aggregate industrial value added by various Spanish industries in 1954, 1960 and 1970. The data show that the largest contributions were made by manufacturers of mechanical and electrical equipment, of transport equipment and of chemicals, as well as by metallurgy.

## Size of Spain's firms

In spite of such industrial achievements, Spain's per capita industrial output in 1970 remained much lower than the corresponding output in the Western world. Worse, Spain's industrial products were not able to compete in world markets, by quality or price, with those produced in the industrialized nations of the 'West'.

Spanish economists have explained Spain's comparatively high industrial production costs and its technological backwardness at the end of the 1960s in terms of the structural dichotomy which characterized the country's industrial sector. A study by Carlos Hornillos García attributed to the small size of the great majority of Spain's industrial firms the major reason for their inefficient production methods. He pointed out that about 90% of all Spanish factories in 1970 employed less than five workers each (Hornillos, 1970, 83). He noted that, on the other hand, the rest of the country's industrial concerns were large industrial enterprises. Spain lacked medium-size industrial firms. The writer concluded that the Spanish structural *'minifundio'* system prevailing in the country's secondary sector was the major obstacle in the way of a more vigorous economic development process.

In a more recent study, María Luisa Ardura Calleja observed that according to the findings of an OECD study of 1971 industrial firms employing less than 50 workers constituted 91% of all industrial firms in industrialized Belgium and 97.3% of all such firms in France. The corresponding percentage exceeded 90% in Japan, Norway and Sweden. It was as high as 83% in Switzerland.

Ardura Calleja affirmed that the number of workers employed by a given firm is by itself a poor measure of the size of the firm. It is only because of pragmatic reasons that national statistics use the number of employed workers in a firm as a measure of its size, even though such a measure, based on a single criterion, is necessarily flawed. For this writer, a correct measure of the size of an industrial firm should also take into consideration other criteria such as the firm's cash flow, the value-added it periodically produces, the quantum of its sales and of its net profits. Each of these criteria, if considered alone, will lead to an inexact estimate of the size of the firm. Only a conjoint evaluation of the various criteria will allow an analyst to formulate a correct categorization of the economic or social importance of an industrial concern (Ardura Calleja,

M.L., 1973, 345). Additional characteristics of a small- or medium-size industrial firm may be the absence of internal R & D activity and funding, its difficult access to capital markets and the major limiting influence of a small market.

To select the size of the firm's labour force as the single criterion determining the firm's size can be misleading. Suppose we consider two firms, A and B, which are engaged in the same activity and which operate in similar locations at the same time. Firm A employs 100 workers; firm B operates with 200 workers. The plant and equipment of firm A are however more modern and efficient than those of firm B and the value of A's sales is twice that of B. Which is the larger firm? To classify A as smaller than B is to place greater weight on socio-economic considerations, i.e. numbers of employed persons, than on purely economic ones such as labour productivity and value of output.

If we accept as our guiding criterion of a firm's size the number of persons it employs, a new problem arises; we must assign quantitative limits to such numbers to differentiate small-, medium- and large-size firms. The International Labour Organization has defined the small firm as one whose labour force does not exceed 10 persons, although it has recognized that this number may vary from country to country. Thus, it has designated as small enterprises in the United States and in former West Germany firms with not more than 100 workers. French statistics have often defined as a small French enterprise firms employing between six and 500 workers. The EC has viewed a small enterprise in Italy as one operating with not more than 100 workers. Spanish writers have generally defined a small firm in Spain as one employing less than 50 persons; enterprises employing between 50 and 500 workers are deemed to be of medium size.

According to the data presented by Ardura Calleja, 94.9% of all Spanish industrial enterprises in 1969 employed fewer than 50 workers each, the average size of their labour force being seven. These firms employed 44.7% of all Spanish industrial workers in that year. The same data source indicates that in 1958 industrial firms of less than 50 workers represented 94.6% of all industrial firms in Spain and that these firms employed 38.9% of all Spanish industrial workers (Ibid., 349). The reader, looking at these figures, will tend to believe that the average size of Spanish industrial firms diminished between 1958 and 1969. Firms employing less than 50 workers, i.e. small firms, employed 38.9% of all Spanish industrial workers in 1958 and 44.7% of such workers eleven years later. In fact, the average size of these firms may not have diminished, or may not even have remained stationary, in this period. Ignoring the effects of possible improvements in statistical evaluations, the significance of a larger portion of small firms in the aggregate of Spain's industrial firms in 1969 as compared to 1958 may be questioned.

Table 24  Average size of the labour force in industrial firms in Spain and in selected countries

| Country | Firms with a labour force of 50 to 1,000 persons | Firms with a labour force of more than 1,000 persons |
| --- | --- | --- |
| USA (1963) | 263 | 2,580 |
| German FR (1961) | 265 | 2,680 |
| Netherlands (1962) | 254 | 2,519 |
| Belgium (1963) | 240 | 2,331 |
| France (1962) | 215 | 2,311 |
| Japan (1963) | 192 | 2,266 |
| Italy (1961) | 198 | 2,245 |
| Spain (1969) | 166 | 2,136 |

Source: Ardura Calleja, M.L., 1973, p. 351

One cannot conclude from the observation of these data that the average size of the industrial firm had failed to increase in this period of time. The data do not exclude the possibility that in the course of these eleven years the capitalization of these firms increased and that they were able to produce a larger output with fewer workers. A rising capital/labour ratio in these years would have raised the productivity of such firms and would have improved their efficiency. The fact that most of them operated with fewer workers did not necessarily mean that they had become economically smaller in size.

A more detailed analysis of firms in the various subsectors of Spain's secondary sector in the course of the 1960s, however, shows that most industrial firms failed to reach optimum size. Looking at a relatively new Spanish industry, that of plastic products, data show the existence of 636 firms in that industry in 1960, the average size of their labour force being 18 workers. In 1969, the number of such firms had increased to 1,706 but the size of their labour force remained practically unchanged, i.e. 22 workers. In 1960, the average size of the labour force of a West German plastic products firm was 75 and in this industry, German labour productivity was much higher than in Spain. For Spanish firms, the most burdensome problem faced by the small industrial enterprise was not the relatively small size of its labour force, but its inadequate capitalization and the continued utilization of old and obsolete techniques of production.

Table 24 shows that in the case of industrial firms operating with more than 50 workers but less than 1,000, Spanish firms employed by far the smallest labour force when compared with similar firms in seven industrialized countries. The differential was smaller in the case of large concerns operating with more than 1,000 workers (Ibid., 351).

The relatively small size of most Spanish industrial firms was largely due to the protectionist policies of the Franco regime. During the course of three decades, the Spanish government effectively protected Spanish manufacturers against foreign competition. The government assured these entrepreneurs that they could sell in the home market without fear of having to face the competition of cheaper and better imported goods. The high Spanish tariff wall allowed domestic manufacturers to earn high rates of return on their investment because of large profits; these profits remained anchored to the high prices imposed by Spanish manufacturers on their Spanish customers, not to more efficient production methods. Because the domestic market was small, Spain's manufacturers had no incentive to expand the scale of production of their plants to take advantage of economies of scale. Because they went on producing on the base of ever more inefficient methods, they were unable to export. This state of affairs led to increasing Spanish technological backwardness and to economic stagnation at a time when the industrialized economies of Western Europe were recording spectacular economic advances.

## Trade relations

As late as 1959, the drafters of the Stabilization Plan showed little interest in negotiating with the young European Economic Community a reciprocal trade agreement that could have been advantageous to Spain even though Spain's trade with the EC-6 was recording an increasing annual deficit. And this at a time when the Community and the European Free Trade Association, EFTA, competed for economic predominance in Western Europe and were thus eager to negotiate special trade arrangements with non-member European nations. The EC in particular showed great willingness to enter into special commercial treaties with African countries and with countries bordering the Mediterranean. The Second Convention of Yaundé, signed on 29 July 1969 with a number of African countries, gave preferential tariff treatment to African products entering the EC area while it allowed the participating African nations to maintain protective tariff barriers burdening the import of Community goods in order to encourage industrialization in the latter countries and to help them overcome balance-of-payments difficulties. The EC also agreed to increase the technical and financial help it extended to those countries. The EC also granted preferential trade treatment to countries forming part of the Mediterranean Basin. Many of these countries were closely linked through trade to EC countries. The EC tried to boost this trade through two types of commercial treaty with the Mediterranean countries. It signed special trade agreements with Mediterranean countries which were possible candidates for membership in the EC and also with other Mediterranean countries. In the 1960s, the EC signed Association Agreements with both

Greece and Turkey. In the 1970s, Agreements for Commerce and Cooperation were signed with second group countries, such as the countries of the Mahgreb (Morocco, Algiers, Tunisia), of the Mashrek (Egypt, Syria, Lebanon and Jordan) and finally with Israel. With minor exceptions, the industrial goods produced in such countries were allowed to enter the EC area free of any import duty.

In Spain, the Franco regime left the study of Spain's economic integration into either the EC or EFTA to a committee of ministers headed by P. Gual Villalví, a Minister without portfolio who presided over endless debates on the question of whether or not Spain should start negotiations with the EC or with EFTA. The *Generalissimo* appeared to remain indifferent to the economic achievements of the two organizations, at least until August 1961, when the United Kingdom, the very country which had proposed EFTA in an effort to hinder the establishment of the Community, petitioned for membership in the latter organization.

Spain's new interest in negotiating an Association Treaty with the Community was probably spurred by the enactment by the latter of regulations dealing with its international trade in agricultural goods. Spain's government had reasons to fear that such regulations could produce a sharp fall in the country's exports of agricultural commodities to the EC-6 countries. On 9 February 1962 Spain's Minister for Foreign Affairs, Fernando Ma. Castiella, wrote a letter to the President of the EC Council, Maurice Couve de Murville, in which he requested that the Community extend to Spain 'an association susceptible of reaching in time complete integration . . .' (Alonso, A., 1985, 24). (The Council's feelings toward the Spanish government probably deteriorated when in June General Franco ordered his government to enforce harsh punitive measures against the Spanish delegates to the European Movement Congress meeting in Munich because the latter had urged the Community not to negotiate with the Franco government. The Council did not respond to Castiella's letter.)

Spain's chances of negotiating a commercial treaty with the European Community appeared to be further limited by the EC Council's approval of the Birkelbach Report drafted by a committee representing the EC European Parliament. This Report in effect prohibited any association between the Community and any European non-EC member country which could not satisfy the political conditions imposed by the Community on nations seeking full membership in the EC. The Council, by supporting the mandate contained in this Report, appeared to forbid the EC Commission from entering into negotiations for the formulation of a preferential trade accord with any country whose political system made it ineligible for membership in the Common Market. Spain's ability to negotiate an Association Agreement with the EC Commission appeared to be further jeopardized when on 4 May 1964 the Italian government sent a declaration to the EC Council reaffirming Italy's support of the Birkelbach Report.

A letter to the Spanish government from the President of the EC Council, Paul Henri Spaak, and dated 2 June 1964, was received with great surprise by the Spanish authorities. M. Spaak notified the Spanish government that the EC Council had allowed the EC Commission to enter into conversations with Spanish officials so that both sides could jointly examine the economic problems faced by Spain which stemmed from the economic development of the European Community and propose appropriate solutions. These conversations were initiated in December of 1964.

During the early 1960s, Spain's trade deficit with the Community had expanded because the latter limited Spanish exports of agricultural goods to the EC area while Spain's imports of capital goods from the EC countries had risen quite rapidly. This deficit, which in 1962 fell short of US$ 200 million, had increased to about US$ 800 million in 1965. Spain's authorities pointed out to the EC Commission that unless Spain could enter into an advantageous preferential trade agreement with the EC, Spain would have to suspend her new policy of foreign trade liberalization. A major difficulty in the way of such trade agreement was that the EC jurists interpreted such agreement to be equivalent to an Association Agreement, an Agreement the EC could not enter into with Spain under the terms of the Birkelbach Report.

Officials of the Spanish Ministry of Foreign Affairs finally convinced the EC Commission that Article 113 of the Treaty of Rome allowed the Community to negotiate with third countries preferential trade agreements which could not be construed as being part of, or leading to, an Association Agreement. Conversations between Spanish officials and representatives of the EC Commission were renewed in January 1966. Both sides attempted to formulate an accord which would not be inconsistent with the political tenets of the Community and which would benefit Spain economically. Both parties recognized that any trade agreement concluded between Spain and the EC would have to honour GATT regulations. The formula developed by the negotiators established a 'Provisional Accord' which would facilitate the progressive establishment of either a customs union between the EC and Spain or a free trade zone between them as sanctioned by Article XXIV, section 5c, of the GATT. The representatives of the EC Commission made the point that the agreement with Spain would make it quite clear that it would never be a stepping stone leading to a future customs union between Spain and the EC; such a possibility implied that the Community would eventually accept Franco's Spain as a full EC member nation. The Spaniards, on the other hand, rejected an agreement with the EC which could be understood as allowing the eventual establishment of a free trade zone including Spain and the EC; their objection rested on the possible eventual power of the Community to demand a total removal of Spanish import duties on the entry into Spain of EC industrial goods. Both sides solved this dilemma by drafting a 'staged agreement' which left to an uncertain future the goals of such agreement as required by Article XXIV, section 5c, of the GATT. These difficulties solved, both parties declared their willingness to negotiate the terms of what became the Accord of 1970.

In July 1967, the European Community opened formal negotiations with Spain by offering that country a reciprocal tariff reductions arrangement as detailed by a First Mandate drafted by the European Council. The EC offered to reduce its duties on imports of most Spanish industrial goods by 60%, such reductions being gradual and extending over a period of four years. Specified EC imports of Spanish goods would have their duties lowered by only 40%, and still others were not to benefit from any duty reduction. The Community did not extend any tariff concessions to imports of Spanish agricultural goods. The EC in turn requested Spain to lower its duties on imports of Community industrial goods by 40% and to completely abolish all quantitative restrictions burdening the entry of such goods into Spain. That country was given a period of six years to effect the proposed changes.

Spain's negotiators were anxious to obtain tariff concessions for Spanish exports of agricultural commodities to the EC countries. In order to induce the Community to widen the scope of its tariff concessions so that the latter would include EC imports of Spanish agricultural products, they formulated a surprising counter-offer. Their strategy offered the Community tariff concessions for its industrial products which were more generous than those requested by the EC itself. The *quid pro quo* consisted of EC tariff reductions for Spanish exports of agricultural goods to the Community. Spain thus requested the Community to formulate a Second Mandate so that the negotiations would cover Spanish exports of agricultural commodities to the EC countries. The Community approved a Second Mandate in October 1969 whose terms met the demands of Spain's negotiators. This Mandate extended privileged tariff treatment to a number of Spanish agricultural exports, including exports of oranges and of olive oil of great importance to Spain. On 29 June 1970 a Commercial Accord between Spain and the EC was signed in Luxembourg. The terms of this Accord were to become effective on 1 October 1970.

It must be noted that the Accord was a preferential agreement, i.e. an agreement under whose terms both parties extended each other partial tariff reductions, reductions which were not automatically extended to third countries participating in the GATT. Even though Article I of the GATT required that any tariff concession extended by one member country to another be granted to all other countries participating in the GATT, the 'provisional accord' between Spain and the EC was exempt from the 'most favoured nation' mandate because Article XXIV of the GATT exempted from the requirements of Article I 'provisional accords leading to the establishment of a customs union or of a free trade zone'. The Accord of 1970 was recognized as a 'provisional agreement' as defined by Article XXIV which left to an unspecified future 'second stage' in the commercial relations between Spain and the EC their decision touching the eventual formation of a customs union or of a free trade zone. It should also be remembered that the tariff reductions mandated by the Accord of 1970 were not imposed on EC and Spanish tariff structures as they existed on 1 October 1970, but on current structures.

## 1971

The year 1971, just like 1970, was characterized by a weakening domestic demand and by a very good export performance of the economy. Large inflows of capital helped Spain record a large external surplus at the end of 1971, as well as a significant increase in official reserves. Reacting to the expanding unused industrial capacity and to the large surplus on current account, the government cautiously embraced expansionary policies in the face of rising prices and wages. The authorities adopted a number of stimulative measures, mostly of a monetary nature, and increased the rate of budgetary spending. The mandatory price-to-import deposit was reduced to 10%. At the start of 1971, the discount rate was reduced by 0.25% to 6.25%, and in April, this rate was further reduced to 6%. In June, the prior-to-import deposit was abolished; in August, the discount rate was reduced to 5%. Banks were freed of the requirement of prior official authorization for the extension of industrial loans exceeding 18 months, and the peseta was allowed to appreciate against the dollar by 2% (OECD, 1972, 10–11). By mid-1971, bank credit to the private sector was about 17% above its level one year earlier while the government's budgetary expenditures exceeded by 19% their 1970 level (Ibid., 14).

In spite of the expansionary effects of increased public spending and in spite of the strong foreign demand for Spain's exports, economic recovery remained weak until the end of the summer of 1971. Capital equipment imports remained below their 1970 value until the third quarter of the year and slowly expanded afterwards. Because of inflation, real purchasing power increased by only 6.5% during the year. Aggregate demand was further limited by a decline in fixed investment;

Table 25 Spain's foreign trade: 1970–1

|  | 1971 change over 1970 in percentages | | |
|---|---|---|---|
|  | Jan.–June | July–Oct. | Jan.–Oct. |
| Imports (cif) | 1 | 9 | 4 |
| Agricultural | 22 | 18 | 20 |
| Non-agricultural | −3 | 7.3 | 1 |
| of which: | | | |
| Oil | 31 | 43 | 38 |
| Iron and steel | −44 | −20 | −35 |
| Machinery | 3.3 | 6.7 | 4.7 |
| Exports | 24 | 26 | 25 |
| Agricultural | 9.3 | – | 6.2 |
| Non-agricultural | 34 | 38 | 35 |
| of which: | | | |
| Machinery | 41 | 6.5 | 26 |
| Ships | 126 | 56 | 95 |
| Footwear | 55 | 84 | 66 |
| Iron and steel | 48 | 109 | 80 |

Source: OECD, *Economic Surveys, Spain*, Paris, 1972, p. 18

in the capital goods industries plant utilization diminished throughout the year.

The principal growth factor of domestic aggregate demand was Spain's export activity. As Table 25 indicates, the value of total Spanish exports in the period January–October 1971 was 25% higher than it had been one year earlier. Exports of non-agricultural goods in 1971 stood at 35% above their value in 1970. In the former year, the value of exports of ships rose by 95% above that registered in 1970; the corresponding increase in the case of iron and steel was 80%. Such export performance placed Spain's external current account surplus expressed as a percentage of GNP the second highest for all OECD countries, second only to that of Japan. By the end of 1971, Spain's official reserves had risen by more than US$ 1.6 billion, nearly twice their increase in 1970 (Ibid., 21).

## 1972

The year 1972 witnessed the highest rate of economic growth the Spanish economy had attained in the course of the decade ending in that year. The rate of Spanish economic growth in 1972 surpassed all estimates. Official studies calculated the rate of growth of the country's GDP in that year to be 7.7% in real terms, a significant jump over the previous year's rate of 4.6%. The Studies Service of the Bank of Bilbao reported for 1972 a rate of growth of real GNP of at least 8% (Banco

## GROWTH AND CRISIS IN THE SPANISH ECONOMY

*Table 26* Selected economic indicators: 1971–2

| Indicator | Annual percentage growth | |
|---|---|---|
| | 1971 | 1972 |
| Gross Capital Formation | −1.4 | 16.0 |
| Investment Index | −0.4 | 21.0 |
| Industrial Output Index | 2.1 | 17.1 |
| Cost of Living Index | 9.7 | 7.3 |
| Wholesale Price Index | 8.4 | 6.4 |

Source: Muñoz, J. et al., *La Economía Española en 1972*, Madrid, EDICUSA, 1973, p. 23

de Bilbao, 1973, 41). In that year, Spanish industrial production expanded in real terms by 10.7%, a major change from a growth rate of 3.9% attained in 1971. Duplicating the rapid growth of the secondary sector's output, that of the tertiary sector increased by 7.5% in terms of constant prices. On the other hand, agricultural output increased by only 0.8% because of the failure of cereal crops (Ibid., 42).

These unequal results on the supply side also appeared on the demand side of the economy. Though all the components of aggregate demand showed rising trends in 1972, these trends differed. The growth of public consumption in the latter year showed a slight decline when compared to that of 1971. In 1972, investment gave the strongest stimulus to the recuperation of total demand. Whereas the rate of growth of Gross Capital Formation had declined by 1.4% in real terms in 1971, it rose by 16% in 1972. In the latter year, private consumption, representing about 67% of aggregate demand, showed a relatively moderate pace of growth of about 6.5%. This rate reflected the impact of inflation in 1972. Indeed, the cost of living rose by about 7.3% in that year. Rising prices were translated into a rate of growth of real wages and salaries of not more than 6%, a rate of growth which was lower than that of the GDP in the same year. These differing trends showed a reduction in the percentage share of National Income commanded by the country's workers. The effect on consumers' spending was obvious since 75% of consumption spending was based on wages and salaries (Muñoz, J. *et al.*, 1973, 20–1).

Exports expanded in 1971 largely because of the weakening of internal demand. In 1972, Spain's exports, valued in terms of US dollars, grew at a rate of 25.6% in spite of an expanding domestic demand. The ability of Spain's export sector to strengthen the national balance of payments in a year of expanding internal demand indicated a major structural change in the Spanish economy. An important indicator of such change was the strong increase in investment demand which characterized the entirety of 1972. Table 26 lists a number of key economic indicators for 1971 and 1972.

## THE 1970s

*Graph 14* Investment index: 1962–72

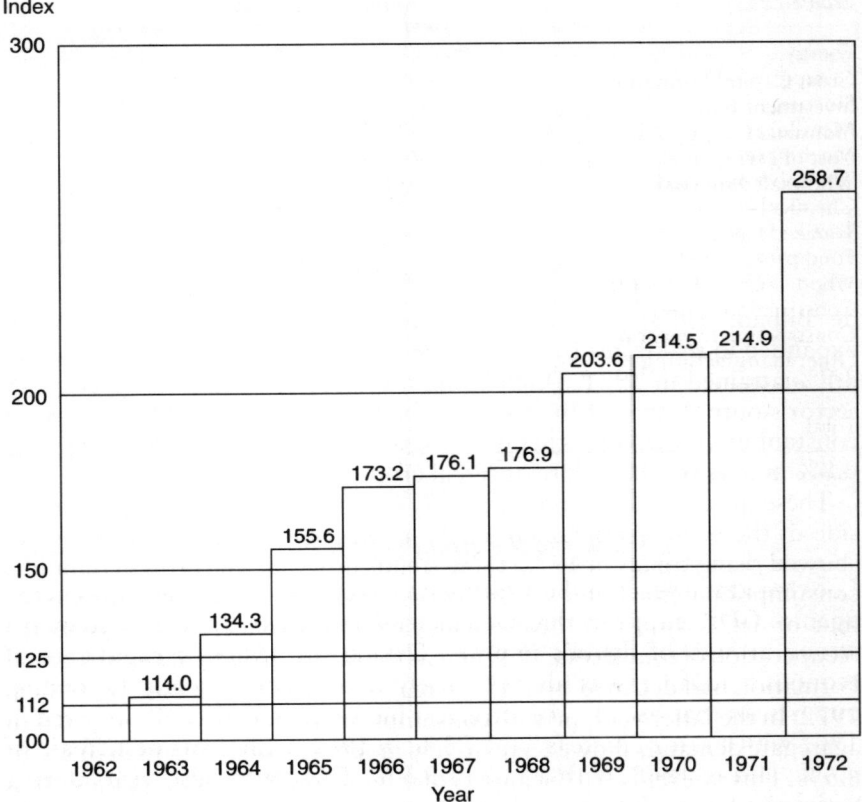

Source: Ibid., p. 25

As shown in Table 27 industrial investment in nominal terms increased by 15.1% in 1972, while it had slightly declined in 1971 when compared to its growth in the previous year. The sudden expansion of investment in 1972, (Graph 14), boosted the outputs of transport materials, chemicals, machinery, wood and cork products as well as construction in general. That year also recorded strong increases in industrial productivity. Productivity per employed worker rose by 8.5% and productivity per work hour increased by 9.8% (Ibid., 32). The year 1972 brought to Spain a renewal of the rapid pace of industrialization the country had experienced in the early 1960s. Graph 15, (p. 135), illustrates how rapidly idle industrial capacity in Spain diminished between March and December 1972.

Table 27  Industrial investment in 1972: Percentage variation 1972/1971

| Sector | Percentage change |
| --- | --- |
| Energy | 8.4 |
| Mining | 9.1 |
| Siderurgy | −0.7 |
| Metallurgy | 19.1 |
| Machinery | 20.1 |
| Transport materials | 35.0 |
| Chemicals | 37.5 |
| Textiles | 13.2 |
| Food processing | 6.4 |
| Wood, cork and furniture | 32.7 |
| Construction materials | −21.9 |
| Construction in general | 52.0 |
| Other manufacturing | 16.2 |
| Miscellaneous | 15.1 |
| Total | 15.1 |

Source: Ibid., p. 31

## Trade and the growth of the economy

Looking at the years in the 1960s which recorded strong increases in the Spanish GDP, it appears that such increases were closely correlated with a strong growth of Spain's imports. During the 1960s, a rapid rate of economic advance was always closely tied to concurrently expanding imports. In that decade, the strongest increases in real GDP occurred in 1961 with a rate of increase of 11.3%, in 1962, with a rate of increase of 9.6%, and in 1963, with a rate of 9.5%. These were also years during which the country's imports showed strong growth; in real terms, imports increased by 39.8% in 1961, 34.1% in 1962, and by 23.2% in 1963. Except for 1965, the rate of growth of real GDP declined during the balance of the decade and so did the annual rate of growth of Spanish imports (Ibid., 42). As the rapidly growing cost of imports became harder to cover with the earnings from tourism and from the remittances of Spaniards working abroad, the Spanish government tried to contain the pace of import growth at the expense of the rate of economic growth. External disequilibria led the government to devalue the peseta in 1967 in order to boost the country's exports and to discourage import growth. While the country's GDP expanded by about 9% during the period 1961 to 1965, imports rose at an average annual rate of 27.6%. It grew by only 6% during the second half of the decade, with imports showing an average annual rate of growth attaining only 8.5% in the period 1966 to 1970 (Ibid.). It thus appears that import expansion was a major determinant of the rate of economic growth of the Spanish economy in the 1960s.

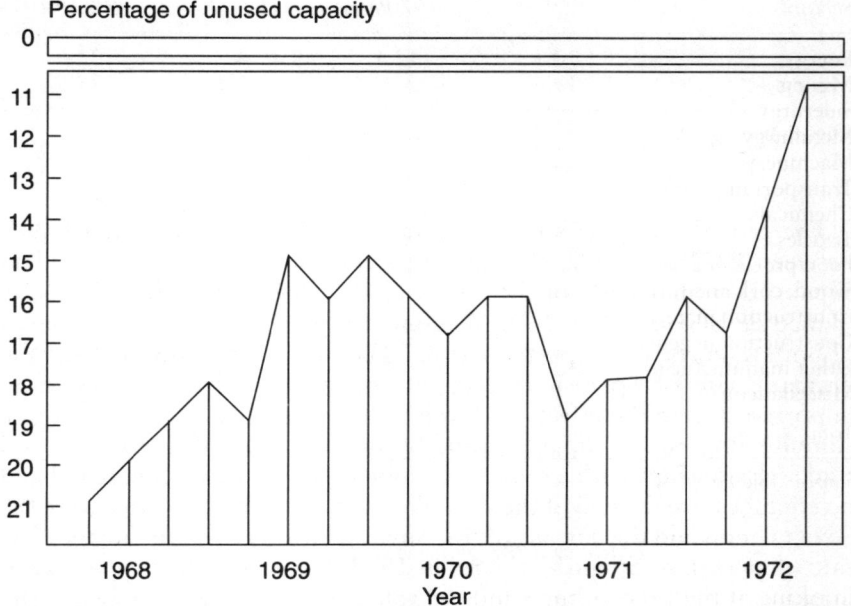

Graph 15 Utilization of productive industrial capacity: 1968–72

Source: Ibid., p. 38

The relationship between the pace of economic growth and the growth of imports is easy to explain in the case of an economically backward country in great need of modernizing its capital equipment, of adopting more efficient technologies, of solving the problems of resource scarcities and of raising its workers' productivity. Spain in the 1960s was an economically poor and backward country in Western Europe. Spain's economy, then characterized by limited resources, by the survival of obsolete production technologies in both the agricultural and the industrial sectors of the economy, by an excessively protected domestic market and by relatively low levels of productivity, had great difficulty in financing the imports the country needed to develop and to modernize. Since the 1950s, Spain had relied on her earnings from tourism and on remittances sent to the home country by Spaniards working abroad to finance much needed imports. In later years, the entry into Spain of increasing volumes of foreign capital facilitated the financing of expanding imports. During the 1960s, Spain's exports, though continuously rising in value, were unable to reduce the country's trade deficit. Table 28 shows annual percentage increases in the value of Spanish imports and exports.

Table 28 Percentage annual increases in Spain's external trade: 1969–72

|         | 1969/68 | 1970/69 | 1971/70 | 1972/71 |
|---------|---------|---------|---------|---------|
| Imports | 20.1    | 12.1    | 4.7     | 33.0    |
| Exports | 19.6    | 25.7    | 23.1    | 25.6    |

Source: Ibid., p. 47

The growth of Spain's foreign trade in 1972 was quite remarkable. Between 1971 and 1972, the value of this trade expressed in US dollars expanded from 1.23% of the world trade's aggregate value to 1.45% (Banco de Bilbao, 1973, 130). A number of factors explain the growth of both imports and exports in 1972. The most important one was the dramatic rise of Spanish investment spending in that year. Next in importance were the effects of commercial policy liberalization and the stimulus imparted to Spain's trade by the initiation of diplomatic and trade relationships with a number of countries with which Spain had had no contact since the end of the Civil War. Among such countries were the Soviet Union and the nations of the 'Soviet Block' in Eastern Europe. The rate of growth of Spanish exports in 1972 was surpassed by the rate of increase of both the volume and the value of the country's imports. The strong growth of imports in 1972 resulted in an expansion of the country's trade deficit as shown by Graph 16. Global inflation accounted for part of the increase in the value of Spanish imports. Their volume was larger than that of 1971 and helped Spain to modernize her productive structures and to contain the pace of internal inflation.

As in 1971, about half of Spain's imports consisted of raw materials and of semi-finished manufactured goods. The share of capital equipment in total imports rose from 24.4% in 1971 to 27% in 1972, while that of foodstuffs declined from 16.8% to 15.7%. Table 29 compares the breakdown of Spanish imports according to principal component groups in 1971 and 1972. The possible inflationary impact of import growth in Spain was undoubtedly restrained by the devaluations of the gold parity of the US dollar in both December 1971 and February 1973. These changes in the gold parity of the dollar were equivalent to a *de facto* revaluation of the peseta in terms of the dollar. Such an indirect revaluation had a stabilizing effect on Spanish prices.

Manufactured goods generated most of Spain's export growth in 1972. As shown by Table 30, manufactured consumer goods constituted the most dynamic export component in that year and represented about a quarter of the aggregate value of Spain's exports. Exports of capital equipment were discouraged by the strong rise of internal demand for such goods and their exports in 1972 increased by only 2.9% above their

*Graph 16* Spain's foreign trade: 1964–72

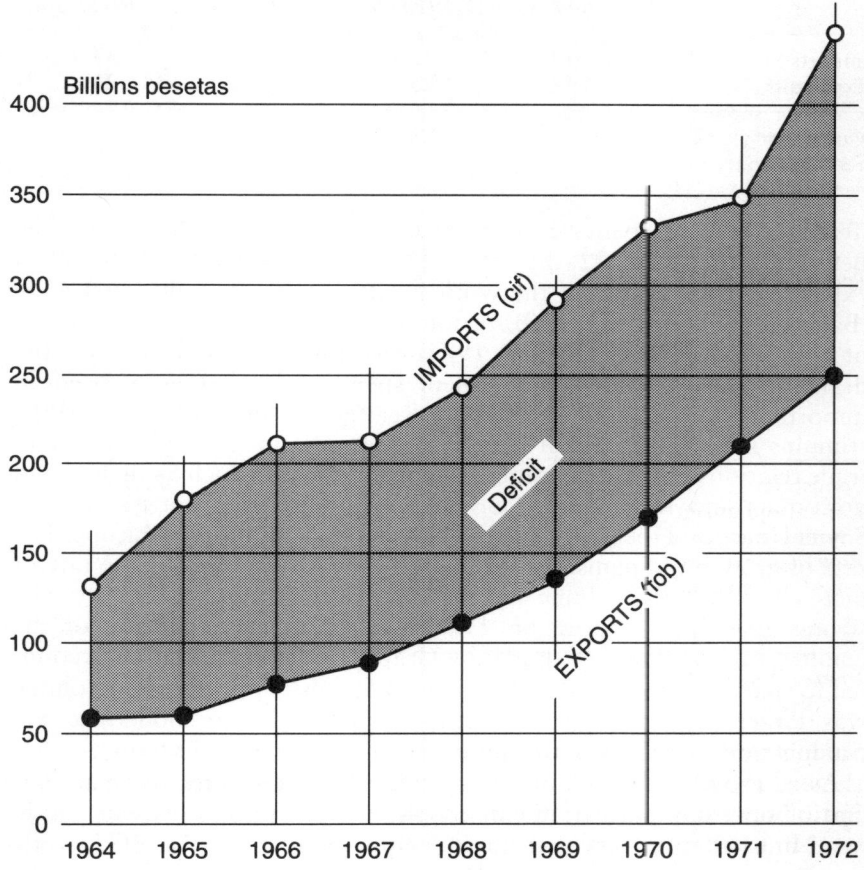

*Source*: Banco de Bilbao, *Informe Económico 1972*, 1973, p. 133

1971 growth rate. Foodstuffs, as a component of total exports declined in relative importance while the export of raw materials and of semi-finished goods retained the share of total exports they commanded one year earlier. It should be noted that Spain's export performance in 1972 strengthened in spite of a growing internal demand for manufactured exportables, in spite of an increase in the domestic prices of manufactured goods in the order of 6% and in spite of the *de facto* revaluation of the peseta in terms of the US dollar following the devaluation of the dollar in terms of gold in December 1971.

Examining the evolution of Spain's commerce with European nations,

Table 29  Principal components of imports: 1971–2

|  | Percentage of the total in 1971 | Percentage of the total in 1972 |
|---|---|---|
| Foodstuffs | 16.8 | 15.7 |
| Capital equipment | 24.4 | 27.0 |
| Consumer goods | 6.8 | 7.1 |
| Raw materials and semi-finished goods | 52.0 | 50.2 |
| Total | 100.0 | 100.0 |

Source: Ibid., p. 137

Table 30  Principal components of exports: 1971–2

|  | Percentage of the total in 1971 | Percentage of the total in 1972 |
|---|---|---|
| Foodstuffs | 30.7 | 27.9 |
| Capital equipment | 18.2 | 18.7 |
| Consumer goods | 22.3 | 25.1 |
| Raw materials and semi-finished goods | 28.8 | 28.3 |
| Total | 100.0 | 100.0 |

Source: Ibid., p. 141

Spain's trade with her most important European trade partner, the EC, showed growing disequilibrium in 1972. While the surge of demand in Spain boosted imports of raw materials, manufactured consumer goods, semi-finished products and capital equipment from the EC, it also weakened Spanish exports to the Community. Compared to their aggregate value in 1971, Spain's exports to the EC increased in 1972 by 13.9%, while Spain's imports from the Community rose by 28.6%. Although trade with the EFTA countries amounted to only one half the value of Spain's trade with the EC, trade with EFTA in 1972 not only increased at a faster pace than that with the EC but also showed a greater balance between imports and exports from and to the European Free Trade Area. Spanish imports from EFTA rose by 28.9% above their 1971 aggregate value, while Spanish exports to EFTA increased by 22.7%. Spain's new trade with the countries of Eastern Europe, though representing a small portion of Spain's total foreign trade, contributed nevertheless to intensify Spain's trade disequilibrium in 1972. While Spanish exports to these countries increased by 40%, Spanish imports from Eastern Europe rose by 104% (Ibid., 146–7).

Spain's expanding trade with the United States, representing 15.5% of the country's total foreign trade in 1971 and 16.02% in 1972, showed in the latter year a 27% increase in the value of Spanish exports, mostly composed of manufactured consumer goods, and a 28% increase in Spanish imports from America, constituted mainly of capital equipment goods and foodstuffs. On the other hand, Spain's trade with Latin America diminished in importance, the share of such trade in total Spanish foreign trade declining from 10% in 1971 to 8.5% in 1972.

Though Spain's trade with the rest of the world expanded in 1972, it also tended to concentrate largely on commercial exchange with a limited number of nations, particularly with the United States and the German Federal Republic. Foreign trade, so vital to Spanish economic growth, was becoming too dependent on Spanish commercial exchange with these two countries.

## 1973

The strong pace of economic growth in 1972 was strengthened in 1973. The Spanish economy in the latter year was characterized by a major advance of its Gross National Product and by rising inflation. The rate of growth of real GNP exceeded 8% and Spain's per capita income reached US$ 1,700 at the exchange rate of 58 pesetas to the dollar. Gross real investment in fixed capital increased by about 20% over its 1972 level. This strong growth process was accompanied by accelerating inflation. During 1973, the cost of living index rose by 14.2% and the general price index increased by 10.4%. This pace of inflation weakened the international competitiveness of Spanish exports while discouraging private saving, and therefore, private investment (Banco de Bilbao, 1974, 63).

On the positive side of the 1973 picture the Spanish economy attained full employment of its active population. The rate of utilization of the country's productive capacity had never been so high; the optimistic mood of Spanish entrepreneurs was evidenced by their rapidly expanding orders for raw materials and manufactured products. Expanding investment and consumption demands, coupled with strong inflationary pressures, started limiting the expansion of bank credit during the last quarter of the year and caused a slight deceleration in the pace of economic growth. The oil and raw materials crises in October further worsened entrepreneurial expectations and caused a decline in investment demand at the start of 1974.

Three important sectors performed as follows:

1 Agriculture produced in 1973 an aggregate output which, in real terms, was about 8.4% higher than that obtained in the previous

year. Concurrently, agricultural prices rose by about 9.2%.
2   The Ministry of Industry reported an increase in real industrial production of 10.1%. This increase was estimated to have reached 11% by the Studies Service of the Bank of Bilbao.
3   A slowdown in the rate of growth of tourism produced a deceleration in the rate of growth of the tertiary sector which nevertheless attained 7.2% in real terms in 1973 (Ibid., 64–5).

The principal explanatory variable accounting for Spain's strong economic growth in 1973 was the surge of investment in fixed capital which in terms of constant prices attained a growth rate of 20.6%. Such a rate surpassed the rate of 19.7% obtained in 1972. Inflation limited the growth of consumers' demand to 6.8% in real terms, a decline from a rate of 7.9% obtained one year earlier.

Foreign trade also expanded in 1973. Real imports increased by 21% above their 1972 level, while exports expanded by 15.9%. The balance of physical trade and of services deficit increased in 1973 by US$ 673 million. This deficit was however easily covered by the surplus shown by the transfers and capital transactions balance. At the end of the year, the Spanish balance of payments showed a surplus of about US$ 1.8 billion. Total employment increased by 3.3% in 1973 and real wages and salaries per employed person rose by 4.6%.

The negative side of Spain's economy in 1973 was its strong inflation. Only five countries in the OECD experienced in that year a higher rise in the cost of living than that in Spain. These were Greece (30.6%), Iceland (28.4%), Portugal (20.1%), Japan (19.1%) and Finland (15.5%).

## The political background 1969–73

In spite of strong economic growth in 1973, dissension and opposition between 'reformists' and 'conservatives' in the Cabinet continued. The former were mostly Falangists and members of the Catholic Action group who wanted to liberalize the existing political regime. During the summer of 1969, they had hoped that the much publicized 'MATESA scandal' would induce the Caudillo to purge the government of the conservative followers of *Opus Dei*. General Franco did not do this.

MATESA was a textile machinery firm which had been founded in 1956 by a Catalan industrialist, Juan Vilá Reyes, a man who claimed that MATESA would improve the French loom 'Iwer' and export it in large quantities. In order to finance this project MATESA acquired official credits to an amount exceeding 10 billion pesetas. MATESA's management had promised to manufacture and export more than 20,000 looms. In fact only one-tenth of the promised quantity was sold.

The government discovered that instead of using the credits received by MATESA to facilitate the export of its looms, the firm's management had used these credits to acquire other Spanish firms, to purchase foreign textile concerns and, worst of all, to finance the personal investments and the personal expenses of MATESA's directors and officers (Tamames, R., 1979, 489–90).

Although the government's leaders appeared willing to enter into an agreement with MATESA and keep silent about the incident, a number of reformist Cabinet ministers facilitated the publication of the scandal. Among these were the Minister for Foreign Affairs, a member of the Catholic Action group, Fernando Ma. Castiella, the Minister for Information and Tourism, the Falangist Manuel Fraga Iribarne, and the Secretary General of the Movement, the Falangist José Solís Ruiz. It was reported that these men had hoped that the publication of the 'affair MATESA' would bring about a wholesale dismissal of members or supporters of *Opus Dei* in the government. If this was their hope, it did not materialize.

On 29 October 1969 General Franco replaced thirteen out of eighteen government ministers in order to constitute a new 'monocolour' government in which members of *Opus Dei* appeared to have a strong majority. Among the dismissed ministers were José Solís Ruiz and Manuel Fraga Iribarne (Ibid.).

The new Secretary General of the Movement, Torcuato Fernández Miranda, lost no time in denouncing the legalization of the political associations favoured by his predecessor on the grounds that the latter would lead to the formation of political parties which, according to Fernández Miranda, were inconsistent with a regime of 'organic democracy'. The powerful Vice-President, Luis Carrero Blanco, was also opposed to any government concession which could resurrect political parties.

The reactivation of the economy in the period 1971 to 1973 did not weaken dissension within the government and within Spanish society. Church–State relations deteriorated while university students and workers demonstrated in favour of a democratization of the country's political regime. Though prohibited by law, local general strikes were carried out in Vigo, in El Ferrol and in Pamplona in 1970. Terrorism intensified in 1972 and 1973. To the violent acts of the Basque ETA group were added those of a new terrorist organization, FRAP. The government responded through harsh police measures. A number of labour leaders were arrested and given long jail sentences. Liberal publications were banned or heavily fined. Carrero Blanco's efforts to silence critics of the regime failed. The daily press started printing the views of non-communist opposition leaders. Newspapers such as *Ya* and *Informaciones* started advocating reform. The new magazine, *Cambio*

16, did not hesitate to print sharp criticisms of the Francoist regime (Carr, R. and Fusi, J.P., 1979, 191–2).

Franco's political apparatus was showing deep cracks. While right-wing toughs attacked bookshops selling reformist literature and while staunch Francoists in the *Cortes* denounced the efforts of Gregorio López Bravo to renew diplomatic and trade relations with the countries of Eastern Europe, the press allowed criticisms of the existing regime to be studied by their readers. In the words of R. Carr and J.P. Fusi,

> Something deeper than a mere ministerial malaise was afflicting the Francoist state: a crisis of the regime which had begun with debates over political associations in 1967–9, a crisis of contradictions. Spain was officially a Catholic state; yet the church was at odds with the regime. Strikes were illegal but there were hundreds of them every year. Spain was an anti-liberal state yet desperately searching for some form of democratic legitimacy. It was a state whose official ideology was 'an integrating national Socialism', but which nevertheless had transformed Spain into a capitalist society. 'In Spain', the ultra right-winger Blas Piñar said in October 1972, 'we are suffering from a crisis of identity of our own state.'
>
> Ibid., p. 194

On 29 June 1973 the *Generalissimo* appointed Luis Carrero Blanco as President of a new government. Carrero Blanco was to succeed Franco and assure the continuation of a Francoist regime even though Prince Juan Carlos de Borbón would be crowned King of Spain. Carrero had served for twenty-two years as Minister Sub-Secretary of the Presidency and almost seven years as Vice-President of the government. He had well proved his loyalty to Franco and to his regime. It was only natural that Franco chose him as his successor. Torcuato Fernández-Miranda retained his position as Secretary General of the Movement and became in addition Vice-President of the government. A close friend of Franco, and until then Mayor of Madrid, Carlos Arias Navarro, became Minister of Governance, while Laureano López Rodó was appointed Minister for Foreign Affairs.

The first Carrero government was also the last. The new President of the government was assassinated by members of the Basque terrorist group ETA on 20 December 1973. The violent death of Luis Carrero Blanco led to the establishment of the last government constituted by General Franco, a government presided by Carlos Arias Navarro and which remained in power from 5 January 1974 until 12 December 1975. It was Franco's tenth and last government.

## THE 1970s
## Relations with the EC

Franco's monocolour government showed greater flexibility in its negotiations with the European Economic Community than in its relationships with Spain's students, workers and priests. On 30 June 1970, the day following that on which the EC and Spain had signed the Accord of 1970, the Community initiated negotiations with the United Kingdom, Ireland, Denmark and Norway in order to define the conditions under which these countries would be admitted to full membership in the European Economic Community. The Spanish government was very concerned with the possible adverse effects on Spanish exports brought about by an enlargement of the Community. Spanish exports of fresh and processed agricultural goods and of wine to the United Kingdom amounted in 1970 to half the value of these exports to the EC-6. Spain also sold smaller quantities of such products to Ireland and Denmark. Until then, such exports had entered the United Kingdom practically free of any import duty. By joining the Community, Britain would have to adopt the Community's common external tariff and Spanish exports to the United Kingdom could suffer as a result.

Because a number of EFTA countries had signed free trade agreements with the EC, Spaniards had also reason to apprehend that their exports of industrial products to countries in Western Europe would face tariff barriers in the EC as well as in the EFTA countries.

At that time, the EC-6 had signed preferential trade Accords with Spain and with Israel, had extended similar preferences to Morocco and Tunisia and had entered into Association Agreements with Greece and with Turkey. Two major problems faced the Community in the summer of 1970. France and Italy feared that the Mediterranean countries with which the EC had signed preferential trade agreements, the so-called co-contracting nations, could displace French and Italian agricultural products from their markets in the Community. In addition, the enlargement of the Community diversely affected the trade of each EC country with the countries of the Mediterranean Basin. In turn, Spain and Israel worried about the effects on their exports to the United Kingdom once the Community's common external tariff would be imposed on British foreign trade.

In order to ascertain the wishes of the co-contracting countries in the Mediterranean Basin, the EC Commission held a number of individual meetings with the governments of the latter countries during June 1971. In a Report the Commission presented to the EC Council in September, the former suggested the Community should extend individualized concessions to each co-contracting nation before 1 January 1973, in an attempt to leave the relative export position of these countries in the Community's market undamaged by the latter's enlargement. Such strategy required the renegotiation of all the EC's preferential trade agreements. Spain's Minister for Foreign Affairs, Gregorio López Bravo, supported the Commission's recommendation.

In March 1972, the French Minister for Foreign Affairs, Maurice Schumann, recommended to the EC Council that the Community should enter into free trade agreements with the various co-contracting parties which would cover agricultural as well as industrial products. Such a proposal was opposed by the Spaniards who feared the consequences of a free entry into Spain of Western European industrial products.

The Council resolved to ask the EC Commission to draft a concrete proposal detailing the Community's 'global Mediterranean policy'. The Commission responded to such request in October and advised the Council that preferential trade agreements with all the EC's co-contracting countries should be renegotiated. The renegotiated agreements should include mutual concessions which would take into account the relative level of economic development of each co-contracting nation. The EC Commission recommended that the Community should follow the following strategy: first, the EC's common tariff on the industrial products of the co-contracting nations should be gradually lowered and should be abolished in 1977; second, the Community should extend deeper and wider tariff concessions for the agricultural products of co-contracting nations and these concessions should cover at least 80% of the exports of agricultural products of the co-contracting nations to the EC; third, the new trade agreements should include clauses detailing the movements of capital, movements of workers, and movements of other production inputs which could take place between the Community and a co-contracting nation; and fourth, the extent of concessions granted by the EC would depend on whether the co-contracting country was a European country which fulfilled all the conditions necessary to become a member country in the Community, or a European country which was eligible for such membership provided it satisfied in the future certain political and/or economic conditions, or was a non-European country unable to join the Community.

The Council partially agreed with the Commission's recommendations. However, it allowed the co-contracting nations to continue trading for a limited period of time with the three new member countries on the basis of their trade agreements pre-dating 1 January 1973. After the expiry of this transition period, the EC–9 would renegotiate its preferential trade agreements with the co-contracting nations in the light of the Community's global Mediterranean policy.

The Council approved Spain's request that the provisions of the Accord of 1970 entered into between Spain and the Community would not apply to Spain's trade with the new Three during the year 1973.

During that year, Spain's important trade with the United Kingdom would thus remain free of increased British import duties.

## The industrialization of the Spanish economy

It is useful at this point to interrupt the chronological examination of Spain's economic development and to try to synthesize the main features of such development during the thirteen years which elapsed between 1960 and 1973. A study of the key indicators of industrial growth in Spain clearly shows that Spain's industry expanded at very high rates during these years and that the country's strong industrial growth acted as the major stimulant of overall economic growth in Spain. The growth of the secondary sector, together with Spain's earnings from tourism, were the dynamic variables which produced the country's 'economic miracle' of those years.

In terms of constant 1972 pesetas, the value of the country's Gross Industrial Product more than trebled in the course of the thirteen years considered, as shown in Graph 17. This value climbed from 325 billion pesetas in 1960 to 1,037 billion in 1973, the increase in value over the time span of thirteen years being equivalent to an average annual real growth rate of 9.4%. Such a rate implied that Spain's industrial production doubled every seven and a half years, an economic achievement surpassed only by Japan. Although Spain's annual rate of growth of industrial output varied from year to year, it remained positive throughout this period and at least equal to 6%, with the exceptions of 1967 and 1971. Between 1961 and 1964, this annual rate attained the remarkable level of 12.5%, such rates being partially explained by the very low starting level of industrial production. Between 1965 and 1973, the rate declined to 7.8%.

During the same period, Spain's industrial sector experienced rapid advances in productivity as its capital equipment was modernized and as new and more efficient production methods were adopted. The structure of this sector also changed in the same period. As shown in Table 31, the contribution of the mining industries to aggregate industrial income declined while that of the manufacturing industries rose. By 1972 manufacturing contributed more than 75% of total industrial income. Among the manufacturing industries recording the largest gains in relative importance as producers of industrial income were those denoted as means of transport, construction materials, chemicals and rubber, and basic metallurgy. Traditional industries such as foodstuffs, beverages and tobacco, textiles, and wood and cork experienced a decline in their relative importance in the industrial sector.

A breakdown of industrial production into consumer goods, intermediate goods and capital goods will show an evolution of industrial

*Graph 17* Evolution of the domestic industrial output and its annual growth rates: 1960–73

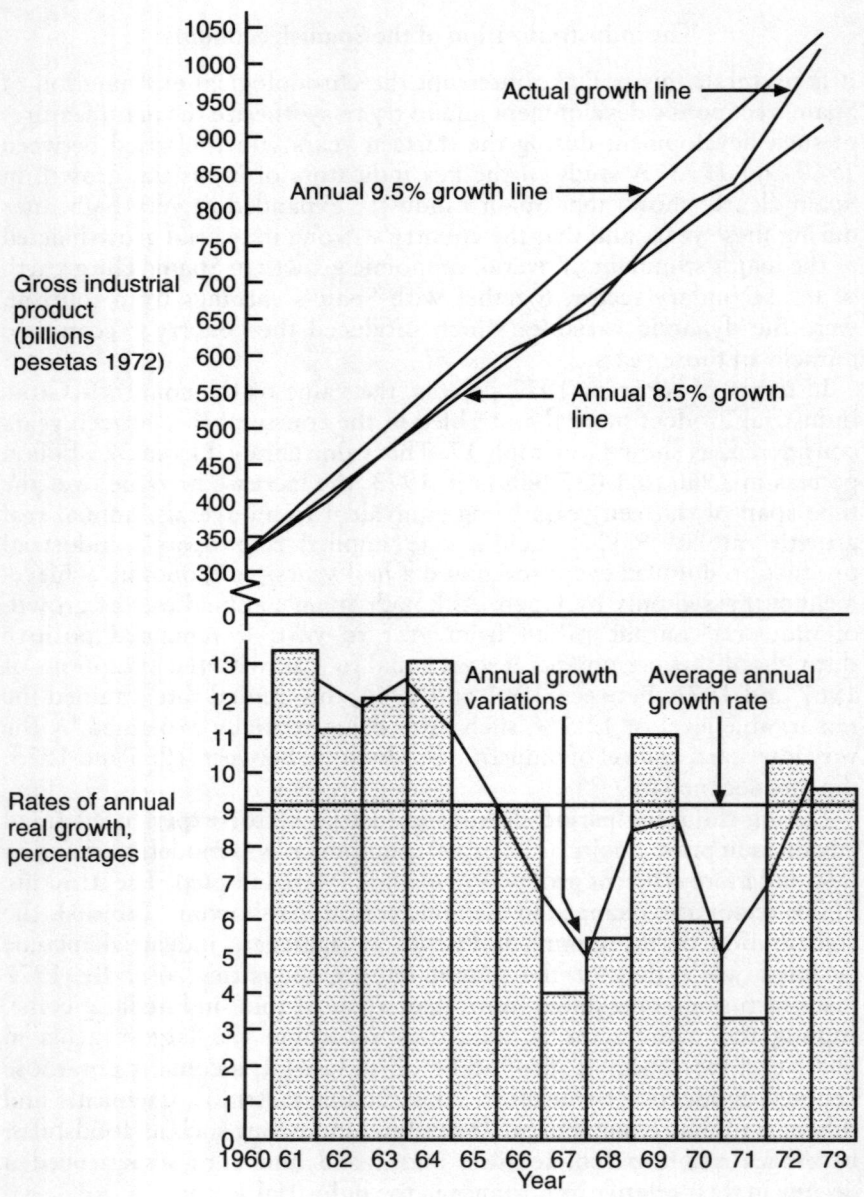

*Source*: Banco Urquijo, *El Crecimiento de la Industria Española*, Madrid, 1974, p. 16

Table 31 Evolution of the relative weight of industrial sectors in the value of aggregate industrial output: 1960–72

|  | Relative weight percentage 1960 (1) | Relative weight percentage 1972 (2) | Change (2) – (1) | Production index in 1972 (1960 = 100) |
|---|---|---|---|---|
| Mining | 6.8 | 3.0 | –3.8 | 120.7 |
| Coal | 3.0 | 1.2 | –1.8 | 102.3 |
| Other | 3.8 | 1.8 | –2.0 | 137.2 |
| Manufacturing | 70.2 | 75.9 | 5.7 | 312.5 |
| Foodstuffs, beverages, tobacco | 14.7 | 11.0 | –3.7 | 216.5 |
| Textiles | 6.9 | 4.6 | –2.3 | 193.3 |
| Footwear, garments, leather | 9.2 | 9.5 | 0.3 | 297.3 |
| Wood, cork | 4.3 | 3.8 | –0.5 | 259.1 |
| Paper, paper products | 3.3 | 3.9 | 0.6 | 334.8 |
| Chemicals, rubber | 7.1 | 8.6 | 1.5 | 352.6 |
| Construction materials | 3.0 | 4.7 | 1.7 | 445.6 |
| Basic metallurgy | 4.8 | 6.1 | 1.3 | 369.3 |
| Metal products | 9.8 | 10.4 | 0.6 | 309.5 |
| Means of transport | 5.3 | 10.2 | 4.9 | 553.3 |
| Other manufacturing | 1.8 | 3.1 | 1.3 | 489.7 |
| Construction industry | 17.8 | 15.9 | –1.9 | 264.5 |
| Electricity, gas, water | 5.2 | 5.2 | 0 | 292.3 |
| All industry | 100.0 | 100.0 | 0 | 289.3 |

Source: Banco Urquijo, *El Crecimiento de la Industria Española*, Madrid, 1974, p. 18

production during the period under consideration in favour of the capital goods industries. The share of the latter in aggregate industrial income advanced from 39.7% in 1960 to about 50% in 1973 (Banco Urquijo, 1974, 19). The increase in the relative weight of the capital goods industries in the composition of aggregate industrial income developed largely at the expense of the relative importance of the consumer goods industries, and to a lesser extent, of that of the intermediate goods industries.

Among the capital goods industries showing most rapid growth in terms of production volume were those manufacturing automobiles and machine tools. The output of automobiles in 1972 was fifteen times that of 1960; that of machine tools, fourteen. The number of ships produced in 1972 was seven times that produced in 1960; that of industrial vehicles, five times. The output of steel in 1972 was five times larger than that of 1960. Among the intermediate goods industries rapid advances

Table 32 Physical growth of selected Spanish industries: 1960–72

| Industry | Units | 1960 | 1972 | Index in 1972 1960 = 100 |
|---|---|---|---|---|
| Coal | 1,000 metric tons | 13,286 | 14,230 | 107.1 |
| Iron ore | " | 2,798 | 6,710 | 239.8 |
| Wheat flour | " | 2,812 | 2,824 | 100.4 |
| Artificial fodders | " | 294 | 3,789 | 1,288.8 |
| Beer | 1,000 hl | 3,433 | 12,010 | 349.8 |
| Cotton yarn | 1,000 metric tons | 115 | 144 | 125.2 |
| Cotton fabrics | " | 93 | 131 | 140.9 |
| Footwear | 1,000 pairs | 33,535 | 119,450 | 356.2 |
| Paper pulp | 1,000 metric tons | 292 | 1,711 | 585.9 |
| Sulphuric acid | " | 1,132 | 2,559 | 226.1 |
| Tyres | 1,000 units | 6,587 | 17,285 | 262.4 |
| Cement | 1,000 metric tons | 5,232 | 19,510 | 372.9 |
| Nitrogenous fertilizers | " | 102 | 681 | 667.6 |
| Penicillin | 1,000 million IU | 21,696 | 138,660 | 639.1 |
| Steel | 1,000 metric tons | 1,919 | 9,530 | 496.6 |
| Aluminium | " | 29 | 148 | 510.3 |
| Wooden boards | 1,000 m³ | 100 | 832 | 832.0 |
| Television sets | 1,000 units | 39 | 677 | 1,735.9 |
| Machine tools | " | 21 | 297 | 1,414.3 |
| Typewriters | " | 69 | 704 | 1,020.3 |
| Industrial vehicles | " | 20 | 95 | 475.0 |
| Automobiles | " | 40 | 601 | 1,502.5 |
| Ships | 1,000 reg. gross tons | 161 | 1,134 | 704.3 |
| Electricity | million kWh | 18,614 | 68,350 | 367.2 |
| Petroleum refining | 1,000 metric tons | 5,826 | 37,675 | 646.7 |

Source: Ibid., p. 21

in terms of volume produced characterized the production of nitrogenous fertilizers and paper pulp. In the case of the consumer goods industries, the manufacturing of television sets, electrical appliances and footwear recorded significant growth. The industries showing fastest expansion of their output were generally those which incorporated into their production processes new and more sophisticated technologies. Table 32 shows the expansion of Spain's physical industrial production in the period under consideration.

Table 33  Industrial productivity levels in selected European countries: 1960

|  | Industrial gross value added in $ per inhabitant 1960 | Production per inhabitant 1960 | | |
|---|---|---|---|---|
|  | Industrial sector total | Electricity kWh | Steel kg | Cement kg |
| German FR | 742 | 2,187 | 641 | 468 |
| Sweden | 725 | 4,652 | 425 | 375 |
| France | 648 | 1,584 | 379 | 315 |
| UK | 582 | 2,608 | 470 | 257 |
| Belgium | 454 | 1,656 | 785 | 479 |
| Norway | 432 | 868 | 137 | 321 |
| Netherlands | 381 | 1,438 | 169 | 157 |
| Italy | 239 | 1,133 | 167 | 324 |
| Spain | 111 | 609 | 63 | 171 |

Source: Alcaide Inchausti, J., 'Productividad, Costes y Precios', in Fraga Iribarne, M. et al., *La España de los Años Setenta*, Madrid, Editorial Moneda y Crédito, 1973, p. 484

A major characteristic of the Spanish economic miracle of the 1960s was the rapid increase in the productivity of the country's industrial labour. Such productivity gains were made possible by expanding imports of capital goods which allowed Spain to provide her workers with better equipment and permitted the modernization of existing industries and the creation of entirely new ones. As noted earlier, Spanish imports of capital goods could be paid for by the country's expanding net earnings from tourism. Economic boom conditions in Western Europe provided Spain with rapidly increasing numbers of tourists and the means to launch a true industrial take-off. This take-off required the creation of new industries as well as the modernization of existing industrial concerns. It allowed a much needed increase in the productivity of Spain's industrial labour and a rise of the country's comparatively low wages. At the start of the decade, increases in real wages and salaries were the *sine qua non* of rising internal demand. A rapid expansion of the country's industrial output and the achievement of improvements in the quality and diversity of such output would not have taken place without a strong increase in domestic demand.

Table 33 shows Spain's relative economic backwardness in Western Europe in 1960. Compared to the corresponding figures for a number of European countries, Spain's industrial gross value added per inhabitant in 1960 was the lowest; so was the country's production per inhabitant of electrical energy, steel and cement. Spain's poor industrial performance at that time was due to a number of factors: the country's technological backwardness at the start of the twentieth century; the disastrous economic impact of the Civil War; and policies of economic autarky pursued by the Franco governments in the 1950s and their excessive control over Spain's foreign trade in that decade. It was only after the Stabilization Plan of 1959 liberalized foreign trade that Spain was able to expand her imports and start restructuring and modernizing her industrial sector.

Once existing industries started receiving new foreign capital equipment and new industries began to appear, Spanish industrial productivity achieved remarkable gains in the 1960s. In spite of the deficiencies in the statistical material available to him, Julio Alcaide Inchausti, a Spanish statistician, estimated the growth of such productivity in the 1960s (Fraga Iribarne, M., 1973, 483–506). According to his calculations Spanish industrial labour productivity in the 1960s rose at an annual rate of 8.4%, a rate which exceeded corresponding rates recorded by other Western European countries at the time. In the latter countries this rate varied between 4% and 6% throughout the 1960s. It remained below 4% in the case of the United Kingdom. Only Japan exceeded the Spanish rate, the Japanese rate attaining 11%. Spain's strong productivity performance was, of course, largely due to her comparatively low productivity level in 1960.

In Spain, annual rates of productivity growth in the 1960s attained 10.8% in the chemical industries, 10.4% in those producing transport materials, and 9% in those producing electricity, gas and water. Productivity growth rates were lowest in the traditional industries such as those producing processed foodstuffs, beverages, tobacco, textiles and leather goods; the rate of annual productivity growth in the latter industries attained only 4.2% (Ibid., 490).

As expected, the industrial subsectors showing the largest productivity gains were those characterized by the highest levels of investment in new capital equipment. Even though Spain's industrial sector remained burdened by institutions which impeded its restructuring and modernization, (shortages of skilled workers, labour market rigidities created by Francoist labour legislation, below-optimum size of plants, etc.) its growth in the 1960s was truly spectacular. This growth was largely the result of the advance in industrial productivity. Table 34 shows calculations of gross industrial product per employed person in 1960 and in 1970 in a number of selected European countries, the values having been calculated in terms of US dollars. Looking at the dollar value of Spain's total gross industrial product per employed person, it increased from $923 in 1960 to $2,525 in 1970. The value of this statistic thus rose from a level representing 35.3% of the average dollar value of the gross industrial product per employed person for the ten selected European countries in 1960 to 45.5% of this average value in 1970.

Table 34 Dollar value of the gross industrial product per employed person in ten selected European countries in 1960 and 1970

| Country | Total industry 1960 | Total industry 1970 |
| --- | --- | --- |
| Sweden | 3,543 | 7,768 |
| France | 3,214 | 6,910 |
| Norway | 3,121 | 6,458 |
| German FR | 3,098 | 7,823 |
| UK | 2,666 | 3,961 |
| Belgium | 2,640 | 5,525 |
| Netherlands | 2,549 | 6,117 |
| Austria | 2,484 | 4,502 |
| Italy | 1,596 | 3,524 |
| Spain | 923 | 2,525 |
| Average ten countries | 2,614 | 5,547 |

Source: Alcaide Inchausti, J., supra, p. 492

During the 1960s, industrial labour costs rose faster than productivity. Industrial costs of production increased in addition because of rising depreciation costs; expanded investment in capital goods and the more rapid obsolescence of the latter increased costs of depreciation. The rising cost of labour, coupled with increasing costs of depreciation, resulted in a decline in the percentage share of the industrial value added representing entrepreneurial profits. This percentage share declined from 49.2% in 1960 to 37.8% in 1970. It was still large enough in the early 1970s to preserve the willingness of Spanish entrepreneurs to invest. Optimistic entrepreneurial expectations regarding the profitability of new investment and real rates of interest which were low maintained domestic investment as a key variable in Spain's economic expansion. Increasing labour costs did not impede economic growth because they allowed in turn rising levels of consumer spending and of domestic saving.

Because industrial prices rose by 80.9% of the increase in the general price level during the 1960s, 19.1% of the income generated by the industrial sector was transferred to the other sectors of the Spanish economy and facilitated the growth of the latter (Alcaide Inchausti, J., 1973, 495). Prices increased least for products of the high productivity industries, such as electrical energy, chemicals, metal manufacturing, etc. Table 35 shows the evolution of the composition of the industrial gross value added between 1960 and 1970.

Table 35 Evolution of the composition of the industrial gross value added: 1960–70

|  | Composition of the gross value added by industry, 1960 | | |
|---|---|---|---|
| Sector | Labour costs percentage | Depreciation costs percentage | Profits percentage |
| Mining industries | 66.9 | 5.2 | 27.9 |
| Manufacturing industries | 41.3 | 6.3 | 52.4 |
| Foodstuffs, beverages, tobacco | 20.9 | 5.0 | 74.1 |
| Textiles, leather | 24.6 | 4.8 | 70.6 |
| Paper and printing | 55.0 | 6.9 | 38.1 |
| Chemicals | 36.6 | 9.1 | 54.3 |
| Glass, pottery | 50.4 | 6.4 | 43.2 |
| Metal industries | 55.2 | 7.2 | 37.6 |
| Transport materials | 64.1 | 8.3 | 27.6 |
| Others | 67.6 | 5.0 | 27.4 |
| Construction | 67.4 | 2.4 | 30.2 |
| Electricity, gas water | 23.1 | 14.4 | 62.5 |
| Sector total | 44.5 | 6.3 | 49.2 |

|  | Composition of the gross value added by industry, 1970 | | |
|---|---|---|---|
| Sector | Labour costs percentage | Depreciation costs percentage | Profits percentage |
| Mining industries | 78.2 | 7.0 | 14.8 |
| Manufacturing industries | 52.4 | 7.5 | 40.1 |
| Foodstuffs, beverages, tobacco | 33.8 | 5.0 | 61.2 |
| Textiles, leather | 46.5 | 6.2 | 47.3 |
| Paper and printing | 54.2 | 7.8 | 38.0 |
| Chemicals | 39.4 | 11.3 | 49.3 |
| Glass, pottery | 52.2 | 7.6 | 40.2 |
| Metal industries | 65.8 | 8.1 | 26.1 |
| Transport materials | 62.7 | 8.6 | 28.7 |
| Others | 56.2 | 5.4 | 38.4 |
| Construction | 70.5 | 3.1 | 26.4 |
| Electricity, gas water | 31.4 | 21.7 | 46.9 |
| Sector total | 54.5 | 7.7 | 37.8 |

Source: Ibid., p. 504

## The effects of the oil crisis of late 1973 in 1974

During the last quarter of 1973, representatives of the Arab oil-exporting nations met in Teheran and agreed to abide by a joint petroleum exporting policy in order to utilize crude oil exports as a powerful weapon in their

*Graph 18* Trend of the index of industrial orders: 1970–4

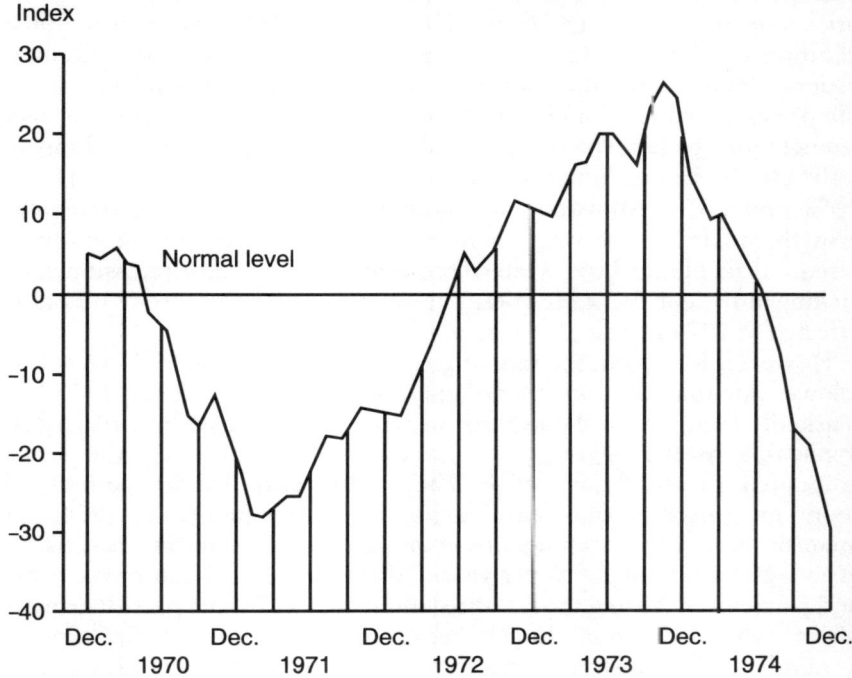

Source: Ministerio de Industria, *La Industria Española en 1974*, 1976, p. 8

fight against Israel. The newly formed Arab oil-exporting cartel immediately raised the price of exportable crude by 386.9% above its level at the beginning of the Arab-Israeli war and announced that the monthly output of crude oil in the member countries would be reduced by 5%. Concurrently, exports of oil to nations which had openly supported Israel, i.e. the Netherlands and the United States, were to be stopped.

The spectacular increase in the price of imported crude oil, together with a sharp global increase in the prices of primary commodities, the latter caused by the rapid economic growth of the industrialized countries, resulted in a drastic fall of the rate of growth of GNP in many nations and an alarming increase in their levels of unemployment. In the OECD area the GNP fell by 0.1% in the course of 1974 while it had risen by 6.3% in 1973. Among the countries which experienced a diminishing GNP in 1974 were Japan (−1.8%), the United States (−2.1%) and the United Kingdom (−0.2%). Concurrently, inflation intensified. The index of prices implicit in the calculation of the GNP in the major countries of the OECD rose by 12.1% in 1974. This increase was nearly twice that registered for 1973 which attained 7.1% and more than three times the average annual increase in the period 1960–72 which was 3.6%. The price index increase in 1974 varied between the OECD member nations. It attained 24.4% in Japan but registered only 7.3% in the German Federal Republic. Inflation was not only fuelled by the sharp increases in the prices of crude oil and of primary commodity imports but was also strengthened by large increases of industrial wages. In Denmark, France, Italy and the United Kingdom industrial money wages rose by between 20% and 23% (Ministerio de Industria, 1976, 7). Weak economic growth, inflation, growing unemployment and deteriorating external disequilibria plunged the Western economies into a major recession and, lacking sufficient domestic energy resources, Spain's economy was also affected in 1974 by this global economic deterioration.

However, for Spain, the rate of growth of real GNP in 1974 was 5%, a lower rate than the corresponding rates attained in 1972 and 1973 but markedly higher than the average negative rate of growth of real GNP applicable to the aggregate of all the OECD countries; the latter amounted to −0.1% in 1974. There were two distinct periods of economic growth in that year. During the first six months of 1974, the Spanish economy continued to exhibit great dynamism, real GNP growing at a rate of 6.5% per year. During the second half of the year, and particularly during the last three months of 1974, the pace of growth of real GNP decelerated, largely because growth started diminishing in a number of industrial subsectors; the construction industry also experienced diminished expansion (Ministerio de Industria, 1976, 8).

In spite of the energy crisis in late 1973, conditions of full employment still characterized the Spanish economy during 1974. The rate of unemployment in December 1974 was 2% of the total active population; it had been only 1.3% at mid-year and increased during the latter half of the year not only because of the slowdown in the secondary sector but also because the flow of Spanish emigration to the rest of Europe contracted (Ibid.).

The movement of the index of industrial orders is a good indicator of Spain's industrial performance in 1974. As shown in Graph 18, between June 1972, when the level of industrial orders already exceeded what Spanish entrepreneurs considered to be their 'normal level', industrial orders followed an ascending trend until October 1973 when they reached a maximum never attained during the five preceding years. From the latter month, the index started falling, reaching its normal level in June 1974 and continuing to decline until the end of that year. The weakening of industrial activity caused the coefficient of industrial plant utilization to fall from 86% in June to between 83% and 81% at the end of 1974 (Ibid., 10). During that year the rate of increase of industrial productivity per working person in the secondary sector attained only

Table 36 Percentage change in the value of key industrial variables: 1971–4

| Variable | 1971 | 1972 | 1973 | 1974 |
|---|---|---|---|---|
| Gross industrial product in constant prices | 4.6 | 10.9 | 10.1 | 5.7 |
| Prices of industrial products | 5.6 | 6.0 | 10.3 | 17.7 |
| Employed industrial labour force | 0.8 | 2.2 | 2.4 | 1.9 |
| Utilization of productive capacity | 83.0 | 87.0 | 89.0 | 84.0 |
| Productivity per employed person | 2.9 | 8.3 | 7.5 | 3.7 |
| Industrial investment | −0.9 | 15.1 | 25.1 | 20.5 |

Source: Ibid., p. 13

3.7%, about half the rate achieved one year earlier.

According to the data of the Ministry of Industry, the 1974 rate of growth of real Gross Industrial Product was 5.7%, about half the corresponding rate for 1973. Table 36 shows the rates of growth of key variables affecting the secondary sector for the years 1971 to 1974.

The international energy crisis had various adverse effects on the Spanish economy. Tourism, one of the country's key industries, was seriously weakened by Europe's economic deterioration. The number of foreign tourists entering Spain in 1974 was 12.2% lower than for 1973 (Banco de Bilbao, 1975, 84). As already noted, economic stagnation in Western Europe also reduced the number of Spanish emigrants and the decline in net emigration had an immediate impact on the level of Spanish unemployment. In 1974 the number of registered Spanish emigrants leaving for Europe was about 50,000 persons, compared to 96,000 in 1973. In the former year between 125,000 and 150,000 Spaniards who had resided abroad returned to Spain; the country thus received in 1974 a net immigratory inflow of about 100,000 people (Ibid., 91). Imported inflation and the weakening of external demand for Spanish products worsened entrepreneurial expectations and resulted in a deceleration in the rate of growth of domestic and foreign investment. Though Spain recorded in 1974 the highest rate of growth of real GNP in the OECD area, this rate was nevertheless 60% smaller than it had been in 1973.

The rise in Spain's cost of living in 1974 also had an adverse impact on the pace of growth of domestic consumption spending. The annual growth rate of real consumer demand fell from 7.6% in 1973 to 4.7% in 1974. Large salary and wage increases in that year prevented an even stronger decline of consumer demand but made for stronger inflationary pressures in 1975 (Ibid., 88). Strong domestic wage increases, as well as the higher costs of imported raw materials and of manufactured goods, were at the base of a significant increase in the cost of fixed investment and slowed down the 1974 rate of growth of real fixed investment to 6%.

In that year the prices of Spanish merchandise imports rose by about 47% and brought Spain's balance of trade deficit to a record high of US$ 4 billion, given a rate of exchange of 57.5 pesetas to the US dollar. In spite of the strong increase in import prices, Spain's real imports in 1974 increased by 7.5% (Ibid., 90). In the same year, Spain's real exports expanded at a rate of 7% while their prices rose by 15.6%. Spain experienced a loss of US$ 774 million in reserves in that year and its worsening real terms of trade acted as a brake on the pace of domestic economic development. The sharp rises in internal and external prices brought an increase in the ratio of the aggregate value of the totality of Spain's merchandise imports and exports to the country's GNP. Expressed as a percentage figure, this ratio increased from 31.8% in 1973 to 36.6% in 1974, the trend being indicative of the fact that because of internal and external inflations, Spain's economy became more open.

In spite of major efforts taken by the government in 1974 to stabilize the domestic prices of crude oil and of primary goods, Spain's economy registered a general deterioration in the values of all key economic variables. This led the government to decide to adopt a number of corrective measures in October 1974: it announced that it would attempt to maintain an annual rate of growth of real GNP of 4.5% in 1975; it would try to reduce the 1975 rate of inflation by four points below its 1974 average; and would take steps to limit the 1975 external current account deficit to US$ 2.5 billion (Ibid., 90–2).

## The political events of 1974–5

On 20 December 1973, Admiral Luis Carrero Blanco, the President of the Government, was assassinated in Madrid. His death heralded the beginning of a political crisis which developed alongside the economic crisis brought about by the spectacular increase in the price of imported crude oil in October 1973. On the last day of that year, General Franco chose Carlos Arias Navarro to form a new government. This government began operating on 4 January 1974. Arias Navarro retained eight ministers who had participated in the Carrero Blanco Cabinet. However, he replaced a number of ministers in that Cabinet with personal friends or collaborators who were not members of *Opus Dei*. Among the ministers being replaced were Laureano López Rodó, Minister of Foreign Affairs under Carrero Blanco, José Ma. López de Letona, the Minister of Industry and Fernando de Liñán, the Minister of Information and Tourism. Their positions were taken by Pedro Cortina y Mauri, a technocrat, Alfredo Santos Blanco and Pío Cabanillas Gallas, a man who had been close to the ex-minister, Manuel Frago Iribarne. A number of Cabinet positions were also given to Falangists.

The Arias government, though dedicated to the continuation of the Francoist regime, appeared at first to be inclined toward reformism. Arias Navarro appeared to take an *aperturista* position and was acclaimed by Francoist reformers, the *aperturistas*, people loyal to Franco but supporting the modification of existing legislation in order to extend the life of the regime after the Caudillo's death. In a speech delivered on 12 February 1974, in the *Cortes*, Arias Navarro declared that his government would support a new Statute of Associations which would allow the formation of political associations by the end of 1975. He also promised the democratization of the existing political system. Concurrently, the new Minister of Information, Pío Cabanillas, tolerated an unprecedented freedom of the press, a freedom which came to a sudden end when Cabanillas resigned in October of that year in order to comply with Franco's mandate. His successor, León Herrera, lost no time in reimposing restrictions and fines on publications which were considered too liberal by General Franco.

The 'spirit of 12 February' came to a rapid end. The *aperturista* reformism failed for a number of reasons. It encountered the opposition of the *bunker*, ultra-conservative Francoists who insisted on the maintenance of the political status quo. The political and economic strongmen of the *bunker*, a group known as the *integristas*, had become alarmed by the Portuguese revolution of April 1974 and by the renewal of labour unrest and of terrorism in Spain. Among these men were José Antonio Girón, the leader of the 'National Confederation of ex-Combatants', Blas Piñar, the head of '*Fuerza Nueva*' (FN), and Mariano Sánchez Covisa whose '*Guerrilleros de Cristo Rey*' did not hesitate to engage in acts of ultra-right terrorism. Wealthy members of the Francoist economic oligarchy, mainly bankers, supported the *bunker*, men such as Mssrs Fierro, Botín and Aguirre Gonzalo (Tamames, R., 1979, 595). The revolution in Portugal induced the *integristas* to initiate a political offensive against the reformers. The attack was even directed against reformist members of the Roman Catholic Church. In March, the *bunker* launched a campaign against the 'red priests' following a proclamation by the Bishop of Bilbao, Monsignor Añoveros, to the effect that the government should respect the rights of the various ethnic groups living in Spain, and more particularly, the right of the Basques to communicate in their own language. This statement, part of the bishop's homily, led to his temporary house arrest. On 28 April in an article in the Falangist daily *Arriba*, José Antonio Girón harshly denounced the tolerance shown by the Arias government to the press and claimed that the liberal ministers in that government were being disloyal to Franco (Carr, R. and Fusi, J.P., 1979, 198–9).

These attacks by the ultra-right induced Arias Navarro to try to appease the *bunker*. Arias also had to recognize that he could not follow for long policies which did not have the support of the Caudillo. In the face of mounting strike activity, terrorism and economic problems he decided to become more conservative.

During a short period of forty-six days in the summer of 1974, the reformers had reason to hope that General Franco would leave politics for the rest of his life and that political reform could be achieved. On 19 July Franco had to be hospitalized because of cardiovascular problems. He transferred his powers as Chief of State to Prince Juan Carlos. Franco recovered, however, and took back the powers he had transferred to the Prince.

A difficult political development gave stronger evidence of the seriousness of the political crisis which engulfed Spain in 1974. Groups opposing the Franco regime, the proponents of a new democratic Spain who advocated a complete 'rupture' with the Francoist regime and the abolition of all laws enacted between 1936 and 1973, felt strengthened by the fall of the Greek and Portuguese dictatorships and by the victory of the socialist Mitterrand in France. They called for an immediate restoration of democratic freedoms in Spain and for the establishment of a provisional government representing all political views in the country. They asked for free elections and for a new national constitution. The *rupturistas* established two distinct opposition organizations.

Encouraged by the possibility that Franco could give up his powers as Chief of State because of his illness various opposition groups founded the 'Democratic Junta of Spain' (JDE) on 29 July 1974. The Junta was initially formed by the Communist Party of Spain (PCE) and by politicians who wanted Don Juan de Borbón to be King of Spain. They were joined by the Popular Socialist Party of Professor Enrique Tierno Galván, by the Carlists of Carlos Hugo, by the 'Workers' Commissions' (CC.OO.) and by the Marxist 'Party of Labour' (PTE). The Junta demanded the formation of a new democratic provisional government, amnesty for political prisoners, the legalization of all political parties, the restoration of democratic freedoms and regional autonomy.

The more moderate Christian Democrats, Social Democrats, Socialists and Liberals did not join the Junta, feeling that it was too strongly dominated by the Communists. This moderate opposition formed a second political organization in June 1975, the 'Platform of Democratic Convergence' (PCD). This organization included: the Spanish Socialist Workers' Party (PSOE), whose First Secretary was a young labour lawyer from Seville, Felipe González Marquez; the General Labour Union (UGT), a socialist labour federation which had been strong in pre-Civil War times; the Democratic Left (ID), representing the Christian Democrats and led by Joaquín Ruiz Giménez; the Social Democratic Party

(USDE) of Dionisio Ridruejo; and Catalan and Basque political groups.

During the autumn of 1974, the government of Arias Navarro came under severe attack by both the ultra-right and labour. As noted, the Minister of Information and Tourism, Pío Cabanillas, was forced to resign on 29 October. Antonio Barrera de Irimo, the Minister of the Treasury, also resigned. Concurrently, a wave of strikes extended over the whole country. By the end of November 200,000 workers were on strike. They not only demanded salary increases to safeguard their purchasing power in the face of inflation but also wanted the right to organize freely and they clamoured for an immediate amnesty for political prisoners. The opposition to the Franco regime was further strengthened by the Roman Catholic bishops of Spain. On 30 November the latter demanded that the government guarantee all Spaniards the rights of free speech and free association (Tamames, R., 1979, 583).

The response of the Arias Navarro government to these developments clearly indicated that it had abandoned any serious intent to democratize the existing political system. On 21 December the government enacted a Decree-Law titled the 'Statute on the Right of Political Association'. It restricted the establishment of legal political associations to those approved by the National Council of the Movement. The latter had to accept the legitimacy of the Francoist regime; such proviso automatically excluded from legalization all opposition associations. Furthermore, only associations with at least 25,000 members, this membership being distributed over at least fifteen provinces, could be given legal status by the National Council of the Movement. This latter requirement prevented in effect the formation of regionalist associations.

The Arias Navarro government was not successful in its attempt to divide the opposition. It tolerated the Platform on Democratic Convergence, the more moderate opposition groups, in order to isolate the 'Democratic Junta'. Arias Navarro was however unable to gain the support of the groups in the Platform. The moderate opposition remained committed to the rejection of the Francoist regime and continued to advocate *ruptura*, a clean break with the existing political system. The socialists of the PSOE, under the leadership of Felipe González, insisted on the restoration of democratic freedoms, on free elections within one year and on immediate amnesty for all political prisoners. They rejected the government's Statute on Political Associations and the democratization programme of the Arias Navarro government.

The policies of the government came also under attack by prominent Francoist reformers. Manuel Fraga Iribarne, ex-minister and ambassador to London since 1973, a well-known political leader, started demanding the formation of an 'association of the centre' which would unite all the reformists loyal to the regime. Francisco Fernández Ordóñez, the former president of INI, asked for constitutional reform.

In order to counteract the reformist efforts of Manuel Fraga Iribarne, the *bunker* founded in June 1975 the 'Union of the Spanish People', UPDE. The major goal of this organization was *continuismo*, the continuation of the existing political system. Its president was Adolfo Suárez, a friend of Fernando Herrero Tejedor, the Minister of the Movement since April 1975. The creation of the UPDE gave Spaniards reason to believe that the Arias Navarro government had decided to give its support to the *bunker* in order to impede the materialization of the association of the centre as proposed by Fraga Iribarne. This belief was supported by the fact that only eight political associations had applied for recognition by the National Council of the Movement by September 1975. Most of these adhered to the Falangist ideology and were dedicated to *continuismo*; only one of them, the UDPE, had the required 25,000 members.

Nineteen seventy-five was a year of economic deterioration and of mounting terrorism. Yet, as late as 1 October 1975, General Franco still explained the country's economic and political problems as being caused by 'a masonic leftist conspiracy' (Carr, R. and Fusi, J.P., 1979, 205). The government, fearing both economic disaster and the strength of the *bunker*, was unwilling and unable to embrace a clear reformist course of action and reverted to acts of repression to discourage the opposition. The latter did not lower its voice and continued to demand 'democracy without adjectives' and political amnesty.

On 20 November 1975, the day when General Franco died, Spain faced an uncertain choice between three courses of political action: *continuismo*, *apertura* or *ruptura*.

## FROM MONARCHY WITHOUT A MONARCH TO THE BEGINNING OF THE REIGN OF DON JUAN CARLOS I: THE ECONOMIC CRISES OF THE LATE 1970s

Spain's annual rate of growth of real GNP fell from 8% in 1973 to 0.7% in 1975. Writing in 1979, Professor Enrique Fuentes Quintana observed that this dramatic economic slowdown was much more than a temporary pause in a long-term process of rapid economic growth as had been the short-term recessions of the 1960s (Fuentes Quintana, E., 1979, 85). The severe fall in the pace of Spanish economic growth which followed the global energy crisis of 1973 represented a lasting break with the previous long growth trend which had brought prosperity to Spain in the 1960s.

The short-lived recessions of 1967, 1969 and 1970 had been largely manifestations of a domestic economy adjusting to disequilibria in major economic variables. They were not part of a global economic crisis which affected both capitalist and socialist economies, both

Table 37 Annual percentage increases in the rates of inflation in selected countries: 1974 and 1975

| Country | 1974 | 1975 |
|---|---|---|
| German FR | 6.8 | 8.0 |
| France | 11.1 | 12.0 |
| UK | 12.5 | 26.3 |
| Italy | 16.9 | 19.0 |
| Netherlands | 9.5 | 11.0 |
| Belgium | 12.7 | 14.3 |
| USA | 10.3 | 9.0 |
| Japan | 21.1 | 7.0 |
| Spain | 13.9 | 16.0 |

Source: Ministerio de Industria, *La Industria Española en 1975*, Madrid, 1977, p. 13

industrialized and developing nations. This world crisis attained alarming proportions in 1975 and did not disappear during the second half of the 1970s. In the case of Spain, it weakened the pace of economic growth for a whole decade. For the OECD area as a whole, the average rate of growth of real GNP became negative in 1975 and attained –2.0%; in the same year, this rate averaged –3.0% for all the EC countries (Ministerio de Industria, 1977, 12). This alarming negative growth was accompanied by severe inflation whose rates in 1975 attained 26.3% in the United Kingdom and varied between 7% and 9% in the German Federal Republic, Japan and the United States. Table 37 shows annual percentage increases in the rates of inflation in selected countries in 1974 and in 1975. Concurrently, the rate of unemployment in the industrialized countries increased while the rate of growth of productivity in many of these countries declined, as shown by Tables 38 and 39.

Another adverse consequence of the energy crisis of 1973 was a declining world trade. In 1975, compared to their level in the previous year, intra-OECD imports declined by 9.5% in real terms and intra-OECD exports fell by 5.5% (Ibid., 13).

Although the decline of the rate of economic growth in Spain began later than in most advanced economies and was not as severe as it was in many OECD economies, it resulted in a deceleration of the rate of investment growth which reduced in turn the country's annual rate of economic growth to between 2% and 3% during the rest of the 1970s (Fuentes Quintana, E., 1979, 85–7). This deceleration in the pace of investment growth reflected a serious deterioration of entrepreneurial expectations regarding the future of Spain's economy.

The economic downturn of 1974–5 marked indeed the end of a long period of strong growth which, with a few exceptions, Spain had enjoyed since the enactment of the Stabilization Plan of 1959. This growth trend

*Table 38* Unemployment rates at the end of 1975 in selected countries (as a percentage of active population)

| Country | Percentage |
|---|---|
| German FR | 4.9 |
| France | 4.0 |
| UK | 4.7 |
| Italy | 3.4 |
| Netherlands | 4.4 |
| Belgium | 5.3 |
| USA | 8.6 |
| Japan | 1.9 |

*Source*: Ibid.

*Table 39* Percentage annual changes in productivity growth in selected countries: 1974 and 1975 (GNP/employed population)

| Country | 1974 | 1975 |
|---|---|---|
| German FR | 2.5 | 0.0 |
| France | 2.8 | −1.5 |
| UK | −0.2 | 0.0 |
| Italy | 1.2 | −4.5 |
| USA | −3.9 | −1.8 |
| Japan | −1.3 | 1.8 |

*Source*: Ibid.

culminated in the years 1971 to 1973 when the rate of growth of investment in Spain attained an annual value of about 8.7%. 1974 introduced a new long-term trend characterized by a persistent fall in the values of key economic variables.

## The world economy in the early 1970s

Professor Enrique Fuentes Quintana has detailed the causes of the global economic crises of the early 1970s (Ibid., 102–13). He points out that continuing large American external deficits in the 1960s allowed countries with which the United States had commercial and financial relations to accumulate large dollar reserves. These countries refused to revalue their currencies and failed to neutralize the monetary effects of their rapidly growing foreign exchange reserves. The resulting expansion of their money supplies led to a major price inflation in the 1970s. Though the United States dollar was devalued in terms of gold in 1971 and in 1973, the then existing international Bretton Woods monetary system collapsed as a result of the abandonment by the United States in August 1971 of the system's 'rules of the game' and because nations participating in the system started floating their currencies, a practice inconsistent with the system of relatively fixed foreign exchange rates adopted by the Bretton Woods Agreement.

From the late 1960s, a booming world demand for foodstuffs and for agricultural primary commodities was translated into sharp increases in the international prices of such products. There were several causes explaining such price increases. Investment in agriculture had generally been deficient during the 1960s and increased the supply inelasticity of agricultural products. Most countries producing these goods suffered severe droughts in the late 1960s and the latter strengthened the supply rigidities of agricultural outputs. As early as 1972 import prices of industrial primary goods started a rapid climb. The external accounts of industrialized countries dependent on imports of foodstuffs and primary commodities started deteriorating. Such deteriorations were intensified by the strong increase in the price of imported crude oil at the end of 1973.

As a result of such developments, the advanced economies experienced a strong deterioration of their real terms of trade which were translated into losses of real national income. The external deficits of industrialized countries lacking internal primary commodities or crude oil supply sources continued to expand while the pace of their economic growth experienced a major setback. As entrepreneurial expectations regarding the profitability of planned new investment ventures worsened and such investment declined, the fall of real national income accelerated and unemployment grew.

Concurrently, the sharp increase in the prices of imported foodstuffs, primary commodities and crude oil triggered the outbreak of cost inflation. Stronger inflationary pressures were transmitted to all markets. The general price level was pushed up, a trend which benefited certain groups in society and penalized others. The rising rate of inflation intensified tensions and hostilities between various social and economic groups in these economies as each group tried to have other groups shoulder the burdens of inflation. A consequence of such behaviour was increased social and political unrest.

As governments tried to reduce the rate of domestic inflation by resorting to restrictive monetary and fiscal measures, they brought down the level of domestic aggregate demand. Their economies not only suffered the economic and social consequences of cost inflation, they also had to endure the effects of a weakening internal aggregate demand. As a result of the economic impacts of these various trends, entrepreneurial profits tended to decline, investment flows diminished, the rate of economic growth continued to fall and unemployment continued to rise.

Fuentes Quintana also points out that the global crisis of the 1970s was intensified by rising governmental budgetary deficits in the advanced countries. In the developing 'welfare states', the citizenry pressured their government to subsidize ever wider public services, services such as national health insurance, increased job security and an easier access to higher education. Concurrently, the economic crisis induced governments to increase public investment in order to boost employment and to expand domestic productive capacity. At the very same time public spending increased, taxpayers started opposing tax increases with greater militancy. Because of such developments, a widening gap between public spending and public revenue developed in most advanced economies. Rising public outlays reinforced the process of inflation. This process was also strengthened by the demands of workers for salary and wage increases, demands reflecting attempts by the workers to protect their purchasing power in times of strong price inflation. Governments generally tried to satisfy the wage demands of workers employed in the public sector at a time when the latter was becoming a larger proportion of the total economy. In the early 1970s, salaries and wages rose faster than productivity, the rapid rise in workers' remunerations intensifying the pace of inflation.

Fuentes Quintana mentions one more aspect of the crises of the 1970s. The large increases in the prices of foodstuffs, as well as those of primary commodities and energy, ended the ability of a number of commercial and industrial sectors in many countries to earn profits. In the advanced economies, a number of industrial sectors were no longer able to adjust to the changed demand and supply conditions of the time and ceased operating to avoid long-term losses. The closing down of firms in these sectors aggravated the domestic unemployment problem. Although governments tried to facilitate the transformation of their national economic structures to make them more adaptable to the new cost conditions, they were unable to formulate reasonable decisions about what new lines of production they should support. The uncertainty about the future course of the cost of energy made it impossible to predict the profitability of possible new investment projects.

The energy crisis of 1973 was duplicated six years later. The adverse effects of such crises plagued the industrialized economies well into the 1980s. Because technology failed to offer industrialized nations a cheap substitute for petroleum, the possibility of continuing increases in the price of imported crude oil acted as a brake which slowed down the rate of growth of industrial production.

Comparing the crises of the 1970s with the Great Depression of the 1930s Fuentes Quintana notices that the two periods of depression were radically different in nature. The Great Depression of the 1930s was fundamentally a demand crisis, while the economic slump of the 1970s represented a supply crisis. In the 1930s, John Maynard Keynes accurately identified the main cause of depression in most of the world as originating in a deficient level of aggregate demand; the depression of the 1930s was characterized by the existence of large primary commodities surpluses and by falling prices. The opposite was true in the 1970s. The crises of that decade were characterized by rapidly rising prices of foodstuffs, of primary commodities and of energy. Instead of fearing the impact of falling prices as in the 1930s, the entrepreneurs of the 1970s apprehended the effects of continuing cost inflation.

The writer observes that all the characteristics of the global crisis of the 1970s were present in Spain's economic downturn in 1974 and in 1975. As a matter of fact, these characteristics were more pronounced in Spain than elsewhere in Europe. Among the reasons for the retarded, but severe, impact of the crisis on the evolution of the Spanish economy, Fuentes Quintana notices the particularly strong growth of the pre-crisis Spanish demand. Such demand had been boosted in the years 1970 to 1973 by the rapid expansion of Spain's United States dollar reserves and by the continuing entry into the country of foreign capital. The Spanish government failed to sterilize the inflationary effects of the expanding foreign exchange reserves and internal credit was able to grow at an annual rate of about 30% (Ibid., 112). The rapid growth of the money supply supported an excessive expansion of internal spending; investment spending alone increased at the rate of 17.5% in 1972 and 15.5% in 1973. Inflationary pressures inevitably became stronger. The rate of increase of consumer goods prices attained 11.8% in 1973. In that year, the Spanish rate of inflation was already much higher than the rate of inflation in the other countries of Western Europe. Then the price of imported crude oil increased fourfold in October 1973. This event brought to Spain in the last quarter of 1973 a rate of increase of consumer goods prices of 14% – the highest at that time in Western Europe.

The effects of the deterioration of the country's real terms of trade were also more severe in Spain compared to the impact of similar trends elsewhere. Spain's balance on current account changed from a surplus of US$ 500 million in 1973 to a deficit of US$ 3.26 billion one year later. Such adverse developments were intensified by internal measures taken by the government to stabilize the purchasing power of the people. The government reduced tax rates and subsidized energy consumption. Whereas such consumption declined in 1973 in the rest of Europe, it rose in Spain.

## The Spanish economy in 1975

The Spanish economy faced two important dangers at the start of 1975: a high rate of domestic inflation and a rapidly growing external deficit. During the first quarter of 1975, prices of consumer goods were rising at an annual rate of 18.7%. Spain's balance of payments registered at that time an overall deficit equivalent to 4% of the country's GNP (Ibid.). To appease workers' discontent, the government allowed salaries and wages to rise at a rate equivalent to the rate of inflation twelve months earlier plus two-thirds of that inflation rate. Large salary and wage increases strengthened the rapid rise in production costs and contributed to the deterioration of investors' expectations regarding the profitability of new investment.

1974 had been the first year in which the Spanish economy felt the full impact of the global crisis. Spain experienced both inflation and economic recession in 1974. The beginning of 1975 developed in an environment marked by strong increases in factor costs, by workers' demands for higher wages, by a worldwide industrial recession and by pessimistic entrepreneurial expectations about the future of the domestic economy. Industrial production contracted in 1975. The annual moving average of change in industrial production for November 1975 was −7.9%; it had been +15.6% two years earlier and +10.4% in 1974 (Ministerio de Industria, 1977, 9). The Ministry of Industry estimate of the rate of growth of Spain's real GNP in 1975 was 0.7%, a rate slightly lower than the rate of demographic growth in that year, which indicated a small decline in per capita income in 1975, a trend which had not been experienced in the country since 1960.

Employment in Spain's secondary sector declined by 1.9% in 1975, following an increase of 1.8% in 1974. The rise of unemployment in that sector in 1975 was strongest in the construction industry which employed 5% fewer workers than in the previous year. For the whole of the industrial sector, 1975 witnessed a loss of 63,900 jobs in the construction industry and of 27,400 jobs in manufacturing and mining. The Ministry of Industry reported that the number of unemployed workers in the industrial sector during the last quarter of 1975 had risen to 246,200, a figure representing 5% of the country's total active population (Ibid., 10).

In 1975, investment was the critical variable affecting Spain's economic performance. Measured in real terms, the rate of growth of investment continued to decelerate and became negative. This rate which had attained 13.9% in 1973 declined to a positive rate of 3.2% in 1974 and became negative in 1975 at −9.2%. The decline of industrial investment in 1975, measured in constant pesetas, was more than twice the corresponding fall in 1971 which had been −4.8% (Ibid., 10).

Productivity per employed person in the secondary sector also fell in 1975, declining by –0.6% from its 1974 level. The decline in the level of productivity in 1975 was even larger at –1.3%, if the construction sector is not taken into consideration. Causes for such productivity decline were the industrial recession which hindered an efficient use of available resources, as well as the intensification of labour conflicts in 1975 and the rigidity of the government's labour policies.

The global economic crisis had also a very adverse effect on Spain's foreign trade; the weakening of the country's exports reduced Spain's import capacity and thus adversely affected Spain's economic development process. In real terms, merchandise imports fell by –2.8% in 1975 and merchandise exports declined by –3.0%. Considering only imports and exports of industrial products, these declined from their 1974 levels by –5.4% and –2.7% respectively.

The government of Carlos Arias Navarro faced other than purely economic difficulties in 1975, problems which further contributed to the deterioration of the economy. Labour unrest and terrorism strengthened the determination of the *bunker* to fight for *continuismo*. Afraid of the Francoist right, Arias Navarro decided to appease it. In February 1975 he made it clear that he rejected any constitutional reform. Following acts of terrorism in the Basque region, the government imposed martial law in that area in April; this led to acts of unprecedented repression by the police. In June, Arias Navarro appointed José Solís Ruiz, the leader of the *bunker*, as Minister of Labour. In August, the government enacted a new Anti-Terrorist Law following the assassination of a number of policemen and Civil Guards.

The opposition, though factionalized into a Democratic Junta and a Platform of Democratic Convergence, was nevertheless committed to the goal of replacing the Francoist regime with a 'democracy without adjectives'. Both opposition groups rejected the government's Statute of Associations and the plan of Manuel Fraga Iribarne to create a Great Association of the Centre which would unite all Francoist reformers. The Francoist extremists determined to crush any attempt by any group to abandon Francoist orthodoxy. In June 1975, they established a *Unión del Pueblo Español*, UPDE, led by a Falangist leader, Adolfo Suárez.

Terrorist and anti-terrorist violence continued. In his last public appearance on 1 October General Franco attributed the political and economic problems of the country to 'a masonic leftist conspiracy of the political class in collusion with Communist-terrorist subversion in the social sphere' (Carr, R. and Fusi, J.P., 1979, 205). Franco died on 20 November. The political timidity of Arias Navarro and the serious effects of the economic crisis made Spaniards wonder whether Francoism without Franco would continue in Spain. The answer to that question could only be given by Spain's new King, D. Juan Carlos I.

## Politics in the first years of the new monarchy

Under Spanish law, King Juan Carlos could only nominate for the position of President of the Government one of the three candidates selected by the Council of the Realm. The Council was controlled by strong Francoists. King Juan Carlos, unable to nominate a liberal Prime Minister, decided to reappoint Carlos Arias Navarro as President of the Government. The first government of the King included conservative Francoists such as José Solís Ruiz, the Minister of Labour, and *aperturistas* such as José Ma. Areilza, the Minister for Foreign Affairs and Manuel Fraga Iribarne, the Minister of the Interior.

The new reign started with a very uncertain economic and political outlook. The economy remained in conditions of recession. The political scenario showed Spain's main political organizations – the Council of the Realm, the National Council of the Movement and the *Cortes* – still controlled by staunch Francoists opposed to any political reform. Many believed that the clashing interests of the members of the *bunker* and of those of the democratic opposition would bring a new civil war to the country. Santiago Carrillo, the Secretary-General of the Spanish Communist Party, believed that the new reign would have such a short life that he gave the King the nickname 'Juan the Brief'. The opposition, strengthened by the belief that Western Europe would not tolerate the continuation of a Francoist regime in Spain, demanded a quick break with that regime, either through negotiations or through new elections, and demanded immediate amnesty for all political prisoners, the legalization of all political parties, free trade unions, the abolition of the Francoist Movement and of the syndicates and the establishment of a new constituent *Cortes* through free elections (Ibid., 209). The government of Arias Navarro opposed any *ruptura* and promised only vague, gradual improvements of the existing political system. On 28 January 1976 Carlos Arias Navarro presented to the Francoist *Cortes* a proposal for political reform. His plan included the legalization of political parties with the exception of the Communists and of 'separatist organizations'. The programme was mute on questions such as awarding limited autonomy to the country's regions and new elections to the *Cortes* whose membership had not changed since 1971. Conforming with the established Francoist usage, Arias Navarro denounced the 'hidden enemies' of Spain and glorified the achievements of the defunct Caudillo. The main concern of Arias Navarro appeared to be the appeasement of the *bunker*.

Although the Prime Minister's speech of 28 January pleased conservative Francoists, it infuriated most Spanish workers. Strikes and street demonstrations multiplied during the early months of 1976. On 1 February 75,000 people demonstrated in Barcelona in support of amnesty for political prisoners and in favour of Catalan autonomy (Ibid.,

210). Terrorism intensified in the Basque region. The *bunker* reacted by loudly proclaiming its opposition to any departure from Francoist orthodoxy. The situation worsened when on 3 March police opened fire on a crowd in Vitoria, killing five workers. This incident induced the two main groups of the democratic opposition to unite and to fuse into a new political organization known as 'Democratic Coordination'.

Carlos Arias Navarro was caught between the determination of the opposition to do away with the totality of the Francoist regime and the equally strong commitment of the *bunker* leadership to preserve intact Franco's political system. Probably feeling that he lacked the support of the King and that of the *Cortes*, Arias Navarro resigned on 1 July 1976.

In the summer of 1976 the principal political organizations in Spain were still controlled by dedicated Francoists. The *bunker* appeared to have won the battle for *continuismo*. The King received from the Council of the Realm a list of three candidates for the position of President of the Government. Two of the nominees had held ministerial positions under Franco. They were Gregorio López Bravo, former Minister of Industry and former Minister for Foreign Affairs, and Federico Silva Muñoz, a former Minister of Public Works. The third nominee was Adolfo Suárez, the current Minister of the National Movement. King Juan Carlos selected Suárez.

The King was anxious to replace Arias Navarro with a new President of the Government. Arias Navarro remained more devoted to the protection of the policies of the deceased Caudillo than to the new course of political strategy supported by the Crown. It was reported that even after the coronation of Don Juan Carlos, a large portrait of Franco in Arias's office continued to overshadow a small picture of the King (Coverdale, J.H., 1979, 43). The King preferred to have a Prime Minister who would know how to further the King's aim of gradual political change. It had to be a man able to convince the Francoist *Cortes* that changes in the political system could not be avoided and that such changes did not necessarily mean political suicide for the sitting *procuradores*.

Arias had proved to be unwilling and unable to alter basic Francoist practices. In April 1976 he had rejected the opposition's demand for a Constituent Assembly and denied the latter any participation in the formulation of reform proposals. On 25 May in the course of a parliamentary debate regarding a proposal to legalize political parties, a proposal initially strongly opposed by most *procuradores*, Adolfo Suárez González, the Minister of the National Movement and a man with excellent Francoist credentials, rose to present to his colleagues an astute argument in favour of the proposal. Suárez made the point that the legalization of political parties was not only consistent with the Caudillo's views, but would 'complete the work of Franco'. In his words,

'The government, which is the legitimate manager of this historic moment, has the responsibility of setting in motion the necessary mechanisms for the definitive consolidation of a modern democracy. To achieve this, the starting point lies in the recognition of a pluralistic society' (Ibid., 41).

On 9 June the *Cortes* approved a measure which provided that any political party seeking legalization had to request it from the Minister of the Interior. The latter was given two months to accept or reject such request. Arias's weak reformist efforts were not well received by any political or economic group in the country. Conservative Francoists condemned them. The democratic opposition felt that a 'negotiated break' with the Francoist regime could only be initiated with a new Prime Minister. Few were amazed when the King demanded and obtained the resignation of Arias Navarro.

The King clearly understood that political and social change without bloodshed could best be effected by having men truly loyal to him controlling the two key political positions in Spain. These positions were the Presidency of the *Cortes* and the Presidency of the Council of the Realm. It happened that Alejandro Rodríguez Valcárcel, a staunch Francoist, resigned in 1975 as both President of the *Cortes* and as President of the Council of the Realm. The King replaced him with his former tutor and friend, Torcuato Fernández Miranda. Fernández Miranda had been a professor of public law at the University of Madrid. Franco chose him to tutor the Prince Juan Carlos in political philosophy. Fernández Miranda became a Minister and the Secretary-General of the National Movement under Franco and served as Vice-President of the Government in the Cabinet of Carrero Blanco. The Francoist right-wing considered Fernández Miranda to be a loyal supporter of the Francoist regime who would strongly oppose both the *aperturistas* and the democratic opposition. What the *bunker* failed to perceive was that Fernández Miranda attached more importance to serving the King than favouring his own political preferences.

The King's intention was to liberalize the old regime gradually, using for this purpose existing institutions and avoiding any sudden break with past practices, a break which could easily lead to a civil war. He wanted a new Prime Minister willing to implement in Spain the political changes which all of Western Europe desired, a man not much older than himself, loyal above all to the King and worthy of the Crown's trust. Fernández Miranda succeeded in placing the name of Adolfo Suárez González on the *'terna'*, the list containing the names of three candidates for the position of President of the Government, from which the King had to choose one.

Adolfo Suárez González was 43 years old when the King chose him to succeed Carlos Arias Navarro as Spain's Prime Minister. He had used his friendship with Fernando Herrero Tejedor, the Minister of the National Movement in the government of Carrero Blanco, to rise rapidly in the hierarchy of the National Movement. With the help of Herrero Tejedor, Suárez became President of the conservative 'Union of the Spanish People'. The death of Herrero Tejedor allowed Suárez to be part of the first government of the monarchy in the capacity of Secretary-General of the National Movement. The announcement of his nomination as President of the Government pleased the ultra-right and many military leaders. It produced great dismay among the regime reformists and among the leaders of the opposition. The latter failed to see that Adolfo Suárez was a pragmatic politician who had used the National Movement to further his career without seriously embracing Falangist ideology. A well-known columnist writing in the left-of-centre newspaper *El País* reacted to the news of Suárez's nomination with the words: 'What an Error, What an Immense Error!'. Areilza, Fraga Iribarne and three other *aperturista* ministers promptly announced that they would not serve in a government presided over by Suárez. Their conviction that Suárez's appointment to head a new government represented the *bunker*'s victory was shared by most Spaniards. Faced by growing unemployment and strong inflation, Spaniards contemplated an intimidating return to the authoritarian government practices of the past.

To demonstrate his conservatism, Suárez retained in his Cabinet the former military ministers. He filled the remaining ministerial positions with relatively young, politically unknown men selected from *aperturista* Francoist political associations such as the Spanish Democratic Union, an organization representing the conservative Christian Democrats in Franco's regime. The government's Vice-Presidency, the ministries of Foreign Affairs, Finance, Information and Justice were given to members of a Christian Democratic group, *Tácito*, which had advocated three years earlier a 'democratic and pluralistic' system. The *Tácito* Christian Democrats had demanded a number of basic reforms they believed were needed to effect a peaceful transition to democracy. Among them: the recognition by Spanish law of the basic freedoms contained in the Universal Declaration of Human Rights of the United Nations and in the European Convention; election by universal suffrage of persons over the age of eighteen; the establishment of an independent judiciary; the recognition of regional demands for autonomy; and the pardon of political prisoners (Abel, C. and Torrents, N., 1984, 27).

Suárez deliberately chose to centre his efforts on political reform and to ignore for the time being serious economic problems in the country such as stagnation, growing unemployment, rising inflation and a worsening of the country's external accounts. In the words of Professor Coverdale,

The new president and the king were determined to give Spain the freer, more democratic institutions most Spaniards wanted. They both rejected, however, the opposition's call for a clean break with the Francoist past through the convening of a constituent assembly, as well as its contention that democracy could not be handed down from above. Suárez opted to continue to work within the framework of the institutions established by Franco: the Cortes, the National Council of the Movement, and the Council of the Realm...

Coverdale, J.F., 1979, p. 47

The main goal of the new Prime Minister was to create a more democratic *Cortes* able to draft in the future a new constitution. Suárez's hope was that the opposition would in time support his programme out of fear that the alternative to the Prime Minister's plan could be a right-wing coup. Suárez also counted on the probability that both the right and the military would support his proposed reforms as long as these appeared in the form of a continuation of the Francoist regime and as long as the Communist Party would not be legalized by the government.

The government's political reform programme was presented to the *Cortes* on 12 September 1976. The political reform bill called for free elections to the *Cortes* and explicitly stipulated that the new democratic system would be 'based on the rule of law, [on the] expression of the sovereign will of the people' (Share, D., 1986, 103). The bill provided for a bicameral legislature whose members were to be elected by direct, secret universal suffrage, though the King retained the power to appoint one-sixth of the senators. The *Cortes* was given the power to draft a new constitution. The King was to be allowed to submit directly to the people by means of a referendum any constitutional amendment he proposed. In order to make the bill more acceptable to the sitting Francoist parliament, it was titled the eighth Fundamental Law of the Francoist political system, even though it contradicted in many respects the Fundamental Laws passed during the lifetime of General Franco. This clever tactic pleased the right because it gave in effect 'retroactive legitimacy' to the Caudillo's laws.

Before they introduced the bill in the *Cortes*, Suárez and Fernández Miranda received assurances from Spain's military leaders that they would support the government's programme. This *entente* with the country's ranking military officers nearly collapsed when on 22 September the Vice-President for Defence, General Fernando de Santiago y Díaz de Mendivil, a staunch Francoist, left the government to protest a meeting that had taken place between the Minister for Syndical Relations and representatives of the clandestine communist-influenced Workers' Commissions organization. De Santiago's resignation threatened a military opposition to the government's reform proposal. Suárez nevertheless accepted the resignation and replaced General de Santiago with General Manuel Gutiérrez Mellado, a strong supporter of the King and a man who favoured political reform.

In accordance with the practices of the Franco regime, the National Council of the Movement was the first Francoist agency to debate and to vote on the bill. It found the bill consistent with the orthodoxy of the Movement and approved it on 9 October 1976. The Francoist *Cortes* accepted it on 18 November even though the bill called for the end of the sitting Francoist parliament. The majority of the *procuradores* voted in favour of the government's reform programme for a number of reasons. The programme was silent about the status of the National Movement. It did not propose the legalization of the Communist Party. It was vague about the new electoral system and most members of the *Cortes* believed that they would be able to run again for office as representatives of the right. Finally, many *procuradores* voted in favour of the bill feeling that the King supported it. Once approved by the *Cortes*, the law was submitted to a national referendum on 15 December 1976, and received the overwhelming support of the Spanish people.

The Suárez victory induced the democratic opposition to abandon its demand for a provisional government. In exchange for a number of concessions extended to it by the government, the opposition decided to accept the Suárez political reform programme. The government allowed the Spanish Socialist Workers Party to celebrate its first congress in Spain in forty years; it also signed the International Agreement on Civil and Political Rights of the United Nations and legalized independent trade unions on 1 April 1977.

### The economy in 1976

Neither the government of Carlos Arias Navarro, nor that of Adolfo Suárez, made a serious effort in 1976 to strengthen the national economy. Whereas the annual rate of growth of Gross Domestic Product in 1976 in the entire OECD area averaged 5%, it attained only 2.4% in Spain. The Spanish economy in that year was weakened by major disequilibria.

The devaluation of the peseta in February 1976 caused an increase of 14.2% in the prices of Spanish imports of goods and services. The prices of Spanish exports rose by only 10.3% in 1976 (Banco de Bilbao, 1977, 69). The country's balance of trade deficit increased by US$ 5.6 billion. In spite of the worsening of Spain's real terms of trade, Spanish imports of goods and services rose by 9.5% in 1976.

Another major disequilibrium was evidenced by the fact that whereas the rate of growth of domestic capital formation declined by 1.6% in

1976, the consumption of goods and services expanded by 4%. Consumer goods prices increased by 17.6%. The cost of living index, which had risen by 14.1% in 1975, increased by 19.8% in 1976. Prices of industrial products had risen by 8.9% in 1975; they rose by 12.7% in 1976 (Ibid., 70). Strong salary and wage increases in 1976 strengthened the process of price inflation. Gross salary and wage increases rose by 21.7% in 1975; they increased by 23% in 1976.

In 1973, the employed active population had represented 37.3% of the total Spanish population. This percentage figure declined to 35% in 1976. The unemployment rate, including persons seeking employment for the first time, rose from 3.22% in 1974 to 4.66% in 1975 and to 5.50% in 1976 (Ibid., 71).

Looking at the structure of Net National Income, income from salaries, wages and social security contributions paid by employers increased from 61.85% of Net National Income in 1974 to 66.67% in 1976. This increase in the share of labour income occurred to the detriment of the aggregate participation in Net National Income of the incomes of farmers, merchants and individual self-employed persons. More important, the share in Net National Income of net business profits experienced a major decline. This share amounted to 9.59% of Net National Income in 1974; it declined to 8.11% in 1975 and to 5.85% in 1976. The private investment index in 1976 was 11% lower than that attained two years earlier.

Spain's Gross Domestic Product rose at the modest rate of 2.4% in 1976. As noted, private consumption spending in that year increased by 4% while real investment in fixed capital declined by 2%. A result of such trends was an increase in real imports at the rate of 9.5% which was translated into an expansion of the external deficit even though the value of the peseta in terms of the US dollar fell by 16.6% in 1976. Spain's balance of payments on current account in that year registered a deficit of US$ 4.3 billion, a sharp increase over the corresponding 1975 figure of US$ 3.5 billion.

Throughout 1976, Spain's economy faced a number of serious problems which the government did not attempt to solve. Spain's rates of price and wage inflation were higher than in other Western European countries. While private consumers' demand grew at positive rates, private investment in fixed capital declined. The rate of unemployment went on rising, and by December 1976 about 800,000 persons were looking for work. The fall in the share of business profits in Net National Income and the adverse effect of inflation on private saving worsened entrepreneurial expectations and acted as major obstacles to the financing of investment. The deterioration of the country's external account produced a rising foreign debt and a decline in the country's foreign exchange reserves.

## THE 1970s
## THE TRANSITION TO DEMOCRACY: 1977, 1978

The two years which followed December 1976 when Spaniards overwhelmingly approved the Political Reform Law of Adolfo Suárez and ended in December 1978 when the Spanish electorate voted in favour of a new democratic constitution formed a period of political transition during which the country moved from Francoist authoritarianism to a new parliamentary democracy.

Suárez's efforts to gradually democratize Spain on the basis of an apparent *continuismo* were immediately opposed by both the extreme right and the extreme left. The President of the Government was forced to act in an environment marked by mounting terrorism carried out by both extremist groups. On 24 January 1977 rightist gunmen shot nine communist labour lawyers in their offices in Madrid, killing five of them. Four days later, armed thugs killed two policemen in Madrid and shot at four members of the Civil Guard. Terrorism in Madrid and in Barcelona declined in February, but it continued in the Basque region, maintained not only by rightist and leftist extremists, but also by the police and by Basque nationalists.

Political parties, now legalized with the exception of the Spanish Communist Party, started preparing their electoral campaigns for the parliamentary elections scheduled for June 1977. A major party was the Popular Party, PP, a centrist alliance led by two former ministers of Franco, José Ma. de Areilza and Pío Cabanillas; the PP had been legalized by the Arias Navarro government. Its membership was made up by centrist and by right-of-centre politicians generally supporting conservative Christian Democracy. In January 1977 the PP entered into an alliance with other Christian Democratic groups, forming a Democratic Centre, CD. The most important political groups forming the CD were the Federation of Democratic and Liberal Parties of Joaquín Garrigués Walker, the Christian Democratic Party of Fernando Alvarez de Miranda, the Spanish Democratic Union of Alberto Monreal Luque, the Liberal Party of Enrique Larroque and the Popular Democratic Party of Ignacio Camuñas. The Social Democratic Grouping of Francisco Fernández Ordóñez joined the CD in February (Coverdale, J.F., 1979, 62).

Suárez welcomed the establishment of the CD as a political power block which would be able to defeat in June both the rightist Popular Alliance, AP, of Manuel Fraga Iribarne and the PSOE of Felipe González. The President did not openly identify with the CD however until late in April. It was only after he had successfully negotiated with the CD leadership his entrance into the coalition and his right to place the names of his own followers on the CD's electoral lists that he announced on 4 May his campaign for a seat in the *Cortes* as a deputy representing the

CD, now renamed Centre Democratic Union, UCD. The head of the renamed alliance was Suárez's lieutenant, Leopoldo Calvo Sotelo.

The UCD's main rival party was the Spanish Socialist Workers' Party, PSOE. This party lacked the support of all socialists in Spain; other socialist groups were politically active. There was the Historical Spanish Socialist Workers' Party, the Popular Socialist Party of Professor Tierno Galván, as well as a Federation of Socialist Parties, FPS. The first group allied itself with the Spanish Social Democratic Party, while the latter two entered into a coalition named the Socialist Unity Coalition. The PSOE remained however the most important socialist political block. At its 27th Congress, illegally held in Madrid in December 1976, the moderates in the party prevailed over the radicals. Felipe González Márquez was re-elected as First Secretary and Alfonso Guerra became Organizational Secretary. Although this Congress professed to embrace Marxian ideology, the party leadership limited its rhetoric to statements generally acceptable to European Social Democrats.

The Spanish Communist Party, PCE, led by Santiago Carrillo, a party unexpectedly legalized by Adolfo Suárez on 9 April 1977, assured its followers that it was dedicated to the restoration of democracy in the country and that its moderate 'Eurocommunism' would remain free of Soviet influence. The rightist Popular Alliance, AP, led by known political figures of the Franco era, recognized the need for political reforms but attacked the Suárez government for being unable to maintain law and order in the country and for supporting the advocates of regional autonomy. Its leader, Manuel Fraga Iribarne, proclaimed that he was a supporter of the Franco regime and claimed that the government was opening the nation to Marxism (Ibid., 66). Christian Democrats were unable to join in a single party and many of them decided to join the UCD.

In the Basque region, a number of political parties were formed, all of them demanding regional autonomy. The most moderate of these parties was the Basque Nationalist Party (PNV), a strong party in the days of the Second Republic, supportive of both centrist policies and regional autonomy. To its left, *abertzale* parties, claiming independence from all Spanish political groups, ranged from Social Democrats to Marxist-Leninist groups. Some claimed only regional autonomy, some, independence from Spain. Autonomists were supported by the PSOE which advocated the establishment of a Spanish federation of autonomous regions; the Communist Party of Euzkadi also favoured such a process, a federation rejected by the UCD.

As in the Basque region, all political parties in Catalonia demanded autonomy for the region. Even the Catalan right, led by Laureano López Rodó, Franco's Commissar for the Plan of Economic Development, made strong demands for Catalan autonomy. The political centre was dominated by the Democratic Pact for Catalonia, PDC, founded by Ramón Trias Fargas and by the banker Jordi Pujol. Joan Reventós led the left, having united his Catalan Socialist Party with the Catalan section of the PSOE to form the Socialists of Catalonia, SC. Further to the left were the Unified Socialist Party of Catalonia (PSUC) and the Catalan left (EC); the PSUC was a pure communist party. EC was a conglomerate of leftist groups extending from Catalan Republicans to the Leninist-Maoist Spanish Work Party.

The elections took place on 15 June 1977. These gave the UCD 34.7% of the popular vote and 47.1% of the seats in the Parliament. The PSOE obtained 29.2% of the popular vote and 33.7% of the seats. The Spanish Communist Party received only 9.2% of the vote and 5.7% of the seats. The Popular Alliance followed with 8.4% of the vote and 4.6% of the seats (Ibid., 73). Spain's electorate had rejected both Francoism and the extreme left.

The two great victors in the election were the UCD and the PSOE which, between them, controlled 80% of the seats in the *Cortes*. Spain's first democratic parliament convened on 13 July 1977. It was no longer a Francoist stronghold. One of its deputies was the aged Dolores Ibarruri, the passionate communist leader in the days of the Civil War known to all Spaniards as 'La Pasionaria'; Adolfo Suárez, the former minister of the Francoist National Movement was another *procurador*.

The new monarchy was legitimized and strengthened by the dissolution of the Republican government in exile in the summer of 1977 and by the renunciation, by Don Juan de Borbón, of his right to the throne of Spain in favour of his son, Juan Carlos. On 4 July King Juan Carlos asked Adolfo Suárez to form a second government.

Suárez's new Cabinet was constituted almost entirely of UCD men. The Prime Minister re-established the position of Vice-President for Economic Affairs in view of the seriousness of the contemporary economic crisis. Enrique Feuntes Quintana, a professor of public finance in Madrid, a man who supported Spain's move toward a free market economy and who had denounced the inequities of the national distribution of income and the unfairness of the existing tax system, was selected for the new position. This appointment signified that after years of relative indifference to the worsening of the economy, the government had decided to take action to lower the national rate of inflation which reached 26.4% in 1977, to reduce the country's balance-of-payments deficit which reached about US$ 5 billion at the end of the year and to contain the rise in unemployment.

Suárez decided to weaken the voice of the military in his government by abolishing the three traditional armed forces ministries. He substituted for the old military ministries a Vice-President for Defence. This position was given to Lieutenant General Manuel Gutiérrez Mellado, a strong supporter of the King. A new Associate Minister for Relations with the Regions revealed Suárez's concern with the problem of regional autonomies. The Social Democrat Francisco Fernández Ordóñez became Minister of Finance. Several new ministers were former reformist Francoists. No socialists participated in the Cabinet.

The government quickly took measures to reduce the country's external debt and to weaken the inflationary process. On 12 July 1977 the peseta was devalued by 19.6%. The government urged employers and trade unions to limit salary and wage increases to a maximum of 17% and promised that it would expand the unemployment insurance fund. It committed itself to the achievement of fiscal reform in order to distribute more fairly the burden of taxes among all citizens. In August the government drafted bills providing for a tax on wealth, a tax on the purchase of luxury goods and an income tax surcharge. The new legislative measures also provided for tax cuts for businesses hiring new employees.

Disenchanted businessmen and trade unions started proclaiming their dissatisfaction with the government. Businessmen and bankers resented the government's fiscal reforms; trade union leaders disliked the government's attempt to mandate a wage increase ceiling. Fearing a weakening of the UCD, Suárez tried to obtain the support of the opposition, not only that of the Socialists and the Communists, but also the aid of Catalan and of Basque parties. Suárez appealed to the Catalan longing for regional autonomy by restoring in September the Catalan *Generalitat*, even though for the time being this regional government was deprived of any real power. To please the Basque population, Suárez published in October the draft of a new amnesty law which would give freedom to all those who had been found guilty of a political crime committed before 15 June 1977, with the exception of crimes 'carried out for profit or with the deliberate aim of destabilizing the democratic process begun 14 December 1976' (Ibid., 91). The Prime Minister knew that the proposed amnesty would please the Basques given the fact that most political prisoners still in jail belonged to the Basque region.

On 5 October 1977 President Suárez invited the leaders of Spain's major political parties to meet with him at the Moncloa Palace in Madrid to discuss and prepare jointly an 'emergency plan' needed to solve the country's 'grave difficulties'. These leaders met for twenty hours and reached an agreement on a programme of economic and political reform known as the Moncloa Pact. They signed the agreement on 25 October. J.F. Coverdale has described the contents of this Pact in these words:

> The economic part of the Moncloa Pact was essentially an austerity plan that offered social reforms and more parliamentary control over the economy in exchange for wage restraint. The government

and the parties agreed to raise pensions 30 percent, increase unemployment benefits to the same level as the legal minimum wage, substitute progressive income taxes for indirect taxes, and undertake other fiscal reforms including new corporate taxes and a permanent tax on wealth. They pledged the creation of new classrooms for 700,000 more students in the public school system as part of a move towards completely free education. In addition, they promised to introduce the distinctive languages and cultures of the various regions into the school curriculum. Programs of slum removal, control of urban land speculation, and construction of subsidized housing would be undertaken ...

In return for these reforms, workers were asked to accept a ceiling of 22 percent on wage increases in 1973. This would represent stagnation of real wages, but not their decline since monetary and fiscal policy would be designed to keep inflation at or below 22 percent. Government expenditures and outlays of the social security system would increase no more than 21.4 percent, and growth of the money supply would be held to about 17 percent.

Coverdale, J.F., 1979, p. 92

The Prime Minister in effect asked the workers to forego an increase in real wages in 1978 as a *quid pro quo* for his abolition of the Francoist ban on independent labour organizations in April of the same year. Indeed, a Decree-Law of 4 March 1977, provided for and regulated the right to strike, a right Franco had taken away from the workers. A debate over a new law on labour organization began in the *Cortes* on 30 March. On 28 April the government allowed the then illegal independent trade unions to acquire legality through the simple process of registry. The Francoist Syndical Organization, established by a Law of Syndical Unity of 26 January 1940, disappeared. As of 1 July 1977 employers and employees were no longer forced to belong to a Francoist 'syndicate'. Spanish workers were free to join, or to refrain from joining, any newly legalized independent labour organization (Lieberman, S., 1982, 328).

The signing of the Moncloa Pact was not followed by a diminution of regionalist disturbances in the country. Strikes and demonstrations in support of regional autonomy were an added burden to the national economy. The government was not opposed to extending pre-autonomy statutes to regions asking for such laws, still it encountered opposition by certain groups. The Suárez government had agreed to support a pre-autonomy statute for the Basque region. The proposed law was, however, opposed by many Basques because the government intended at first to incorporate Navarre into the region. Many Navarrese were also opposed to having their province treated as part of the Basque area.

Navarrese opposed to the proposed law demonstrated in Pamplona on 3 December 1977. They were supported by UCD politicians. The PSOE, the PNV and ETA insisted on the inclusion of Navarre in the Basque area. The government succeeded in having these opposing groups agree on a compromise. At the end of the year, it proposed the enactment of a pre-autonomy law which would only apply to the provinces of Alava, Guipúzcoa and Vizcaya. Navarre could decide to join the Basque region in the future. The government in Madrid also allowed the establishment of a Basque Council which, like the Catalan *Generalitat*, had at the time only symbolic significance. Demonstrations in favour of real autonomy continued. Regionalist violence was now directed at the nuclear power plant at Lemóniz, near Bilbao. Basque nationalists and the Basque left denounced the plant as representing an act of genocide perpetrated by Madrid against the Basque people. In December 1977, the quarters of the Civil Guard protecting the plant were bombed by ETA.

Strikes and threatened or actual violence soon weakened the Basque economy. Industrialists in the region, eager to avoid paying the 'revolutionary tax' imposed on them by ETA or fearing being kidnapped and held for ransom by that organization, moved their plants out of the Basque region, creating thereby a rising number of unemployed workers.

The willingness of the central government to grant autonomy powers to both Catalonia and the Basque region had a knock-on effect on other Spanish regions. Regions without a distinctive economy or culture started demanding autonomy. The Suárez government, feeling that such demands represented little political or economic danger to the nation, was willing to please the regionalist forces. By the middle of 1978, ten regions containing between them about three-fourths of Spain's total population, obtained pre-autonomy statutes. The central government extended such laws to Andalusia, Aragón, the Balearic Islands, the Canary Islands, Castile-León, Extremadura, Galicia and Valencia. Spain was quickly becoming a federation of autonomous regions.

Uncertainty about the future course of internal politics, a weak global economic recovery and a marked fall in domestic economic activity were the main factors which impeded a satisfactory recovery of the Spanish economy in 1977. Until the elections of June, the government centred its attention on political rather than on economic problems. Its permissive economic policies facilitated the further increase in inflation and in unemployment, a decline in productive investment as well as a fall in productivity, and a deterioration of the country's external accounts. During the first half of 1977, the annual rate of expansion of bank credit attained 26%. In the summer months, the rate of inflation exceeded 35%. The balance-of-payments deficit on current account threatened to reach US$ 5 billion by the end of the year. The government finally reacted to the country's increasing external deficit and devalued the peseta in July. The new rate of exchange approximated 85 pesetas to the US dollar. Measures were taken to slow down the rates of monetary and of bank credit expansion. A new Ministry of Economics started preparing the economic reform programme which would become part of the Moncloa Pact in October (Banco de Bilbao, 1978, 61).

The study of the national economy by the Studies Service of the Banco de Bilbao reported the following macroeconomic trends. In terms of 1976 prices, Spain's GDP increased in 1977 by 2.4%. Industrial production rose by 3.8% in that year and that of services by 3%. The potential beneficial impact of such increases on the domestic economy was however limited by a decline of 2.2% in the output of the primary sector and by a fall of 1.5% in that of the construction industry.

Industrial production showed a slight recovery during the first half of 1977 but cost inflation and the weakening of domestic demand for capital goods caused it to decline during the second half of the year. In the latter period, industries such as metallurgy, shipbuilding, capital goods and textile industries faced serious difficulties. Service industries showed dissimilar trends. While the tourist trade strengthened, commerce and maritime transport showed a significant decline.

The GDP's rate of growth of 2.4% in 1977 was largely due to an improvement in Spain's external balance. Internally, all the components of private domestic demand had an adverse effect on the economy. Household incomes, diminished by rising inflation and by a heavier tax burden, rose by only 1.8% between 1973 and 1976, compared to a growth rate of 7.8% for the years 1970 to 1973 (OECD, 1978, 8). The growth rate of per capita private consumption fell from an average rate of 5.8% for the period 1970 to 1973 to 2.3% for the period 1973 to 1976 and was practically zero in 1977. Shrinking profit margins, as well as political and economic uncertainties in Spain caused investment to fall from 1975. Since that year, fixed capital formation declined at an annual rate of 6.5%. The growth of GDP in 1977 was entirely based on expanding exports and on the strong growth of public consumption.

Table 40 shows the eroding effect taxes and transfers had on household incomes in the period 1970 to 1977.

The fall in investment was the major cause of the rise in unemployment which reached 6.3% of the active population at the end of 1977. At the start of the 1970s, the decline in the agricultural labour force had been compensated by an increase in non-agricultural employment. Total employment grew at the rate of about 1% per year. As of 1975, aggregate employment started declining as shown in Table 41. By the middle of 1977, non-agricultural employment stagnated. In spite of the adverse trend in total employment, the movement of workers out of the primary sector continued after 1974. In spite of the net migration out of the agricultural sector, agricultural employment still represented 20% of

*Table 40* Net effect of taxes and transfers on household incomes: 1970–7

| Percentage of household income | 1970 | 1974 | 1975 | 1976 | 1977 |
|---|---|---|---|---|---|
| Transfers received | 10.5 | 10.8 | 11.4 | 12.0 | 12.0 |
| Income tax | 1.3 | 1.9 | 2.1 | 2.4 | 2.8 |
| Social security contributions | 9.1 | 10.3 | 11.5 | 12.0 | 12.8 |
| Net effect of taxes and transfers | 0.1 | –1.4 | –2.2 | –2.2 | –3.6 |

Source: OECD, *Economic Surveys, Spain*, 1978, p. 8

*Table 41* Employment trends in Spain: 1960–77

| Sector | Structure of civilian employment in thousands, 1977 | Percentage change in annual rate of employment | | |
|---|---|---|---|---|
| | | 1960–70 | 1970–4 | 1974–7 |
| Total | 12,468 | 0.7 | 0.9 | –1.1 |
| Agriculture | 2,606 | –2.8 | –4.9 | –4.5 |
| Non-farm sector | 9,862 | 2.7 | 3.1 | 0.0 |
| Industry | 3,433 | 2.2 | | –1.0 |
| Construction | 1,224 | 2.7 | | –0.5 |
| Services | 5,205 | 3.2 | | 1.1 |

Source: OECD, *Economic Surveys, Spain*, 1978, p. 9
Note: The breakdown of non-farm employment for 1970–4 is not available because of a change in treatment of categories

the total Spanish labour force in 1977, though the share of agriculture in GDP had fallen to 9% (Ibid., 9).

Unemployment rose rapidly between 1974 and 1977. It expanded from 3.4% of the total labour force at the start of 1974 to 6.3% at the end of 1977. Although the main cause of this development was the decline in investment, another contributing factor was the sharp reduction in the number of foreign workers admitted to European countries which up to 1974 had attracted Spanish emigrants. An estimated 575,000 Spaniards left Spain in 1974. During the next three years, fewer than 100,000 Spaniards migrated abroad during the entire period.

In addition to a weakening of economic activity and the rise in unemployment, Spain experienced a rate of inflation which was appreciably higher than that in the rest of the OECD nations. Between 1963 and 1973 the annual Spanish rate of inflation had averaged 7.3%; this rate rose to 17% between 1974 and 1976 and reached about 25% in 1977. The acceleration of inflation in Spain was fed by rapidly rising import prices and by the acceleration in the rise of domestic wage costs. If rising social security contributions paid by employers are included in the wages bill, the latter increased by 27.7% in 1977. While the share of wages and salaries in the Net National Product expanded, the share of entrepreneurial profits became smaller. In 1974, net profits commanded 36.4% of the NNP; this share fell to 31.4% in 1976 and to 30.9% in 1977. The continuous fall in the profits share of the NNP constituted a major obstacle to the growth of investment (Banco de Bilbao, 1978, 64).

Up to 1973, the cost impact of rapidly rising wages was in part absorbed by productivity gains. After that year, a weakening demand reduced the ability of entrepreneurs to incorporate rising wage costs into the prices of their products or services; Francoist labour laws prevented employers from reducing their labour force. The net result was a declining profit margin followed by a deterioration in entrepreneurial investment expectations.

The devaluation of the peseta in the summer of 1977 also stimulated the rise of domestic costs during the latter half of the year. During the last quarter of 1977, consumer prices rose by 26.9% over their level in the corresponding period in 1976; during the same quarter, food prices increased by 28.9% (OECD, 1978, 14). Such rates of inflation meant that the purchasing power of wages declined in 1977 in spite of their sharp nominal increases.

Between 1970 and 1973, Spain's balance of payments on current account had shown a surplus. Between 1974 and 1976 this surplus gave way to a deficit averaging about US$ 3.7 billion per year. The deterioration of the country's terms of trade following the energy crisis of 1973 worsened Spain's trade deficit. Global recession limited the growth of Spanish exports and speculation about the devaluation of the peseta during the first half of 1977 encouraged the outflow of short-term capital. During this period, the external current account deficit threatened to reach US$ 5 billion by the end of the year.

The trend in the balance-of-payments current account deficit improved however during the second half of 1977 and economists then predicted that this deficit would amount to only US$ 2.5 billion for the entirety of 1977, a significant decline from the US$ 4.3 billion level this deficit had attained in 1976. The improvement in the country's balance-of-payments position was probably the major positive aspect of Spain's economic scenario in 1977.

A major factor explaining such development was an increase in net current invisible earnings following the devaluation of the peseta in July. During the second half of 1977, the number of foreign tourists in Spain rose by 16% but their spending in the country, calculated in US dollars, increased by 50%. Concurrently, there occurred an expansion in the net inflows of private capital. This increase in the inflow of foreign capital was closely related to the government's expanded borrowing abroad.

Spain's external indebtedness increased from about US$ 3.5 billion at the end of 1973 to US$ 13 billion at the end of 1977 (Ibid., 36).

A further positive development experienced by the country's economy beginning in the late summer of 1977 was a decline in the rate of inflation. A fall in the rate of increase in the prices of foodstuffs caused a decline in the overall rate of inflation which remained below 15% between September 1977 and February 1978. The new trade unions and the workers, by respecting the wage increase norm set by the Moncloa Pact, also contributed, through their restraint regarding demands for wage increases, to reducing the pace of inflation.

A more discouraging aspect of the Spanish economic picture revealed that by the end of 1977 industrial orders had fallen to a record low. The fall in investment in capital goods accelerated during the second half of the year and economists predicted a further fall of domestic demand during the first half of 1978. Events proved that they were not mistaken.

Indeed, the slowdown of the process of inflation and the improvement in the country's external position were not due to an increase in domestic economic activity, but resulted from the government's austerity programme. Entrepreneurial expectations, already darkened by the uncertainty clouding estimates of trends in energy costs, were further disturbed by the legalization of independent trade unions whose Marxist ideology frightened potential investors.

Although the new independent trade unions showed great restraint in their demands, they constituted nevertheless an element of uncertainty in the investment evaluations of businessmen. Under such circumstances, production declined in many economic sectors. Utilized industrial plant capacity at the end of 1977 attained only 82%. In the early months of the following year this figure declined to 80%. Official data reported that there were 831,000 unemployed persons in the country at the end of December 1977. In the first quarter of 1978, the unemployment figure reached nearly one million, representing 7% of the total active population. Concurrently, many major Spanish enterprises were threatened by bankruptcy. In Bilbao, the large industrial firm Babcock-Wilson had to close down (Coverdale, J.F., 1979, 103).

On 24 February 1978 Professor Enrique Fuentes Quintana resigned his position as Vice-President for Economic Affairs, probably feeling that the head of the government was not paying due attention to Spain's serious economic problems. Indeed, it appeared that Adolfo Suárez was excessively concerned with political matters. He did not select a new Vice-President for Economic Affairs, but handed the duties of the latter to his Vice-President for Political Affairs, Fernando Abril Matorell. Following the resignation of Fuentes Quintana, Suárez rearranged his Cabinet. The most significant change touched the Ministry of Industry. Suárez appointed Agustín Rodríguez de Sahagun as new Minister of

Industry. Rodríguez de Sahagun was a former Vice-President of the conservative Confederation of Spanish Business Organizations, CEOE. The PSOE quickly denounced what appeared to be the government's move to the right.

Demonstrations, acts of terrorism and police violence continued unabated in the Basque region. In Navarre, conflict originated in clashes between Navarrese supporting and opposing the inclusion of their province in the Basque region. Such a clash occurred in the bullring in Pamplona on 8 July at the time of the San Fermín festivities. Following the armed intervention of the police, rioting extended to the whole city. Terrorists, apparently members of ETA, murdered Brig. Gen. Juan Sánchez Ramos in Madrid. ETA terrorists went on killing police and military officers in Spain in the autumn (Ibid., 106–10).

Doubts about the future course of the world economy, internal social tensions related to the uncertain direction of domestic politics and lack of interest on the part of the government in renewing the Moncloa Pact when it expired in the autumn of 1978, were all factors which impeded an adequate recovery of the Spanish economy. As a result, unemployment rose in 1978. Government officials who supported a policy of rationalization of the national economy asserted that the level of unemployment could not be reduced and that the economy could not be invigorated unless a prior correction to the two major disequilibria burdening the Spanish economy could be effected. These disequilibria were price inflation and the deterioration of the country's external accounts. In addition, the contemporary economic crisis required a restructuring of those sectors of the economy most affected by such crisis. The invigoration of the economy could require measures which in the short-run could impede the growth of economic activity and intensify unemployment.

Although the rate of increase of consumer prices between December 1977 and December 1978 was 16.5%, a rate markedly lower than the average rate of increase of 24.6% for 1977, and that of 26.4% for the period December 1976 to December 1977, the problem of price inflation in Spain was not solved by the Suárez government. A Spanish rate of inflation of about 16% in 1978 was more than twice the corresponding rates of price inflation in the industrialized countries of Western Europe existing at that time. Unless the Spanish rate could be reduced to a level lower than 8%, Spanish exports would lose competitiveness abroad and Spanish interest rates would remain much higher than rates in the OECD area generally.

Two fortuitous events helped the Spanish economy in 1978. Good weather and abundant rain combined to produce bumper crops in that year and the latter not only limited the pace of increase of food prices, but also strengthened the country's exports. In addition, the number of foreign tourists visiting Spain in 1978 rose by 16.6% over the number recorded for 1977; more important, their spending in the country, calculated in terms of US dollars, increased by 38% (Banco de Bilbao, 1979, 80). Such spending strengthened activity in the country's tertiary sector, particularly commerce, transport and the operation of hotels. In addition, the July 1977 devaluation of the peseta continued to boost Spanish merchandise exports. The growth of tourist spending largely explained the 3.3% rate of growth of the tertiary sector.

Household demand for consumer goods increased by 2%, a result of the fact that household disposable income rose faster than consumer goods prices. On the other hand, gross investment in capital goods declined. The level of investment in construction was 3% below that of 1977. The drop in investment in the production of equipment and transport materials was even stronger at 4.5%. While both imports and the domestic production of machinery declined, exports of such goods rose. On the whole, industrial production in Spain rose by 2.6% over its 1977 volume.

The declining share of profits in national income constituted a major explanatory factor explaining the poor performance of the economy. This share had represented about 10% of the national income in the pre-crisis years; it had declined to 5% in 1978 (Ibid., 84).

Spanish forecasters had predicted in 1977 that the Spanish GDP would rise by 1.1% in 1978. They had also estimated that the numbers of the unemployed would rise by 100,000 persons. In both instances, these predictions proved to be erroneous. The GDP rose by 3% in 1978. While private consumption in the latter year increased by about 2%, with public consumption rising by 4.7%, gross capital formation declined by 3.6%, a larger fall than that predicted earlier. In spite of the growth of the GDP, unemployment rose by 250,000 in 1978. Unemployment became Spain's major economic problem. The regionalization of the country under the new Constitution rendered the solution of the problem more difficult. Furthermore, as the relative cost of labour increased, a higher level of investment was not necessarily the way to increase employment. An increase in investment could bring with it a switch to labour-saving production techniques. There existed no consensus of opinion among Spanish economists in 1978 about how best to boost employment in the country and invigorate the weak domestic economy. Government officials and business leaders insisted on further reducing the rate of inflation in order to encourage investment. The labour unions demanded rising public investment in order to help create more jobs.

Meanwhile, Abril Matorell, the Minister of Industry, showed little interest in initiating negotiations in order to obtain a new agreement between the political parties, or between the representatives of business and labour, which would replace the Moncloa Pact. Spaniards centred their attention on the December referendum which could place the country on a new political track. Indeed, on 6 December 1978 the Spanish electorate approved a new constitution which established a parliamentary monarchy in Spain. The Franco era soon became a memory, cherished by some, deplored by most.

## THE CLOUDED DAWN OF THE NEW DEMOCRACY

The approval of a new constitution by a large majority of the Spanish people in December 1978 did not automatically eradicate all dangers the newly established democratic monarchy was exposed to. The right and the military had so far abstained from an attempt to abort the government's Political Reform Law through an act of insurrection. Many conservatives had hoped that Adolfo Suárez, once a Franco political appointee, would in due time impose limits on the process of political democratization. By the end of 1978, however, it had become too evident that the President of the Government had not remained faithful to the Francoist ideology he had once apparently embraced. Indeed, Suárez had ignored the assurances he had given to the right and to the military to the effect that he would not allow the legalization of the Spanish Communist Party. The PCE, the 'bête noire' for all Francoists, was given legality. Suárez further scandalized conservatives in Spain by supporting a policy of regionalization, a policy strongly opposed by the military. The right became convinced that Suárez had betrayed the cause for which the Caudillo had fought.

Following the approval of the new constitution in December 1978, Adolfo Suárez dissolved the Parliament and called for new elections to be held in March 1979. A major reason for this action was that municipal elections, already postponed once, were to take place in April. Fearing that the left would do very well in such elections, Suárez decided to hold the national parliamentary elections before April so that the outcome of the municipal elections would not have an influence on the vote at the national level.

Five major political parties competed for seats in the *Cortes*. The right was constituted by the Democratic Coalition, led by Fraga Iribarne's Popular Alliance. Adolfo Suárez's UCD represented the centre-right. To its left were the socialists of Felipe González, now joined by the PSP of Professor Tierno Galván. Farther to the left were the Communists under the leadership of Santiago Carrillo. Finally, a number of regional parties campaigned as independent parties, with the centrist Basque and Catalan parties being the most important in this group.

The elections were held on 1 March 1979 and were won by the UCD.

This party won 167 seats in the *Cortes* out of a total of 350. The PSOE became the second strongest party by obtaining 121 seats, a gain of three. Fraga Iribarne's Popular Alliance lost seven of the 16 seats it received in 1977. The PCE got 23 seats, a gain of three also. The Catalan regionalists obtained nine seats and the Basque PNV seven (Abel, C. and Torrents, N., 1984, 33). Adolfo Suárez continued his Presidency.

It was the quest for autonomous powers by a number of Spanish regions, a quest Suárez had supported, that would weaken the popularity of the President of the Government. Autonomy Statutes for the Basque region and for Catalonia were approved by the *Cortes* and by regional referenda held in October. The Constitution recognized that these two regions contained 'historic nationalities' and were thus entitled to receive autonomous powers quickly. The Autonomy Statutes provided for the establishment of regional parliaments and for the operation of a regional Supreme Court in the two regions. Regional parliaments received wider powers than they had in the days of the Second Republic.

The regionalist policy of the central government encouraged other regions, particularly Andalusia and Galicia, to request similar treatment. These were regions without historic nationalities. The Constitution provided that for such regions, the way to autonomy would differ from that available to regions containing historic nationalities. Article 143 of the Constitution of 1978 provided that in the case of regions without historic nationalities, before a regional referendum on autonomy could take place, every province in the region would have to approve autonomy by an absolute majority in a pre-referendum vote.

Andalusia requested regional autonomy. Provincial referenda were then held. Because voters in the province of Almería did not support autonomy by a majority vote, a region-wide referendum on autonomy was never held. Andalusians resented the operation of the law and their discontent weakened Suárez's popularity in Andalusia.

Other developments further reduced such popularity. The wealthy economic oligarchy opposed the tax reforms introduced by the Social Democrat Francisco Fernández Ordóñez. Catholics and the Church denounced the government's proposed divorce law. Many military officers felt that Suárez had betrayed his initial commitment to Franco's ideology. Aware that his popularity was waning, Adolfo Suárez resigned as President of the Government in January 1981.

## 1979

Economic 'stagflation' continued in 1979. Although the rate of inflation diminished and the country's external balance improved, unemployment continued to rise. The national elections of March 1979 intensified entrepreneurial uncertainty and delayed the passing of the National

Budget which adversely affected public investment. In June, OPEC effected a second sharp increase in the price of crude oil and as a result economic growth weakened in most industrialized countries. This second oil crisis had serious consequences for the Spanish economy. Not only did Spain have to transfer a larger part of its national income to the oil producing countries, but the international economic slowdown caused by the higher imported oil price brought a decline in foreign tourism in Spain and a weakening of foreign demand for Spanish exports.

The government failed to push the re-structuring of productive sectors to render them more adaptable to the economic crisis. The drop in external demand had a negative impact on the rates of growth of industrial output and of services. Inflation derived from the increase in the price of imported crude oil diminished the real income of Spaniards and acted as a brake on the rise of domestic consumer demand. Entrepreneurial expectations deteriorated and depressed investment levels even further.

Official forecasts made in 1978 had predicted a rate of growth of real GDP in 1979 of 4%. On an annual average basis, GDP grew by only 1.4% in 1979 (Banco de Bilbao, 1980, 80). Agricultural output declined by 2.5% in that year and construction fell by 4.7% with the real value of construction in 1979 being 16% below the level attained in 1973. The overall growth of the services sector was estimated at 2.3%, a rate that was lower than that attained the previous year. The Research Service of the Bank of Bilbao estimated that Spanish industrial production rose by 2.3%, a slight improvement over the 1978 rate (Ibid., 81).

Spain's foreign trade in 1979 expanded much faster than that of most other European countries. Though exports expanded, so did imports. For the first time since the occurrence of the first oil crisis, the value of imports in real terms grew faster than that of exports. As a result, the trade deficit expanded as shown in Table 42. The acceleration in the growth of imports started during the second half of 1979. This acceleration was explained in part by the increased cost of oil imports, but it was also due to the rise in the prices of imported raw materials and to the government's reduction of import tariffs.

In regard to export volumes, while exports of farm products rose by 25% in 1979, exports of manufactured products declined by between 34 and 22% and exports of minerals fell by between 9% and 5% (Ibid., 150). As Table 42 indicates, the country recorded a balance of trade deficit of US$ 7.2 billion at the end of 1979, up from US$ 5.6 billion at the end of 1978.

Although the balance of invisibles recorded a significant surplus at the end of 1979 in spite of a decline in the number of foreign tourists visiting Spain in that year, this surplus could not counteract the increased trade

## GROWTH AND CRISIS IN THE SPANISH ECONOMY

Table 42  Spain's foreign trade: 1973–9

|  | 1973 | 1975 | 1977 | 1978 | 1979 |
|---|---|---|---|---|---|
| Imports (cif, millions of US dollars) | 9,533 | 16,262 | 17,889 | 18,665 | 25,407 |
| Exports (fob) | 5,129 | 7,690 | 10,253 | 13,082 | 18,192 |
| Deficit | 4,405 | 8,572 | 7,635 | 5,583 | 7,215 |
| Percentage change over previous year |  |  |  |  |  |
| Imports |  |  |  |  |  |
| Value | 44.4 | 5.5 | 2.4 | 4.3 | 36.1 |
| Volume | 8.3 | −2.7 | −5.7 | 1.7 | 12.1 |
| Exports |  |  |  |  |  |
| Value | 39.0 | 8.6 | 17.6 | 27.6 | 39.1 |
| Volume | 3.5 | −3.3 | 14.4 | 14.1 | 3.8 |
| Deficit (value) | 51.3 | 2.8 | −12.7 | −26.9 | 29.2 |

Source: Banco de Bilbao, *Informe Económico 1979*, Bilbao, 1980, p. 147

Table 43  Spain's balance of payments: 1978 and 1979 (million US$)

|  | 1978 | 1979 |
|---|---|---|
| Goods | −4,084.0 | −7,495.9 |
| Services: | 4,307.8 | 5,168.4 |
| Tourism and travel | 4,920.9 | 5,561.8 |
| Freight, insurance, transport | 754.1 | 1,155.1 |
| Technical aid and royalties | −324.1 | −402.1 |
| Investment income | −1,095.7 | −1,078.6 |
| Other services | 67.7 | −53.8 |
| Transfers | 1,451.8 | 1,514.9 |
| Balance on current account | 1,675.6 | −812.6 |
| Long-term capital | 1,495.2 | 2,511.4 |
| Basic balance | 3,322.8 | 1,838.9 |

Source: Banco de Bilbao, *Informe Económico 1979*, Bilbao, 1980, p. 179

deficit. As a result, Spain's balance on current account showed a deficit of US$ 812.6 million at the end of 1979. On the other hand, Spain received in that year a net inflow of capital which allowed Spain's basic balance at the end of 1979 to show a surplus of US$ 1.8 billion (Table 43).

Spain's main trade partner in 1979 was the European Community. The EC was Spain's best customer and largest supplier. Spanish imports from the EC amounted to 35.9% of Spain's total imports in 1979 and Spain exported to the EC 48% of its total exports (Ibid., 173). Within the EC, France replaced West Germany as Spain's largest supplier in 1979.

Spain retained in 1979 one of the highest inflation rates in Europe.

Though this rate was lower than that of 1978 by one percentage point, i.e. 15.5%, it still impeded an adequate recovery of the Spanish economy. The rate of Spanish unemployment rose from 8.2% to 10.1% in 1979. The continuation of 'stagflation' and rising unemployment showed that the government of Adolfo Suárez had been unable to pull the national economy out of a crisis which had weakened Spanish economic growth for over half a decade, a crisis intensified by the second OPEC oil increase and by the economic and political uncertainties Spaniards faced in 1979.

## REFERENCES

Abel, C. and Torrents, N. eds, *Spain, Conditional Democracy*, New York, St. Martin's Press, 1984.
Alcaide Inchausti, J., 'Productividad, Costes y Precios', in Fraga Iribarne, M. et al., *La España de los Años Setenta*, Madrid, 1973.
Alonso, A., *España en el Mercado Común, Del Acuerdo del 70 a la comunidad de los Doce*, Madrid, Espasa Calpe, 1985.
Ardura Calleja, M.L., 'El Sector Industrial', in Fraga Iribarne, M. et al., *La España de los Años Setenta*, Madrid, Editorial Moneda y Crédito, 1973a, pp. 323–36.
———, 'Dimensión y concentración de empresas', in Fraga Iribarne, M. et al., *La España de los Años Setenta*, Madrid, Editorial Moneda y Crédito, 1973b, pp. 337–448.
Banco de Bilbao, Servicio de Estudios, *Informe Económico*, (various issues), Bilbao, Editorial Eléxpuru Hnos.
Banco Urquijo, *El Crecimiento de la Industria Española, Evolución Reciente, Comparación Internacional y Expectativas*, Madrid, 1974.
Carr, R. and Fusi, J.P., *Spain, Dictatorship to Democracy*, London, George Allen & Unwin, 1979.
Coverdale, J.F., *The Political Transformation of Spain after Franco*, New York, Praeger, 1979.
Fraga, Iribarne, M. et al., eds, *La España de los Años Setenta*, Madrid, Editorial Moneda y Crédito, 1973.
Fuentes Quintana, E., 'La Crisis Económica Española', in *Papeles de Economía Española*, Nr. 1, Madrid, 1979, pp. 84–142.
Hornillos García, C, *Problemas de la Pequeña y Mediana Industria en España*, Madrid, Confederación Española de Cajas de Ahorros, 1970.
Ministerio de Industria, *La Industria Española*, (various issues), Madrid.
Muñoz, J. et al., *La Economía, Española en 1974*, Madrid, EDICUSA, 1974.
Share, D., *The Making of Spanish Democracy*, New York, Praeger, 1986.
Tamames, R., *Historia de España, La República, La Era de Franco*, Madrid, Alianze Editorial, Alfaguara, 1979.

# 4

# ECONOMIC CRISIS IN THE 1980s: 1980–5

## REVIEW OF THE SPANISH ECONOMY AT THE START OF THE 1980s

The long period extending from the end of the 1950s to 1973 was characterized by a rapidly increasing domestic demand and by a strong growth of the Gross Domestic Product in the countries of the OECD. The widespread apprehension of an economic slowdown in 1970 and in 1971 induced most national governments in the OECD area to embrace expansionary monetary policies whose effects were intensified by the ever continuing balance-of-payments deficits of the United States. At the end of this period in 1972 and in 1973, economic growth in these countries was accompanied by rising external deficits and by a strengthening of domestic inflationary pressures.

These two major disequilibria were present in Spain's economy in both 1972 and 1973. An average annual rate of growth of the money supply of 24% in the years 1971 to 1973 had facilitated a strong rise in domestic demand which caused a rising external deficit and an increase in inflation. The latter trend was strengthened by large wage increases which were obtained by workers' councils from managers who apprehended the possibility of work stoppages at a time of booming demand. Such wage increases became relatively uniform throughout the economy and tended to surpass productivity gains. In addition to these wage increases, a rise in employers' social security contributions from 1971 increased per unit labour costs, reduced profits and weakened the growth of a number of economic sectors.

During the summer of 1973, the governments of many OECD countries started enacting deflationary measures. The energy crisis of October nullified the effects of these restrictive measures and added strength to inflationary pressures. The rate of inflation increased. The growing inflation was once again accompanied by a deterioration of the countries' external accounts; as their income declined, their governments began to enact new restrictive economic measures.

Table 44 Structure of Spanish demand: 1973–80 (percentages of participation in GDP at constant prices)

| Year | Private consumption | Public consumption | Aggregate consumption | Gross capital formation | National demand |
|---|---|---|---|---|---|
| 1973 | 65.0 | 10.0 | 75.0 | 28.4 | 103.4 |
| 1974 | 64.8 | 10.4 | 75.2 | 29.4 | 104.6 |
| 1975 | 65.6 | 10.9 | 76.5 | 28.0 | 104.5 |
| 1976 | 67.1 | 11.3 | 78.4 | 26.9 | 105.3 |
| 1977 | 66.1 | 11.4 | 77.5 | 25.2 | 102.7 |
| 1978 | 65.8 | 11.8 | 77.6 | 23.5 | 101.1 |
| 1979 | 66.7 | 12.3 | 79.0 | 23.1 | 102.1 |
| 1980 | 66.3 | 12.7 | 79.0 | 23.3 | 102.3 |

Source: Myro Sánchez, R., 'La evolución de las principales magnitudes: una presentación de conjunto', in García Delgado, J.L., (ed.), *La Economía Española de la Transición y la Democracia*, Madrid, CIS, 1990, pp. 527–58

Because of the strongly optimistic expectations of Spanish entrepreneurs, the Spanish economy maintained a satisfactory pace of economic growth in 1974 in spite of the restrictive monetary policy adopted by the government at the end of 1973. As imports of costlier crude oil went on increasing in 1974, Spain's balance of trade worsened and domestic prices rose.

Entrepreneurial expectations drastically changed in 1975. Reasons for such change were both economic and political in content. Sharp wage increases and more burdensome social security contributions imposed on firms by the government reduced the expected profitability of investment. Greater uncertainty about the political and economic future of Spain developing after the death of General Franco moved entrepreneurs' expectations regarding the profitability of new investment from optimism to gloom. From 1975 the annual flow of investment diminished.

The decline in investment was eventually followed by a fall in private consumption spending. The Spanish consumer, observing expanding employment in the secondary and tertiary sectors of the economy until 1975 as well as rising nominal salaries and wages, gave little importance for some time to the unavoidable consequences of the global economic crisis. Moreover, the slow and gradual decline of private consumption spending after 1975 was offset, at least until 1977, by a rising share of public consumption in the Gross Domestic Product. Aggregate consumption spending remained stable until the latter year. It was only after 1977 that a sharp increase in unemployment started alarming the Spanish private consumer.

In spite of the stability of aggregate consumption spending until 1977,

Table 45 Percentage annual rates of change in consumption: 1967–80 (in 1980 prices)

| Product | 1967–70 | 1971–5 | 1976–80 |
|---|---|---|---|
| Agriculture and fish | 2.2 | 3.9 | 2.5 |
| Energy and water | 22.9 | 13.1 | 10.2 |
| Basic metallurgy | 10.1 | 8.0 | 2.8 |
| Metallic products | 10.4 | 14.8 | 3.1 |
| Non-metallic mining products | 10.2 | 11.7 | 3.2 |
| Chemicals | 15.3 | 7.8 | 0.9 |
| Rubber and plastics | 11.9 | 10.8 | −1.5 |
| Office machinery and computers |  |  | 0.9 |
| Mechanical machinery | 10.4 | 4.9 | 1.2 |
| Electric and electronic machinery | 9.1 | 12.6 | 3.5 |
| Transport materials | 9.6 | 8.3 | 3.0 |
| Precision instruments | 3.2 | 10.9 | 2.1 |
| Foodstuffs, beverages, tobacco | 4.7 | 6.2 | 3.3 |
| Paper | 15.8 | 8.5 | −2.4 |
| Textiles and leather | 7.9 | 0.2 | −0.3 |
| Footwear and apparel | 5.9 | 0.6 | −5.0 |
| Wood and furniture | 6.1 | 3.6 | 1.7 |
| Other manufacturing | 37.3 | 4.4 | −1.1 |
| Construction | 7.7 | 11.3 | −1.4 |
| Transport | 9.1 | 8.0 | 0.8 |
| Other Services | 11.1 | 3.4 | 5.2 |

Source: Ibid., p. 532

the decline in gross capital formation during the second half of the 1970s caused a sharp deceleration in the rate of growth of aggregate demand in the latter period (See Table 44). Professor Rafael Myro Sánchez observed that the deceleration in the pace of growth of domestic demand induced Spanish firms to attach greater importance to the development of external markets and that as a result of the energy crises of 1973 and of 1979, there followed a wider opening of the Spanish economy (Myro Sánchez, R., 1990, 531). Professor Myro has pointed out that while the rate of growth of Spanish imports declined from 1975, Spanish firms attempted to boost their exports as of 1976.

The weakening of aggregate internal demand had a stronger negative impact in Spain on industrial production than on the activities of the primary and tertiary sectors of the economy. While the share of industrial production in GDP declined, the shares of the outputs of the primary and tertiary sectors expanded. This was a potentially dangerous departure from the trend in the demand structure which had prevailed in the prosperous 1960s and which had registered an expanding share of industrial production in the aggregate national demand. Table 45 shows the annual evolution of spending on the products constituting aggregate consumption in terms of constant prices.

An understanding of the problems faced by Spanish industry at the close of the 1970s necessitates not only a comprehension of the effects of changes in the strengths of domestic and foreign demands during that decade, but requires in addition a recognition of the effects of Spain's industrial structure and of the significance of its slow evolution over time.

In the 1950s, the slow reconstruction of the Civil War-damaged economy, excellent harvests which allowed Spain to expand its exports of agricultural goods and American aid allowed the country to reduce its energy, industrial equipment and raw materials shortages. An expansionary monetary policy supported a strong domestic demand. While the government continued to adhere to a policy of strong protection, it softened its autarkic position and relaxed its controls over prices and wages while hesitatingly opening Spain's door to foreign capital. Such developments revived industrial activity in the country during the second half of the 1950s.

In that decade, domestic industrial production was exclusively directed at the satisfaction of domestic demand. Spain's leadership believed that its principal mission was to widen the internal market by facilitating the development of import-competing, private and public enterprises, with little importance being attached to the comparative economic and technological inefficiencies of the newly created manufacturing concerns. Spanish industry, highly protected from foreign competition, remained technologically backward and continued to be based on small production units whose costs of production were so high and the quality of their products so poor that they could sell only in the domestic market they monopolized.

Spanish exports remained limited to agricultural products. The international competitiveness of such exports was weakened by the domestic inflation resulting from the government's expansionary monetary policy. While domestic inflation impeded the growth of Spain's exports, the widening of the internal market required expanding imports. Spain's external position in the 1950s deteriorated to such an extent that the government started paying its foreign debts by drawing on the country's gold reserves. By the end of the decade, Franco's economists had to recognize the pressing need for a change in official commercial policy and the government enacted the Stabilization Plan of 1959. The value of the peseta in terms of gold was defined and the authorities established a fixed rate of exchange between the peseta and the American dollar. The traditional policy of limiting imports through a system of quantitative restrictions was replaced by a strongly protectionist tariff. The government's decision to slowly and gradually open the domestic economy was expressed through a number of new official measures: the latter were designed to facilitate the inflow of foreign capital and to encourage the migration of Spanish surplus labour to other countries in order to reduce domestic unemployment. The government did not renounce however its determination to limit domestic industrial growth to the expansion of the internal market and to facilitate the growth of the latter by means of an expansionary monetary policy. In spite of booming foreign economies in the 1960s, Spain's industrial growth in that decade remained totally dependent on the growth of Spain's GDP.

Nevertheless, Spain's industrial output in the decade 1965 to 1975 registered a growth rate second only to that of Japan and larger than that obtained by the EC countries. This growth rate allowed Spanish industries to boost the productivity of their labour and capital and to increase their contribution to the country's exports. By 1970, industrial exports represented 65.6% of Spain's aggregate exports (Myro Sánchez, R., 1988, 191–230).

In order to study more meaningfully the evolution of Spanish industry in recent decades, Professor Myro grouped Spanish industries into three categories, those of strong-, medium- and weak-demand, this categorization being based on the rates of growth registered by such industries within a broad area representing the European Community, the United States and Japan in the period 1971 to 1983.

Myro's category of strong-demand industries included the following industrial production: airplanes, computers, office machinery, electrical machinery, electronic machinery, pharmaceutical products, chemicals and precision instruments. The output of medium-demand industries included automobiles, mechanical machinery, transport materials, rubber and plastic products, paper, processed foodstuffs, beverages and tobacco. The refining of crude oil also appeared in this category. The products of the weak-demand industries included iron and steel, non-ferrous metals, metallic products, wood and cork products, textiles, leather products, footwear and apparel, as well as ships (Ibid., 198).

This Spanish economist noted that by the mid-1970s, most of Spain's industrial production was concentrated in the weak-demand industries. Such industrial output exceeded the needs of the domestic market, while the production of the country's strong- and medium-demand industries failed to satisfy domestic demand. This conclusion was based on the computation of export to import ratios for each industrial group as shown by Table 46. The table shows comparative data for the year 1975.

A Spanish export/import ratio of 0.28 for strong-demand industries and of 0.73 for medium-demand industries meant that Spain's efforts to come closer to the economic levels attained in the EC countries were bound to result in expanding balance of trade deficits. While Spain's

Table 46 Characteristics of industrial foreign trade in the EC countries and in Spain: 1975

| Sectors | German FR | France | UK | Italy | Belgium | Netherlands | Spain |
|---|---|---|---|---|---|---|---|
| Export/Import ratios | | | | | | | |
| Strong-demand | 1.94 | 1.15 | 1.38 | 1.08 | 1.08 | 1.37 | 0.28 |
| Medium-demand | 2.24 | 1.45 | 1.14 | 1.22 | 0.91 | 1.16 | 0.73 |
| Weak-demand | 1.03 | 1.08 | 0.83 | 1.78 | 1.31 | 0.66 | 1.21 |
| Percentage of exported output | | | | | | | |
| Strong-demand | 32.5 | 30.2 | 32.2 | 25.5 | 78.7 | 86.3 | 7.2 |
| Medium-demand | 25.4 | 21.4 | 19.3 | 17.8 | 44.5 | 41.2 | 7.9 |
| Weak-demand | 17.0 | 18.8 | 20.0 | 19.1 | 68.5 | 48.0 | 9.3 |

Source: Myro Sánchez, R., 'La Industria: Expansión, Crisis y Reconversión', in García Delgado, ed., *España, Economía*, Madrid, Espasa-Calpa, 1988, p. 201

Table 47 Characteristics of Spanish industrial sectors: 1975

| Sector | Labour productivity (in millions of pesetas of gross value added per worker) | Spending on R & D as a percentage of net value added by large firms | Percentage of total industrial output | Effective protection rate |
|---|---|---|---|---|
| Strong-demand | 2.0 | 3.6 | 13.7 | 20.6 |
| Medium-demand | 1.4 | 3.0 | 46.1 | 27.2 |
| Weak-demand | 1.3 | 0.7 | 40.2 | 24.3 |

Source: Ibid., p. 202

labour remained relatively cheap by international standards, the country retained a comparative advantage in the production of labour-intensive goods, goods mostly produced by its weak-demand industries. In order to modernize her economy Spain needed, however, to expand her strong- and medium-demand industries, industries which could only grow in Spain in the 1970s because they were financed by foreign capital and/or because they were able to utilize imported foreign technology. The growth of such industries was actually hampered in that decade by a national commercial policy which gave stronger protection to weak- or medium-demand industries than to strong-demand industries. Table 47 indicates that in 1975 strong-demand industries received less protection than the other two industrial groups.

Throughout the 1960s, a major economic goal of the Francoist government was to have industrial growth serve nearly exclusively the internal market by reserving the latter to domestic manufacturers. It showed utter disregard for the inability of Spanish firms to compete in world markets. The exports of Spanish industrial concerns remained minimal.

The commercial policy of the EC countries followed a very different direction. These countries not only strove to expand their intra-EC trade, but tried in addition to increase their trade with the rest of the world. The moderate common external tariff of the EC and preferential trade agreements entered into by the EC with third nations helped the Community countries to boost both their imports and exports. In spite of the signing of a preferential trade treaty with the EC in 1970, Franco's government appeared reluctant to follow the commercial policy orientation of the Community. The government's short-sighted determination to have Spanish industry produce almost exclusively for the domestic market discouraged the establishment of large firms in Spain, firms which under different policy conditions could have engaged in the large-scale production of technology-intensive products to be sold in multinational markets. The Francoist governments persisted in their effort to protect Spanish industry from foreign competition and attempted in addition to minimize competition within the home market by regulating domestic prices. In the 1960s, the entry of foreign capital into Spain was eased and the government facilitated the import of foreign technology. On the other hand, the Spanish authorities paid no attention to the development of truly Spanish technology. Industrial advance in Spain became ever more dependent on foreign capital, on foreign management and on foreign technology. '*Que inventen ellos!*' – 'Let others invent!' – appeared to be the motto of Franco's economists.

In the 1960s, the government attempted however to boost the exports of some of the most protected industries – weak-demand industries – by extending tax privileges to such exports and low interest credits to Spanish exporters. The bulk of such exports was supplied by the weak-demand industrial group, particularly by firms registering excess capacity. Still, by 1975 Spain remained a practically closed economy.

As noticed above, the raw materials and energy crises of the early 1970s, global recession and the political and economic uncertainties which developed in Spain following the death of General Franco brought a major crisis to the country's internal market. As domestic demand declined, the privileged position of Spanish manufacturers in the home market was threatened. Concurrently, the repercussions of the global energy crisis impeded Spanish export growth.

The expansionary measures adopted by the government in 1971, the determination of Spanish authorities to stabilize the internal prices of petroleum products by subsidizing the sale of such products to

*Table 48* Spanish industrial demand: 1971–86
(annual change rates in 1980 pesetas)

| Sectors | 1971–5 | 1976–80 | 1981–3 | 1984–5 | 1986 | 1971–86 |
|---|---|---|---|---|---|---|
| Strong-demand | 10.5 | 1.6 | 0.8 | 1.4 | 14.5 | 4.9 |
| Medium-demand | 5.1 | 3.9 | −1.4 | 2.6 | 7.3 | 3.3 |
| Weak-demand | 5.9 | 0.9 | −6.2 | −2.4 | 8.3 | 1.1 |
| Total | 6.1 | 2.4 | −2.7 | 0.9 | 8.8 | 2.8 |

Source: Ibid., p. 208

consumers following the events of October 1973, rapidly rising nominal wages and labour laws which prevented employers from reducing their labour force, postponed until 1975 the beginning of a major domestic economic crisis in the country. During the early 1970s, Spanish labour costs had risen more rapidly than in most developed nations. Although the share of salaries and wages in gross value added increased for all three Spanish industrial groups between 1970 and 1975, the increase was strongest for the weak-demand group (Ibid, 207). During the same period, domestic industrial demand rose most rapidly for the products of strong-demand industries, and to a lesser extent, for those of weak-demand industries. As shown by Table 48, the weakening of industrial demand after 1975 affected mostly these two industrial groups, and to a lesser extent, the medium-demand industries. It was only at the end of Spain's internal economic crisis in 1986 that the trend in industrial demand which had existed during the first half of the 1970s was re-established.

The crisis of the domestic economy during the second half of the 1970s induced Spanish industrial concerns to expand their foreign sales. In their attempt to expand their exports to compensate for the effects of a weakening domestic demand, these firms faced two major difficulties. Global recession induced industrial firms in other countries to follow a similar course of action; as a result, Spanish exporters found sharpening multinational competition in world markets. They faced, in addition, the competition of the Newly Industrializing Countries, the NICs, countries such as Brazil, Hong Kong, Mexico, Singapore, South Korea and Taiwan, countries whose development policies gave emphasis to the export of manufactured goods of both low and high technological intensity. Their relatively low labour costs gave their products a comparative advantage in foreign markets. On the other hand, Spain had experienced sharply rising labour costs during the first half of the 1970s. Increasing labour costs particularly burdened Spain's weak-demand industries so that their products had difficulty competing abroad with those of other industrialized nations or with those of the NICs. Another

Table 49 Annual rates of growth of the foreign trade of Spanish industries: 1971–86 (in 1980 pesetas)

| Sectors | 1971–5 | 1976–80 | 1981–3 | 1984–5 | 1986 | 1971–86 |
|---|---|---|---|---|---|---|
| Exports | | | | | | |
| Strong-demand | 12.8 | 15.2 | 9.5 | 18.2 | –3.6 | 12.4 |
| Medium-demand | 5.7 | 10.7 | 6.3 | 7.3 | –3.2 | 7.0 |
| Weak-demand | 13.6 | 7.3 | 9.6 | 5.5 | –17.5 | 7.7 |
| Imports | | | | | | |
| Strong-demand | 11.5 | 5.1 | 6.3 | 8.3 | 20.2 | 8.6 |
| Medium-demand | 8.4 | –2.6 | 9.7 | 1.2 | 25.7 | 5.1 |
| Weak-demand | 8.8 | 2.3 | –11.2 | 10.0 | 36.3 | 4.3 |

Source: Ibid., p. 212

difficulty faced by Spanish exports during the latter half of the 1970s resulted from the determination of Spain's monetary authorities to maintain at all costs a stable rate of exchange between the peseta and other currencies. Given the fact that internal prices were rising faster in Spain than in most of the countries with which Spain traded, the international competitiveness of Spanish exports was diminished. Indeed, the peseta appreciated in terms of the currencies of non-EC countries between 1976 and 1980.

Table 49 shows that during the second half of the 1970s the value of Spain's industrial exports in constant pesetas registered significant annual growth, this growth being weakest for the weak-demand industries. The exports of the latter group were hampered by the relatively large increase of its labour costs, by the strong competition offered by the NICs in world markets and by the fact that most of the foreign markets of Spain's weak-demand industries were in non-EC countries, countries against whose currencies the peseta had shown strong appreciation after 1976.

A major problem faced by the Spanish economy during the second half of the 1970s was the rapid rise in the country's level of unemployment. Between the last quarter of 1977 and the last quarter of 1978, the number of unemployed in Spain grew by 252,000 persons. By the end of the latter year, there were over one million jobless workers in the country who constituted 8% of the total active population. Between 1974 and 1978 the percentage of unemployed workers in the total active population increased threefold.

The Spanish unemployment problem in the 1970s cannot be understood exclusively in terms of the deceleration of Spanish economic growth. It would be both simplistic and erroneous to assert that a higher

GDP growth rate would have reduced, if not eliminated, unemployment in Spain. Even during the prosperous decade of the 1960s, neither the secondary nor the tertiary sectors of the Spanish economy were able to provide employment to the young people entering the labour market for the first time and to the masses of agricultural workers who migrated every year out of the primary sector in search of industrial or service jobs. If unemployment in Spain did not intensify until 1974, it was because the country's surplus labour was able to emigrate to other countries in search of employment that labour was not able to find in the home country.

A number of factors limited the ability of Spain's secondary and tertiary sectors to create sufficient jobs for former rural workers and for young people looking for their first job. Low interest rates, a fiscal system which allowed entrepreneurs to rapidly depreciate capital equipment, imported capital-intensive technology financed by foreign capital, burdensome enterprise contributions to the social security system imposed by the government on firms and a government policy which attempted to achieve a fairer distribution of national income by means of mandated salary and wage increases gave priority to the adoption of new labour-saving methods of production in the secondary and tertiary sectors of the economy. The 'reconversion' of many Spanish industries was based on new methods of production involving a high capital/output ratio; Spain's industrial and business managers, eager to modernize their operations, paid little attention to the creation of new jobs. As a result, Spain's industrialization in the prosperous 1960s failed to create sufficient job opportunities for both new entrants in the labour market and for the workers who had abandoned their activities in the primary sector. In the 1960s, about 150,000 annually entered the labour market for the first time while about 100,000 agricultural workers left the agricultural sector every year in search of new employment (García de Blas, 1979, 8).

The annual large exodus of agricultural workers out of the primary sector did not necessarily constitute a growing burden on Spanish economic performance. This exodus provided the two other sectors of the economy with abundant and cheap labour which facilitated the growth of these sectors. As the number of workers in Spain's manufacturing and service industries increased, internal demand was strengthened because these workers were not as prone as agricultural workers to consume self-produced goods. Finally, this exodus provided the great majority of emigrating workers. Once these workers were able to earn an income abroad, the remittances they sent to their family in the home country allowed Spain to strengthen its external balance on current account.

The point emphasized by A. García de Blas was that the continuous emigration out of Spain's primary sector was not exclusively connected with the country's rate of overall economic growth. Factors not directly related to the rate of growth of GDP triggered the net outflow of workers out of the country's primary sector: agricultural wages were significantly lower than wages of workers employed in the two other sectors, the quality of housing in the primary sector was highly deficient, so were educational facilities in that sector, a sector also characterized by the absence of basic public health facilities and by the inadequacy of available medical services. The economic and social backwardness of Spain's primary sector explains why as late as 1974 nearly half of the country's agricultural workers were illiterate (Ibid., 9). A. García de Blas asserted that the main cause of the endless rural exodus originated in the primitive and harsh living conditions of Spanish agricultural workers.

Starting in 1974, Western European countries started closing their borders to the immigration of foreign workers. Emigration, the safety valve Spain had relied on for years to minimize and stabilize domestic unemployment, ceased to be a key parameter determining the *modus operandi* of Spain's economy. Once emigration was no longer available to Spanish unemployed workers, an increase in the national level of unemployment could only be prevented if the secondary and tertiary sectors of the economy could create every year about 245,000 new jobs; 145,000 to accommodate the young people entering the labour market for the first time, and 100,000 to accommodate workers who had left the primary sector. The economy was unable to do so, even during the booming 1960s.

As noticed, new investment mainly took a capital-intensive form and mostly benefited industries operating on the basis of a high capital/output ratio. New investment hardly penetrated labour-intensive industries and did not flow to agriculture or mining. In addition, national fiscal policy extended tax advantages to investment in new labour-saving technologies and encouraged Spanish firms to move away from labour-intensive methods of production. Imported technology was of a labour-saving nature and provided therefore no immediate support for employment growth.

The creation of new jobs in the secondary and tertiary sectors of the Spanish economy was further hindered by two important institutional factors. The average age at which employed workers retired in those sectors was higher than in the same sectors in other Western European nations. In 1977, 23% of the retirees in the Spanish sectors were older than 65, and 5% of them were older than 70 years at the time of retirement (Ibid., 9). The relatively advanced age at retirement in Spain was largely due to the inadequacy of retirement incomes. In December 1976, Spain's average monthly retirement income was 7,751 pesetas, a sum which was 32% lower than the minimum legal monthly salary at that time. Another major deterrent to job creation was based on the heavy cost burden of mandated firms' social security contributions. Unlike the situation prevailing in most Western European countries, the share of the Spanish state in the finance of the country's social security system was quite small; in Spain, this share averaged about 8% of the system's total cost; it averaged about 16% in France. In Spain over 70% of the aggregate cost of the social security system was financed by firms. Under such conditions, Spanish entrepreneurs had little interest in expanding their labour force. Finally, under the Francoist regime, illegal workers' organizations concentrated on the prevention of workers' dismissals. Such efforts tended to discourage job creation.

The Moncloa Pact of 1977 represented the first serious attempt by the government and political parties' leaders to correct existing economic disequilibria. The Pact pursued three main objectives. The drafters of the Pact felt that they could no longer count on internal private and public demand to bring the Spanish economy out of its depressed state. Excess productive capacity and gloomy entrepreneurial expectations discouraged any strengthening of private investment. The participants in the Pact agreed that probably the only way out of the crisis was an expansion of the country's exports. In order to boost exports, Spain's high rate of inflation had to be reduced in order to render domestic production costs more competitive with costs in other countries. Further, in order to improve entrepreneurial expectations, an increase in the rate of net profits of Spanish firms was unavoidable. Both of these goals could be achieved through a more effective public control over wage increases. The Suárez government was determined to centre its efforts on slowing down the pace of wage increases and to reduce the country's rate of inflation. Compared to the weight attached to the attainment of such goals, the creation of new jobs commanded only secondary importance. The 'sanitation' of the economy was given precedence over the reduction of existing unemployment. The signers of the Pact adopted an economic strategy centring on the achievement of economic modernization which was believed to be the best remedy, at least in the long-run, for reducing unemployment growth. Many targets stipulated by the Moncloa Pact were achieved and even surpassed in 1978. Inflation was contained in the latter year, the country's balance of payments improved and GDP grew at a rate of 2.8%, a rate which was more than twice the predicted 1.1% (Garayalde, I., 1980, 56). On the other hand the number of unemployed in the country increased by 250,000 workers in 1978, a much larger increase than the predicted 100,000. Nevertheless, the government continued to support the Moncloa strategy during the balance of the 1970s. As a result, the level of unemployment increased by 100,000 persons during the first four months of 1979. The most the government did to create new jobs was to allow entrepreneurs to hire on a temporary basis young workers or workers receiving unemployment insurance benefits. The government stuck to its position that only productivity increases and improving entrepreneurial expectations could solve in due time Spain's employment problems. Meanwhile, the hardships of the crisis would have to be endured by the working class. The restoration of an acceptable level of employment was not an immediate concern of the Suárez government.

How effective were the attempts of the Suárez government to boost Spain's export capacity? The government devalued the peseta in July 1977; the currency was devalued by 19.2% in terms of the value of a basket of currencies belonging to countries Spain traded with. In spite of such devaluation, the international competitiveness of Spanish exports weakened in 1978 and by October of that year the favourable effects of the 1977 devaluation on Spanish exports had vanished.

Juan Badosa Pagés estimated the trend in such competitiveness for the years 1976–8. The international competitiveness of Spain's exports was directly affected by differentials in cost of production trends in both Spain and in the countries trading with Spain. The dissimilar trend in costs was largely due to different rates of inflation in these countries. Badosa Pagés's Index of Relative Prices, IRP, measured annual changes in the relative competitiveness of Spanish exports due to inflation rate differentials in the relevant countries. Rising indices show that Spain's production costs rose more rapidly than the corresponding costs in trade partner countries, diminishing thereby the competitiveness of Spanish exports in foreign markets. An Index of the Relative Value of the Peseta, IRVP, showed how Spanish exports were affected by changes in the external value of the peseta. Rising index values show an appreciation of the peseta in relation to the currencies contained in the selected 'basket', while falling index values signify a depreciation of the peseta in terms of such currencies. Badosa Pagés then computed an Index of Trends of Spanish Competitiveness, ITC, by combining the two other indices. Falling index values in the ITC indicate a deterioration of the international competitiveness of Spanish products (Badosa Pagés, J., 1978, 74). Table 50 shows the various monthly index values for the years 1976–8.

As an example, the ITC index for July 1977 was 112.54. This index figure indicates that Spain's international competitiveness in July 1977 had improved by 12.54% over what it had been in January 1976. The IRP index shows that during this period, Spanish prices increased by 21.18% more than those of the country's competitors, thus worsening Spain's competitiveness. This deterioration of Spain's international competitiveness was, however, more than compensated by the effects of the devaluation of the peseta in 1977. Indeed, this devaluation depreciated the peseta in terms of other currencies as indicated by the decline

Table 50 Spanish international competitiveness indices: 1976–8

| Date | IRP | IRVP | ITC (100–IRP × IRVP + 100) / 100 |
|---|---|---|---|
| **1976** | | | |
| Jan. | 100.00 | 100.00 | 100.00 |
| Feb. | 100.44 | 89.93 | 109.67 |
| Mar. | 102.03 | 91.25 | 106.90 |
| Apr. | 103.05 | 91.77 | 105.43 |
| May | 107.10 | 91.77 | 101.71 |
| Jun. | 105.94 | 91.59 | 102.97 |
| Jul. | 106.08 | 91.44 | 103.00 |
| Aug. | 106.32 | 91.39 | 102.83 |
| Sep. | 107.42 | 91.62 | 101.59 |
| Oct. | 107.68 | 91.53 | 101.44 |
| Nov. | 109.07 | 91.11 | 100.63 |
| Dec. | 109.42 | 90.32 | 101.17 |
| **1977** | | | |
| Jan. | 112.03 | 90.23 | 98.91 |
| Feb. | 112.73 | 89.70 | 98.88 |
| Mar. | 114.32 | 90.64 | 96.38 |
| Apr. | 115.02 | 90.26 | 96.18 |
| May | 115.03 | 89.96 | 96.52 |
| Jun. | 117.73 | 89.27 | 94.90 |
| Jul. | 121.18 | 72.17 | 112.54 |
| Aug. | 124.70 | 72.83 | 109.18 |
| Sep. | 125.53 | 72.84 | 108.56 |
| Oct. | 126.79 | 72.94 | 107.52 |
| Nov. | 127.13 | 73.20 | 106.94 |
| Dec. | 128.04 | 72.58 | 107.07 |
| **1978** | | | |
| Jan. | 129.16 | 72.67 | 106.14 |
| Feb. | 129.67 | 72.32 | 106.22 |
| Mar. | 130.18 | 72.08 | 106.17 |
| Apr. | 131.94 | 72.19 | 104.75 |
| May | 132.28 | 72.92 | 103.54 |
| Jun. | 132.94 | 73.20 | 102.69 |
| Jul. | 134.97 | 73.63 | 100.62 |
| Aug. | 136.77 | 76.14 | 95.86 |
| Sep. | 136.82 | 76.70 | 95.06 |
| Oct. | 136.88 | 77.59 | 93.79 |

Source: Badosa Pagés, J., 'La evolución de la competividad de la exportación', in *Información Comercial Española*, Nr. 544, Madrid, Dec. 1978, p. 74

in the IRVP index from 100.00 in January 1976 to 72.17 in July 1977. The combined effects of both the IRP and the IRVP index values for July 1977 resulted in an increase of Spain's international competitiveness of 12.54% in that month as compared to the country's competitive position in the base year.

Between July 1977 and October 1978, the ITC index fell from 112.54 to 93.79, indicating a loss of Spain's international competitive position of 20%. This loss was due both to Spain's rising inflation, the IRP index value rising from 121.18 to 136.88, and to the relative appreciation of the peseta indicated by an increase in the IRVP index from 72.17 to 77.59.

The ITC index figures show that in spite of the devaluation of July 1977, a devaluation which depreciated the peseta by 19.2% in terms of other currencies, the positive effects of such devaluation on Spain's exports had vanished by October 1978. In that month the ITC index stood at 93.79, lower than it had been immediately prior to July 1977 when its value was 94.90.

Spain's relative high rate of inflation during the period considered was the principal variable explaining Spain's weakening international competitiveness over the three year period. The rate differential started diminishing during the summer of 1977. Since July of that year, the weakening of Spanish competitiveness was increasingly due to the appreciation of the peseta. Badosa Pagés calculated that between July 1977 and October 1978 the appreciation of the peseta in terms of other currencies was about 5.4% (Ibid., 76). According to this writer, Spain's loss of competitiveness during this fifteen-month period was of 20%; of these 20%, 13% was explained by Spain's higher rate of inflation and the remainder by the appreciation of the peseta.

Spanish economists recognized in the 1970s the destabilizing effects of Spain's strong inflation. José Luis Raymond stressed the role of expectations about the future rate of inflation in the actual process of inflation. He showed in an econometric model how these expectations about the future course of inflation are determined by differentials in the actual and expected rates of inflation in the immediate past (Raymond, J.L., 1978, 151–6). Raymond recognized that during any given period of time, an economy's actual rate of inflation is determined by the effects on the home economy of exogenous 'shocks', e.g. the sudden major increase in the price of imported crude oil at the end of 1973. This actual rate is also the result of the particular interrelationships between trends in wages and prices in the home economy. Because wages are a basic element of costs, wage increases will necessarily lead to a rise in prices, unless such wage increases are compensated by equal increases in labour productivity.

Raymond also presented the hypothesis that economic actors make in a given period of time an efficient use of the information they have regarding the actual rate of inflation in the home economy in an immediately earlier period in order to predict the rate of inflation in the subsequent period. The hypothesis states that the rate of inflation predicted by these economic actors for a year n+1 will equal that recorded in the previous year n, but increased by a fraction of the differential between the actual rate of inflation in the year n and the predicted rate of inflation in the latter year. In other words, Raymond assumed that expectations regarding the rate of inflation in year n+1 will be based on the recorded rate of inflation in the year n, adjusted for prediction errors made by the economic actors in year n. An unpredicted acceleration of inflation in the year n will result in gloomier inflation expectations in the year n+1 which will contribute to accelerate the process of inflation in the latter year.

Following Raymond's notation, if $\Delta P_n^*$ is the expected rate of inflation in the year n and if $\Delta P_n$ is the actual rate of inflation in the year n, and if $\Delta P_{n+1}^*$ is the expected rate of inflation in the year n+1, then we can write:

$$\Delta P_{n+1}^* = \Delta P_n + \theta\,(\Delta P_n - \Delta P_n^*) + \mu$$

in which the constant $\mu$ is affected by any acceleration or deceleration in inflation expectations.

In the case of the Spanish economy in the period 1954 to 1978, Raymond arrived at the following equation:

$$\Delta P_{n+1}^* = \Delta P_n + 0.188\,(\Delta P_n - \Delta P_n^*) + 0.02$$

This equation means that if in any year n in the period under study the actual rate of inflation in year n exceeded by one point the expected rate of inflation in the same year, the expected inflation rate in year n+1 will equal the actual rate of inflation in year n augmented by 0.02 points due to expectations of growing inflation and by 0.188 points because of an upward adjustment of such expectations due to the prediction error of economic actors in the year n. Raymond concluded that because of expectations of rising inflation over time due to prediction errors made in an immediately earlier period, the rate of inflation in the home economy may continue rising over a number of years.

This review of Spain's economic trends in the latter half of the 1970s clearly shows that at the start of the 1980s the Spanish economy faced a serious crisis. A new democratic Spanish state had been inaugurated in December 1978. It was Spain's misfortune to embrace democratic institutions at a time of world recession. The country had already experienced such a situation in the early 1930s; the attempt to democratize the country at a time when many nations experienced both major economic depression and the rise of fascist demagoguery led to a bloody civil war whose outcome turned Spain into a political and economic pariah in Europe for too many years.

It appeared in 1980 that successive Spanish governments had failed to control the growing economic disequilibria which became apparent from 1975. The worst consequences of such disequilibria were a major fall in domestic investment and a weakening of internal demand, rising unemployment and an accelerating rate of inflation.

As observed, the internal demand crisis induced Spanish firms to expand their sales abroad. However, a number of developments limited the growth of Spanish exports. Rapidly increasing domestic wage costs eroded the international competitiveness of Spanish exports. The comparatively high rate of Spanish inflation, strengthened as noticed by J.L. Raymond by expectations of a rising rate of inflation, further burdened the country's export capacity during the very same period when Spanish exports had to face intensifying competition in world markets not only from industrially advanced nations but also from the NICs.

The UCD government appeared little interested in curbing the rise of the unemployment level. Its principal economic goals were to modernize the country's industrial facilities and to encourage the growth of domestic private investment by trying to widen the share of GDP going to entrepreneurial profits. Such goals required a more effective limitation of wage increases. Meanwhile, the continuing migration of workers out of the primary sector, the ending of the earlier migratory flow of Spanish workers to other countries and the inability of the secondary and tertiary sectors of the home economy to employ workers who had left agriculture or potential new workers looking for their first job, forced a rising number of Spaniards into the ranks of the unemployed and of the poor. It is not surprising that under such circumstances the UCD government found it increasingly difficult to survive.

## THE FALL OF THE UCD GOVERNMENT

Adolfo Suárez intended to minimize the political repercussions of a probable leftist victory at the municipal elections scheduled for April 1979 when, immediately following the approval of the new Constitution in December 1978, he decided to dissolve the *Cortes* and called for new national elections to a new Parliament in March. The UCD emerged victorious at the March elections. The outcome of these elections weakened both the UCD's rightist and leftist opponents. Fraga Iribarne's rightist Popular Alliance obtained only 6% of the national vote and the PSOE, the UCD's major leftist rival, lost a number of seats in the new *Cortes*.

And yet Suárez's prestige in the country weakened. It was not only the deteriorating economy which constituted the main reason for the mounting criticism directed at the Prime Minister. A major cause of such criticism was Suárez's inability to follow a course of action which would please both the supporters of regional autonomy and their rightist opponents.

The Francoist regime had harshly suppressed all activities in support of regional autonomy. Anti-government acts of terrorism, often directed at the military, followed as a reaction to Franco's intransigent position regarding the regionalist problem. Such acts of terrorism started gaining the support of an increasing number of people in the Basque region and in Catalonia. The various political parties campaigning for the elections of June 1977 offered different proposals to remedy the country's regionalist problem. Fraga Iribarne's *Alianza Popular* courted the Francoist military and the anti-regionalist right but had to recognize the presence of strong regionalist sentiment in some parts of the country; it therefore advocated a limited grant of autonomous powers to certain regions by the central government. The leftist parties, particularly the PSOE and the PCE, argued in favour of the establishment of a federalist political system based on fully autonomous regions. The UCD had no clear proposals touching the regionalist problem. At best it recommended that each region negotiate separately with the central government the possible transfer by the latter of limited autonomous powers. Regionalists in Andalusia, in the Basque area and in Catalonia became increasingly dissatisfied with the UCD. The PSOE and regionalist parties started winning local elections. Concurrently, the Prime Minister came under sharper criticism. Members of his own party started accusing him of trying to impose his personal decisions on the party and on the country. The UCD itself started losing public confidence as increasing factionalism within the party brought open dissension between party Christian Democrats, Social Democrats and Liberals. Observing how his control of the UCD was vanishing, Adolfo Suárez resigned in January 1981 from his positions as President of the UCD and President of the Government.

Adolfo Suárez had another important reason for leaving his position as Prime Minister. The Francoist military had been left untouched by the government's efforts to democratize the country following the death of the Caudillo. Unlike the situations in Greece and Portugal, no internal revolution had ended the tenure of generals still devoted to the Francoist regime and to the maintenance of an authoritarian state. Most Spanish generals belonged to the extreme right, the *bunker*, which opposed the country's democratization. These generals had tolerated Suárez's political reforms because they believed, at least for some time, that such reforms would not abolish the Francoist centralized state. The military command saw in Suárez, the former head of the National Movement, a man loyal to Franco's regime and a new political leader supported by the King. Their confidence in Suárez started disintegrating as soon as he legalized the Communist Party and showed tolerance for the growing regionalist movements. Military officers particularly resented the intensification of Basque terrorism, not only because it was generally directed at military personnel, but also because it was perpetrated by people advocating separatism and Marxism, both of which the military abhorred.

Military opposition to the democratizing efforts of the government strengthened. The Spanish secret police aborted a planned coup against the government which was to be carried out in September 1978. The two coup leaders, Lt Col Antonio Tejero of the Civil Guard and Cpt. Ricardo Saenz de Ynestrillas were tried by a military court which sentenced the two conspirators to a prison term of less than seven months (Shaer, D., 1986, 172). It is interesting to notice that this same Antonio Tejero was a major actor in the second coup attempt of 1981 February 23, when, on the day Parliament was about to perform the ceremony of investiture of Leopoldo Calvo Sotelo as Spain's new Prime Minister, Tejero and his men invaded the *Cortes* and held all deputies hostage for some hours. Tejero's dramatic action in parliament was accompanied by a movement of military tanks through the streets of Valencia and by the taking of control of key communications centres in the nation by military officers. This serious threat to the country's young democracy was set aside by a courageous King who refused to negotiate with the rebellious officers. This attempted coup did not stop the ongoing democratization process in the country but it did contribute to the disintegration of the UCD party.

Leopoldo Calvo Sotelo proved unable to control growing dissension among the various groups in the UCD. In the summer of 1981 infighting intensified as the rightists in the party tried to prevent the enactment by the *Cortes* of a divorce law which was supported by the Social Democrats. The electorate's reaction to the evident lack of party unity proved to be disastrous for the UCD. It lost to the rightist Popular Alliance at the elections for a regional parliament of conservative Galicia. The UCD lost again at the Andalusian elections for a regional parliament in the spring of 1982. As the national elections scheduled for 28 October 1982 approached, UCD Christian and Social Democrats started abandoning the party.

The national elections gave victory to the PSOE. The party of Felipe González obtained 46% of the votes, 57.8% of the seats in the Lower House and 66.3% of the seats in the Senate. The Popular Alliance was second with 25.3% of the votes, 30.3% of the seats in the Lower House and 26.3% of the seats in the Senate. The UCD obtained only 7.2% of the votes, 3.4% of the seats in the Lower House and could muster only four senators (Ibid., 177). Unable to survive its defeat, the UCD disbanded in 1983.

# ECONOMIC CRISIS, 1980-5

The elections of 1982 brought to Spain its first leftist single-party government. For the first time in the country's history, a socialist majority dominated the *Cortes*. The Popular Alliance, in spite of its strong political comeback, failed to become a serious political rival of the PSOE. Only seven years after Franco's death, Spain had elected what in fact was a moderate Social Democratic government.

## THE SPANISH ECONOMY UNDER UCD LEADERSHIP

The Suárez–Calvo Sotelo governments had had to face the adverse economic effects of the two imported oil crises of the 1970s. These governments were unwilling to adopt the necessary adjustment measures required by the domestic and global economic situations. The economic effects of the first oil crisis were particularly disastrous for Spain. Until 1974, the Spanish economy had experienced one of the highest economic growth rates within the OECD area. Between 1974 and 1980, this growth rate fell to about 2%, a rate inferior to the average OECD rate of 2.75% (OECD, 1981, 5). During this latter period, Spanish private gross capital formation declined continuously in real terms, this fall being accompanied by a steady rise in unemployment. These trends are shown by Table 51.

The two oil price shocks not only weakened Spain's domestic demand, but also reduced Spain's net earnings from tourism and initiated a reversal in the net annual migratory flows of Spain's surplus labour. The first oil crisis seriously worsened Spain's terms of trade causing the country an annual income loss equivalent to about 3.75% of Spain's GDP in 1974. The second oil shock imposed on the Spanish economy a further worsening of its terms of trade, equivalent to between 2.5% and 3% of

*Table 51* Selected Spanish macroeconomic trends: 1977–80

| Indicator | 1964–70 | 1970–4 | 1974–80 | 1977 | 1979 | 1980 |
|---|---|---|---|---|---|---|
| Gross fixed capital formation: annual growth rate | 9.5 | 8.2 | –1.5 | –0.2 | –2.0 | 0.5 |
| Consumer price index: annual growth rate | 6.4 | 10.9 | 17.8 | 24.5 | 15.7 | 15.5 |
| Unemployment rate, as percentage of civilian labour force | 1.4 | 2.2 | 6.5 | 5.7 | 9.2 | 11.2 |
| External balance, millions US dollars | –290 | –236 | –2,263 | –2,450 | 1,126 | –5,095 |

Source: OECD, *Economic Surveys, Spain*, Paris, 1981, p. 7

*Table 52* Percentage share of selected weak-demand industrial products in total national industry: selected countries, early 1970s

| Country/Year | Iron and steel | Shipbuilding and repairs | Textiles, clothing, leather goods | Total |
|---|---|---|---|---|
| Spain (1972) | 5.56 | 2.25 | 20.07 | 27.88 |
| Greece (1970) | 3.69 | 3.03 | 16.25 | 22.97 |
| Italy (1970) | 6.17 | 0.47 | 15.42 | 22.06 |
| Austria (1971) | 7.31 | — | 12.17 | 19.54 |
| Japan (1975) | 6.60 | 2.81 | 9.21 | 18.62 |
| Norway (1975) | 4.28 | 8.72 | 3.92 | 16.92 |
| Sweden (1972) | 6.14 | 2.73 | 6.49 | 15.36 |
| France (1970) | 4.58 | 3.10 | 6.53 | 14.21 |
| UK (1975) | 4.71 | 1.80 | 7.68 | 14.19 |
| Germany FR (1970) | 6.19 | 0.62 | 6.86 | 13.67 |
| Canada (1971) | 4.03 | 0.58 | 6.64 | 11.25 |

Source: OECD, *Economic Surveys, Spain*, Paris, 1981, p. 11

the country's GDP (Ibid., 7). The oil crises also restricted the growth of Spain's export markets.

A number of structural problems made the Spanish economy very vulnerable to the exogenous energy shocks. Among the various OECD countries, Spain showed greatest dependence on oil. Moreover, Spain's secondary sector still concentrated on the production of manufactured goods whose world supply exceeded world demand in the 1970s. As noticed, too many Spanish industries were weak-demand industries. Table 52 shows the relative weight of weak-demand production in total national industrial output in a number of countries in the early 1970s. As indicated by this table, the combination of iron and steel, shipbuilding and repair, textiles, clothing and leather goods represented a much higher percentage of total national industrial output than in other OECD countries in 1972. The export of such products in the 1970s was increasingly burdened by the intensifying competition presented by the NICs, including some Eastern European nations. Because of the increasing international competition, Spanish exporters had to accept both a declining share of their foreign export markets and lower profit margins. A major deficiency of the Spanish economy was its inability to produce high-technology industrial products, products for which world demand strengthened. These products included aircraft, aircraft parts, consumer electronics, data-processing equipment, electronic components, telecommunication equipment, etc.

Construction was one of the Spanish industrial sectors hardest hit by a number of adverse developments in the 1970s. The disappearance of the earlier housing shortage, the steady decline of foreign tourism in the country, as well as reduced labour mobility resulting from growing unemployment, restricted the growth of the construction sector.

Because about two-thirds of the country's industrial energy requirements were based on imported oil, and because more than 80% of the country's freight moved by road, Spain remained highly dependent on imported oil throughout the 1970s. Spain was unable in the short-run to convert her industries to different forms of energy use. Rising prices of imported oil, rising wages, rising social security contributions and a comparatively high rate of inflation lowered the international competitiveness of Spain's exports and had a strongly negative impact on entrepreneurial expectations. The government was slow in reducing the country's high dependence on imported energy. A National Energy Plan was not approved until July 1979. It was only in October 1980 that specific measures needed to implement the Plan were approved by the *Cortes*. Workable industrial restructuring plans were only finalized in 1979 and their implementation began in 1981 (OECD, 1981, 18–19).

The government's fiscal policy remained expansionary in this period. The entire responsibility for inflation control was given to monetary policy. The latter never achieved a significant deceleration of the growth rate of the money supply largely because the monetary authorities feared that strong restrictions on the expansion of bank lending to the private sector could further reduce the flow of private investment.

## 1980

As Spain's terms of trade deteriorated in 1980, and as the rate of export growth declined, aggregate demand weakened. Tax increases reduced the growth rate of households' disposable income and brought a deceleration in the growth rate of private consumption. The second oil crisis of 1979 had an adverse effect on the Spanish tourist industry in 1980. Private fixed investment declined for the sixth consecutive year. Real Spanish GDP increased by only 1.75% in that year (Ibid., 30).

Concurrently, Spanish consumer prices rose by 15.4% in 1980, keeping Spain's inflation level above that of the OECD area. Table 53 compares average annual rates of consumer price increases in Spain and in other countries between 1977 and 1980.

The level of total employment in 1980 was about 3% below that of 1979. Such decline was largely due to a fall in employment in both the construction industry and agriculture. Table 54 shows the weakening of the Spanish labour market in 1980.

Although in 1980 the primary sector's real value added increased by 9% because of good harvests, the value of industrial output in that year rose by only 1% while the rate of growth of the output of the tertiary

Table 53 Comparative consumer price trends: 1977–80
(average annual rates)

| Area | 1977 | 1978 | 1979 | 1980 |
|---|---|---|---|---|
| Spain | 24.5 | 19.8 | 15.7 | 15.4 |
| Seven major countries | 8.1 | 7.0 | 9.3 | 12.2 |
| EC | 9.9 | 7.0 | 8.9 | 12.1 |
| OECD Europe | 11.3 | 9.4 | 10.6 | 14.2 |
| Total OECD | 8.9 | 7.9 | 9.8 | 12.9 |

Source: OECD, *Economic Surveys, Spain*, Paris, 1981, p. 32

Table 54 Employment trends: 1976–80

| | Thousand persons | Percentage of total employment | Percentage annual change | | | | |
|---|---|---|---|---|---|---|---|
| | | | 1976 | 1977 | 1978 | 1979 | 1980 |
| Employment[1] | | | | | | | |
| Total | 11,896 | 100.00 | −1.8 | −0.0 | −1.2 | −2.4 | −3.1 |
| Primary sector | 2,343 | 19.7 | −7.6 | −6.5 | −2.8 | −6.3 | −7.0 |
| Industrial sector | 3,251 | 27.3 | 0.6 | 1.5 | −1.3 | −3.2 | −4.5 |
| Construction | 1,109 | 9.3 | −1.4 | 2.2 | −2.8 | −5.6 | −6.2 |
| Tertiary sector | 5,194 | 43.7 | −0.3 | 1.9 | 0.2 | 0.8 | 0.2 |
| Labour force | 13,101 | | −0.9 | 1.0 | 0.8 | −0.5 | −0.1 |
| Unemployment[2] | 1,205 | | 4.8 | 5.7 | 7.6 | 9.2 | 11.9 |

Source: Ibid.
Notes: 1 Includes marginal workers, i.e. people who worked at least one hour per week, but less than one-third of normal weekly work hours
2 Measured as percentage of labour force

sector decelerated from 2% in 1979 to only 1.25% in 1980.

The rise in the price of imported oil and the poor performance of the tourist industry caused the country's trade deficit to rise from US$5.7 billion in 1979 to US$12 billion in 1980 (Ibid., 35). Given a continuing inflow of long-term capital from abroad, the country's basic balance showed a deficit of US$1.29 billion at the end of 1980. The deficit on current balance for the same year amounted to US$5 billion.

In an effort to strengthen their profit margins, Spanish exporters increased their prices by as much as 19% in 1980. The depreciation of the peseta in terms of the US dollar should have supported their sales while preventing an expansion of Spanish imports. In fact, though exports to the EC area expanded, exports to North America declined. In the same year, Spanish imports of consumer goods rose sharply and imports of crude oil were not reduced. The net result of these trends was a doubling of the trade deficit.

The measures taken by the Adolfo Suárez government in 1980 addressed various problems faced by the domestic economy but were unable to slow down the pace of its deterioration. In order to boost demand, public investment was increased. An investment tax credit, introduced in 1979, was continued. The government transferred 230 billion pesetas to the social security system to lighten the burden of the mandatory contributions to the system imposed on private firms. The government hoped that the increase in the budget deficit would be justified by a decline in the level of unemployment. To help finance increased public investment, the government relied on an improved system of tax collection and on a slowdown in the rate of increase of salaries and wages paid to public servants.

Two important labour laws were enacted in 1980. A new Workers' Statute gave employers greater ease in dismissing workers while recognizing, with certain limitations, the workers' right to strike. It raised the minimum age of workers from 14 to 16, reduced the maximum weekly working time from 44 to 42 hours and lowered the maximum monthly length of overtime work from 20 to 15 hours. It facilitated temporary and part-time hiring by employers and set the maximum retirement age at 69 (Ibid., 27). A Basic Law on Employment separated the administration of unemployment insurance from the social security system and established new ways for the determination of insurance payments and for the duration of such payments.

The government also adopted a series of measures designed to facilitate the implementation of the National Energy Plan enacted in 1979. In December 1980, the *Cortes* approved a Rational Use of Energy Law which aimed to encourage by means of tax incentives intra-firm generation and consumption of electricity. To induce the private sector to switch from the use of oil to that of coal in the generation of electric power, a public corporation, CARBOEX, was established to provide the country with sufficient quantities of imported coal. Concurrently, domestic energy prices were raised. In the course of 1980, the price of gasoline increased by 33%, that of electricity rose by 67%, that of diesel fuel increased by 77% and the price of fuel oil went up by 90%.

The government's industrial policy for the private sector followed three main principles. First, the initiative for the restructuring of any industrial sector facing economic difficulties had to rest with that sector. Second, the government would not provide special assistance to an individual firm, but would try to help the sector as a whole. Third, this public assistance could be fiscal and/or financial and the government would monitor the progress achieved by the recipient sector.

A Royal Decree of 3 October 1980 provided for the reconversion of the northern steel industry. It established a joint-stock company which would be in charge of all the private firms in the given sector. This joint-stock company was to be entirely responsible for all necessary reconversion operations. It had the power to determine the level of the sector's output, to effect cost reductions, to set limits to the numbers of workers employed in each participating firm, to market their products and to facilitate mergers between such firms. The government planned to extend this arrangement to the entirety of the Spanish steel industry and possibly to other industries.

## 1981

In 1981, the international economy still suffered the consequences of the second oil crisis of 1979–80. For the industrialized countries, the loss of real income due to the higher price of imported crude oil was augmented by the economic effects of the deflationary trends which developed in 1980. As a result, and largely because of adequate economic growth in Japan in 1981, the rate of growth in the industrialized countries in that year averaged 1%. The rate of economic growth in the EC countries declined by half a percentage point. The United States economy, stagnant in 1980, fell into recession in the last three months of 1981. In all these countries, the level of unemployment rose. In the German Federal Republic, the number of unemployed people at the end of 1981 was 54% higher than it had been at the end of 1980; 5.8% of the German active population was unemployed at the end of 1981. In the United Kingdom, the number of unemployed rose by 45% in the latter years. Over nine million persons were unemployed in the United States at the end of the same year.

The deflationary effects of rising unemployment were reinforced by the monetary policies followed by the industrialized nations in 1981. The United States' prime rate of interest stood at 20.5% in August 1981. The high American rates of interest were duplicated in the Western economies because the industrialized countries tried to prevent a depreciation of their currencies in terms of the US dollar. These countries had to pay for most of their imports, among them imports of crude oil, in terms of American dollars. A depreciation of their currency in terms of the American dollar would have pushed up the domestic price of their imports and would have intensified inflationary pressures at home. High rates of interest weakened in turn internal investment demand; in these countries, the demand for durable consumer goods, for housing and even for capital goods weakened.

Reduced economic activity in the industrialized countries brought stagnation to world trade. The prices of internationally traded primary goods fell by 19.6% in 1981, measured in US dollars. In terms of the same currency, the international prices of primary industrial raw materials declined by 11.7% (Ministerio de Industria y Energía, 1982, 3–5).

Spanish economic growth weakened in 1981. Real GDP rose by only 0.25%. Internal demand fell by as much as 2%, this decline being compensated by export growth (OECD, 1982, 8). The main factors explaining the deterioration of Spanish internal demand were a decline in real household disposable income and a fall in construction investment. The slight growth of GDP was due to a rise in public investment and to a strengthening of private investment in capital goods as well as of exports. Both peseta earnings from exports and from tourism expanded during the second half of 1981.

The gross value added by agriculture fell, however, by 11% as a result of severe drought conditions prevailing in 1981. The drought caused the internal prices of foodstuffs to rise. The gross value added of the industrial sector did not show any appreciable gain over its 1980 level. Though investment in the communications, energy and transport sectors increased, it stagnated or declined in other industrial sectors. An excess housing stock and declining demand for new house-building caused the gross value added of the construction industry to decline in spite of increased government spending on public works. The tertiary sector alone was able to register a 2% gain in gross value added, a gain due to the recovery of the tourist industry (Ibid., 9).

The practical stagnation of Spanish industry in 1981 was largely the result of the inability of Spain's secondary sector to contribute to the growth of GDP for the third consecutive year. During 1981, the most dynamic component of Spanish industrial activity was the production of equipment goods which was stimulated by the implementation of the National Energy Plan and by the modernization of the country's railroad company, the RENFE.

Private consumption, weakened by growing unemployment and by a slowdown of the growth of salaries and wages, was unable to stimulate domestic demand. It was domestic investment in capital goods, a renewed growth of foreign tourism and an expansion of the volume of exports that allowed GNP to rise by 0.3% measured in terms of market prices (Ministerio de Industria y Energía, 1982, 7).

Employment conditions in 1981 continued to deteriorate, though less drastically than in the previous year. The number of persons employed at the end of that year, including workers as young as sixteen but excluding marginal workers, was 288,000 below that registered at the start of 1981; this number was significantly lower than that of 442,000 recorded in 1980 (OECD, 1982, 10).

Inflationary pressures also weakened in 1981. The rate of increase of consumer prices fell from 15.4% in 1980 to 14.6% in 1981. The deceleration of Spanish inflation growth was however weaker than the corresponding trend in the European OECD countries, largely because the depreciation of the peseta in terms of other currencies boosted the domestic prices of Spanish imports. Other factors supporting a relatively high rate of inflation in Spain were the rise of internal agricultural prices caused by the drought and the increase of domestic energy prices.

On the other hand, a more moderate rise of salaries and wages contained the pace of inflation growth and was of great benefit to the Spanish export industry. Wage increases provided by collective trade agreements in 1981 did not surpass 13.1%. They had attained 15.3% one year earlier (Ministerio de Industria y Energía, 1982, 7). The resulting reduction in per unit labour costs and an increase in labour productivity in 1981 of about four percentage points allowed the share of profits in the firms' gross value added to increase, facilitating thereby the process of equipment and plant renovation.

In 1981, the value of Spanish exports, measured in terms of pesetas, exceeded that of the previous year by 26.5%. Because of the depreciation of the Spanish currency in relation to the American dollar, the value of these exports, measured in terms of US dollars, was 2% below their dollar value in 1980. Spanish exporters succeeded in expanding their foreign market shares in 1981. Such foreign market shares particularly expanded in markets where buyers of Spanish products gained most from the depreciation of the peseta. While the volume of Spanish exports to the EC countries declined, it grew in the case of exports to the United States, to the Latin American and OPEC countries and to those of the COMECON.

Depending upon the type of currency in which they were measured, the performance of Spanish imports in 1981 could be interpreted differently. Valued in pesetas, Spanish imports rose by 21.2% in 1981. Measured in terms of US dollars, this value diminished by 5.8% compared to the dollar import value in 1980. Import activity was affected by Spain's reduced demand for imported energy. In 1981, the volume of Spanish petroleum imports was 7.6% smaller than that of 1980; in spite of this decline in import volume, Spain's dollar payment for imports of petroleum in 1981 was 2.1% larger than it had been in the previous year (Ibid., 9). The 1981 decline in the volume of imported crude oil was in part explained by Spain's internal economic crisis. It was also due, however, to a smaller dependence of Spain's industry on imported crude oil. Indeed, the Spanish consumption of crude oil as a percentage of the aggregate Spanish consumption of energy fell from 64.3% in 1980 to 61% in 1981 (Ibid.).

OECD data indicate that Spain's trade deficit fell from US$11.5 billion in 1980 to US$10.1 billion in 1981. Declining tourism and

Table 55 Spain's external accounts: 1979–81 (in US$ million)

| External accounts | 1979 | 1980 | 1981 |
|---|---|---|---|
| Exports, fob | 18,352 | 20,929 | 20,450 |
| Imports, fob | 24,022 | 32,389 | 30,570 |
| Trade balance | –5,670 | –11,461 | –10,120 |
| Services, net, of which: | 5,014 | 4,424 | 3,410 |
| Tourism | 5,559 | 5,720 | 5,708 |
| Investment income | –1,088 | –1,548 | –2,374 |
| Technical aid and royalties | –403 | –464 | –413 |
| Transfers, net | 1,782 | 2,048 | 1,696 |
| Current balance | 1,126 | –4,989 | –5,014 |
| Long-term capital | 3,010 | 3,800 | 4,148 |
| Basic balance | 4,136 | –1,189 | –866 |

Source: OECD, *Economic Surveys, Spain*, Madrid, 1982, p. 14

transfer earnings, however, caused the current balance deficit to rise from US$4.9 billion in 1980 to slightly over US$5 billion in 1981 (OECD, 1982, 14).

Net inflows of long-term capital were higher in 1981 than they had been in 1980. This aggregate trend reflected a small decline in private capital inflows but this latter trend was more than offset by large public borrowing abroad. Table 55 shows the trends in Spain's external accounts in 1979, 1980 and 1981.

Throughout 1981, the government's fiscal policy remained expansionary. Public investment rose to stimulate domestic economic activity, with fixed investment spending rising by about 30% in nominal terms. Transfers to state-controlled enterprises and to autonomous government agencies expanded and the central government allotted 27 billion pesetas for the restructuring of a number of industries (Ibid., 17). Public consumption spending was reduced. The rise in public spending was facilitated by an increase in aggregate public revenue of about 23% made possible by a sharp increase in revenue from indirect taxes.

The monetary authority had the heavy responsibility of containing inflation growth, of financing the external deficit at a time of high interest rates, of controlling the expansion of the money supply so as to promote economic recovery and of stabilizing the external value of the peseta.

Hoping to achieve a rate of GDP growth of between 1% and 2% in 1982 with a rate of inflation of between 13.5% and 15%, these authorities set a target growth rate of the money supply (M3) of 16.5%. During the first half of 1981, a weak domestic demand for credit limited the rate of expansion of M3 to 13.5%. During the second quarter monetary policy was tightened to contain the depreciation of the peseta; domestic interest rates rose. The growth rate of M3 rose to 17.5% during the second half of the year but Spanish interest rates remained higher than those in the OECD area.

Reviewing the weaknesses of the Spanish economy in 1981, the OECD enumerated the following structural problems which the UCD governments had not been able to solve. First, to be able to control the rate of inflation, an effective incomes policy was needed. Not much had been done to improve the latter since 1977. In 1981 the government, the trade unions and the employers' associations signed a National Employment Pact, ANE, in order to limit the rate of growth of contractual wages in 1982. The parties agreed to limit this rate to between 9% and 11%. The compensation received by civil servants was not to rise above 9%. Social security pensions were not to be increased by more than 10%. The parties understood that one of the country's major economic problems was cost-push inflation. Second, it was observed that compared with industrial sectors in other countries, Spain's industry was too heavily represented by sectors facing either worldwide excess capacity or increased NIC competition. It was also noted that programmes designed to restructure Spain's secondary sector started being implemented relatively late. Third, plans advanced to reduce Spain's dependence on imported energy were delayed for too long. Domestic energy prices were not sufficiently increased before mid-1970.

The heavy social security contributions firms had to pay and the survival of costly dismissal procedures imposed on employers by old Francoist legislation constituted additional obstacles to the growth of employment.

## 1982

The year 1982 was one of the worst years the Western economies had experienced since the 1940s. Instead of bringing an expected end to the worldwide recession which followed the first oil crisis, 1982 witnessed a deepening of depressed economic conditions, whether measured in terms of production, employment or volume of international trade. World trade was hampered by the growing use of the devices of the 'New Protectionism' by major trading countries. The resulting distortions in the flows of international trade limited the exports of developing nations and rendered the latter unable to service their foreign debts. World trade was further weakened by a decline in the growth rate of the major industrialized countries. Table 56 shows that the rate of growth of GNP in the seven major economies of the OECD fell by 0.5% in 1982. The average rate of growth for the OECD economy as a whole was particularly weakened by a deceleration in the pace of economic growth

Table 56 Annual percentage changes in key variables in seven major OECD countries: 1980–2

| Variable | 1980 | 1981 | 1982 |
|---|---|---|---|
| GNP | 1.0 | 1.3 | −0.5 |
| Contributing to the growth of GDP: | | | |
| Private consumption | 0.7 | 0.7 | 0.7 |
| Public spending | 0.4 | 0.2 | 0.2 |
| Private residential construction | −0.4 | −0.1 | −0.2 |
| Other private investment | 0.3 | 0.2 | −0.5 |
| Changes in stocks | −0.7 | −0.1 | −0.2 |
| Exports | 1.1 | 0.9 | 0.0 |
| Imports | −0.2 | −0.4 | −0.5 |
| Industrial production | −1.2 | 0.8 | −4.2 |
| Unemployment (annual average percentage of active population) | 5.6 | 6.5 | 8.0 |
| Annual percentage increase in consumer prices | 12.2 | 10.0 | 8.1 |

Source: Ministerio de Industria y Energía, *Informe Anual sobre la Industria Española, 1982*, Madrid, 1983, p. 12
Note: The countries are Canada, France, German FR, Italy, Japan, UK and USA

in Japan and by a deepening recession in both the United States and Canada.

The generally poor economic performance of the Western world in 1982 was mostly due to a fall in both the private investment and the exports of the pertinent countries. Most of the latter recorded a decline in their industrial production, a major consequence of the continuing American recession. This recession negatively impacted demand conditions in the developing countries, including the OPEC nations. In the major OECD economies, the rate of growth of industrial production fell by 4.2%. Such conditions produced a general rise in unemployment which attained about 10% of the active population in the European zone of the OECD. This rate reached 11% in the United States. The recession not only affected the countries of the OECD, but also extended to the nations of Latin America which suffered an average decline of 1.6% in their rates of economic growth in 1982 (Ministerio de Industria y Energía, 1983, 12–13). Only the NICs of Asia appeared to be able to maintain a rate of economic growth averaging 5.5%.

The intensity of the 1982 recession was largely due to a general change in economic policy following the second oil crisis of 1979–80. The first energy crisis had boosted the international price of imported crude oil from US$3 in 1973 to US$11 per barrel one year later. Such drastic price increase generated both deflationary and inflationary repercussions in the oil-consuming nations. The transfer of real income from the latter to the OPEC countries had deflationary effects in the industrialized and in the industrializing countries. The dramatic increase in the price of imported crude oil had in turn an inflationary impact on the economies of the oil-importing nations. Their governments tried to compensate for the deterioration of internal demand conditions and for their loss of real income by adopting permissive or expansionary fiscal and monetary policies.

Following the second oil crisis during which the international price of a barrel of crude oil increased from US$13 in 1979 to US$34 in 1981, the oil-importing nations adopted a very different economic strategy. They tried above all to control inflation and to weaken inflation-based expectations. Mrs Thatcher in the United Kingdom and Mr Reagan in the United States gave priority to inflation control over unemployment reduction. Both of them claimed that the government's attention should centre, not on the Keynesian concept of demand, but on the supply side of the economy. Inspired by the neo-classical 'Say's Law', they argued that a more efficient and rational allocation of resources in a freer market and a necessary restructuring of productive sectors in the economy would in time generate an adequate level of demand. Misinterpreting John Maynard Keynes, they argued that governments' Keynesian economic policies had been mostly responsible for growing inflationary pressures. They condemned the widening role of the public sector in the economy on the grounds that this sector impeded an efficient allocation of resources.

The supporters of 'Reaganomics' claimed that monetary policy should be the major weapon governments should use to fight inflation. The restrictive monetary policy they embraced added to the deflationary effects produced by the rise in the price of imported crude oil. The high American rates of interest produced by the Reaganite monetary policy started attracting to the United States large inflows of foreign funds and caused the value of the American dollar to rise in world financial markets.

Other industrialized countries tried to prevent a depreciation of their currency in terms of the US dollar. They naturally apprehended that such depreciation would strengthen inflation in their home economy. They too adopted restrictive monetary policies. Such monetary strategy intensified the recession they had experienced since 1979.

The appreciation of the US dollar and high rates of interest proved to be catastrophic for most developing nations. Since the beginning of 1980, a number of dramatic changes in the world economy seriously damaged the economies of the developing countries. Among these changes were the appreciation of the US dollar, the continuing recession in the industrializing nations, the rapid rise of interest rates in the world's financial markets, the decline in the volume of world trade and the resulting fall of the international prices of primary commodities. From mid-1982, a number of developing countries had to announce their inability to service their external debts and the possibility that they would have no other alternative but to repudiate the latter. Indeed, the ability of these countries to pay interest or principal on such debts had been seriously impaired since 1980 by a concurrent decline of the quantities and the prices of their exports. On the other hand, rising interest rates in world financial markets increased the difficulty of servicing their external debts. The fall in the volume of their exports was mainly due to the deterioration of economic activity in the economically advanced nations. Falling prices of primary commodities, the chief export of most developing nations, weakened the ability of the latter to earn the foreign exchange they needed to remain externally solvent. The external solvency of the developing nations ultimately depended on the ability of the industrialized nations to overcome their internal economic crises and to import more commodities from the developing nations.

In the 1960s, industrialized countries exporting manufactured goods started facing the new competition offered by the NICs in years marked by a slowdown in technological advance. The early 1970s brought an end to the general boom period caused by the reconstruction and development activities which followed the end of World War II, and the collapse of the Bretton Woods international monetary system which was replaced by highly unstable international monetary arrangements. The two energy crises of that decade unleashed recessions throughout the Western world which seriously impeded the resumption of adequate economic growth in the industrialized nations. In view of these changes, a necessary adjustment of the advanced economies required restructuring of their industrial sectors in favour of high-technology production to reduce competition with the NICs producing low- or medium-technology products. Such industrial transformation was however rendered difficult because world markets for high-technology goods were narrow. Worldwide recession was another major impediment to such industrial reconstruction.

Western economists could not agree on how best to move the advanced economies out of their stagnating state. Keynesian macroeconomists argued that the economic difficulties developing in the late 1970s originated in inadequate demand conditions. Supply-side economists argued on the other hand that the main economic problem was one of lack of proper adjustment of productive sectors. At a time of general economic stagnation, governments found it difficult to strengthen economic activity by using either demand-oriented or supply-centred policies. Supply-side solutions required an adequate financing of industrial renovation and a reduction in production costs. Though the fall in the prices of primary commodities and a slowdown in the rate of increase of wages allowed production costs to decline in 1982, the rise of interest rates in world financial markets and the increasing use of new protectionist devices by most trading nations rendered the process of industrial adjustment extremely difficult. Moreover, though the US dollar price of imported primary goods declined, the impact of such decline in the industrialized nations was limited or cancelled out by the depreciation of their currency in terms of the US dollar.

Since 1979 excess productive capacity, the rise of financial costs and deteriorating entrepreneurial expectations had weakened industrial investment in the advanced economies. While the developing countries' external indebtedness increased in the early 1980s, the indebtedness of firms in the advanced economies also expanded as harsh monetary policies added to the weight of their financial burdens.

Continuing conditions of recession and the acceleration in the growth of unemployment intensified the use of protectionist measures by the governments of the trading nations of the Western world. Indeed, unemployment rose by 44% in the German Federal Republic and by 30% in the United States in 1982 (Ibid., 24). Governments did not turn to the traditional tariff-type protectionism; political reasons impeded it. Instead, they made greater use of the various trade-restricting devices which the 'New Protectionism' had developed in the 1970s (Lieberman, S., 1988, 125–66). Imports were discouraged through complex administrative restrictions purporting to ensure that imports met national 'health and safety' standards. Foreign governments and suppliers were pressured into 'voluntary export restraint agreements'. Multinational discriminatory trade agreements were concluded or renewed in order to limit imports of certain goods originating in certain countries. This new hidden protectionism aimed above all to curb imports of textiles and of steel in view of the excess supplies of such goods in the domestic market. It also extended to imports of automobiles, colour television sets and machine tools. In December 1982, the strongly discriminatory Multi-Fibre Agreement was renewed for the third time. In the same year, the United States took measures to reduce imports of steel from both the European Community and Japan. The New Protectionism effectively reduced the volume of world trade and distorted the directions of its flows.

The Spanish UCD governments clearly recognized the connecting ties linking the deterioration of domestic economic activity to the poor performance of the country's industrial sector. It had become obvious that decelerating rates of growth of internal and external demands had brought conditions of excess productive capacity to the secondary sector and that such development discouraged private investment in fixed capital. As a result, existing plant and equipment were becoming increasingly obsolete. Burdened by rapidly rising production costs and by technological retardation, a number of Spanish industrial subsectors faced the alternative of restructuring and modernizing their operations or collapsing.

The UCD governments embraced a policy of 'industrial reconversion' whose details were specified in the Decree-Law of June 1981 and in the Law 21/1982. An industrial policy was announced in Spain five or six years after similar policies had been adopted in many other countries of Western Europe. The Decree-Law of June 1981 provided for financial and fiscal aid to certain industrial subsectors designated as 'industries of preferred interest' and as 'concerted action industries'. No government assistance was to be granted to individual firms, although exceptions were made. The type of public assistance extended by the government to a 'reconversion' group of industrial firms depended on a tripartite agreement entered into by such firms, the relevant trade unions and the government.

At the end of 1982, the government had decided to extend reconversion aid to eleven industrial subsectors. This aid was intended to improve the financial conditions of recipient firms and help them operate with a more efficient and smaller labour force; the reconversion plans largely by-passed the problem of group restructuring and failed to provide for a government monitoring mechanism able to evaluate the effectiveness with which recipient firms used reconversion aid.

A brief examination of the economic conditions prevailing in the early 1980s in the selected industrial subsectors and of the public assistance they received will illustrate the industrial strategy adopted by the Suárez–Calvo Sotelo governments.

## Government aid to selected industrial subsectors

### The steel industry

The Royal Decree 971/1982 provided for a reconversion plan for 'non-integrated producers of common steel'. This subsector consisted of thirty-one firms which had produced in 1981 about 36% of the total national steel output. These firms employed 12,900 workers and rapidly rising production costs imposed great financial difficulties on them at a time when their excess capacity expanded. The reconversion plan specified by the Decree purported to reduce the productive capacity of these firms by one million tons and to close down obsolete plants. The government was to assist the restructuring of this subsector through the grant of 6.3 billion pesetas over the years 1982, 1983 and 1984; in addition, firms participating in the plan would receive an aggregate of 5.5 billion pesetas in credits in 1982 and of 5.2 billion pesetas in 1983 (Ministerio de Industria y Energía, 1983, 43–6). Only six firms in the subsector agreed to participate in a reconversion plan. The boards of the other firms were unable to agree on proposed measures to reduce the group's excess capacity.

Outside this group were three large integrated steel producing firms, ENSIDESA, Altos Hornos de Vizcaya and Altos Hornos del Mediterráneo. These firms also faced problems of excess capacity even though their exports had risen from 3% of their sales in 1974 to 40% in 1982 (Ibid.). Their rising per unit costs brought them net losses which amounted to 38 billion pesetas in 1982. The Reconversion Plan of 1981 agreed to by management, the trade unions and government provided for a reduction of labour costs in total production costs and for public financial aid to be extended over the years 1981 to 1985, aggregating 230 billion pesetas. These firms agreed to coordinate their production plans and to close down high cost plants, as well as plants consuming high levels of energy. The Plan allowed the postponement of their tax debts. It also stipulated that workers between 60 and 65 years of age who had lost their jobs because of renovation activities would receive full retirement benefits. In spite of the financial aid extended to these firms by the government, their indebtedness continued to rise and they were unable to finance planned investments. Their international competitiveness continued to weaken.

Within the Spanish steel industry, seventeen firms produced 'special steel products', products required by the capital goods industries, the armament industry, the petroleum industry and shipbuilding. These firms also faced a declining demand for their products. Between 1974 and 1982, these firms invested about 25 billion pesetas in new productive capacity, doubling thereby their total capacity. Given a widening gap between supply and demand, the lack of coordinated production plans and an excessively large labour force, these firms recorded annual net losses aggregating 7 billion pesetas (Ibid., 41).

In order to avoid the immediate bankruptcy of major firms in this group, a Royal Decree 2206/1980 providing for the reconversion of the Special Steel subsector was enacted on 3 October 1980. Under its terms, a Reconversion Society for this group of firms was established with the major special steel producers participating in it. The Society was to implement necessary measures to enhance the international competitiveness of participating firms; among these were S.A. Echevarría, Orbegozo, S.A., Aceros de Llodio, S.A., Aceros de Irura, Fundiciones Echevarría, S.A., Babcock Wilcox, S.A. and Olarra, S.A. Public assistance to these firms was financed by both the Ministry of Industry and Energy and the Basque government. Such financial aid was to extend over the years 1980, 1981 and 1982 and aggregated 6 billion pesetas. Though in 1983 the Ministry of Industry reported that the objectives of the Plan of 1980 were attained, the management of the firms in this group and the relevant trade unions started negotiating a Plan for the Reindustrialization of this subsector to facilitate a decline of its production costs to internationally competitive levels.

## Shipbuilding

Shipbuilding was another industrial subsector facing serious difficulties in 1982. Since the mid-1970s, Spanish shipyards experienced mounting problems. The principal reason for the dramatic drop in construction contracts they received in the early 1980s was the fall in global demand for ships which had started in 1974. The problem was common to all shipbuilding countries in the OECD area. Governments and shipbuilding firms in other nations responded to the deterioration of the world market by closing down high cost shipyards, by diversifying their products and by restructuring the entire industry. Such efforts were initiated in Spain only at the start of the 1980s.

The shipbuilding industry at the beginning of that decade consisted of two large shipbuilding enterprises, ASTANO and AESA, both of them belonging to the INI, and thirty-five medium-size and small enterprises, five of them being public concerns and the others private firms. The large public enterprise Bazán which built only navy ships was not part of this subsector.

The shipbuilding subsector was characterized by a low utilization of productive capacity, by declining sales, by rapidly rising production costs and by a labour force too large for efficiency. The government decided to assist the restructuring of this subsector in 1981 when a Royal Decree 9/1981 first formulated a reconversion plan for the subsector. It was followed by the Royal Decree 643/1982 which detailed the financial aid available to firms in the country's shipbuilding industry (Ibid., 55). Only two firms applied for such financial aid in 1982: Astilleros del Cantábrico y Riera, S.A. received government credits amounting to 300 million pesetas; Unión Naval de Levante, S.A. was given a grant of 1.2 billion pesetas and government credits aggregating 900 million pesetas.

The Decree of 1981 established a Society for Naval Reconstruction, SORENA, which was to direct and supervise the restructuring of medium-size and small shipbuilding companies. In the case of large firms, the Reconversion Plan of 1981 proposed a greater specialization in production and the development of greater technological independence, the closing down of low productivity facilities and the reduction of labour costs to 25% of the value of the final product. The large shipbuilders were to reduce their productive capacity by 40%; the other firms in the industry were directed to reduce their capacity by 35%. The firms responded poorly to such directives. In general, they limited the reduction of their labour forces to early retirements only (Ibid., 57).

## Textiles

The government intervened to promote the restructuring of other industrial subsectors, generally sectors of weak demand, burdened by deteriorating financial conditions and by rapidly rising production costs. The textile industry was one of them. It was one of the oldest and most important industries in the country. At the start of the 1980s, it was constituted by medium-size and small enterprises, as well as by processing activities carried out in private homes. The managers of most textile firms were poorly trained. The subsector included two types of firms. Most of them clung to traditional and obsolete methods of production; co-existing with these, were a number of modern enterprises operating on the basis of capital-intensive advanced technology. The subsector comprised 3,500 textile firms in 1982 which employed 208,000 workers. There were also 3,700 apparel producers with an aggregate work force of 200,000 and ten chemical fibres producers employing 12,000 persons (Ibid., 61).

The composition of the subsector's output changed markedly over time. Synthetic fibres, which in 1960 represented only 2% of the national fibre consumption, attained 55% of such consumption in 1980. In the case of cotton, the corresponding percentages fell from 67% in 1960 to 29% in 1980.

In the 1960s and 1970s, this subsector started facing the rising competition of a number of developing countries. Its firms were threatened by bankruptcy as internal and external demands for their products weakened, as new investment in the subsector became scarcer and as rising petroleum prices increased the cost of producing synthetic fibres. The government's attempt to save the industry was tardy. A Royal Decree 2010/1981 established a reconversion plan for the textile industry. The Decree-Law 9/1981 and the Law 21/1982 detailed the public financial assistance available to the subsector. It was to receive subsidies amounting to 626 million pesetas in 1982, 685 million in 1983 and 456.6 million in 1984. Official credits and guarantees were also available to its firms (Ibid., 60). What the government was unable to do was to improve the course of domestic and foreign demand for the products of this industry. Private investment in this sector continued to stagnate.

## Other subsectors

Another deteriorating, weak-demand industry the government decided to assist in 1982 was footwear. Firms in this subsector were burdened by rapidly rising production costs, low productivity and an excessive labour force. Most of these firms were either medium-size or small and 56% of them were located in the province of Alicante. A Royal Decree 1002/1982 provided this subsector with fiscal and subsidy benefits. An Executive Committee for the Reconversion Plan was given the task of complementing the goals of the Plan and of supervising their fulfilment. The Ministries of Economy and Commerce, of Industry and Energy and of Labour participated in this Committee.

In a few instances, the government showed that it was not only interested in assisting industries in financial difficulty, but that it was also concerned about Spain's industrial future. Thus, even though the national electronic components industry had barely made a start in the 1970s, the government was quite aware that it offered strong growth potential. This industry had been officially declared to be one of preferential interest in 1974. A Royal Decree 769/1982 provided for the raising of the industry's productivity to levels prevailing in the industrially advanced countries. A Plan of Reconversion of the Electronic Components Industry was formulated. This industrial subsector, though in its infant stage, was to receive government subsidies, official credits and fiscal privileges. These subsidies amounted to 305.2 million pesetas in 1982.

The UCD governments also maintained the preferential treatment the Franco governments had extended to designated industries. Economic and fiscal benefits granted to industries of preferential interest as defined in 1963 and to concerted action industries as provided for by the First Development Plan were continued. Ten lines of industrial activity were recognized as being preferential interest activities in 1982; among them, the manufacturing of automobiles, the production of electronic equipment and components and zinc mining. Three major automobile producers, Fasa Renault, Ford Española y Seat and Talbot, obtained in 1982, as preferential interest industries, subsidies aggregating 27.5 billion pesetas. The government also extended financial assistance in that year to other industries, particularly the chemical industry.

## Energy policy

The National Energy Plan of 1979 intended to limit the growth of real consumption of energy during the decade 1980 to 1990. One of its main objectives was to reduce the country's dependence on imported crude oil. The government planned to partially replace petroleum as a source of energy by coal, natural gas and nuclear energy. The national supply of coking coal was to be raised through subsidies to the coal mining industry. Government subsidies were to facilitate the growth of the supply of nationally produced hydroelectric and thermoelectric energy.

The government's energy policy targets were attained in 1982. Compared to the level of national petroleum consumption in 1981, that in 1982 declined by 8%. The real consumption of nuclear energy fell by 9.3% (Ibid., 66). The decline in the real consumption level of these two sources of energy was helped by the country's low level of economic activity. On the other hand, the real consumption of coal-based energy rose by 16.6% above its 1981 level; that of hydroelectric power increased by 13%. There was also an increase in the consumption of natural gas in 1982.

In that year, the aggregate gross domestic consumption of primary energy derived from all sources declined by only 0.54% below its 1981 level. The slight fall was made possible by an increase of 9.8% in the output of domestic coal over its 1981 level and by an increase of 2.6% in the national production of electric energy. Spain's industry moved from petroleum to coal for its energy needs. Coal had represented 15.4% of the aggregate supply of domestic energy sources in 1977. In 1982 this percentage had risen to 26% (Ibid., 69). In 1977, the supply of domestically produced energy constituted 28.4% of the aggregate available energy supply in the country; in 1982 this figure had risen to 36.3% (Ibid.). The UCD governments' achievements in the field of energy policy involved the decline in the national real consumption of petroleum and the increased use of domestic coal as a source of energy. The larger use of coal brought also a greater pollution of the environment. Air pollution worsened as over two million tons of sulphur dioxide were released into Spain's sunny skies in 1981.

## Employment policy

The UCD governments followed a regional industrial policy whose main purpose was to create new industrial jobs. The governments' main objective was to contain the growth of industrial unemployment. Firms located in zones designated as 'zones of preferential industrial location' and as 'large areas of industrial expansion' were to receive a subsidy for each new job they created. A Decree-Law 2,993/1982 extended the existence of these preferential zones until the end of 1983. A new 'large area of industrial expansion', that of Castilla-La Mancha, was established in 1982, an area which included the provinces of Albacete, Ciudad Real, Cuenca, Guadalajara and Toledo. The Royal Decree 2,635/1982 continued the existence of the 'Development Pole of Oviedo' until the end of 1983.

Government subsidies were not only granted to industrial firms which created new jobs, but also to firms which refrained from dismissing workers, as well as to small and medium-size firms located in the preferential zones which presented modernization plans to the authorities. The subsidy paid by the government for each newly created industrial job increased from 6.9 million pesetas in 1981 to 9.8 million

Table 57 Fixed investment, job creation and public subsidies in preferential industrial zones: 1981 and 1982

|  | Fixed investment (billion pesetas) | | New jobs | | Subsidies (billion pesetas) | |
| --- | --- | --- | --- | --- | --- | --- |
|  | 1981 | 1982 | 1981 | 1982 | 1981 | 1982 |
| LAIE Galicia | 10.17 | 21.78 | 3,026 | 1,985 | 1.42 | 2.55 |
| LAIE Andalucía | 77.75 | 37.07 | 6,586 | 2,394 | 9.65 | 1.73 |
| LAIE Extremadura | 4.05 | 11.79 | 1,893 | 1,090 | 0.71 | 2.17 |
| LAIE Castilla León | 11.52 | 20.23 | 2,263 | 3,338 | 1.02 | 3.20 |
| Polo Oviedo | 1.87 | 0.38 | 375 | 124 | 0.11 | 0.03 |
| ZPIL Campo Gibraltar | 1.52 | — | 201 | — | 0.14 | — |
| ZPIL Valle del Cinca | 0.57 | 4.88 | 20 | 87 | — | 0.09 |
| ZPIL Islas Canarias | 1.91 | 0.82 | 449 | 160 | 0.36 | 0.13 |
| Total | 116.85 | 94.84 | 16,712 | 9,586 | 13.98 | 10.18 |

Source: Ministerio de Industria y Energía, *Informe Anual sobre la Economía Española, 1982*, Madrid, 1983, p. 74

in 1982. In spite of the increase of this subsidy, the total number of newly created industrial jobs in 1982 amounted to 12,500, a decline from the 16,700 new jobs established in 1981 (Ibid., 74). Table 57 compares fixed investment, new job creation and public subsidies in the various preferential zones of Spain in 1981 and in 1982.

## SPAIN'S INDUSTRIAL STRUCTURE IN THE EARLY 1980s

### Size of firms

During the years of economic crisis in the early 1980s, Spain's industrial structure remained anchored to the traditional prevalence of small and medium-size firms. The excessive weight of small, suboptimal firms in the distribution of industrial firms' sizes explained the country's relative technological backwardness and the weak competitiveness of its exports.

No major merger movement developed which would have established in Spain's secondary sector firms matching the size and the productive efficiency of large Western European enterprises. Only one major merger occurred in Spain in 1982. Fuerzas Eléctricas del Noroeste, S.A., a distributor of electric power in Galicia, was absorbed by Unión Eléctrica, S.A., a producer and distributor of electricity serving Castilla-León, Castilla-La Mancha and Asturias. The merger created a new Unión Eléctrica, S.A. with a capital of 89.5 billion pesetas.

In a study of Julio Segura and his associates for the period 1980 to 1984, Spanish industrial firms were categorized into size groups, size

*Table 58* Percentage distribution of numbers of industrial firms per size group: 1980–4 (number of workers)

| Year | 1–9 | 10–19 | 20–49 | 50–99 | 100–499 | >500 | Total | Index |
|---|---|---|---|---|---|---|---|---|
| 1980 | 77.2 | 10.9 | 8.0 | 1.9 | 1.7 | 0.3 | 187,134 | 100.0 |
| 1981 | 78.6 | 10.1 | 7.4 | 1.9 | 1.7 | 0.3 | 177,904 | 95.1 |
| 1982 | 80.1 | 8.7 | 7.3 | 1.9 | 1.7 | 0.3 | 168,972 | 90.3 |
| 1983 | 80.6 | 9.4 | 6.1 | 1.9 | 1.7 | 0.3 | 169,876 | 90.8 |
| 1984 | 81.2 | 8.6 | 6.4 | 1.8 | 1.7 | 0.3 | 164,546 | 87.9 |

Source: Segura, J. et al., *La industria española en la crisis, 1978–1984*, Madrid, 1989, p. 71

being determined by either the number of workers employed or by the amount of value added produced by these firms. The authors observed the annual percentage changes in the numbers of firms in each size group. Size being determined by numbers of workers employed. The numbers of firms in each size group, as a percentage of the aggregate number of industrial firms, either declined or remained stationary during the five-year period with the exception of the smallest size group, i.e. the group of firms employing between 1 and 9 workers. (Segura, J. *et al.*, 1989, 71). Table 58 shows these trends.

What was typical of Spain's industrial structure was that those industrial subsectors dominated in other countries by large enterprises were, in Spain, represented mainly by small firms. In the case of the Spanish steel industry, firms with less than 9 workers represented over one-third of all firms in the subsector, whereas firms with over 500 workers constituted only 10% of the firms in this group (Ibid., 74).

During the early 1980s, only Spain's smallest firms, i.e. firms employing between 1 and 9 workers, showed an increase in their numbers. The number of firms employing between 10 and 49 workers declined. During the period 1980 to 1984, the percentage of firms employing between 10 and 99 workers in the totality of the country's industrial firms declined.

On the other hand, if size is measured in terms of value added by the firm, such size increased for all groups with the exception of the group of firms employing between 1 and 9 workers. Size in terms of value added increased most strongly for firms employing between 50 and 500 workers. These trends are illustrated by Table 59. The data indicate that labour productivity increased most markedly in the latter group of firms. Conversely, labour productivity declined in small firms employing between 1 and 9 workers. As noticed above, this group of small firms represented 80.1% of all industrial firms in 1982, 81.2% of them in 1984.

The Segura *et al.* study found that industrial firms in Western European countries whose gross industrial product was larger than that

*Table 59* Distribution of firm sizes in terms of their value added: 1980–4
(million 1980 pesetas)

| Year | 1–9 | 10–19 | 20–49 | 50–99 | 100–499 | 500 |
|---|---|---|---|---|---|---|
| 1980 | 2.26 | 15.53 | 38.64 | 99.45 | 348.39 | 2,415.76 |
| 1981 | 2.18 | 15.47 | 39.66 | 102.20 | 359.22 | 2,276.50 |
| 1982 | 2.02 | 17.01 | 41.51 | 107.70 | 367.68 | 2,398.62 |
| 1983 | 2.25 | 16.50 | 43.47 | 107.11 | 360.75 | 2,803.38 |
| 1984 | 2.17 | 15.85 | 42.83 | 118.30 | 399.22 | 2,681.89 |

*Source*: Ibid., p. 77

of Spain were generally larger than their Spanish counterparts. Their sales were also more multinational. This was particularly the case in France, Germany and the United Kingdom. On the other hand, industrial firms in Belgium and in the Netherlands were often smaller than corresponding Spanish firms, with the exception of firms in a number of industrial subsectors such as the manufacturing of electrical machinery, the foodstuffs industry and that of petroleum in the case of the Netherlands, and non-electrical machinery in the case of Belgium. Italian industrial firms were comparable in size to those of Spain (Ibid., 93).

Unlike France, Germany and the United Kingdom, Spain lacked multinational firms. Compared with large industrial firms in Belgium, France, Germany, Italy, the Netherlands and the United Kingdom, the only Spanish industrial subsectors containing larger concerns were the plastics industry and the refining of crude oil. On the other hand, several Spanish industrial subsectors contained firms whose size averaged only half that of corresponding firms in the other Western European nations. Among these were the following industries: chemical products, electrical machinery, mining, non-electrical machinery, pharmaceutical products, precision and scientific instruments and wood and paper products.

Even the largest Spanish industrial firms were in general appreciably smaller than their counterparts in the European Community area. In view of this fact, Segura recommended that the Spanish government's industrial policy should not emphasize the adoption of more efficient methods of production by existing Spanish industrial concerns, but should give priority to the development of a more dynamic Spanish industrial management able to effect an internationalization of their firms' sales (Ibid., 95).

## R & D

Another major aspect of Spain's industry in the early 1980s relates to the efforts of Spanish industrial firms in the development of the technology they used. Such activities cover both managerial attempts to promote technological progress internally as well as the acquisition of new external technology. National technological advance is not produced by managerial efforts alone. Although so-called research and development activities mostly take place in specialized departments and laboratories of private firms in the industrially advanced countries, they are also carried out by profit-making research enterprises, by universities and by public agencies. This group of research organizations is not a country's only source of new technology. Industrial firms and public agencies in all countries also import technology developed abroad.

The national research and development effort can be thought of as a production process whose inputs are constituted by domestic and foreign spending on domestic R & D efforts and whose output can be measured in terms of the numbers of patents registered by the relevant country's residents in that country or in other countries.

The acquisition of external technology can be measured by the cost of importing such foreign technology, including royalties paid to foreign patent holders, expressed either in terms of domestic or foreign currency.

A country's 'technological effort' during a given year expresses the percentage of that country's aggregate industrial value added in that year which is devoted to R & D. The Segura research group found that for the period 1975 to 1984 the Spanish index of technological effort remained much lower than that recorded for the various countries of the EC-9. Table 60 shows that the Spanish technological effort index in 1983 was 0.8%. The corresponding index attained 3.9% in the EC-9 countries in the same year (Ibid., 242). Moreover, R & D spending was much more concentrated in Spain than in other Western European nations. Spanish industrial firms with over 1,000 workers, a small minority of Spanish industrial firms, financed 59.7% of the national R & D effort in 1984 (Ibid., 243). These researchers concluded that even accounting for differentials in productive capacity, Spain's industrial technological effort in the early 1980s was much weaker than in the countries of the EC-9.

When considering imports and exports of technology, only contractural arrangements dealing with traded technology are considered. Foreign trade in capital goods which may incorporate new technology is excluded from consideration in order to avoid double counting in the calculation of external accounts.

The Segura study covers the period 1975 to 1984 and is based on data supplied by the Bank of Spain. Foreign exchange earnings from the country's export of technology were reported as 'Technological Assistance', a meaningful title because Spain exported mostly technological know-how acquired from the industrially advanced countries to

Table 60  R & D activities of Spanish industrial firms: 1975–84

| Year | R & D spending (in million 1980 pesetas) | Index[1] | Technological effort[2] |
|---|---|---|---|
| 1975 | 25,398 | 100.0 | 0.6 |
| 1976 | 23,233 | 91.5 | 0.6 |
| 1977 | — | — | — |
| 1978 | 23,787 | 93.6 | 0.6 |
| 1979 | 24,690 | 97.2 | 0.6 |
| 1980 | 27,997 | 110.2 | 0.7 |
| 1981 | 24,794 | 97.6 | 0.6 |
| 1982 | 32,300 | 127.2 | 0.8 |
| 1983 | 31,357 | 123.5 | 0.8 |
| 1984 | 36,110 | 142.2 | 0.9 |

Source: Segura, J. et al., *La industria española en la crisis 1978–1984*, Madrid, Alianza Editoria, 1989, p. 242
Notes: 1 Index of R & D spending, base year 1975.
2 Percentage of R & D spending in industrial value added

Table 61  Industrial technological coverage ratios: 1975–84

| Year | Technological Assistance coverage ratio | Patents, Designs and Trade marks coverage ratio | Technological coverage ratio |
|---|---|---|---|
| 1975 | 16.7 | 3.4 | 9.7 |
| 1976 | 12.8 | 3.7 | 10.1 |
| 1977 | 10.7 | 5.5 | 9.1 |
| 1978 | 13.3 | 5.4 | 10.9 |
| 1979 | 15.6 | 4.3 | 11.6 |
| 1980 | 14.2 | 6.6 | 12.5 |
| 1981 | 22.8 | 8.0 | 20.6 |
| 1982 | 11.9 | 12.9 | 12.0 |
| 1983 | 12.3 | 7.3 | 11.2 |
| 1984 | 19.8 | 6.0 | 15.8 |

Source: Ibid., p. 256

developing nations. Payments for imports of foreign technology were recorded under the title 'Patents, Designs and Trade Marks'.

During these years, Spain's industry paid on the average 92% of the national payments for the import of technology, while its earnings from the export of technology amounted to only 55.2% of the national total (Ibid., 253). Spain's industrial 'technological coverage ratio' in 1984, i.e. the ratio of national earnings from industrial technological exports to national payments for industrial technological imports, amounted to only 15.8%. It must also be noticed that the largest part of the country's earnings from its 'industrial technological exports' were represented by payments in Spain by foreigners registering patents and trade marks with the Spanish authorities. The very low technological coverage ratio indicates the high dependence of Spanish industry on foreign technology.

Most of the foreign trade in industrial technology was limited to a few industrial subsectors of strong demand. These were constituted by producers of electrical materials, energy, chemicals and transport materials. Table 61 shows the various technological coverage ratios for the years 1975 to 1984.

## The financial structure of firms

An important aspect of Spain's industrial sector in the early 1980s was the financial structure of its firms. Their high degree of indebtedness limited their potential for growth because of the high cost of their investment in fixed capital. The degree of a firm's indebtedness is measured by a 'coefficient of indebtedness' determined by the ratio of the value of resources used but not owned by the firm to that of owned resources. A sectoral coefficient of indebtedness can be calculated by the ratio of the value of sectoral resources used but not owned by the sector to that of resources owned by it. The sectoral coefficient can also be computed by taking the simple average of the coefficients of the component firms.

Table 62 shows that the coefficient of indebtedness of Spanish industrial firms was high. For the secondary sector as a whole, as well as for the country's manufacturing industries, the value of their debt exceeded that of owned resources. Moreover, the coefficient increased in the period 1982 to 1984. The coefficient was largest for public enterprises and for these their debt was more than twice as large as the value of their own resources.

If the industrial firms' indebtedness is disaggregated in terms of its

*Table 62* Coefficients of indebtedness for public and private firms: 1982–4

|  | 1982 | 1983 | 1984 |
|---|---|---|---|
| General industry | 110.9 | 117.3 | 117.7 |
| Public firms | 218.4 | 205.6 | 183.7 |
| Private firms | 87.8 | 98.1 | 103.1 |
| Manufacturing | 109.3 | 111.7 | 107.5 |
| Public firms | 275.2 | 287.0 | 273.5 |
| Private firms | 83.8 | 86.6 | 84.9 |

*Source*: Ibid., p. 221

Table 63  Cost of borrowing for public and private firms: 1982–4

|  | 1982 | 1983 | 1984 |
|---|---|---|---|
| General industry | 15.6 | 14.7 | 15.3 |
| Public firms | 13.5 | 13.4 | 13.8 |
| Private firms | 16.7 | 15.3 | 16.0 |
| Manufacturing | 16.8 | 17.2 | 16.7 |
| Public firms | 14.0 | 15.0 | 14.4 |
| Private firms | 18.2 | 18.2 | 17.8 |

Source: Ibid., p. 230

maturity structure, and if we define short-run maturities as those with a duration of less than one year, medium- and long-run maturities extending over periods longer than a year, it appears that public enterprises were able to rely more than private firms on medium- and long-run debt. This was largely due to the fact that public concerns had better access than private firms to medium- and long-run finance. Because of this privileged financial position, public enterprises were less exposed than private firms to the risks and uncertainties of short-term fluctuations in interest rates. On the other hand, the cost of servicing the firm's debt could be higher for enterprises financed to a large extent by long-run indebtedness. Indeed, *ceteris paribus*, the longer the maturity of a given debt, the greater will be the risk taken by the lender that the borrowing firm may encounter financial difficulties in the future and therefore the higher will be the interest rate charged by the lender.

When the borrower is a public enterprise the risk of financial default appears to be smaller to the lender than in the case of a private firm. This was true of the Spanish case in the early 1980s. The cost of borrowing was between 2.5% and 4% lower for public enterprises than for private firms. This is shown by Table 63.

The Segura group also observed that during these years, and in the case of the fourteen industrial subsectors they studied, there existed an *inverse* relationship between the amount of borrowing and its cost. This is surprising because one would expect that firms face a very elastic supply of borrowable funds whose cost starts rising because of risk after a critical (high) quantity is reached. These researchers found that the cost of borrowing also depended on factors such as the size of the borrowing firm, measured by its labour force, the ease or difficulty of the firm's access to privileged financial markets and the maturity structure of its indebtedness. They found, for instance, that large firms paid a relatively low interest rate though their coefficient of indebtedness was high. The rate of interest paid by firms also varied markedly according to the industrial subsector to which they belonged. The average cost of borrowing per subsector is

Table 64 Cost of borrowing by industrial subsector: average 1982–4 (percentages)

| Sector | Total private and public firms | Private firms only |
|---|---|---|
| Energy | 14.7 | 15.2 |
| Metallic minerals and steel | 14.1 | 14.1 |
| Non-metallic minerals | 19.1 | 19.1 |
| Chemicals | 18.5 | 18.9 |
| Metallic products | 19.4 | 19.4 |
| Machinery | 16.0 | 15.9 |
| Office machines | 15.7 | 20.6 |
| Electrical materials | 15.5 | 15.5 |
| Transport materials | 17.0 | 17.5 |
| Foodstuffs | 20.4 | 21.3 |
| Textiles, apparel, footwear | 22.1 | 21.4 |
| Paper and paper products | 16.9 | 18.4 |
| Rubber and plastics | 17.5 | 17.5 |
| Wood, cork | 23.8 | 23.8 |

Source: Ibid., p. 231

shown in Table 64. In general, the high dependency of Spanish industrial firms on borrowed funds kept the cost of their potential investment projects high and limited their growth and modernization.

## SPAIN AND THE EUROPEAN COMMUNITY: 1975 TO 1982

The imposition of death sentences by a Spanish court on a number of political prisoners in September 1975 brought a sudden end to ongoing negotiations between Spain and the European Community regarding the adoption of a new trade Accord between the two parties. The EC Commission and the governments of the EC-9 countries had requested the Spanish government to commute the death sentences. The execution of the sentenced men on 27 September induced the EC Commission to advise the EC Council to order the stoppage of all negotiations with Spain. The Council decided to suspend the negotiations.

Following the death of General Franco on 20 November King Juan Carlos predicted in his coronation speech that Spain would become an integral part of Western Europe (Alonso, A., 1985, 122). The presence of the President of France and the Chancellor of the German Federal Republic at the coronation ceremony indicated that major Western European governments were willing to give their support to a new democratic Spain. This European hope in Spain's political transformation was evidenced by the EC Council's declaration of 20 January 1976 announcing that the EC-9 were willing to renew negotiations with Spain. In February, Spain's Minister for Foreign Affairs, José María de Areilza, started a round of visits to the capitals of the EC countries and assured their peoples that Spain would embrace democracy. The Spanish government, in turn, informed the EC Commission that it was ready to renew negotiations with the Community in order to adapt the Accord of 1970 between Spain and the EC to the conditions attending Spain's eventual entry into the European Community.

Areilza was particularly interested in maintaining for the time being the commercial relationships Spain had had with the United Kingdom, Ireland and Denmark before these countries joined the EC in 1973. The new Three gave their support to Areilza's wishes. The EC Commission took the position that it would refrain from enforcing Community rules applying to Spain's trade with the new Three until the EC Accord with Spain was revised.

Between 1975 and 1977, the EC appeared to be more interested in developing its Mediterranean Basin economic policy than in concluding a new trade Accord with Spain. The EC signed a new Accord with Malta in December 1975; one month later, it finalized negotiations with the three Mahgreb countries, Algeria, Morocco and Tunis. Accords with the latter countries were signed in April 1976. Negotiations with Egypt, Jordan, Lebanon and Syria followed. The EC intended to enter into similar agreements with all the countries of the Mediterranean Basin, including Greece, Israel, Spain, Turkey and Yugoslavia, but excluding both Albania and Libya, countries which had not shown any interest in entering into trade negotiations with the EC-9. The EC Accords entered into with Israel and with the Mahgreb countries disadvantaged Spanish exports of agricultural products to be the Community area.

Spain protested that her exports of citrus fruits, olive oil and wines were being discriminated against by the EC. An 'exploratory meeting' between the EC and Spain followed on 28 April 1976. The purpose of the meeting was to allow each party to inform the other what commercial policy changes it desired. Spain demanded an end to EC discrimination against her agricultural exports. The EC urged the Spanish delegates to lower Spanish customs duties imposed on Community industrial goods. In its Report of July 1976 the EC Commission advised the EC Council to reduce the EC tariff on Spanish industrial goods by 80% and requested Spain to lower her import duties on the entry of Community industrial products by a maximum of 80% and a minimum of 40% (Ibid., 127). The conditions governing the trade in agricultural products between the EC and Spain were to remain those agreed to by the parties in 1974.

Spain immediately protested the Commission's recommendations. Spanish negotiators argued that Spain was moving rapidly in the direction of political democracy and would therefore soon be able to become a full Community member. They pointed out that the Commission's recommendations ignored this possibility. Indeed, the Suárez government scheduled free general elections for mid-1977. A strong indication that the new Spanish government broke all ties with the Francoist regime was the ending of Alberto Ullastre's tenure as head of Spain's Mission to the European Community in September 1976. The strong support given by the Spanish referendum of 15 December 1976 to democratic political reform convinced the governments of the EC-9 countries that the Community should bolster political change in Spain by admitting Spain to full membership in the EC.

A further development enhanced Spain's chances of becoming a full EC member nation. On 6 January 1977 the Englishman Roy Jenkins became the new President of the EC Commission. Jenkins favoured the extension of the Community to Greece, Portugal and Spain.

Following the Spanish elections of 15 June 1977, and the instauration of the UCD government, Adolfo Suárez decided to request Spain's full membership in the EC without further delay. Such membership was requested on 26 July 1977. The EC Council took notice of it on 20 September and instructed the EC Commission to supply it with a Report analysing the implications of the Spanish request.

This Report was presented to the EC Council on 20 April 1978. The Commission's main concern centred on the fact that the economies of the three applicant nations differed sharply from those of the EC-9 nations. The Greek, Portuguese and Spanish economies were relatively poor and backward and the Commission was apprehensive of the possibility that the admission of the three countries to full membership at a time when economic crisis prevailed within the EC area could jeopardize the Community's efforts to create an economic and monetary union.

In view of this situation, the Commission recommended that the three applicant countries should be granted sufficient time to bring their economic systems closer to those of the EC-9 countries. Following their incorporation into the EC, each one of the three new member countries should be granted varying 'transition periods', whose duration could differ among the various economic sectors of each country and cover between five and ten years.

Regarding Spain, the EC Commission recommended that the country should adopt the Community's tariff system as soon as possible. Spain would have to accept the Community's Common Agricultural Policy, as well as the Community's Commercial Policy, including the preferential trade agreements entered into by the EC with third countries. The Commission advised the EC Council that following the EC's enlargement, the intra-Community trade in 'Mediterranean products' would have to be regulated and restricted in order to avoid serious supply problems in the Community markets for such goods. The free movement of Spanish workers within the EC area would have to be restricted during a transition period.

Following the people's approval of a new Spanish Constitution on 6 December 1978 the EC Council scheduled the beginning of negotiations regarding Spain's entry into the Community for February 1979. The first negotiating session was held in Brussels on 5 February 1979. At that meeting, Leopoldo Calvo Sotelo urged the EC Commission to grant his country a uniform transition period exceeding ten years; he also urged the EC negotiators to take account of Spain's economic problems when preparing new Community policies, particularly when working on a reform of the Common Agricultural Policy. François Poncet, then President of the EC Council, requested in his speech that at the following negotiating session, scheduled to take place during the summer, the parties should try to agree on an overview, a *'vue d'ensemble'*, of the various problems which could affect both the Community and Spain following the latter country's acquisition of full membership in the EC. Poncet probably intended to postpone discussions dealing with the actual terms of Spain's membership.

Six additional meetings between Spanish and EC negotiators took place during the rest of 1979. They did not produce any significant results. At the most, these meetings allowed the two parties to identify problems they deemed important. The EC Commission argued in favour of a short period of transition while the Spaniards demanded a uniform period of at least ten years. The EC requested Spain to introduce the value added tax as soon as possible, and not later than the date of Spain's formal entry into the Community; the Spaniards insisted on an adequate transition period before such tax would replace the existing cascade tax in Spain.

Additional meetings dealing with a *vue d'ensemble* of the relevant problems connected with Spain's entry into the Community were held during the first half of 1980. Their failure to produce any significant advance in the solution of the problem they addressed was largely due to the fact that the EC authorities were focusing their attention on other developments. Their interest centred on two problems: the first involved the large budgetary spending for agricultural purposes; the second related to the large Community transfers to the United Kingdom. France's President, Valéry Giscard d'Estaing, let it be known that there could be no meaningful discussion about the terms of Spain's entry into the EC until the latter had solved its financial problems and had decided how to reform its agricultural policy. A new Community agricultural policy would have to protect the interests of French farmers producing Mediterranean crops.

On 30 May 1980 the EC Council instructed the EC Commission to prepare a Report, the so-called 'May 30 Report', in which the Commission would present and explain three main proposals. These were to deal with the reform of the existing Common Agricultural Policy, the restructuring of the Community's budget and the development of new Community policies.

The Spanish government was quite disenchanted with the lack of progress in its negotiations with the EC. Spaniards started doubting the diplomatic effectiveness of the Suárez government. In order to strengthen its image at home, the government announced that it would pressure NATO to accept Spain's membership in that organization. The government predicted that such membership would not only induce the United Kingdom to surrender Gibraltar to Spain, but that it would also facilitate and hasten Spain's entry into the European Community.

On 8 September 1980 Leopoldo Calvo Sotelo, appointed Vice-President of the Government for Economic Affairs, was replaced as Minister for Relations with the European Community by Eduardo Punset. Roy Jenkins visited Madrid in the first days of October and informed Spaniards that the approval of Spain's membership in the EC was held up by unresolved internal Community problems. He believed that such problems would not be solved until the meeting of the European Council in Dublin in December 1981. Adolfo Suárez had hoped that Spain's formal entry into the EC would take place on 1 January 1983. Jenkins's prediction cast cold water on such hope.

On 25 June 1981 the EC Commission transmitted its 'May 30 Report' to the EC Council. Its recommendations were not limited to budgetary matters and to agricultural policy reform. It proposed a general overhaul of the totality of Community policies. In the words of the new President of the EC Commission, Gaston Thorn, the Community's institutions had to be reshaped in order to allow it to face 'the challenge of the 80s' (Ibid., 149). The EC Commission noted that the Community had left behind an era of rapid industrialization and of strong consumer demand; that it had entered a long period of economic crisis and of rising unemployment.

1981 ended without any action taken by the European Council to implement the recommendations contained in the Commission's 'May 30 Report'. Nothing significant was achieved in the course of negotiations held between Spain and the EC in 1981. The situation did not change in 1982. The responsibility for ending the standstill in the negotiations fell on the PSOE once this party emerged victorious in the late 1982 elections.

The frustration and disappointment of the UCD leadership caused by the lack of a significant breakthrough in Spain's negotiations with the EC can be easily understood. Spain's entry into the EC was of great importance for both Adolfo Suárez and Leopoldo Calvo Sotelo for political and for economic reasons. Politically, such entry would end the misgivings and the ill feeling Western European governments and

Europeans in general had shown for Francoist Spain. After a hiatus of more than forty years, Spain's incorporation into the European Community would re-establish Spain as a true part of Western Europe. Economically, Spain's full membership in the EC would open to Spanish industrialists a wide foreign market and rising Spanish exports would compensate them for diminished sales in the domestic market. The UCD leaders strongly hoped that Spain's entry into the EC would quickly improve entrepreneurial expectations in Spain and reactivate economic activity in the home country.

What was to happen to the trend of Spanish exports in a post-entry period depended, of course, on whether or not their international competitiveness could improve. What had happened to the external competitiveness of Spain's industrial exports since the death of General Franco? Segura and his research group attempted to give an answer to this question in their econometric study (Segura, J. *et al.*, 1989, 353–88).

Initially, the external competitiveness of a country's exports was evaluated on the basis of the Ricardian notion of comparative advantage in production costs and was thus expressed in terms of relative costs and prices alone. More recently, theoreticians attempted to include in the measurement of international competitiveness additional factors such as the quality and design of exported products, factors which did not lend themselves easily to quantitative analysis.

Having developed an 'index of revealed comparative advantage', the Segura group found that the evolution of Spain's industrial competitiveness in the EC area in the period 1978 to 1984 was positive. The researchers obtained the opposite result when they evaluated Spain's external industrial competitiveness in terms of costs and prices alone (Ibid., 377–88).

A question these researchers did not address themselves to was whether Spain's improving external competitive position in the EC area during the years 1978 to 1984 was a result of more effective Spanish entrepreneurial efforts or was simply the fruit of non-Spanish expertise and of foreign capital invested in Spain. Were expanding Spanish exports the consequence of a true Spanish 'industrial revolution' or were they mostly due to foreign technology and to foreign capital?

## THE LAST UCD ATTEMPTS TO RESCUE THE ECONOMY

### 1981

On 21 January 1981 Adolfo Suárez resigned as President of the Government. He was replaced on the following day by Leopoldo Calvo Sotelo. Political uncertainty strengthened in the country, an uncertainty which led to the attempted coup of 23 February. In his inaugural speech, Calvo Sotelo identified two major developments which were impeding economic growth. He pointed to the effects of the recent increase in the price of imported crude oil, particularly to the impact it had on Spain's external balance. He then referred to the adverse consequences of an Agreement entered into in February 1980 between the Spanish employers' association, the CEOE, and the major trade union federation, the UGT. That Interconfederal Agreement limited salary and wage increases in 1981 to between 13% and 16%. Economists soon recognized that the *Acuerdo Marco Interconfederal* had established salary and wage increase limits which were too high to reduce the rate of inflation and the rise in real labour costs (Linde, L.M., 1990, 45). Calvo Sotelo wanted Spain's various interest groups to agree on a new plan for economic and social development.

On 20 March the President of the Government requested a meeting of representatives of all political parties, of the employers' association and of the labour federations so that these groups could initiate the joint formulation of a new economic and social plan. The political opposition, i.e. the PSOE and the PCE, refrained from taking a direct part in the negotiations which took place during April and May. On the other hand, representatives of the labour federations which these latter parties supported, the UGT and the Workers' Commissions, took part in the drafting of the Accord which was signed in June. This *Acuerdo Nacional de Empleo*, ANE, the National Employment Accord, represented the principal contribution of the Calvo Sotelo government to the Spanish economy; it constituted the last UCD effort to bring the Spanish economy out of its long period of stagnation.

The drafters of the Accord recognized that in view of the global recession, of weakening domestic demand, of declining internal capital formation and of rising unemployment, real domestic investment had to be stimulated by means of a reduction in the rate of increase of real labour costs and through larger government spending on unemployment insurance and pensions. The ANE provided three major changes which were to become effective in 1982: first, the rate of salary and wage increases was not to exceed a range between 9% and 11%; second, contributions of firms to the social security system were to be reduced by 1%; and third, new labour legislation was to give employers greater freedom in formulating hiring contracts. The government promised to create 350,000 new jobs between 9 June 1981 and 9 June of the following year. It soon became evident that the authorities would be unable to fulfil such commitment. The ANE also included a provision which was strongly opposed by the CEOE. It allowed the government to subsidize workers' organizations out of the national budget.

The Spanish economy continued to weaken in 1981. The Bank of

Spain reported a fall in capital formation of 5.9%, a decline estimated to have reached 9.2% by the National Institute of Statistics (Ibid., 52). Unemployment in the same year represented 15.4% of Spain's active population and the number of unemployed increased by 368,000. Measured in terms of US dollars, the value of Spanish exports in 1981 was 2.1% smaller than it had been in the previous year. Spain's international reserves diminished by US$1.3 billion. The only encouraging aspect of this economic scenario was a slight decline in the rate of inflation amounting to 0.9%.

Spain's economic picture did not brighten in 1982. Indeed, economic disequilibria intensified. The National Institute of Statistics reported that, in 1982, the number of unemployed persons increased by 246,000. The rate of unemployment reached 17.1%. Industry and construction registered a loss of 161,200 jobs (Banco de Bilbao, 1983, 91).

## 1982

An important aspect of the Spanish economy in 1982 was the spectacular increase in the budgetary deficit which nearly doubled since 1981, rising from 605 billion pesetas in the latter year to 1,132 billion in 1982 (Ibid.). Spain's balance on current account at the end of 1982, payments for the import of crude oil excluded, showed a larger deficit than that of December 1981. The country's foreign debt in December 1982 surpassed its December 1981 figure by US$1.5 billion. The deterioration of Spain's external financial position was evidenced by the country's loss of US$3.8 billion in its international reserves.

In December 1982 the government devalued the peseta by 8%. The rate of exchange of the peseta in terms of the US dollar fell from 96.81 pesetas to the dollar to 125.93 pesetas.

In spite of growing economic disequilibria, Spain's GDP grew by 1.2% in 1982, a rate of growth exceeded only in France and Japan. Unlike Spain, most industrialized countries sacrificed growth in order to reduce their rates of inflation and to re-establish economic equilibria. Spain's permissive economic policies failed to strengthen entrepreneurial expectations and private investment continued to decline.

The new government, coming to power following the national elections of 24 October 1982, had announced that it would take measures to reduce internal economic disequilibria. Trying to please the country's workers and the labour federations, it allowed salary and wage increases of between 9.5% and 12.5% and reduced the maximum number of ordinary weekly hours of labour per worker. Such policy led to an increase of hourly labour costs of more than 14% and threatened to further discourage private investment in 1983.

The GDP's growth of 1.2% in 1982 was largely due to a rise of

*Graph 19* Evolution of the components of Spain's GDP: 1970–88

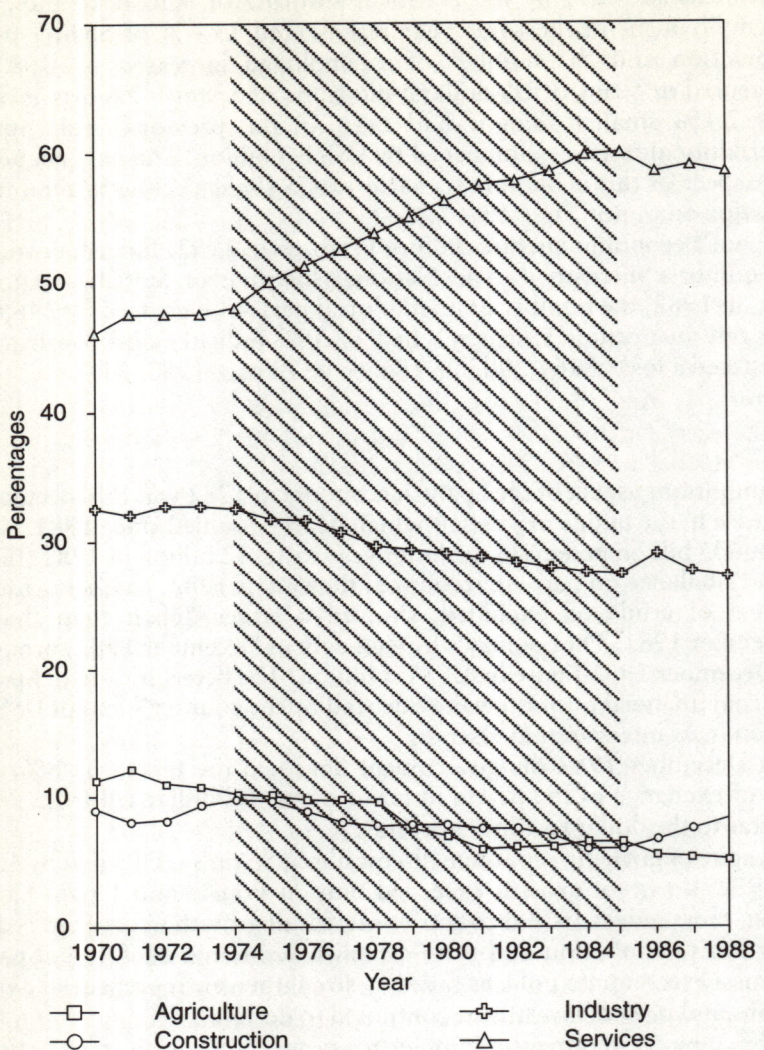

Source: Cuadrado Roura, J.R., 'Cambio estructural, terciarización y remodelación territorial', in García Delgado, J.L., ed., *La Economía Española de la Transición y la Democracia*, Madrid, CIS, 1990, p. 177

agricultural production above its 1981 level and to the expansion of the tertiary sector's activity. Aggregate industrial production stagnated in 1982. The industrial production index calculated by the National Institute of Statistics was 1% below its 1981 figure.

The tertiary sector grew by 1.9% in 1982 on the basis of an expansion of tourism by 5% and the growth of public services by 4% (Ibid., 95). In 1973, the tertiary sector had produced 49.4% of Spain's GDP; this figure rose to 60% in 1982. Spain's economic structure experienced a 'tertiaryzation' in the 1970s and 1980s.

Professor Juan R. Cuadrado Roura observed a salient trend in the evolution of Spain's economic structure since the beginning of the 1960s. The primary sector experienced a continuous decline. The secondary sector expanded in the 1960s, but stagnated and even retrogressed in the latter period of economic crisis. The tertiary sector grew during the three periods extending until 1990 (Cuadrado Roura, J.R., 1990, 174).

As of 1960, the contribution of industry and construction to Spain's GDP was 15% larger than it had been at the start of the twentieth century. During the 1960s, the participation of these sectors in the GDP expanded by 2.1%. The oil crises of the 1970s brought an end to its further growth. The tertiary sector, which during the long span of time elapsing between 1900 and 1960 increased its participation in the GDP by only 6.5%, enlarged its participation by 8.3% in the 1960s.

Following the first oil crisis, Spain's GDP components experienced a significant change. From 1974 on, the industrial sector retrogressed both in terms of output and in terms of employment. The economic crisis slowed down the relative decline of the primary sector, but did not end the continuous fall of its participation in the GDP. In spite of the oil crises, the tertiary sector went on expanding. Graph 19 shows the evolution of Spain's GDP components between 1970 and 1988.

Looking at the evolution of the structure of the GDP in terms of sectoral employment, Professor Cuadrado Roura noticed that between 1974 and 1985 employment in the primary sector fell by 1,172,000 workers and that it also fell in the secondary sector with a loss of 804,000 jobs. On the other hand, employment in the tertiary sector increased by 343,000 workers (Ibid., 176). Employment in the services sector grew largely because of a rapid increase in the numbers of public service jobs during the period of economic crisis.

Between 1974 and 1985, Spain's tertiary sector grew more rapidly than the country's GDP. During this period, industry and construction either stagnated or registered negative rates of growth. The relative economic importance of agriculture steadily diminished. Spanish economic development throughout this period was indeed characterized by a continuing process of tertiaryzation.

## THE FIRST THREE YEARS OF THE PSOE GOVERNMENT: 1983-5

The new Felipe González government came to power at a time of world economic recession when Spain's economy, burdened by high rates of inflation and of unemployment, appeared unable to move away from a state of low income equilibrium. It was not until after the mid-1980s that the government efforts helped the economy to experience a spectacular recovery. During the second half of the decade, rapid economic growth allowed the Spanish standard of living to approach Western European levels.

The transformation of the Spanish economy after 1985 was not based in any way on orthodox socialist prescription. Both Miguel Boyer and Carlos Solchaga, Ministers for the Economy in the 1980s, embraced a programme of deregulation and privatization to strengthen the role of the market in the domestic economic system. A major step in this direction was taken when Spain became a full member of the European Community in 1986.

In 1982, however, the international economic scenario looked quite threatening to the political leaders and entrepreneurs of the western world. The real GDP of the industrialized countries had fallen by 0.3% in that year. The US economy experienced in 1982 a negative rate of economic growth of –1.7%; the West German economy also experienced a negative growth rate of –1.2%. Developing countries started defaulting on their international indebtedness (Rodríguez Braun, C., 1992, 52).

There were however a number of encouraging aspects in this bleak global economic scenario. The price of imported OPEC oil started declining and this trend was maintained until the start of the Gulf War. In many industrialized countries, rates of interest and rates of inflation also began a descending trend.

In Spain, the new PSOE government faced serious economic problems: as noted above, Spain's GDP had increased by only 1.2% in 1982; the Spanish rate of inflation stood at 14.4%; and unemployment covered about 17% of the active population. The most important economic goal the new government tried to achieve was the reduction of the fundamental disequilibria present in the Spanish economic system. These disequilibria touched the external deficit, the budgetary deficit, inflation and unemployment. While the governments of other Western European countries engaged in a major effort to adjust their economies to the global economic crisis, in Spain the PSOE government attempted to pursue an economic adjustment policy and, concurrently, a social policy aiming at a more equitable distribution of income. Conflicts between these two policies soon became apparent. Wage increases and an expansion in current government spending ran counter to the government's efforts to reduce the rate of inflation.

The conflict between public economic and social policies was not new in Spain. During the period 1973 to 1981, Spain's secondary sector experienced a loss of 800,000 jobs and employed in the latter year a labour force which was only 83% of that employed in 1973. And yet, during this same period, real industrial labour costs rose by 37% while industrial profits declined by 41% (Banco de Bilbao, 1984, 101). In order to survive, industrial firms had to raise their productivity and minimize the size of their labour force; the latter practice restricted employment growth.

## 1983

Rising real wages and increases in public spending produced a more equitable distribution of income but brought about a fall in the rate of national saving from 19% of the GDP in 1973 to 6% in 1983. The decline in the rate of national saving produced a decline in the rate of real investment in fixed capital from 24% of the GDP in 1973 to 18% in 1983 (Ibid., 102).

Spain's GDP increased by 2% in 1983, an increase explained by the growth of industrial and agricultural production, by the expansion of the tertiary sector and by a decline in construction activity. Among the industrial subsectors showing strongest growth were those producing energy, automobiles and processed foods. Consumer goods industries recorded a growth rate of 6.1%, intermediate goods industries advanced by only 1.6% and capital industries recorded a fall of 5.1% in their output. The small increase in aggregate industrial output of 0.5% in 1983 was largely stimulated by foreign demand. Spanish exports of goods rose by 7.4% in terms of constant pesetas. Foreign tourism in Spain also expanded in 1983. On the other hand, real construction activity in 1983 declined by 1.5%, as measured by the National Institute of Statistics, and by 2%, as measured by the Bank of Bilbao. Such decline explained that year's fall in fixed capital investment. The tertiary sector expanded by 2% and its participation in the country's GDP rose from 60.1% in 1982 to 60.4% in 1983 (Ibid., 103–5).

The government's efforts to reduce basic disequilibria in the economy achieved success in the fight against inflation and in the improvement of the country's external accounts. The government's attempts to reduce unemployment and to reduce the growth of the budgetary deficit failed. Spain's consumer price index in December 1983 was 12.2% above its level one year earlier. The rate of consumer goods price inflation remained higher than corresponding rates in other countries and areas. The differential was 4.1% in the case of the European countries of the OECD, 6.9% in the case of the whole OECD area and 5.3% in the case of the countries of the EC (Ibid., 109). Spain's high rate of inflation and the devaluation of the peseta in December 1982 caused the Spanish currency to depreciate in terms of the currencies of the industrialized countries. Between the end of 1982 and that of 1983, the external value of the peseta fell by 36.7% in terms of the yen, by 30.5% in terms of the US dollar and by 24% in terms of the German mark. The depreciation of the peseta strengthened Spain's exports of goods and services while it discouraged imports. The fall in the external value of the peseta coincided in time with a decline in the price of imported crude oil. As a result, the country's external current account deficit fell by 60% below its 1982 level and Spanish foreign reserves increased by US$1 billion (Ibid.).

The government of Felipe González was less successful in its efforts to reduce unemployment and to limit the growth of the budgetary deficit. The public deficit expanded in 1983 to reach 5.9% of Spain's GDP in that year. The large size of the deficit had adverse effects on the country's economic growth because it reduced the volume of bank credit extended to the private sector and therefore undermined private investment in fixed capital. In 1983, the public deficit absorbed 75% of net national saving.

The National Institute of Statistics estimated that gross capital formation in 1983 declined by 2.7% below its 1982 level. The Banco de Bilbao study group estimated this figure at 2.4% (Ibid., 106). The demand for domestically produced capital goods fell by 3% while the demand for imported capital goods decreased by 3.5%. The fall in imports of foreign equipment goods indicated that Spain's effort to modernize her industry was being undermined by the existing economic crisis.

The PSOE government was unable to stop the rise in the level of unemployment. The Spanish economy experienced an additional net loss of 103,000 jobs in 1983. Thousands of jobs disappeared in both the primary and the secondary sectors; the tertiary sector of the economy was the only sector showing a net increase in the number of jobs, but this increase was only 4,000. The net loss of 103,000 jobs in 1983 and an increase of 126,000 persons in Spain's active population in that year amounted to an aggregate increase of 229,000 unemployed people. Unemployment now covered 18.07% of the total active population or slightly over 2.4 million people (Ibid., 10).

The most encouraging aspect of Spain's economy in 1983 was its export performance. In terms of constant prices, Spanish exports of goods and services expanded at a rate of 7.7%, while real Spanish imports grew by only 0.6%. These trade trends allowed Spain's current account deficit to fall by US$1.6 billion from its 1982 level.

Felipe González announced at his inaugural address that he intended to pursue a restrictive monetary policy in order to reduce the rate of inflation. The government's target rate of growth of the broadly defined money supply M3 was 13%, though the actual rate of growth was allowed to fluctuate within a band of two percentage points either side of the target rate. As was customary in Spain, monetary aggregates were to be controlled through the regulation of bank reserves. The Bank of Spain could either strengthen the growth of M3 by expanding its loans to the banking system or could restrict it by selling short-term public debt instruments to the banks. The monetary targets of the government were attained with M3 growing at an annual rate of 12.7% in 1983. Domestic credit expanded at the rate of 15%, a rate slightly lower than the targeted 15.5% (OECD, 1984, 20–2).

Fiscal pressure was also increased in order to reduce the rate of domestic inflation. Such pressure, as measured by the ratio of tax revenue to GDP rose by 1.5% in 1983. It was made possible by an increase in the rates of selected indirect taxes, by a change in the schedule of withholdings for personal income tax and by reductions in the exemptions applicable to direct taxes (Ibid., 25).

The first year of the PSOE administration had brought mixed results to the Spanish economy. Domestic demand remained weak largely because gross capital formation continued to fall while public consumption growth decelerated. Spain's rate of unemployment remained one of the highest within the OECD area. Though the rate of inflation declined, Spain's price differential with the rest of the OECD remained high. On the other hand, economic activity strengthened, stimulated by a strong export performance. The country's external position improved. One of Spain's major economic difficulties in 1983 was the continuing decline in gross fixed capital formation. It was due to a fall in business investment caused by low rates of profits, excess capacity, tight credit conditions and uncertain business prospects.

## The Socialist government

There had never been a PSOE government in Spain before the 1982 elections. The Felipe González government which had come to power in December of that year had no previous experience in the formulation of economic policy. Its leadership had however been able to observe the failure of the expansionist economic policies of the French socialist government and learned thereby a valuable lesson. The PSOE government decided to follow an economic strategy in accordance with the most conservative social-democratic ideals.

The PSOE's pre-election message to the Spanish people contained the promise of creating 800,000 jobs, of safeguarding the purchasing power of the workers and of modernizing the economy so that Spain could become a viable part of the European Community. The details of the

PSOE economic programme were contained in a *Medium Term Economic Programme, 1983–1986*, which identified major flaws in the existing Spanish economic system. It pointed to: the excessive rise of real industrial wages; the uncontrolled growth of public social spending; the Bank of Spain's major role in financing the large budgetary deficit; and the dangerous fall in the rate of national saving. It proposed the adoption of an economic policy strategy which was to follow two lines of action. The first aimed at correcting fundamental internal and external economic disequilibria. The second line of action would reform domestic economic institutions so as to facilitate the implementation of economic adjustment processes and improve the functioning of markets. This strategy was referred to as '*saneamiento y reforma*', i.e. sanitation and reform (Segura, J., 1990, 63).

The *saneamiento* policy was to achieve three main goals. The most important was the reduction in the rate of inflation differential with the EC economies. Such reduction had to be achieved by means of a restrictive monetary policy. Public deficits would have to be financed through the sale of government securities instead of through Bank of Spain loans. In addition, the pace of salary and wage increases had to be restricted. Second, Spain's external deficit had to be reduced by means of a devaluation of the peseta and through an increase in the competitiveness of Spanish exports. Finally, the growth of the budget deficit had to be curbed in order to strengthen saving and investment.

The Programme's reform policy advocated industrial restructuring, a more efficient use of energy sources, the liberalization of labour legislation and the reform of public enterprises and of the social security system (Ibid., 64).

## 1984

The González government continued its *saneamiento* policy in 1984. Its major achievement in that year was the transformation of a balance of payments deficit into a surplus. The rate of inflation declined, but unemployment and public spending went on increasing. The government's efforts to encourage the restructuring of industrial subsectors in economic difficulty was a major factor explaining the increase in the budgetary deficit.

The government's attempts to approximate the domestic economy to existing worldwide conditions were helped by two exogenous developments. The recovery of the US economy strengthened the growth of world trade and Spain took advantage of this trend to expand her trade share in international markets. Spain's exports of merchandise, measured in real terms, increased by 18.8% in 1984, a rate of growth which was more than twice the rate of world trade growth in the same year. The

Table 65  Spain's external accounts: 1983 and 1984 (million US dollars)

|  | 1983 | 1984 | Change |
|---|---|---|---|
| Imports | 28,254.8 | 27,873.2 | −381.6 |
| Crude oil | 9,021.0 | 8,709.4 | −311.6 |
| Other | 19,233.8 | 19,163.8 | −70.0 |
| Exports | 20,867.9 | 24,855.1 | 3,987.2 |
| Balance of trade | −7,386.9 | −3,018.1 | 4,368.8 |
| Services, incomes | 3,733.6 | 4,119.2 | 385.6 |
| Services | 6,082.3 | 6,562.0 | 479.3 |
| Incomes | −2,349.1 | −2,442.8 | −93.7 |
| Transfers | 1,170.6 | 871.5 | −299.1 |
| Current balance | −2,482.7 | 1,972.6 | 4,455.3 |
| Capital balance | 2,181.3 | 2,587.4 | 406.1 |
| Balance of payments | −301.4 | 4,560.0 | 4,861.4 |

Source: Banco de Bilbao, *Informe Económico 1984*, Bilbao, 1985, p. 103

climate also helped the country expand its agricultural output. The participation of the primary sector in the GDP increased by 0.5%. Imports of crude oil and of coal declined in 1984 in response to an increase in the domestic supply of hydroelectric energy. These trends allowed the real GDP to rise at a rate of 2.2% even though internal demand recorded a decline of 0.5% (Banco de Bilbao, 1985, 96).

Except for construction, all the economic sectors contributed to the growth of GDP. A favourable climate expanded the output of the primary sector by 7.2%. Stimulated by growing foreign demand, industrial output recorded a rate of increase of 2.8%. The domestic production of primary energy rose by 8%.

Measured in real terms, Spanish imports of goods and services rose by only 0.7% in 1984. It was Spain's export sector which allowed the country's GDP to register a positive rate of growth in 1984. The remarkable growth of Spain's exports of goods and services in that year allowed the country's external current balance to record a surplus of US$1.9 billion at the end of 1984, a significant change from the US$2.5 billion deficit accumulated one year earlier. As shown by Table 65, Spain's capital balance recorded a surplus of US$2.5 billion, a gain of US$4.5 million over the 1983 surplus. The total balance of payments showed a surplus of US$4.5 billion.

The government's adjustment policies caused private consumption spending and private capital investment to fall in 1984. Real household consumption spending declined by 3%, largely in response to the deceleration in the pace of increase of salaries and wages. Public consumption spending rose by 3% but gross capital formation declined by 2.3%. Productive investment, excluding public and construction

GROWTH AND CRISIS IN THE SPANISH ECONOMY

Table 66 Key Spanish macroeconomic variables: 1982–4

| Variable | 1982 | 1983 | 1984 |
|---|---|---|---|
| **Inflation and costs** | | | |
| Consumer goods prices (per cent) | 14.0 | 12.2 | 9.0 |
| Differential with the EC (per cent) | 5.5 | 5.3 | 3.6 |
| Per unit labour costs (per cent) | 11.7 | 10.1 | 6.2 |
| Gross enterprise profits (percentage of GDP) | 40.5 | 41.4 | 43.7 |
| **Public sector** | | | |
| Budgetary deficit (percentage of GDP) | 5.3 | 5.8 | 5.7 |
| Tax pressure (percentage of GDP) | 26.5 | 28.3 | 28.6 |
| **External accounts** | | | |
| Balance on current account (million US$) | –4,124 | –2,483 | 1,973 |
| Foreign reserves (million US$) | 11,530 | 11,228 | 15,788 |
| Foreign debt (million US$) | 28,772 | 29,462 | 30,000 |
| **Employment** | | | |
| Employment level change (per cent) | –0.74 | –0.92 | –1.83 |
| Unemployment rate (percentage of active population) | 16.54 | 18.07 | 20.85 |

Source: Ibid., p. 105

investment, fell by about 2% in 1984. Construction activity in 1984 recorded a fall of 4.5%. Spain's investment to GDP ratio fell from 17.8% in 1983 to 16.9% in 1984. The decline in productive investment remained a major weakness of the Spanish economy (Ibid., 100).

The PSOE government achieved two of its major policy targets in 1984. Externally, the balance of payments recorded a surplus and internally, the rate of inflation was reduced. On the other hand, an expanding budget deficit and rising unemployment remained unsolved difficulties.

The rate of increase of consumer prices declined from 12.2% in 1983 to 9.0% in 1984. At the end of 1984, Spanish consumer goods prices were still 67% higher than similar prices in the EC. Spain's industrial prices rose by 8.7% in 1984, compared with a rate of 14.3% in 1983.

Agricultural prices declined by 2.5% in 1984.

The pace of growth of per unit labour costs also decelerated in 1984; this trend, combined with a strong rise in productivity largely due to the fall in the numbers of employed workers, allowed the share of enterprise profits in the GDP to expand by 2.3% (Ibid., 106).

The level of employment fell by 103,000 persons in 1983. It fell by an additional 207,000 people in 1984. By the end of the latter year, Spain's unemployment rate amounted to 20.85% of the country's active population. Table 66 presents the values of key macroeconomic variables and summarizes the outcomes of the adjustment policies of the PSOE government in the course of its two first years in power.

An objective evaluation of the achievements of the González administration in 1983 and 1984 must point out the success of its economic policy in the external accounts trends, in the reduction of the rate of domestic inflation and in the expansion of the share of entrepreneurial profits in the GDP. Spanish industry became less dependent on imports of energy and a noticeable restructuring was carried out in a few industrial subsectors such as shipbuilding and steel production. The bulk of Spanish industry had yet to be modernized. A serious problem faced by the government was that the process of industrial modernization required an expanding public deficit. The promised reforms of public enterprises could have the same consequence. Concurrently, employment and private productive investment deteriorated. At the end of 1984, the Spanish economy was still in a state of serious economic crisis.

## 1985

The government's national adjustment policy was continued in 1985. As in 1984, this policy succeeded in reducing the rate of domestic inflation and in maintaining the external equilibrium. Employment conditions improved during the last quarter of the year, but the ratio of the budgetary deficit to the GDP continued to increase.

A major success of the government's market-oriented policy was an increase in private productive investment in 1985. Such increase was mostly used to renovate and modernize existing plant and industrial equipment and resulted in advances in productivity and a stronger international competitiveness of Spanish exports. Though the rate of consumer price inflation was reduced to 8.1%, the inflation rate differential with the EC declined by only half a percentage point.

The rise in the level of real investment was the result of an increase in the rate of enterprise profits which allowed gross national saving to rise from 17.1% of the gross disposable national income in 1983 to 19.3% in 1984 and to 20.1% in 1985 (Banco de Bilbao, 1986, 98). This trend allowed real investment to attain a rate of growth of 6% in 1985, rising from 17.7% of the GDP in 1984 to 18.2% in 1985. As noticed, this increase in investment served to renovate and modernize existing industrial facilities and did not develop any new lines of industrial production. Though beneficial to the rise of productivity, the expansion in productive investment did little to raise the employment level.

As in 1984, the growing budgetary deficit remained Spain's major economic problem. This growth occurred in spite of an increase in the tax pressure which reached 30.1% of the GDP in 1985. The fact that this deficit was mostly used for redistributive purposes and played a minor role in the formation of fixed capital explains why the Spanish economy had great difficulty recovering from its long crisis. The growing deficit had an inflationary effect on prices, it tended to reduce bank credit to the private sector, increased rates of interest and slowed down the pace of economic growth. The public deficit rose by 11.2% in 1985 above its 1984 level.

The government was more successful in controlling the growth of the money supply M3. The monetary authorities had targeted an 11% rate of growth for 1985. For the year as a whole, the average daily rate of M3 growth was 7.1%. The volume of bank credit to the private sector increased at a rate of only 9.6%, but credit to the public sector increased by 25.7% and absorbed 65.3% of aggregate credits (Ibid., 113).

Spain's GDP increased by 2.1% in 1985. Unlike the situation in 1984 when the increase in the GDP was mostly due to a stronger external demand, in 1985 it was the rise of internal demand which accounted for practically the entire increase in GDP. All of the components of domestic demand contributed to the increase in GDP in 1985. An increase of 10.2% in private consumption spending was made possible by an increase of 10.7% in gross disposable household income, an increase which exceeded the rise of 8.8% in consumer goods prices. Household saving rose by 15.4% as non-wage incomes rose faster than salaries and wages. A noticeable change from past trends was an increase in the gross formation of capital and, particularly, an expansion of investment in fixed capital. Gross capital formation increased by 6% in real terms. The year 1985 was the first since 1974 in which investment in fixed capital exceeded a 5% rate of growth. The construction component of such investment grew by only 0.5%. On the other hand, investment in industrial equipment and transport goods expanded by 15% (Ibid., 106).

While in 1984 it was Spain's export sector which had to be credited with maintaining a positive rate of growth of the GDP, with internal demand contributing negatively to such growth, the situation was reversed one year later. In 1985, the increase in Spain's balance of trade deficit meant that the country's foreign trade sector had a negative impact on the growth of the GDP. In addition, the capital balance recorded a deficit of US$4.4 billion. This deficit resulted from a sharp decline in Spanish borrowing abroad. Spain maintained however an aggregate external surplus in 1985 because the services balance recorded a surplus of US$6.2 billion (Ibid., 108).

Though Spain's rate of unemployment in 1985 reached 22.1% of the active population, there occurred a slight increase in the level of employment during the last quarter of the year. At the end of 1985, Spain's economy still faced serious unemployment and the problem of a rising public deficit.

*Summary of the government's economic achievements, 1983–5*

Looking at the three-year period 1983 to 1985, it appears evident that the PSOE administration introduced in Spain the strongest and most sustained effort to restore basic equilibria in the economy any Spanish government had made since the beginning of the economic crisis in the 1970s. The government of Felipe González succeeded in reducing the rate of inflation by maintaining throughout the period a restrictive monetary policy and by restraining the rate of growth of salaries and wages. This achievement had a negative aspect. A restrictive monetary policy coupled with a continuously rising public deficit made for rising interest rates which restricted the pace of economic recovery. The recuperation of the world economy helped the Spanish government to restore equilibrium to its external accounts. At the end of this three-year period, productive investment started growing, a trend facilitated by a rising national saving ratio and by improving entrepreneurial expectations. Two additional factors contributed to the improvement of the Spanish investment climate. In 1985 the government allowed firms to take an instantaneous full depreciation for capital equipment purchased in either 1985 or 1986. The treaty providing for Spain's full membership in the EC was signed in mid-1985.

By the end of 1985, there were indications that the Spanish economy was finally recovering from a crisis that had lasted for eleven years. In spite of a rising rate of unemployment, the end of 1985 witnessed an expansion of employment in the country's tertiary sector. The expansion of the public sector created 114,000 new jobs. Even though the two other sectors experienced a major loss of jobs in 1985, at the end of that year, Spain's employment recorded a net gain of 45,000 new jobs (Segura, J., 1990, 67).

The government's attempt to correct or reduce the existing major macroeconomic disequilibria required, besides the adjustment policies noted above, the adoption of structural and institutional reforms with beneficial long-run effects.

The PSOE government did not hesitate to finance a restructuring programme for industrial subsectors which had been severely hurt by the economic crisis. Among these subsectors were steel production and shipbuilding. Although the government generously financed the early retirement of workers in those subsectors, a managerial belief that national economic recovery was imminent induced most firms to retain their existing labour force and to continue operations in spite of mounting losses. The recently legalized trade union federations also opposed any form of labour force reduction. The government faced difficult choices. Though it was highly interested in industrial modernization, it tried to avoid workers' opposition to its industrial policy. As a result industrial restructuring was slow and costly.

During the period 1983 to 1985 the government attempted to reduce the public sector's absorption of private firms in financial difficulty. In 1983, 70% of the deficit of the National Institute of Industry represented the cost of acquisition of private firms which had been socialized by the UCD governments between 1977 and 1982 (Ibid., 68). The government also attempted to improve the organization of public enterprises.

Curiously, the 'socialist' government favoured a policy of industrial privatization. Leading government officials appeared to share the belief that public enterprises were generally poorly managed. Hence, the government's efforts to rescue from financial disaster, private firms, mainly a large number of private banks, without nationalizing them.

The government's energy policy tried to achieve a number of goals. Among these, a reduction in energy use, a greater diversification of its sources and a solution to the problem of excess capacity in the electric power industry. Very little advance was made regarding the attainment of the first two goals. Fortunately for Spain's economy, the price of imported crude oil declined and its consumption was stabilized by slow industrial growth.

The government's labour reform programme was more successful. At the end of 1984, the government, the employers' association and the trade unions signed an Economic and Social Accord, the AES, whose provisions were to become effective in 1985 and 1986. Besides limiting the rate of growth of salaries and wages in those years, the agreement provided for greater flexibility in hiring arrangements. The Accord allowed hiring contracts of limited duration and permitted employers to hire workers on a part-time basis. It also established a minimum wage for workers under the age of eighteen. The Accord failed to reduce the high dismissal costs established by the Franco regime. In order to obtain the employers' and workers' support of the Accord, the government extended generous tax advantages to the employers and additional social benefits to the workers. Retirement benefits paid by the social security system were raised and unemployment insurance pay was increased to 48% of the daily wage or salary. The government's concessions were one more factor contributing to the expansion of the budgetary deficit. On the other hand, the AES restrained the pace of wage growth and facilitated an increase in the rate of entrepreneurial profit. The adjustment and reform policies of the PSOE government commanded a high cost, a cost which was however accepted by Spain's electorate when it maintained the 'socialist' government in power in 1986.

## REFERENCES

Badosa Pagés, J. 'La evolución de la competividad de la exportación', in *Información Comercial Española*, Nr. 544, Madrid, Dec. 1978, pp. 72–80.
Banco de Bilbao, *Informe Económico*, Bilbao, (various issues).
Cuadrado Roura, J.R., 'Cambio estructural, terciarización y remodelación territorial', in García Delgado, J.L., ed., *La Economía Española de la Transición y la Democracia*, Madrid, CIS, 1990.
Garayalde, I., 'El desempleo como mecanismo de la salida de la crisis', in *Información Comercial Española*, Nr. 558, Madrid, Feb. 1980, pp. 52–62.
García de Blas, A., 'Consideraciones sobre los orígenes del paro en España', in *Información Comercial Española*, Nr. 553, Madrid, Sep. 1979, pp. 7–13.
García Delgado, J.L., ed., *La Economía Española de la Transición y la Democracia*, Madrid, CIS, 1990.
Lieberman, S., *The Economic and Political Roots of the New Protectionism*, Totowa, New Jersey, Rowman and Littlefield, 1988.
Linde, L.M., 'La profundización de la crisis económica, 1979–1982', in García Delgado, J.L., ed., *La Economía Española de la Transición y la Democracia*, supra, pp. 35–57.
Ministerio de Industria y Energía, *La Industria Española*, Madrid, (various issues).
———, *Informe Anual sobre la Industria Española, 1982*, Madrid, 1983.
Myro Sánchez, R., 'La industria: expansión, crisis y reconversión', in García Delgado, J.L., ed., *España, Economía*, Madrid, Espasa Calpe, 1988, pp. 197–230.
———, 'La evolución de las principales magnitudes: una presentación de conjunto', in García Delgado, J.L., ed., *La Economía Española de la Transición y la Democracia*, supra, pp. 527–58.
OECD, *Economic Surveys, Spain*, Paris, (various issues).
Raymond, J.L., 'Expectativas Inflacionistas e Inflación en España', *Papeles de Economía Española*, Nr. 1, Madrid, 1978, pp. 51–6.
Segura, J., 'Del primer gobierno socialista a la integración en la CEE: 1983–85', in García Delgado, J.L., ed., *La Economía Española de la Transición y la Democracia*, supra, pp. 59–77.
Segura, J. et al., *La Industria Española en la Crisis, 1978–1984*, Madrid, Alianza Editorial, 1989.
Share, D., *The Making of Spanish Democracy*, New York, Praeger, 1986.
Tusell, J. and Sinova, J., eds, *La Década Socialista – El Ocaso de Felipe González*, 2nd edn, Madrid, Espasa Calpe, 1992.

# 5

# ECONOMIC RECOVERY DURING THE SECOND HALF OF THE 1980s

## STRUCTURAL EVOLUTION OF THE SPANISH ECONOMY: 1970–85

The harsh impact of the prolonged crisis which started weakening the Spanish economy in the early 1970s could be observed in the fall of the domestic rate of economic growth, in the decline of internal demand, in the diminished industrial production, in the rise of production costs and in the deterioration of entrepreneurial profits and expectations. Table 67 illustrates the diminishing contribution of the secondary sector to the GDP between 1970 and 1985. The fact that during that period industry's participation in the GDP diminished by 6.5 percentage points does not indicate that the Spanish economy experienced a process of de-industrialization during those years; the decline of industry's relative importance in the GDP is explained by the rising participation in the formation of the GDP by the tertiary sector.

An observation of the main indicators of the evolution of Spain's industrial sector reveals that the value of key variables for that sector began a significant decline as of 1978. The rates of growth of industrial value added started falling after that year, reaching negative rates as of 1983. This latter trend evidenced the particular impact of the crisis on Spain's industrial activity.

The crisis also strongly affected the evolution of domestic demand,

*Table 67* Composition of Spain's GDP: sectoral percentages: 1970–85

| Year | Agriculture | Industry | Services |
|---|---|---|---|
| 1970 | 10.7 | 42.0 | 47.3 |
| 1977 | 8.7 | 39.8 | 51.5 |
| 1985 | 6.0 | 35.5 | 58.5 |

Source: Vázquez, J.A., 'Crisis, cambio y recuperación industrial', in García Delgado, J.L., ed., *La Economía Española de la Transición y la Democracia*, Madrid, CIS, 1990, p. 84

Table 68 Evolution of key variables in Spain's industrial sector: 1970–85

| Variable | 1970 | 1975 | 1980 | 1983 | 1985 |
|---|---|---|---|---|---|
| **Consumption** | | | | | |
| Billion 1980 pesetas | 7.5 | 10.1 | 11.4 | 10.5 | 10.7 |
| Annual rate of change | | 6.1 | 2.4 | –2.7 | 0.9 |
| **Production** | | | | | |
| Billion 1980 pesetas | 7.3 | 9.8 | 11.5 | 10.8 | 11.1 |
| Annual rate of change | | 6.1 | 3.3 | –2.0 | 1.5 |
| **Gross Value Added** | | | | | |
| Billion 1980 pesetas | 2.1 | 3.1 | 3.8 | 3.6 | 3.4 |
| Annual rate of change | | 8.5 | 3.9 | –1.6 | –5.1 |
| **Imports** | | | | | |
| Billion 1980 pesetas | 0.7 | 1.1 | 1.2 | 1.4 | 1.5 |
| Annual rate of change | | 9.4 | 1.2 | 3.4 | 5.6 |
| **Exports** | | | | | |
| Billion 1980 pesetas | 0.5 | 0.8 | 1.3 | 1.7 | 2.0 |
| Annual rate of change | | 9.6 | 9.9 | 8.1 | 8.4 |
| External trade balance (billion 1980 pesetas) | –0.2 | –0.3 | 0.1 | 0.3 | 0.5 |
| **Employment total** (1,000 persons) | 3,638 | 3,583 | 3,069 | 2,743 | 2,590 |
| Annual change (1,000 persons) | | –75 | –514 | –326 | –153 |
| Index | 100.0 | 98.5 | 84.4 | 75.4 | 71.2 |
| **Prices** | | | | | |
| Index 1980 = 100 | 29.3 | 49.4 | 100.0 | 149.3 | 181.1 |
| Real labour costs per unit of production | | | 0.60 | 0.54 | 0.53 |

Source: Ibid., p. 86
Note: 1 billion = 1,000 million

employment, prices and investment. Internal demand recorded a negative rate of growth of –2.7% between 1980 and 1983. In those years, the domestic economy avoided a major deterioration by the strengthening of foreign demand for Spanish exports. Employment started declining from 1976, the rate of fall intensifying during the early 1980s. During the decade 1973 to 1983, the industrial sector lost about one million workers which represented about 30% of the industrial labour force in 1974 (Vázquez, J.A., 1990, 88). In addition to the reduction of the industrial labour force during the years of crisis, the average duration of the industrial work day also declined. See Table 68 for the evolution of key variables.

During this long period of economic crisis, rising production costs had a negative impact on the evolution of the domestic industrial output. These costs were raised by the continuous rise in the prices of industrial raw materials and of intermediate industrial inputs, as well as by rising employers' contributions to the social security system and by rising nominal wages. Until 1981, real costs of industrial production increased faster than industrial productivity. The shortening of the work day made for even more rapidly rising costs per work-hour. Industrial prices rose rapidly until 1977, their rate of increase decelerating after that year, particularly during the early 1980s.

Productive investment, particularly industrial investment, fell during the decade of economic crisis, an unavoidable consequence of economic deterioration and of worsening investors' expectations. Internal investment was not only adversely affected by the weakening economy, but also by the political and social uncertainties which developed during the long period of crisis. Given these various trends in the economy, the participation of gross industrial profits in the secondary sector's value added diminished; as a result, firm-generated new investment fell and the indebtedness of industrial enterprises grew.

Compared to other OECD countries, Spain recorded, particularly in the early 1980s, a relatively low rate of growth of Gross Value Added and a stronger decline of the level of employment.

Graph 20 shows the evolution of Spain's industrial production from 1971 to 1984. Graph 21 traces the evolution of the country's industrial investment between 1979 and 1984.

Spain's economic crisis of 1974 to 1985, though it affected the whole economy, hurt particularly the country's industrial sector. As shown by Graph 20 below, it was the manufacturing industry which suffered most from the crisis. Energy production fared much better with intermittent subperiods of rapid growth.

Until 1978, the Spanish governments reacted to the economic crisis by following permissive and compensatory policies intended to minimize the fall in domestic demand. However, these policies strengthened the pace of inflation, stimulated the rise in production costs and contributed to the worsening of the country's external disequilibrium. In 1978, the crisis deepened as the rate of fall of demand, investment and domestic

*Graph 20* Evolution of real industrial output: 1971–84

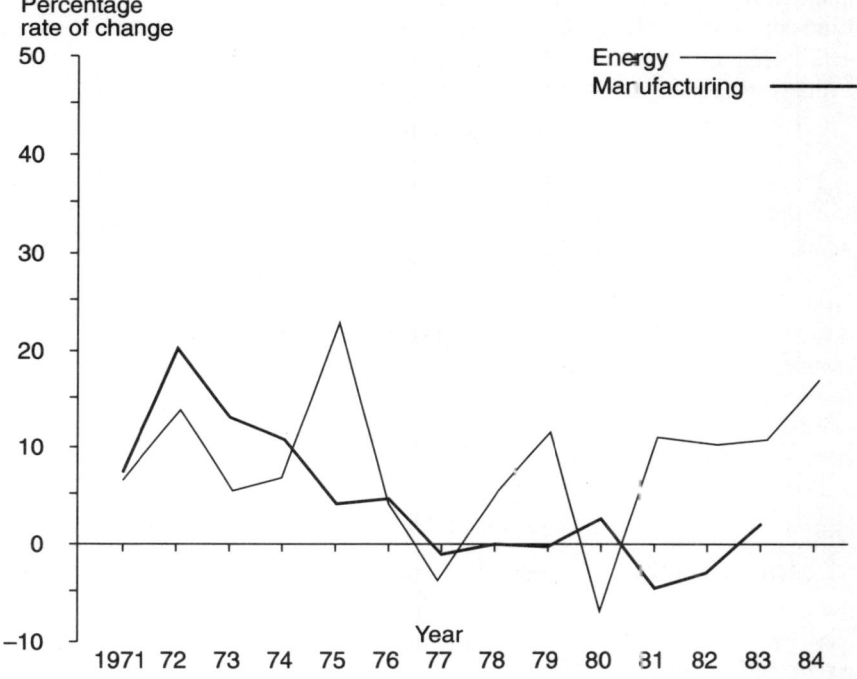

Source: Segura, J. et al., *La industria española en la crisis, 1978–1984*, Madrid, Alianza Editorial, 1989, p. 16

production increased. Though many Spanish businessmen had exclusively operated within the domestic market until then, they felt compelled to sell abroad in order to avoid a complete collapse of their activities. This new attempt to export was hindered by a number of difficulties. Industrial firms faced rising labour costs, in part because of the rigidities of surviving Francoist labour legislation. Old labour laws impeded the dismissal of redundant workers and many industrial firms had to operate with an excessively large labour force. Firms tried to lighten their labour cost burden by reducing the daily or weekly number of hours worked by their employees. They could not escape however the aggressive wage demands of the recently legalized independent trade unions. Most firms tried to finance their rising costs of production by raising their indebtedness at a time of increasing rates of interest. Such practice weakened their financial structure and reduced their rates of profit.

*Graph 21* Evolution of investment in Spain's secondary sector: 1978–84

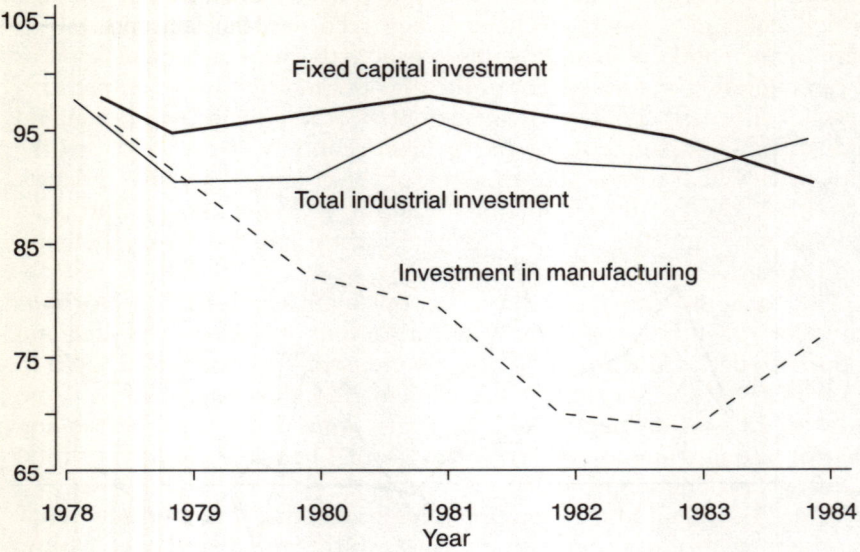

Source: Ibid., p. 201

Compared to the situation in other European OECD countries, the crisis started relatively late in Spain. It also ended much later than in other nations. As the economic crisis intensified in Spain during the early 1980s, the government was compelled to adopt measures to effectively reduce the growing basic disequilibria in the domestic economy. A greater effort was made to modernize the country's production apparatus. As noticed above, the government succeeded in moderating the rise in the per unit of output labour costs of firms by entering into agreements with both employers and trade unions which provided for a slowdown in wage increases. As a *quid pro quo*, conditions of workers' dismissals were eased and the government financed early retirement programmes. With a decelerating rate of increase of labour costs and the adoption of improved, labour-saving technology, productivity increased. Entrepreneurial rates of profit started rising in 1983. By the mid-1980s, entrepreneurial expectations appeared to be improving as firms were able to reduce their indebtedness and to improve their organizational structures. As of 1985, investment showed signs of recovery.

As indicated by Graphs 20 and 21, most of Spain's manufacturing activities were seriously hurt by the economic crisis. Between 1978 and 1984, the rates of growth of their real value added were generally negative. Industrial subsectors such as the production of machinery, of textiles, of transport materials, of steel and of wood and cork products experienced economic deterioration. These were industrial activities for which demand strongly declined. They recorded the sharpest fall in employment and the smallest gains in productivity. Measured in terms of their stagnating technology, or of their lack of international competitiveness or of their poor growth potential, these were weak-demand industries. Unfortunately for the Spanish economy, these were also the industries which represented the bulk of the country's secondary sector activities. Unlike the competing economies of the major European Community countries, Spain's secondary sector had few strong-demand industries.

The economic impact of the crisis on Spain's industrial sector was however not entirely negative. While the output of Spain's weak-demand industries declined from 40% of total industrial production in 1970 to 33% in 1985, the output of medium-demand industries expanded from 40% to 53% of the aggregate industrial output in the same period and that of strong-demand industries rose from 11 to 14% of Spain's total industrial production (Ibid., 95).

Professor Rafael Myro has observed the changing foreign trade trends for the three groups of Spanish industries during the period of economic crisis (Myro, R., 1988, 197–230). As domestic demand weakened during the years 1976 to 1980, total Spanish exports expanded, though their annual average rate of growth was not much higher than it had been during the first half of the 1970s. During the second half of that decade, the growth of aggregate Spanish exports was held back by a decline in the annual rate of growth of the weak-demand industries' exports. As shown by Table 69, the poor export performance of this group of industries was explained by various developments. These industries exported mostly to non-EC countries against whose currencies the peseta appreciated in the period 1976 to 1980. These were also the Spanish industries which experienced the highest rise in labour costs in this period and which faced the strongest NIC competition in foreign markets. The other two industrial groups directed most of their exports to EC countries whose currencies appreciated in terms of the peseta. Spain's weak-demand industries were unable to increase their penetration of the EC market. The declining share of the exports of weak-demand industries in total Spanish exports to the EC is shown in Table 70.

Spain's pattern of foreign trade changed during the years 1981 to 1983. The average annual rate of growth of total exports declined though domestic demand was falling. On the other hand, the annual rate of

Table 69 Trends in Spain's industrial foreign trade: 1971–85
(average annual percentage rate of change, constant 1980 pesetas)

|  | 1971–5 | 1976–80 | 1981–3 | 1984–5 |
|---|---|---|---|---|
| Exports |  |  |  |  |
| Sectors |  |  |  |  |
| Strong-demand | 12.8 | 15.2 | 9.5 | 18.2 |
| Medium-demand | 5.7 | 10.7 | 6.3 | 7.3 |
| Weak-demand | 13.6 | 7.3 | 9.6 | 5.5 |
| Total | 9.6 | 9.9 | 8.1 | 8.4 |
| Imports |  |  |  |  |
| Sectors |  |  |  |  |
| Strong-demand | 11.5 | 5.1 | 6.3 | 8.3 |
| Medium-demand | 8.4 | –2.6 | 9.7 | 1.2 |
| Weak-demand | 8.8 | 2.3 | –11.2 | 10.0 |

Source: Myro, R., 'La industria: expansión, crisis y reconversión', in García Delgado, J.L., ed., España, Economía, Madrid, Espasa Calpe, 1988, p. 212

Table 70 Spain's industrial trade with the European Community: 1975–85
(percentages of Spain's total foreign trade)

|  | Exports | | Imports | |
|---|---|---|---|---|
|  | Weak-demand industries | Total industries | Weak-demand industries | Total industries |
| 1975 | 40.0 | 39.3 | 63.5 | 62.7 |
| 1978 | 40.5 | 49.9 | 61.6 | 64.2 |
| 1980 | 42.4 | 52.8 | 64.6 | 62.0 |
| 1983 | 36.0 | 50.7 | 62.4 | 61.3 |
| 1985 | 36.3 | 57.7 | 65.5 | 64.5 |

Source: Ibid., p. 213

growth of Spanish imports rose as the country's import duties were reduced and as the peseta appreciated in terms of EC currencies. This appreciation of the Spanish currency weakened Spanish exports to the EC, particularly those of the strong- and medium-demand industries. Weak-demand industries, exporting mainly to non-EC countries, benefited from a depreciation of the peseta in terms of non-EC currencies and from the fact that their products received stronger protection in the home market than those of the other two industrial groups.

Spain's trade balance for both strong- and medium-demand industries deteriorated in the period 1981 to 1983. These industries reacted to this situation by trying to reduce their production costs; they made a serious effort

*Table 71* Spain's industrial production: 1976–86 (average annual rate of change in 1980 pesetas)

| Sectors | 1976–80 | 1981–3 | 1984–5 | 1986 |
|---|---|---|---|---|
| Strong-demand | 1.9 | 0.3 | 2.1 | 7.8 |
| Medium-demand | 5.1 | −1.4 | 3.4 | 3.9 |
| Weak-demand | 1.5 | −3.5 | −1.7 | 0.7 |
| Total | 3.3 | −2.0 | 1.5 | 3.4 |

Source: Ibid., p. 219

*Table 72* Foreign trade balance of Spain's industrial sectors: 1975–86 (billions of 1980 pesetas)

| Sectors | 1975 | 1980 | 1983 | 1985 | 1986 |
|---|---|---|---|---|---|
| Strong-demand | −253.5 | −250.4 | −278.0 | −265.7 | −408.5 |
| Medium-demand | −141.6 | 168.8 | 150.1 | 248.3 | 64.8 |
| Weak-demand | 65.7 | 185.6 | 456.3 | 485.5 | 244.8 |
| Total | −329.4 | 104.0 | 328.4 | 468.1 | −98.9 |

Source: Ibid.

to dismiss redundant workers and adopted new labour-saving methods of production. Weak-demand industries also reduced their labour force, not because of a serious attempt to reduce their per unit labour costs, but largely in response to the dramatic fall in home demand.

The country's foreign trade pattern changed again in 1984 and 1985. During these years, the peseta ceased depreciating in terms of non-EC currencies. As a consequence, the rate of export growth of the weak-demand industries fell. Concurrently, the appreciation of the peseta in terms of EC currencies in 1984 exposed the weak-demand industries to the rising competition of competing EC products.

The ability of Spain's strong-demand industries to reduce their costs of production in the preceding years allowed them to nearly double the annual rate of growth of their exports. These were the industries most interested in raising the international competitiveness of their exports through product specialization. The exports of medium-demand industries also expanded, although in a much less spectacular way. On the other hand, this latter group faced a very modest rise of imports of competing goods, largely because their products enjoyed greater protection than those of the strong-demand industries.

As already noted, Spain's industrial exports gradually strengthened between 1976 and 1980 as industrial firms tried to compensate the adverse effects of declining domestic sales with rising exports. Table 71

Table 73 Evolution of Spain's industrial structure: 1975–86, percentages of total industrial output (constant 1980 pesetas)

| Sectors | 1975 | 1980 | 1983 | 1985 | 1986 |
|---|---|---|---|---|---|
| Strong-demand | 13.7 | 12.8 | 13.7 | 13.9 | 14.5 |
| Airplanes | 0.2 | 0.3 | 0.5 | 0.3 | 0.4 |
| Office equipment, computers | 0.2 | 0.2 | 0.4 | 0.4 | 0.6 |
| Electrical machines and materials | 3.4 | 3.2 | 3.1 | 3.1 | 3.4 |
| Electronic equipment | 1.2 | 1.3 | 1.8 | 1.8 | 2.0 |
| Precision instruments | 0.4 | 0.4 | 0.4 | 0.4 | 0.4 |
| Pharmaceuticals | 1.0 | 1.4 | 1.6 | 1.5 | 1.5 |
| Chemicals | 7.3 | 5.9 | 5.9 | 6.3 | 6.2 |
| Medium-demand | 46.1 | 50.5 | 51.2 | 53.2 | 53.4 |
| Rubber and plastics | 3.7 | 2.9 | 3.0 | 3.2 | 3.1 |
| Motor vehicles | 5.5 | 6.7 | 7.1 | 7.6 | 8.2 |
| Mechanical machinery | 3.5 | 4.1 | 3.7 | 4.1 | 4.1 |
| Railroad equipment | 0.5 | 0.4 | 0.5 | 0.3 | 0.2 |
| Other transport goods | 0.3 | 0.3 | 0.3 | 0.3 | 0.3 |
| Foodstuffs, beverages, tobacco | 20.7 | 21.5 | 23.2 | 23.8 | 22.9 |
| Petroleum products | 6.2 | 10.1 | 9.0 | 9.5 | 10.2 |
| Paper | 5.8 | 4.4 | 4.3 | 4.4 | 4.5 |
| Weak-demand | 40.2 | 36.8 | 35.1 | 32.9 | 32.1 |
| Steel | 6.7 | 9.0 | 9.5 | 9.8 | 8.5 |
| Non-ferrous metals | 2.8 | 1.5 | 1.6 | 1.6 | 1.6 |
| Shipbuilding | 2.0 | 1.3 | 1.4 | 0.7 | 0.7 |
| Metallic products | 6.9 | 6.9 | 6.6 | 6.1 | 6.0 |
| Non-metallic minerals | 4.8 | 5.0 | 4.1 | 3.6 | 3.7 |
| Wood and cork | 3.8 | 3.6 | 3.2 | 2.7 | 3.1 |
| Textiles | 4.2 | 4.0 | 3.3 | 3.3 | 3.4 |
| Leather | 1.2 | 0.7 | 0.7 | 0.7 | 0.7 |
| Apparel and footwear | 6.3 | 4.1 | 3.8 | 3.5 | 3.4 |
| Other manufactures | 1.4 | 0.9 | 0.9 | 0.9 | 0.9 |
| Total industry | 100.0 | 100.0 | 100.0 | 100.0 | 100.0 |

*Source*: Ibid., p. 221

indicates that, in spite of the domestic economic crisis, aggregate industrial output expanded at an average annual rate of 3.3% in this period. This output declined during the critical years of 1981 to 1983 to recover a modest rate of growth in 1984 and 1985. The foreign trade balance for products of the medium- and weak-demand industries showed a surplus as of 1980, as indicated by Table 72. This surplus was largely made possible by Spanish exports of steel, motor vehicles, apparel and footwear. The trade balance of the strong-demand industries remained negative, though relatively stable.

Table 73 shows a more detailed breakdown of the evolution of Spanish sectoral industrial production. Between 1975 and 1986, the medium-demand industries recorded the largest percentage gains of industrial production. Such gains were largely the result of an expansion in the production of mechanical machinery, motor vehicles, petroleum products and processed foodstuffs. The table shows the relative loss of importance of the output of the weak-demand industries. The strong-demand sector obtained a slight gain in relative weight in the secondary sector with the largest gains being achieved by the electronic equipment industries.

## SPAIN'S ENTRY INTO THE EUROPEAN COMMUNITY

The 1982 electoral programmes of the PSOE had called for Spain's full membership in the EC. In his inaugural speech of 30 November 1982 Felipe González declared that a main objective of his government was to have Spain acquire full membership in the EC 'within a time horizon given to the present legislature' (Alonso, A., 1985, 164). A few days later, the new President of the Government chose Fernando Morán to be his Minister for Foreign Affairs.

During the first days of December 1982, the Council of Europe, meeting in Copenhagen, had announced its support for the incorporation of Spain and Portugal into the Community and instructed the EC Council to proceed as rapidly as possible with negotiations leading to formal treaties providing for the incorporation of the two countries into the EC. The European Council requested the EC Council to solve any existing problems regarding the intra-EC trade in Mediterranean agricultural products before March 1983.

EC and Spanish negotiators had met in 1982 on thirty-six occasions to determine Spain's conditions of entry into the Community. At the beginning of 1983, many of these conditions had not as yet been agreed to by both parties. Further negotiations between the EC and Spain appeared to be favoured by the moderate political and economic stance of the Felipe González government. On 20 April 1983 the *Cortes* had ratified a five-year extension of Spain's 'Friendship, Defence and Cooperation Accord' initially signed by Leopoldo Calvo Sotelo on 2 July 1982. Subsequently, Felipe González met Chancellor Helmut Kohl in

Bonn and President Ronald Reagan in Washington. Their talks generated increased goodwill on the part of major Western countries toward the 'socialist' government of Spain.

In April 1983, the EC Commission had recommended to the EC Council that, following her entry into the EC, Spain should be granted a seven-year transition period during which she would reduce, and finally abolish, her customs duties on Spanish imports of industrial goods produced in the EC area. Prior to the date of such entry, Spain would have to reduce her *ad valorem* customs duties on the import of EC industrial products exceeding 20% (Ibid., 167).

Regarding Spain's trade in agricultural products, no exceptions being made for the country's trade in wine and olive oil, such trade was to be gradually governed by EC trading practices, the gradual adoption of such practices by Spain being allowed a transition period of seven years. The Commission had excepted from this proposal Spain's trade in fresh fruit and vegetables. In the case of these commodities, the EC Commission recommended that Spain should be allowed to adopt EC trade rules over a long transition period of between ten and twelve years. This period was to be subdivided into two subperiods. During an initial transition stage of between four and six years, Spain's exports of fresh fruit and vegetables to the EC would not receive any favoured customs treatment by the rest of the EC countries; on the other hand, Spanish imports of such products from the EC area would enjoy existing intra-Community trade treatment. The latter recommendation implied that Spain would have to abolish, *ab initio*, her quantitative restrictions on the entry into the country of fresh fruit and vegetables from the EC area. During a second transition period of between six and eight years, Spanish exports of fresh fruit and vegetables to the Community would be treated according to the rules of the EC's Common Agricultural Policy.

Spain's employers' association, the CEOE, strongly opposed the Commission's proposals. The CEOE demanded a longer transition period before Spain abolished her import duties on the entry of EC industrial goods. It opposed the Commission's proposed treatment of Spanish exports of fresh fruit and vegetables to the Community. The Spanish government supported the arguments of the CEOE. It declared that Spain would not accept any differentiated trade treatment for industrial and agricultural goods.

The González government had assumed quite correctly that the integration of both Portugal and Spain into the European Community was unavoidably linked to the Community's problem of financing its agricultural budget. The latter needed to generate larger internal financial resources to finance its agricultural programme adequately. In order to do so, it had to abandon its existing practice of having each member nation contribute a maximum of 1% of the value added tax it collected to the Community's budget. The largest contributing member nation was the Federal Republic of Germany. Given its financial might, Germany had the power to pressure other EC nations to facilitate Spain's entry into the EC. This is why González travelled to Bonn on 3 May 1983. González assured Chancellor Kohl that in exchange for German backing of Spain's candidacy, Spain would support Germany's defence policy and allow 'euromissiles' to be installed on Spanish territory if the USA and the USSR failed to reach an accord in their talks in Geneva.

Following the González–Kohl meeting, the West German government announced that it would agree to an increase in the mandatory contributions of member nations to the EC budget if Portugal and Spain were allowed to join the Community. The integration of these two countries into the Community thus became a necessary condition for the implementation of the Community's necessary financial reform. The Council of Europe, meeting in Stuttgart on 17 to 19 June 1983, accepted the German position.

In spite of the 'Stuttgart resolution', negotiations covering the condition's of Spain's membership in the EC had not terminated in 1983. A final agreement was not reached because of the opposition of the French *Midi* to the entry into the Community of a country which would compete with France in intra-EC sales of Mediterranean agricultural products. France went on opposing Spain's entry in the absence of new Community regulations designed to protect French agriculture from Spanish competition. Such regulations were finally approved on 14 November 1983.

The Spanish government's efforts to obtain EC membership did not weaken. Manuel Marín, Spain's Minister for Relations with the European Community, announced that Spain would engage in 'marathon negotiations' at the ministerial meeting scheduled for 19 June 1984 in Luxembourg. Spain's negotiating position was strengthened by the fact that the government, the political parties and the Spanish employers' association shared similar views regarding the 'minimum economic conditions' under which Spain would become part of the Community. The CEOE detailed such conditions best. Customs duties imposed on the trade in industrial products between Spain and the Community should be gradually reduced in the course of a transition period of seven years during which such duties would receive eight successive reductions. In addition, the terms of Spain's treaty of adhesion to the EC should allow the country's steel industry to complete its modernization programme with the help of public subsidies, and Spanish steel exports to the rest of the Community should be allowed a normal development. In regard to the commercial policy governing the trade in agricultural products between Spain and the rest of the Community, the CEOE suggested that during an identical transition period Spain should be allowed to retain her quantitative restrictions on the imports of milk and milk-based foodstuffs, of beef and pork, of bread grains and of sugar. The trade in fresh fruit and vegetables should receive the same treatment extended to third countries by the Community.

On 19 June the EC negotiators in Luxembourg proposed that with regard to the trade in industrial goods, Spain would receive a transition period of six years during which tariffs on such goods would be lowered on seven occasions without any need for Spain to lower her duties on certain industrial products prior to the date of adhesion. On the other hand, customs duties on industrial products exceeding 20% would have to be rapidly reduced during the first years following Spain's formal entry into the EC. Regarding the trade in agricultural products between Spain and EC countries, Spain should accept a two-stage transition period for the trade in fresh fruit and vegetables, citrus fruit being included in this category. All other agricultural products would be granted a transition period of seven years.

In November 1984, the two parties finally agreed on a commercial policy regarding the trade in industrial products. Spain's negotiators were granted their demands. For the trade in industrial goods between Spain and the rest of the Community, a transition period of seven years was accepted by the EC. During this period, eight tariff reductions would take place, the first of them becoming effective on 1 March following the date of Spain's entry, the remaining reductions becoming effective on 1 January of each of the following seven years. These successive tariff reductions were to be of 10%, 12.5%, 15%, 15%, 12.5%, 12.5%, 12.5% and 10% (Ibid., 195). With the exception of automobiles, there were not to be any accelerated tariff reductions for industrial products burdened by high duties. At the end of the seven-year transition period, Spain's tariff for industrial goods would become the corresponding EC common tariff and Spain would adopt the Community's tariff concessions to third countries. Spain was granted a period of three years to complete the modernization of her steel industry under existing conditions.

No final agreement had been reached on the agricultural policy which would govern the trade in agricultural products between both parties. The eagerness of Spain's negotiators to finalize a partial agreement with their Community colleagues left the Spaniards with little bargaining power in the formulation of an agricultural commercial policy.

On 6 January 1985 Jacques Delors, formerly France's Finance Minister, replaced Gaston Thorn as President of the EC Commission. Lawrence Natali remained the Commission's Vice-President in charge of negotiations regarding the enlargement of the EC. The Community negotiators had not presented as yet a proposal for a commercial policy related to the trade in agricultural products between Spain and the EC. Spain's negotiators were impatient to learn how the Community intended to treat the trade in agricultural products sensitive to Spain. No arrangement regarding the free intra-Community movement of Spanish workers had been proposed by the EC negotiators.

On 8 February 1985 the Commission finally presented a proposal to the EC Council dealing with these questions. The Commission's proposal was about to be accepted by the Council at its meeting of 17 to 21 March when at the last moment the French delegation impeded a vote by claiming that Spain's wine production quota had to be reduced and by insisting that the number of Spanish fishing vessels authorized to fish in Community waters was too large. Spain's negotiators had already accepted the Commission's proposals. The President of the EC Council, Giulio Andreotti of Italy, then scheduled a new meeting of the Council on 28 and 29 March.

It was during those latter days of March 1985 that the Commission's proposals of 8 February were finally accepted by the EC Council. Such acceptance concluded the EC's negotiations with Spain regarding the conditions of that country's entry into the EC.

Spain agreed to the conditions of trade in agricultural products proposed by the Community. She was to reduce her average annual production of wine. On the grounds that Spanish pork meat could have been contaminated by an African porcine disease, Spain was allowed to export only sterilized pork products, whereas all other EC countries were free to export to Spain any type of pork meat. Spanish exports of fresh fruit and vegetables, including citrus fruit, were not to receive any favoured customs treatment from the EC for a period of four years. The EC seriously undermined Spain's ability to expand her exports of her most competitive agricultural products for a total transition period of ten years.

A transition period of seven years was established during which Spanish workers were deprived of free movement within the Community area.

In spite of strong opposition by Spanish farmers to the conditions imposed on them by the terms of their country's agreement with the European Community, most Spanish interest groups acclaimed the ending of the negotiations on Spain's entry into the EC. The CEOE welcomed Spain's integration in the Community. With the exception of the Spanish Communist Party, all other political parties in Spain reacted positively to the achievement of a Treaty of Adhesion. This Treaty was signed on 12 June 1985 in the *Palacio de Oriente* in Madrid. The signing of the Treaty by Spain's President of the Government, Felipe González, was witnessed by King Juan Carlos I, by Giulio Andreotti, the President of the EC Council and by Jacques Delors, the President of the EC

Commission. The Treaty was ratified by Spain's Congress of Deputies on June 26, and by its Senate on 17 July. As of 1 January 1986, Spain became a member nation in the European Community.

The sustained efforts of Spain's government and of its negotiators to acquire for their country full membership in the European Community was based on their perception that in years of domestic economic crisis, expanding exports could keep Spanish firms from financial disaster. In years of economic upswing, growing exports helped these firms to finance their imports of foreign technology.

## Spain's foreign trade before EC entry

During the long time span of 1959 to 1981, Spain's foreign trade had grown more rapidly than world trade. In 1958, Spanish imports amounted to US$872 million and represented 0.76% of the world's imports. In that year, Spanish exports attained a value of US$485 million, or 0.44% of the value of global exports. In 1981, the value of Spanish imports reached US$32,211 million, or 1.73% of the value of total world imports; Spanish exports amounted to US$20,481 million, representing 1.10% of the value of global exports (Granell, F., 1982, 135).

These trends do not indicate however that during those years Spain's became a significantly open economy. Spanish foreign trade continued to represent a much smaller percentage of GNP than the foreign trade of the EC countries. In 1980, the imports of the EC-10 nations amounted to 25% of the aggregate value of the area's GNP; their exports represented 23.7% of such GNP. The corresponding percentage figures for Spain were 13.5% and 9.7%. Table 74 shows the values of imports and exports as a percentage of GNP in 1968 and in 1980 for Spain and for a number of Western European countries. Looking at the values of imports and exports per capita, Table 75 shows that Spain and Portugal recorded the lowest values in comparison with those of EC countries.

The relatively small opening of Spain's economy in the 1960s and in the 1970s was largely the consequence of the strong protectionist policies Spain had maintained in earlier decades. For too long, Spanish businessmen had become used to selling exclusively in a home market in which they were free of foreign competition. Those potentially interested in selling abroad were discouraged from doing so by an overvalued peseta. In spite of the country's adherence to the GATT as of 1963, in spite of the Preferential Trade Accord with the European Community of 1970, in spite of trade agreements signed in 1979 with EFTA nations, Spain retained a high tariff wall and continued to rely on other protection devices which impeded a more effective integration of its economy into the world economy. As shown in Table 76, Spain was able to maintain

*Table 74* Imports and exports as a percentage of GNP, selected countries: 1968–80

| Country | Imports as a percentage of GNP | | Exports as a percentage of GNP | |
|---|---|---|---|---|
| | 1968 | 1980 | 1968 | 1980 |
| German FR | 15.2 | 20.9 | 18.7 | 22.5 |
| France | 11.0 | 18.7 | 10.0 | 17.2 |
| Italy | 13.7 | 24.0 | 13.6 | 22.3 |
| Netherlands | 36.8 | 45.3 | 33.1 | 42.8 |
| Belgium–Luxembourg | 38.7 | 51.8 | 38.0 | 49.3 |
| UK | 18.4 | 25.3 | 14.9 | 22.6 |
| Portugal | 20.7 | 32.0 | 14.6 | 17.0 |
| Greece | 17.8 | 25.0 | 6.0 | 10.1 |
| Spain | 14.0 | 13.5 | 6.3 | 9.7 |

Source: Granell, F. 'La integración en la Comunidad Europea y sus efectos sobre la exportación española', in *Información Comercial Española*, Nr. 588/89, Madrid, 1982, p. 135

*Table 75* Per capita import and export values in Spain and in EC-10 countries: 1980 (ECUs per inhabitant)

| Country | Imports | Exports |
|---|---|---|
| German FR | 1,896 | 2,042 |
| France | 1,454 | 1,337 |
| Italy | 996 | 924 |
| Netherlands | 3,509 | 3,315 |
| Belgium–Luxembourg | 4,161 | 3,959 |
| UK | 1,324 | 1,181 |
| Ireland | 2,131 | 1,550 |
| Greece | 740 | 299 |
| Portugal | 485 | 258 |
| Spain | 499 | 358 |

Source: Ibid.

approximately the annual rate of her exports during the years of economic crisis in the 1970s. A depressed home demand caused however a drastic fall in the rate of growth of the country's imports.

During the 1970s, Spain experienced the highest annual rate of real export growth among the 24 countries of the OECD, even surpassing that of Japan. On the other hand, with an average annual rate of real import growth of only 3.4%, Spain's rate of import growth was seventeenth among those of the various OECD countries.

Such foreign trade trends constituted a marked departure from those prevailing in the 1960s when Spanish import growth exceeded by far the

Table 76 Average annual rates of growth of real imports and exports in Spain and in the industrialized countries: 1960–79

|  | Average annual real percentage growth rates | | | |
|---|---|---|---|---|
|  | Imports | | Exports | |
|  | 1960–70 | 1970–9 | 1960–70 | 1970–9 |
| Industrialized countries | 9.3 | 4.5 | 8.4 | 5.9 |
| Spain | 18.5 | 3.4 | 11.5 | 10.8 |

Source: Ibid., p. 136

growth of the country's exports. Spain's relatively strong export performance in the 1970s was due to a number of factors. Among these were a greater interest in exporting and a better knowledge of foreign markets on the part of Spain's businessmen; increased investment in Spain's export sector, much of it financed by multinationals and by foreign enterprises, boosted the country's export capacity.

In spite of a relatively satisfactory Spanish export performance during the period of internal economic crisis, Spain remained a country whose economy remained isolated from that of the outside world.

## SPAIN'S BANK CRISIS OF 1977–85 AND THE FINANCIAL PROBLEMS OF THE COUNTRY'S INDUSTRIAL FIRMS

Spain's banking system began experiencing severe difficulties as soon as the effects of the first energy crisis started manifesting themselves in the domestic economy by mid-1975. Of the 110 banks operating in Spain at the end of 1977, 52% of them faced serious financial problems (Cuervo, A., 1988, 23). Between 1980 and 1982, the Spanish Bank Deposit Guarantee Fund had to rescue 29 banks which were close to insolvency. Some banks experiencing financial distress were merged into larger banks. Some were helped by the consortium of strong banks to which they belonged. The Bank of Spain intervened to maintain the solvency of the Banco de Exportación and of the Banco Rural y Mediterráneo. Banks experiencing financial difficulties such as the Banco Coca, the Banco Ibérico, the Banco Internacional de Comercio, the Banco de Valencia and the Banco Garriga Nogués were absorbed by other banks (Ibid., 29).

During the first year of the González administration, the government expropriated the twenty banks owned by the holding company RUMASA for the sake of the country's 'economic and social interests'. The political right reacted to such action by accusing the government of following extremist socialist policies. In fact, this unusual act of the government was a response to severe tax evasion practised by the management of RUMASA.

The bank crisis is most easily explained in terms of the overall economic crisis of the period. Spain's GDP growth rate, which during the period 1961 to 1974 had averaged 7% per year, started declining in 1975 and continued falling until 1979 when it bottomed at 0.2%. Between 1979 and 1985 the average annual rate of growth of Spain's GDP strengthened to 1.5%. The long period of economic crisis had two major consequences for the domestic economy. The crisis not only caused a drastic fall in domestic economic activity and in levels of employment, it also caused internal prices to rise rapidly, the rate of Spanish inflation exceeding 20% in 1977.

The fall in the annual rate of economic growth and the increase in the rate of inflation had adverse direct and indirect effects on the country's banking system. Rising inflation caused interest rates to increase and resulted in rising costs of industrial production. Restrictive monetary measures imposed by the government as of 1977 to contain the rise in internal prices and to correct balance-of-payments disequilibria reduced the liquidity of commercial and industrial banks.

Industrial firms were threatened by two developments. In the first place the internal and external demands for their products deteriorated. Second, as the prices of their production inputs rose, they were unable to pass on to the consumer the increase in their costs of production. The latter were boosted in addition by rising real labour costs.

The fall in the annual rate of economic growth and the rise of input prices diminished the profitability of the operations of the industrial firms. Their ability to effect timely interest payments to their banks deteriorated. Many firms started falling behind in such payments or completely suspended them. Such trends adversely affected the financial soundness of the banking system.

Other factors contributed to the rise of Spanish industrial production costs. The methods of production of Spanish firms were more energy-consuming than those of their foreign competitors. The much needed technological 'reconversion' in both the public and the private sectors of the economy was costly and many private firms could not finance it without increasing their already high level of indebtedness.

An important cause of failure of many Spanish industrial firms in the years of economic crisis was their excessive reliance on outside funding. A. Cuervo has estimated the relative importance of the various components of the financial structure of such firms (Ibid., 52). In 1985, 36% of the investment of Spain's industrial firms was financed by borrowed funds. The issue of bonds financed an additional 9.1% and other funds originating outside the enterprises represented 9.8% of the firms' aggregate financial means. 54.9% of these firms' investments were thus

Table 77 Evolution of real interest rates and of the annual rate of growth of bank credit to the private sector: 1975–85

| Year | Real bank interest rate | Real rates of interest charged by savings banks | Annual rate of growth of bank credit to the private sector |
|---|---|---|---|
| 1975 | −7.0 | −7.9 | 22.7 |
| 1976 | −6.6 | −7.6 | 23.5 |
| 1977 | −11.7 | −13.1 | 21.6 |
| 1978 | −6.9 | −9.1 | 14.7 |
| 1979 | −2.4 | −5.0 | 14.9 |
| 1980 | 1.2 | −1.6 | 17.7 |
| 1981 | 1.9 | −0.4 | 16.2 |
| 1982 | 1.8 | −0.1 | 15.0 |
| 1983 | 4.1 | 2.4 | 10.9 |
| 1984 | 5.0 | 2.7 | 2.6 |
| 1985 | 7.1 | 5.5 | 8.9 |

Source: Cuervo, A., *La crisis bancaria en España, 1977–1985*, Barcelona, Ariel, 1988, p. 48

financed by outside funding. Only 45.1% of these investments were supported by self-generated funds. Of these, shareholders contributed 19.8%, the appreciation of the firm's assets, most often an accounting entry arbitrarily calculated for the purpose of giving the firm the appearance of financial soundness, averaged 9.8% while reserves amounted to 10.5% of the self-owned funds. The ratio of outside funding to the aggregate of internally generated funds amounted thus to 1.2%. The high level of enterprise indebtedness to the banks in a period of declining economic activity imperiled the financial soundness of Spain's private banks.

The firms' managers were interested in increasing the indebtedness of their firms as long as the rate of interest paid to their banks remained below the expected rate of profitability of their investments. Table 77 shows that real bank interest rates remained negative until 1979, became positive in 1980 but remained very low until 1983. Interest rates charged by savings banks remained negative until 1983. Given this real interest rate structure, business managers showed little interest in self-financing their investments. The success of such financial strategy was endangered by increases in the real rate of interest, increases usually resulting from the government's imposition of a restrictive monetary policy.

Real rates of interest charged by banks became positive in 1979. These rates averaged 5% in 1984 and 7% in 1985. As the cost of borrowing increased, the annual rate of growth of bank credit to the private sector declined. Table 77 shows that this rate started falling in 1981, when it stood at 16.2%, to reach 2.6% in 1984.

As real rates of interest became positive and started rising, the costs of production of industrial firms increased and the expected profitability rate of their investments declined. The profit margin of their sales fell from 11.3% in 1974 to 6.7% in 1980. Given these trends, industrial firms found it increasingly difficult to service their bank debts. In order to prevent their bankruptcy, creditor banks had to accept delays in the payment of interest by their debtor firms at a time when the compliance by these firms with the arranged payment schedule was of vital importance to the banks.

The soundness of Spain's commercial and industrial banks was further undermined by two concurrent developments. The first involved a stock exchange crisis. The continuing fall in the market value of shares of stock traded in the stock exchange during the years of economic crisis hindered the sale of new stock issues and made it increasingly difficult for firms to self-finance their investments. The resulting decline in the value of the firms' assets discouraged their interest in any new investment. A. Torrero Mañas reported that shares of corporate stock purchased for 100 pesetas on 1 January 1975, had a market value of only 27 pesetas on 31 December 1983 (Torrero Mañas, A., 1990, 345).

Spanish economists have also mentioned the limited managerial abilities of Spain's business leaders. According to them, the ability of Spanish firms to adapt to the changing economic environment was limited by their excessive attachment to traditional business practices. Spain's business managers were trained and acquired their experience in Franco's corporative capitalist system in which business activity was closely regulated and controlled by the authorities which purported to foster domestic industrialization by means of subsidies and of strong protective measures. Competition in the Francoist domestic economy remained weak. Rival firms often colluded to fix product prices and to divide the domestic market between them. Such practices hindered the development of adaptive and innovative managerial talents and acted as an obstacle to the advance of organizational and production technology.

The adjustment of organizational and production structures to the deteriorating economic environment was also hindered by the survival of the Francoist labour legislation during the period of political transition. While in times of economic hardship the newly legalized independent trade union organization succeeded in burdening Spain's industrial firms with rising real wages, the governments failed to provide greater flexibility to labour-management relations. Rising real wages produced rising costs of production at a time of declining internal and external demand. Industrial firms started recording losses which brought an end to the existence of many of them. The closing-down of firms not only intensified the country's unemployment problem, it also damaged financially the shareholders of the insolvent firms and the banks which had extended credits and loans to such enterprises.

A. Cuervo gives an additional reason for the financial deterioration of many Spanish private banks during the years of economic crisis. With the exception of new banks created by established banks in that period, new independent banks were in most cases unable to maintain their solvency in the deteriorating economic environment. Between 1963 and 1979, thirty-five new banks were created in Spain. Twenty-one of these were industrial banks and the rest were commercial banks. Of these thirty-five new banks, seven were industrial banks established by major established banks. Of the remaining twenty-eight, fourteen were industrial banks and the rest were commercial banks. Only two banks in each of the latter categories were able to survive the economic crisis (Cuervo, A., 1988, 66).

Most of these new industrial banks were large shareholders in industrial enterprises whose financial position had been hurt by the state of the economy. These enterprises pressured their bank to expand its holdings of shares of stock in the firm in order to allow the latter to safeguard its solvency by financing new investment projects promising a high rate of return. The bank, apprehending that its existing investment in the firm could become worthless unless it extended additional funds to such firm, bought additional shares of stock in the latter or extended to it new credits and loans. The firm's indebtedness to the bank became larger and the firm's managers found it increasingly difficult to pay interest on the enlarged debt. Given the existing conditions of weakening demand, the firm, instead of improving its financial health, experienced increased financial weakness, a weakness which was passed to its bank.

The problem of impaired solvency was shared by most new banks. This problem was intensified by the lack of expertise and, too often, by the professional misconduct of these banks' managers. To maintain the appearance of their bank's solvency, these managers did not hesitate to overstate in their accounting statements the true market value of the bank's assets. They 'sold' bank assets to firms they controlled at exaggerated prices. Defaulted loans were 'continued' and their 'accruing interest' was reported as a bank asset (Ibid., 66–74).

The managers of nearly insolvent banks often tried to persuade the management of a strong established bank to purchase theirs. In order to induce the latter to do so, the former proposed to finance the acquisition by means of credits extended by their own bank. If the management of the strong bank, for reasons of prestige or because of a belief that the economy would soon recover, decided to acquire the financially distressed bank, the former was soon exposed to danger too.

Finally, falling stock market prices further reduced the actual value of bank assets. Their managers turned to risky investment in real estate promising high rates of return. Unfortunately, the prolongation of the economic crisis impacted negatively on such investments. Real estate market values declined and banks were unable to sell their realty holdings without incurring major losses.

## CRITICISMS OF THE FIRST FELIPE GONZÁLEZ ADMINISTRATION

Critics of the first González government pointed out that during the political campaign of 1982 the PSOE promised to create 800,000 new jobs during the following three years and that in fact the numbers of unemployed rose by 700,000 in that period (Gámir, L., 1992, 187). They question the effectiveness of a government unable to expand employment in spite of rising public deficits. They claimed that a more egalitarian redistribution of the national income had taken place in the period 1974 to 1981 and that hardly any redistribution of such income took place during the first three years of the socialist government (Ibid., 190).

Luis Gámir, a distinguished conservative Spanish economist, felt that the government failed to take advantage of the improvement in the world economy which started as early as 1983. He pointed out that nominal crude oil prices started declining in 1983 and that the recovery of the American and Japanese economies in that year strengthened the economic activity of the European Community countries in 1984. Both 1983 and 1984 remained years of economic crisis for Spain.

González's opponents linked Spain's slow economic recovery to the economic management of the economy by a socialist government. An objective study of the economic policies of that government clearly shows, however, that such policies were closer to neo-classical economic thought than to socialist or social-democratic ideology. It must be noted that the powerful Minister of Economics, Miguel Boyer, had at one time abandoned the PSOE to join the CD party later. Carlos Solchaga, the Minister of Industry, was an MIT graduate. Neither of these men were socialists.

Even Luis Gámir recognized that the incomes policy of the González government was mainly directed at the containment of the rate of growth of labour costs for Spanish firms and did not aim to increase the purchasing power of the country's workers. In this regard, the government's strategy was to enter into broad agreements with both employers and the trade unions to limit the rate of wage increase to the expected rate of inflation in December of the following year, a change from the Francoist formula which tied the rate of wage increase to the existing rate of inflation plus three points. With a diminishing rate of inflation, the new way of calculating the permitted rate of wage increase, based on the expected rate of inflation at the end of the following year and not on the average rate of inflation during that year, allowed the rate of wage increase to lag behind that of prices (Ibid., 177). This incomes policy represented the core of the supply-side of the government's economic policies.

The core of the demand-side was the government's restrictive monetary policy. It alone was charged with the task of minimizing the inflationary effects of the expanding public deficits. Fiscal policy was to have above all a redistributive function. It is difficult to argue that the government of Felipe González had a Keynesian orientation.

Any government programme, whether economic, military, political or social, will forever be criticized by the political opposition, no matter the country, no matter the time. It must be recognized that the moderate economic measures taken by the socialist government during its initial years in power brought a steady decline in the rate of domestic inflation, a rise in the rate of economic growth and an improvement in the country's balance of payments. The economic picture was only darkened by rising unemployment.

The unemployment problem was aggravated by two unavoidable developments. The first sprang from the government-supported managerial efforts to modernize Spain's industry. The process of industrial renovation was capital-intensive in nature. The second development was related to the government's enactment of new labour legislation which allowed employers to dismiss redundant workers. The new labour laws and increasing layoffs in the iron, steel and shipbuilding industries brought rising tensions between the trade unions and the socialist government. The number of strikes in 1984 was 30% higher than it had been one year earlier (Share, D., 1986, 191). Labour unrest centred in the Basque region and in Catalonia. Workers' discontent in Catalonia allowed Jordi Pujol's centrist *Convergencia i Unió* party to defeat the PSOE in the regional elections of 1984.

Attacks against the government came from other sources also. The government's nationalization of the large private holding company RUMASA antagonized most Spanish businessmen. Their denunciations of the government's action gradually disappeared after the government promised to return the RUMASA enterprises to the private sector as soon as possible.

The Popular Alliance and the Church protested loudly in 1984 when the government increased its control over private schools, most of them being Church schools.

In spite of sharp criticisms of the government's policies, most Spaniards continued to give their support to González. He still was the most popular Spanish politician in 1985. The PSOE was the country's strongest political party in that year, impervious to the denunciations of the Spanish Communist Party, now led by the pragmatic Gerardo Iglesias, or of the conservative Popular Alliance of Manuel Fraga

Iribarne. The supporters of González felt vindicated when the Spanish economy showed that it had left behind the long years of crisis.

## THE OECD ECONOMIES IN 1986

1986 was the fourth consecutive year of economic recovery and expansion experienced by the industrial countries of the OECD following the oil crisis of 1979–80. Over four million new jobs were created in those countries in 1986. Concurrently, their rates of inflation declined. The aggregate OECD area production, as measured by its GNP, grew at a rate of 2.5%. This rate had attained 3% in 1985. Important reasons for the lower rate of growth in 1986 were the trade effects of the depreciation of the US dollar and a weakened import demand in the non-OECD countries. Although OECD exports weakened, intra-OECD demand rose at the average annual rate of 3.5% (Banco de Bilbao, 1987, 13). Within the OECD area, private consumption contributed 2.25 points to the 2.5 points of aggregate GNP growth. In other words, 90% of the rate of growth of the area's GNP in 1986 was due to the growth of consumption spending within the area. Foreign trade contributed –1.25 points to the growth of the area's GNP. For the various OECD nations, rates of real GNP growth varied between 2% and 3%. Table 78 shows the rates of growth of real GNP in various countries and country groups in the OECD area in 1985 and in 1986.

Within the OECD area, the growth of consumption spending was largely due to the fall in the international prices of crude oil and of primary commodities. So far as national governments allowed the fall in these prices to reduce the domestic prices of consumer goods, household disposable income rose and strengthened private consumption. The

Table 78 Rates of growth of real GNP in the OECD area: 1985 and 1986
(percentage over previous year)

|  | 1985 | 1986 |
|---|---|---|
| USA | 2.70 | 2.75 |
| Japan | 4.50 | 2.25 |
| German FR | 2.50 | 2.75 |
| France | 1.40 | 2.00 |
| UK | 3.50 | 2.25 |
| Italy | 2.30 | 2.50 |
| Canada | 4.00 | 3.00 |
| OECD–Europe | 2.50 | 2.50 |
| OECD–total | 3.00 | 2.50 |

Source: Banco de Bilbao, Informe Económico 1986, Sondika-Vizcaya, Imprenta Industria, S.A., 1987, p. 14

Table 79  Rates of interest in the OECD countries: 1985 and 1986

|  | 1985 | 1986 |
|---|---|---|
| Short-term rates | | |
| USA | 7.48 | 5.88 |
| Japan | 6.46 | 4.92 |
| German FR | 5.44 | 4.57 |
| France | 9.94 | 7.59 |
| UK | 11.65 | 10.40 |
| Italy | 15.26 | 13.41 |
| Canada | 9.56 | 9.09 |
| Long-term rates | | |
| USA | 11.37 | 9.02 |
| Japan | 6.78 | 5.77 |
| German FR | 6.94 | 5.97 |
| France | 11.87 | 8.66 |
| UK | 10.63 | 9.68 |
| Italy | 13.12 | 10.38 |
| Canada | 11.04 | 9.60 |

*Source*: Ibid., p. 16

decline in these prices constituted a gain in national income which was also devoted by national governments to reduce public deficits in order to lower the rate of national inflation.

With the exception of the United States which embraced an expansive monetary policy, most OECD nations adopted policies designed to keep prices and rates of interest stable. Table 79 shows that both short-term and long-term rates of interest were lower in 1986 than in 1985.

Employment expanded in practically all the regions of the OECD area. For the total OECD area, employment rose at the annual rate of 1.25% in 1986, this rate representing the effects of the creation in that year of 4.2 million new jobs (Ibid., 18). In the OECD–Europe area, employment rose by only 0.75%, an increase made possible by the creation of 1.15 million new jobs. Employment rose by 3% in Canada and by 2.25% in the United States. In most OECD countries, the growth of the active population absorbed the increase in employment, so that the average unemployment rate in the OECD area remained stable at 8.25%. In the OECD–Europe area, this rate was 11% in 1986, a rate which was practically identical to that of the previous year. Unemployment rates in the OECD area for 1985 and 1986 are shown in Table 80.

The rate of unemployment in the OECD–Europe area remained high in 1986 and unchanged from its 1985 figure. On the other hand, the rate of inflation of consumer goods prices in the same area fell from 6.20% in 1985 to 3.75% in 1986. The corresponding decline for the entire OECD area was from 4.50% to 2.75%. The annual rate of change of

Table 80  Unemployment rates in the OECD area: 1985 and 1986
(percentage of the active population)

|  | 1985 | 1986 |
|---|---|---|
| USA | 7.20 | 7.00 |
| Japan | 2.60 | 2.75 |
| German FR | 8.30 | 7.75 |
| France | 10.20 | 10.50 |
| UK | 11.80 | 11.75 |
| Italy | 10.60 | 11.25 |
| Canada | 10.50 | 9.75 |
| OECD–Europe | 10.90 | 11.00 |
| OECD–total | 8.30 | 8.25 |

Source: Ibid., p. 20

Table 81  Index of private consumer goods prices: 1985 and 1986
(percentage annual rate of change)

| Country | 1985 | 1986 |
|---|---|---|
| USA | 3.50 | 2.25 |
| Japan | 2.20 | 0.75 |
| German FR | 2.10 | –0.75 |
| France | 5.50 | 2.25 |
| UK | 5.20 | 4.00 |
| Italy | 9.40 | 6.25 |
| Canada | 4.10 | 4.00 |
| OECD–Europe | 6.20 | 3.75 |
| OECD–total | 4.50 | 2.75 |

Source: Ibid., p. 23

such prices in the various OECD countries is given in Table 81.

The fall in the rate of inflation in the various OECD nations was made possible by the concurrent decline in the international prices of imported crude oil and of primary commodities. By mid-1986 the price of a barrel of crude oil had fallen to US$11.00 and the prices of imported primary commodities were on the average 30% lower than they had been six years earlier (Ibid., 21). As shown by Table 81, the rate of inflation significantly declined in 1986.

The fall in the rate of inflation was due to exogenous developments such as the decline in the international prices of imported crude oil and of primary commodities, as well as to endogenous factors such as a moderate rate of increase in the per unit labour costs of firms which resulted from both low increases in nominal wages and a moderate increase in productivity. Table 82 shows the annual rate of increase of per

*Table 82* Percentage annual change in per unit labour costs in OECD countries: 1985 and 1986

| Country | 1985 | 1986 |
|---|---|---|
| USA | 4.10 | 3.25 |
| Japan | 0.10 | 2.50 |
| German FR | 0.70 | 1.75 |
| France | 4.40 | 2.00 |
| UK | 4.80 | 5.25 |
| Italy | 8.20 | 7.25 |
| Canada | 3.80 | 2.50 |

*Source*: Ibid., p. 23

*Table 83* Current account balances, selected countries: 1985 and 1986 (billion US dollars)

| Country | 1985 | 1986 |
|---|---|---|
| USA | −117.70 | −138.00 |
| Japan | 49.20 | 81.75 |
| German FR | 13.20 | 32.50 |
| France | −0.20 | 3.75 |
| UK | 4.60 | −0.25 |
| Italy | −4.20 | 4.75 |
| Canada | −0.40 | −6.75 |
| OECD–Europe | 21.20 | 54.50 |
| OECD–total | −57.50 | −19.75 |

*Source*: Ibid., p. 27

unit labour costs in various OECD countries in 1985 and in 1986.

The volume of the OECD's international trade grew at a rate of 3.5% in 1986, a rate identical to that of 1985. The current account balance improved significantly in both Japan and the German Federal Republic, as well as in France and Italy. Current account deficits increased in Canada, the United Kingdom and the United States.

As shown in Table 83, the aggregate current deficit of the entire OECD's area fell from US $57.5 billion in 1985 to US$19.75 billion in 1986.

Spain's economy was affected by three major developments in 1986. These were Spain's incorporation into the European Common Market, the fall in the prices of imported crude oil and primary commodities and the depreciation of the US dollar. It was a remarkable year for the Spanish economy. While real GDP increased at the rate of 3%, domestic demand rose at the annual rate of 5.7%. Of the increase in domestic demand 46% had to be satisfied by imports. Rising imports and an unchanged export performance should have caused a deterioration of the country's balance of payments. Real terms of trade changed however so much in favour of Spain that at the end of 1986 the country's balance on current account recorded a surplus of about US$5 billion.

The achievement of an external surplus was the more surprising as Spanish total exports failed to expand in that year, with the exception of a small increase of exports to the European Community. On the other hand, real Spanish imports from the EC rose by 20% (Ibid., 79).

All the components of Spanish demand showed an increase in 1986. Private consumption demand rose by 3.8%, such increase being made possible by the rising disposable incomes of households. Indeed, household disposable income rose at a rate which exceeded the rate of increase of consumer goods prices. Private consumer demand was strengthened by a number of factors: rising wages and an accompanying expansion of employment; increasing entrepreneurial profits; and expanding government transfers. In spite of a rising tax burden, Spanish consumers increased their spending on durable consumer goods such as automobiles, electrical and electronic appliances, furniture, etc.

Productive investment, exclusive of construction, rose at the annual rate of 15%. Spain's entry into the European Common Market induced many Spanish firms to strive for stronger international competitiveness by expanding their investments in capital and in transport goods (Ibid., 80). Such investments boosted Spanish imports. Spain's merchandise imports rose by 16% in real terms in 1986 while Spanish exports grew by only 3.6%. The impact of such adverse trade conditions was however nullified by the decline in the price of imported crude oil, by the depreciation of the US dollar and by a major gain in the services balance. At the end of 1986, Spain was able to record a surplus on current account exceeding US$5 billion. The fall in the international price of crude oil and the depreciation of the US dollar allowed Spain to reduce her payments for oil imports by US$4.3 billion (Ibid.). Spain's current account surplus was also due to the fact that the peseta price of Spanish imports excluding oil experienced a sharper decline in 1986 than that of the peseta price of Spanish exports.

Spain's consumer goods price index in 1986 remained unchanged from its 1985 level. Between December 1985 and December 1986 such prices increased by 8.3%; the average annual rate of increase of such prices in the latter year attained 8.8%.

In the EC area, the consumer goods price index declined from 5.2% in December 1985 to 2.8% in December 1986. Because this index remained unchanged in Spain at 8.3%, the differential between the two indices increased from 3.1 points in 1985 to 5.5 points in 1986. This differential hurt Spain's exports to the EC. It could be partly explained by rising per unit labour costs in Spain.

The liberalization of Spain's labour laws undoubtedly contributed to an increase in the country's employment level in 1986. Employment in that year rose by 2.4%, an increase representing the creation of 250,000 new jobs. Such increase was however insufficient to give employment to the net increase in the active population. Spain's rate of unemployment registered a slight increase (Ibid., 81).

As noted above, national demand increased at the rate of 5.7% in 1986 while the GDP rose at the rate of 3%. Expanding merchandise imports were needed to satisfy internal demand. The various components of the GDP developed quite differently in 1986. The real output of the primary sector decreased by 5.5% and had a negative impact on the growth of GDP equivalent to −0.4 percentage points. The annual rate of growth of industrial production, exclusive of construction, attained 3.2%. However, the production performance of the various industrial subsectors showed great differences. Mining declined by 5% and the production of basic metals showed a decrease of 7%. Manufacturing industries expanded their output by 3%. While the production of chemicals, materials of construction and steel declined, that of automobiles rose by 11% and the manufacturing of machinery increased by 10%. Industrial activity also differed among regions. Industrial production in Aragón, Cataluña, Murcia, Navarra and Valencia expanded by 4%; in Asturias, the Basque region and Cantabria, industrial production remained at the level recorded in 1985 (Ibid., 82–3).

For the first time since 1975, the construction industry experienced growth. In terms of volume, construction expanded at the rate of 6%.

Tertiary activities continued to expand, largely in response to the growth of foreign tourism which in real terms increased by 10%. The tertiary sector contributed 2.7 percentage points to the rate of growth of the GDP. The growing importance of the tertiary sector in the Spanish economy indicated that that economy was becoming increasingly a services economy.

All the components of internal demand showed ascending trends in 1986: private consumption increased by 3.8%; public consumption expanded by 4.2%; and gross capital formation recorded an annual increase of 13.1%. Of great importance to the economy was a rate of increase of investment in fixed capital of 9.6% (Ibid., 84).

In spite of rapidly rising Spanish imports, the improvement in the country's real terms of trade by 16.6% and the expansion of foreign tourism allowed Spain to end 1986 with a balance-of-payments current surplus exceeding US$5 billion (see Table 84).

The resulting increase in Spain's holdings of foreign reserves and the reduction of the country's external debt placed the external financial position on solid ground. However, the opening of the economy,

Table 84 Spain's balance of payments in 1984, 1985 and 1986 (million US dollars)

|  | 1984 | 1985 | 1986 |
|---|---|---|---|
| Imports, fob | 27,062.6 | 27,857.0 | 34,617.2 |
| Crude oil | 7,387.0 | 7,608.6 | 4,040.1 |
| Other imports | 19,675.6 | 20,248.4 | 30,577.1 |
| Exports, fob | 22,727.2 | 23,478.0 | 28,374.9 |
| Trade balance | −4,335.4 | −4,379.0 | −6,242.3 |
| Services and Incomes | 5,197.5 | 5,895.4 | 10,247.1 |
| Services | 7,688.4 | 8,127.9 | 12,389.2 |
| Incomes | −2,490.9 | −2,232.5 | −2,142.1 |
| Transfers | 1,117.9 | 1,137.3 | 1,150.1 |
| Balance on current account | 11,980.0 | 2,653.7 | 5,154.9 |
| Balance on capital account | 2,579.4 | −3,957.7 | −2,311.7 |
| Balance of payments | 4,559.4 | −1,304.0 | 2,843.2 |

Source: Ibid., p. 90

Table 85 Growth in employment and wages: 1983–6 (annual percentage change)

|  | 1983 | 1984 | 1985 | 1986 |
|---|---|---|---|---|
| Annual change in paid employment | −1.59 | −3.92 | −0.01 | 2.85 |
| Change in the consumer goods price index | 12.20 | 11.20 | 8.80 | 8.80 |
| Change in the nominal wage per worker | 14.81 | 11.28 | 9.35 | 9.77 |
| Change in the real wage per worker | 2.33 | 0.07 | 0.51 | 0.89 |

Source: Ibid., p. 96

particularly Spain's incorporation into the EC, imposed on the country's manufacturers the challenge of improving the quality of their exportable goods and of reducing their costs of production. A rising rate of profit encouraged them to do so. Entrepreneurial profits had increased from 10.6% of the GDP in 1983 to 15.6% in 1986. This trend induced firms to expand their investments in fixed capital and in new technology. Concurrently, the share of salaries and wages in the GDP fell from 53.3% in 1983 to 49.8% in 1986. Table 85 shows the trends in Spain's employment and real wages in the years 1983 to 1986.

Gross national saving in Spain benefited from the fall in the prices of imported crude oil and imported primary commodities. In terms of their percentage of the GDP calculated at market prices, gross national saving increased from 18.58% of the GDP in 1983 to 22.31% in 1986. This trend allowed Spain to increase its investment in gross fixed capital from 1985.

Spanish monetary authorities had targeted for 1986 an annual rate of increase of the liquid assets in the hands of the people, i.e. the ALPs, of between 9.5% and 12.5%. They had hoped that this rate would not surpass 11% at the end of the year. This rate of growth of privately held liquid assets would support a growth rate of the real GDP of 3% given an internal rate of inflation of 8%. The government's monetary goals were reached. As noticed above, consumer goods prices increased by 8.3% from December 1985 to December 1986 and by an average of 8.8% during the latter year. The rate of growth of the ALPs amounted to 11.7% when measured from December 1985 to December 1986 and by 12.1% if measured in terms of daily averages throughout 1986 (Ibid., 98).

## THE NEW SPANISH ECONOMIC MIRACLE

In his inaugural speech given at the end of 1982, Felipe González promised to lower the country's rate of inflation. He kept his word. Rejecting the economic instruments of a command economy, his government proceeded to liberalize internal markets instead of embracing economic *dirigisme* or relying on economic planning. The new government's economic strategy was to attempt to remedy basic economic disequilibria and to stimulate the growth of efficiency at the microeconomic level through the exclusive use of both fiscal and monetary policies. The socialist government favoured orthodox capitalist economic policies! Its economic strategy did not totally reject public intervention in the economy, though such intervention was to be limited to public spending. Its economic credo followed the Keynesian prescription that national demand could be strengthened in a market economy operating at a below-full employment equilibrium without the risk of a rising rate of inflation. In spite of a continuous increase in public spending, the government succeeded in reducing the rate of inflation in a significant way. The rate of increase of consumer goods prices had reached 26.9% in 1977. In 1983, this rate amounted to 12.2%. One year later it declined to 9.0%. It remained at 8.8% in both 1985 and 1986. Concurrently, Spain's external financial position strengthened during the first term of the González administration. The balance of payments on current account showed surpluses in 1984, 1985 and 1986.

Though economic recovery after the second oil crisis came relatively late to Spain, the country's real GDP increased by 2% in 1983, by 2.2% in 1984, by 2.1% in 1985 and by 3% in 1986. Spain's major economic problem during that period was the rising rate of unemployment.

## ECONOMIC RECOVERY, 1985-90

The orthodox economic policy orientation of the González government was probably due to the economic failures of the François Mitterrand government of France. However, Spain's government leaders rejected Margaret Thatcher's and Ronald Reagan's loud criticisms of Keynesian economic policy. Under the ministry of Miguel Boyer, Spain's public deficit exceeded 5% of the country's GDP. In 1985 and in 1986, under the ministry of Carlos Solchaga, this deficit attained more than 6% of the GDP (Rodríguez Braun, C., 1992, 57).

The strengthening of the Spanish economy during the period 1983 to 1986 was not entirely due to the Boyer–Solchaga policies. Spain continued to be highly affected by trends in the economies of other countries. Economic growth in Western Europe at that time expanded foreign tourism in Spain and sustained foreign investment in the country. Following Spain's incorporation into the European Common Market at the start of 1986, private foreign investment in the country grew to US$5.2 billion. Over one-third of such investment represented direct investment; another third was portfolio investment (Banco de Bilbao 1987, 92).

As of 1987, Spain's economy benefited from an expanding international economy and from the opening of a large market to Spanish exporters. During the balance of the 1980s, the Spanish economy grew at a rate which exceeded the rate of growth of the industrialized economies. In spite of the stock market crisis of October 1987, Spain's real GDP increased by 5.3% in that year. This rate amounted to 5.1% in 1988, 4.8% in 1989 and 3.7% in 1990 (Banco de Bilbao, various issues). Spain's consumer goods price index fell from 8.8% in 1986 to 5.2% in 1987 and to 4.8% in 1988. It rose to 6.8% in 1989 and declined slightly to 6.7% in 1990.

A brief summary of the evolution of the Spanish economy during the latter half of the 1980s will give emphasis to these data. Spain's economic growth in that period imposed however a heavy price on Spaniards. As of 1988, Spain's balance of payments on current account started recording a growing deficit, a deficit the country was able to cover with its large foreign reserve holdings. Although employment increased in those years, the rate of unemployment remained high. Spain continued to be a high unemployment country in Western Europe. The rate of unemployment, as a percentage of the active population, amounted to 20.54% in 1987. This rate declined to 19.5% in 1988, to 17.28% in 1989 and to 16.25% in 1990 (Ibid.). The slow decline in the country's rate of unemployment was in large part due to an increase in per unit labour costs which rose by 21% between 1987 and 1991, costs which registered an increase of less than 10% in France during the same period (Rodríguez Braun, C., 1992, 59).

As shown by Graph 22, Spain's industrial production stagnated in

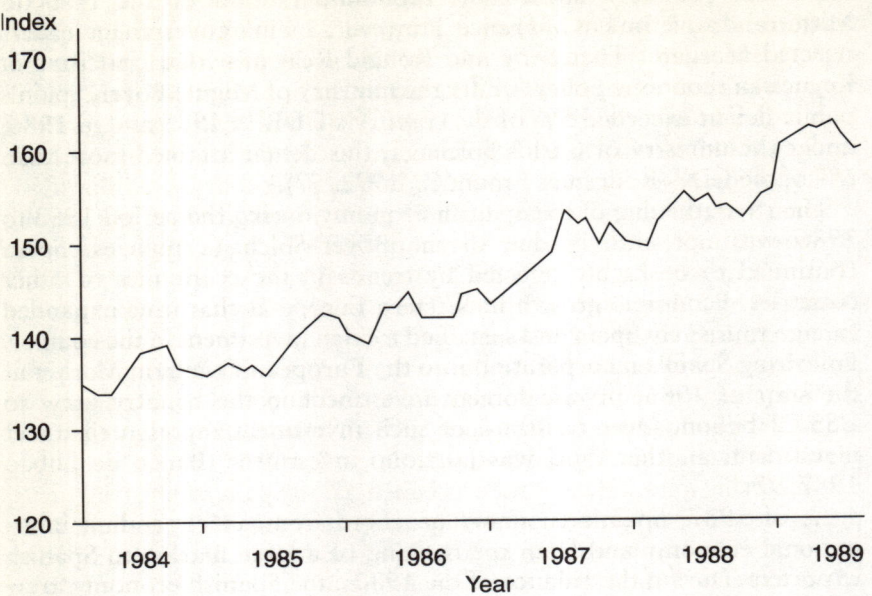

Graph 22  Spain's index of industrial production: 1984–9

Source: Myro, R., 'La recuperación de la industria española', in Velarde, J., García Delgado, J.L. and Pedreño, A., eds, *La Industria Española*, Madrid, Economistas Libros, 1990, p. 15

1984. During the second half of 1985 this production initiated a sharp increase, an increase which continued in 1986 though the momentum of such growth decelerated. The rate of growth of industrial production accelerated again during the first half of 1987, decelerated once more during most of 1988 and resumed an ascending course in 1989. The resumption of growth of domestic production, after years of stagnation, coincided in time with Spain's incorporation into the EC. For the period 1985 to 1989, Spain's industrial output grew at an average annual rate of 4.2%, a rate of growth which was lower than that attained in the 1960s but which exceeded by one percentage point the average annual rate of growth of industrial production in the OECD countries during the second half of the 1980s (Myro, R., 1990, 16).

In his interesting study of Spain's industrial recovery during the second half of the 1980s, Professor Rafael Myro attributed the growth of industrial output and the growth of domestic industrial demand in that period to the growth of Spanish private and public demand during those years. Because the growth of domestic industrial production remained weaker than the growth of internal aggregate demand, the differential in these rates of growth was compensated by expanding imports of industrial goods. Myro calculated that during the years 1985 to 1989 Spain's real imports grew at an average annual rate of 14.3%, this rate reaching a peak in 1987 when it attained 22.7%. The rate of import growth exceeded significantly the rate of export growth in this period. Spanish exports were adversely affected by the appreciation of the peseta in relation to other currencies in 1986, 1988 and 1989. As a result of foreign trade trends, Spain's balance of trade deficit increased from 787.1 billion pesetas in 1985 to 3,017 billion pesetas in 1989 (Ibid., 18).

Spain's internal industrial demand grew in response to the strong growth of domestic aggregate demand which in real terms rose at an average rate of 6%, a rate which surpassed that of the other OECD countries by 2.4 percentage points. The growth in domestic demand was in turn caused by an increase in both private and public consumption spending, as well as by a strong growth of gross capital formation. The strengthening of aggregate domestic demand impelled an expansion of industrial production, though such growth remained weaker than the growth of internal industrial demand.

If the rising national demand was beneficial to Spain's industrial firms, their increasing investment spending contributed in turn to the further strengthening of internal demand. In 1987 and 1988, industrial firms in Spain expanded their investment spending at the annual rate of 30%. Investment growth facilitated employment growth.

This period also recorded a deceleration in the rate of increase of domestic industrial prices. As shown by Table 86, the annual rate of industrial prices increase reached a minimum in 1987, then rose in 1988 and 1989. Myro attributed this latter trend to the inadequate growth of the domestic industrial supply as well as to the continuation of

*Table 86* Key economic industrial indicators: 1985–9 (annual real percentage rates of change)

| Indicator | 1985 | 1986 | 1987 | 1988 | 1989 |
|---|---|---|---|---|---|
| Consumption | 2.7 | 7.8 | 7.9 | 6.5 | 7.6 |
| Production | 2.5 | 3.8 | 5.2 | 4.1 | 5.2 |
| Imports | 2.4 | 10.0 | 22.7 | 17.3 | 16.0 |
| Labour productivity | 5.7 | 3.3 | 2.8 | 2.5 | 2.3 |
| Wages | 10.7 | 11.4 | 7.9 | 5.6 | 6.3 |
| Industrial prices | 8.1 | 1.5 | 0.8 | 2.3 | 4.0 |
| Real per unit labour costs | −3.6 | −6.6 | 3.2 | −0.8 | −1.1 |
| Gross formation of fixed capital in manufacturing | 18.5 | 13.8 | 27.4 | 30.0 | — |
| Trade balance deficit in billion current pesetas | −787.1 | −971.0 | −1,693.6 | −2,286.3 | −3,017.0 |

Source: Ibid., p. 17

protection in a number of internal markets. The rise of industrial prices in 1988 was not due to the effect of wage increases because wage growth decelerated throughout the period, except in 1989. Indeed, an annual rate of increase of industrial labour productivity of about 2.% and the gradual deceleration of the growth rate of wages in the second half of the 1980s resulted in declining per unit labour costs in most years in this period. The modest rise of Spanish industrial prices, a rise which remained smaller than the corresponding increases in other EC countries, strengthened the international competitiveness of Spain's industrial exports.

Myro observed that the strengthening of national demand as of 1985 was largely based on the growth of private consumers' demand for durable consumer goods such as automobiles, as well as on the growth of private and public investment in capital goods. Such demand increases unavoidably strengthened industrial demand in the country. In response to the rising internal industrial demand, Spain's industrial firms concentrated their investment on the modernization of their production technology and refrained from expanding their productive capacity (Ibid., 23).

## CRISIS, RECOVERY AND INDUSTRIAL POLICY

From 1974, Spanish industrial growth had been burdened by the rise in the prices of production inputs, particularly the price of energy. Managers of industrial firms, finding it increasingly difficult to finance production costs, reduced their firms' output and tried to operate on the basis of a smaller labour force. They hoped that by dismissing workers, the productivity of those who remained on the payroll would rise and that a smaller wages bill would prevent a fall in the firm's rate of profit. The immediate result of such policy was an increase in the rate of unemployment. Spain's unemployment conditions were aggravated by the fact that to the extent that firms financed new investment, such investment was mostly devoted to the adoption of labour-saving methods of production. New private investment soon disappeared from the country's economic scenario as entrepreneurial expectations deteriorated.

A number of factors made Spain's secondary sector particularly vulnerable to the energy crises of the 1970s. The fragile Spanish industrial sector was easily shaken by the strong rise in energy prices. The excessive participation of weak- and medium-demand industries in the country's secondary sector made it difficult for Spain to expand her exports to offset the effects of a weakening internal market. In 1981, weak- and medium-demand Spanish industrial subsectors supplied 87.2% of the country's aggregate industrial production, the corresponding

Table 87 Trends in Spain's industrial structure: 1975–86 (percentage of total industrial output, 1980 prices)

| Industrial sectors | 1975 | 1980 | 1985 | 1986 |
|---|---|---|---|---|
| Strong-demand | 13.7 | 12.8 | 13.9 | 14.5 |
| Airships | 0.2 | 0.3 | 0.3 | 0.4 |
| Office machines and computers | 0.2 | 0.2 | 0.4 | 0.6 |
| Electrical machinery | 3.4 | 3.2 | 3.1 | 3.4 |
| Electrical components | 1.2 | 1.3 | 1.8 | 2.0 |
| Precision instruments | 0.4 | 0.4 | 0.4 | 0.4 |
| Pharmaceuticals | 1.0 | 1.4 | 1.5 | 1.5 |
| Chemicals | 7.3 | 5.9 | 6.3 | 6.2 |
| Medium-demand | 46.1 | 50.4 | 53.2 | 53.4 |
| Plastics and rubber | 3.7 | 2.9 | 3.2 | 3.1 |
| Automobiles | 5.5 | 6.7 | 7.6 | 8.2 |
| Mechanical equipment | 3.5 | 4.1 | 4.1 | 4.1 |
| Railroad equipment | 0.5 | 0.4 | 0.3 | 0.2 |
| Other transport materials | 0.3 | 0.3 | 0.3 | 0.3 |
| Foodstuffs, beverages, tobacco | 20.7 | 21.5 | 23.8 | 22.9 |
| Petroleum products | 6.2 | 10.1 | 9.5 | 10.2 |
| Paper | 5.8 | 4.4 | 4.4 | 4.5 |
| Weak-demand | 40.2 | 36.8 | 32.9 | 32.1 |
| Steel | 6.7 | 9.0 | 9.8 | 8.5 |
| Non-ferrous metals | 2.8 | 1.5 | 1.6 | 1.6 |
| Shipbuilding | 2.0 | 1.3 | 0.7 | 0.7 |
| Metal products | 6.9 | 6.9 | 6.1 | 6.0 |
| Non-metallic minerals | 4.8 | 5.0 | 3.6 | 3.7 |
| Cork and wood | 3.8 | 3.6 | 2.7 | 3.1 |
| Textiles | 4.2 | 4.0 | 3.3 | 3.4 |
| Leather | 1.2 | 0.7 | 0.7 | 0.7 |
| Apparel and footwear | 6.3 | 4.1 | 3.5 | 3.4 |
| Other manufacturing | 1.4 | 0.9 | 0.9 | 0.9 |
| Total industry | 100.0 | 100.0 | 100.0 | 100.0 |

Source: Ministerio de Industria y Energía, *España en Europa: Un Futuro Industrial*, Madrid, 1987, reproduced in Petitbò, A. and Saez Barcena, J., 'El papel de la política industrial en la recuperación y reestructuración de la industria española', in Velarde, J., García Delgado, J.L. and Pedreño, A., *La Industria Española, Recuperación, estructura y mercado de trabajo*, Madrid, Economistas Libros, 1990, p. 67

rate in the EC-10 area being 76.2% (Petitbò, A. and Saez Barcena, J., 1990, 65). Strong-demand industries represented only 13.7% of the national aggregate industrial output in 1975 and 14.5% in 1986, as shown in Table 87.

As indicated above, most of Spain's industrial activity was based on the production of medium-demand industrial firms. The relative weight of such production in aggregate national industrial output increased between 1975 and 1986 largely as a result of the expansion in the manufacturing and assembly of automobiles. Weak-demand industries recorded a fall in their participation in total industrial production in that period.

Though strong-demand industries increased their contribution to national industrial output between 1975 and 1986, their participation in such output remained much lower than it was in the industrialized countries of the EC-10. The growth of strong-demand industries in Spain was weakened by an inadequate private investment in research and development. Even though such investment slowly expanded in Spain between 1981 and 1986, its growth remained weaker than it was in the industrialized nations of the EC-10. As a result, Spain failed to close the competitiveness gap which separated her industrial exportables from those of the EC.

The collapse of the Francoist regime during the second half of the 1970s and economic stagnation in those years discredited the *dirigiste* economic policies of the dictator's 'men of development'. During the political transition period, Spanish economists, whether supporters of the UCD or of the PSOE, appeared to embrace a neo-classical way of thinking which cast suspicion on the effectiveness of state intervention in the economy. Academic economists and their colleagues in the Adolfo Suárez, Leopoldo Calvo Sotelo and the Felipe González governments appeared to agree that the role of the government in the economy should be limited; they favoured the deregulation of the economy and the privatization of public enterprises. These economists also believed that the government could not pursue concurrently economic growth and income redistribution. In their view, the paramount goal of the government in the years of economic crisis was an increase in entrepreneurial profits which would stimulate both investment and employment.

The UCD governments, as well as the first PSOE government, attempted however to strengthen national economic activity by participating in multi-party agreements or by signing accords with both employers and trade unions whose main goal was to reduce industrial costs of production and to contain inflation through more effective controls over wage increases. No significant measures were taken until the 1980s to restructure and modernize the country's industrial sector. The early, major emphasis given to an incomes policy as the most effective instrument the government should use in its attempt to strengthen economic activity was evidenced by the broad agreements in which the government participated, such as the Moncloa Pact, the Interconfederal Framework Accord and the National Employment Accord. The main goal of all of these agreements was to contain the rise of industrial labour costs.

The adoption of public measures enacted to facilitate the restructuring and the modernization of industrial subsectors damaged by the economic crisis was tardy. It was only in 1980 and 1981 that the government enacted legislation designed to facilitate the restructuring of specified industries such as those producing household electrical appliances, machinery for the automobile industry and special steels and textiles. The Reconversion Law of 1982 extended public financial assistance to shipbuilding, the production of footwear, of electronic components, of standard steel and to other specified industrial activities (Ibid., 77).

The entry of Spain into the European Common Market induced the government to become more interested in strengthening the international competitiveness of the country's export sector. Spain's scientists and economists recognized that an increase in the competitiveness of the country's industrial exports had to be based on the expansion and better organization of internal Research and Development, R & D, efforts. The country's R & D experts met at Buitrago, near Madrid, in 1985 to debate the best ways to promote the intensification of scientific and technological research in the country and to enlarge the supply and quality of its investigators. Their recommendations were incorporated into a Law for the Promotion and General Coordination of Scientific Research and of Technological Development, commonly known as the 'Science Law', which was enacted in 1986. This Law was to be implemented by a National Plan for Scientific Research and Technological Development which was enacted by the government in 1988. These efforts to advance domestic production technology were accompanied by additional legislation. A National Plan for Electronic and Information Science, PEIN I, had been enacted by Parliament in January 1984. Two years later the government approved a Plan for the Promotion of Research in the Pharmaceutical Industry whose goal was to assist the development of high quality exportable pharmaceutical products. A new Patent Law was enacted in 1986 and a Law on Intellectual Property was passed in 1987.

Alberto Lafuente Félez and Luis A. Oro Giral have studied the effects of the National R & D Plan of 1988 on Spain's scientific research and development efforts during the years 1988 to 1990 (Lafuente Félez, A. and Oro Giral, L.A., 1991, 33–123). These two government R & D experts examined four principal effects of the Plan. They looked at the evolution of the financing for R & D and the spending of R & D funds; they evaluated the mobilization of human resources needed to expand scientific research and the growth of 'scientific output' during the three years; finally, they estimated the effects of scientific output growth on the expansion, the productivity and the international competitiveness of Spanish industrial production in these years.

The variable they chose as the best indicator of the national R & D effort was the ratio of aggregate domestic investment in R & D to GDP.

Table 88  R & D investment efforts in selected OECD countries: 1983–90 (spending on R & D as percentage of GDP)

| Country | 1983 | 1985 | 1987 | 1989 | 1990 |
|---|---|---|---|---|---|
| German Federal Republic[1] | 2.51 | 2.71 | 2.85 | 2.83 | — |
| United Kingdom[1] | 2.25 | 2.28 | 2.27 | — | — |
| Italy[1] | 0.95 | 1.12 | 1.19 | 1.25 | — |
| France[1] | 2.11 | 2.25 | 2.29 | 2.33 | — |
| United States[1] | 2.71 | 2.92 | 2.90 | 2.80 | — |
| Spain[1] | 0.45 | 0.53 | 0.62 | 0.72 | 0.82 |
| Spain[2] | 0.48 | 0.57 | 0.68 | 0.79 | 0.90 |

Source: Lafuente Félez, A. and Oro Giral, L.A., 'Evolución del sistema de ciencia y tecnología en España, El Plan Nacional de I+D', in Dorado, R. et al., eds, Ciencia, tecnología e industria en España, Situación y perspectivas, Madrid, Fundesco, 1991, p. 38
Notes: 1 GDP at market prices. 2 GDP at factor costs

Table 89  Receipts and spending of R & D funds in selected countries

|  | German FR[1] | UK[2] | France[3] | Spain[2] |
|---|---|---|---|---|
| Receipts |  |  |  |  |
| Private firms | 65.1 | 49.7 | 43.1 | 48.8 |
| Public sector | 32.8 | 38.7 | 50.6 | 48.5 |
| Other | 0.6 | — | 0.6 | 1.1 |
| Export sector | 1.5 | 9.2 | 5.9 | 1.5 |
| Spending |  |  |  |  |
| Private firms | 73.0 | 67.0 | 59.8 | 57.3 |
| Higher education | 14.1 | 14.2 | 15.0 | 15.5 |
| Public sector | 12.3 | 15.1 | 25.2 | 26.3 |
| Non-profit entities | 0.6 | 3.7 | 0.9 | 0.9 |

Source: Ibid., p. 41
Notes: 1 1989; 2 1987; 3 1988

They also compared this effort to corresponding efforts in major OECD nations.

As shown in Table 88, Spain's investment in R & D grew rapidly after 1983, the ratio of such investment of GDP rising from 0.48% in 1983 to 0.90% in 1990 when measured in terms of factor costs. This growth rate was larger than that in the selected industrial OECD countries listed in Table 88. This table also shows that the average annual rate of growth of investment in R & D in Spain was nearly twice the corresponding rate in the listed OECD countries in the period 1983 to 1989.

In spite of Spain's significant effort during these years to advance her internally generated technology, the country's spending on R & D was still quite modest at the end of the decade of the 1980s when compared to the spending in neighbouring industrial nations. In terms of market prices, such spending represented 0.72% of Spain's GDP in 1989. The corresponding percentages in the same year were 2.83% in the German Federal Republic, 2.80% in the United States, 2.33% in France.

Table 89 indicates the receipt and spending of the percentage of aggregate R & D funds by various entities in the economy. The pattern of receipts and spending in Spain did not differ very much in the late 1980s from the corresponding patterns in the other listed nations.

An important result of the growth of R & D investment in Spain was an increase in the numbers of the country's research scientists in the 1980s. Per one thousand members of its active population, the number of Spanish research scientists rose from 1.0 in 1982 to 2.1 in 1990 (Ibid., 43). The number of full-time researchers in Spain still remained much lower than in other OECD countries. In 1987 the German Federal Republic counted 5.6 researchers per 1,000 active population; the number was 4.6 in the United Kingdom, 4.0 in France and 2.9 in Italy.

Lafuente Félez and Oro Giral measured the evolution of the 'scientific output' produced by Spain's increased R & D effort in the 1980s in terms of the increase in the numbers of scientific publications published by Spanish researchers. On the basis of data provided by the Institute for Scientific Information, these writers noticed that between 1982 and 1990 the ratio of the annual number of Spanish scientific publications to the total worldwide number of such publications in the relevant year increased from 0.8% in 1982 to 1.6% in 1990. This rate of increase was much higher than the corresponding rate in other OECD countries.

The writers defined an index of Spanish gains in scientific international competitiveness using the formula:

$$I = [((PS/PX)_t / (PS/PX)_b) - 1] \times 100$$

in which I is the index of gain in scientific competitiveness; PS is the number of Spanish scientific publications in the base year b and in the relevant evaluated year t; PX denotes the number of scientific publications produced in a country X in the years b and t. Table 90 shows that Spain registered significant gains in scientific competitiveness in the 1980s when the index of such gains is calculated according to the above-stated formula. The table shows that such competitiveness increased between 1982 and 1990 by 83.5% with respect to France and by 80.2% with respect to the German Federal Republic.

Lafuente Félez and Oro Giral also noticed that Spain recorded in 1987 one of the highest numbers of scientific publications per 100 researchers. These writers concluded that the rising R & D effort achieved by Spain in the 1980s paid off in terms of a national scientific output whose

Table 90 Scientific output in Spain and other countries: 1982–90

| Country | Ratio of Spanish to global scientific output percentage 1982 | 1990 | Gain in Spanish scientific competitiveness with respect to each other country: 1982–90 percentage |
|---|---|---|---|
| German Federal Republic | 6.3 | 6.8 | 80.2 |
| United Kingdom | 7.1 | 7.8 | 75.5 |
| Italy | 2.2 | 2.8 | 54.9 |
| France | 4.9 | 5.2 | 83.5 |
| United States | 36.6 | 37.9 | 87.7 |
| Spain | 0.8 | 1.6 | – |

Source: Ibid., p. 47

Table 91 Trends in the numbers of patents registered in Spain and in other countries: 1982 and 1988

| Country | Penetration rate of foreign patents[1] 1982 | 1988 | Average percentage annual rate of increase of national patents registered abroad by residents of each country |
|---|---|---|---|
| German Federal Republic | 1.3 | 1.6 | 8.2 |
| United Kingdom | 2.0 | 2.9 | 8.7 |
| Italy | — | — | 10.2 |
| France | 3.4 | 4.3 | 7.4 |
| United States | 0.8 | 0.9 | 8.5 |
| Spain | 5.2 | 13.3 | 10.7 |

Source: Ibid., p. 50
Note: 1 The ratio of foreign patents registered by non-residents to those registered by residents

international competitiveness considerably improved over the course of the decade (Ibid., 50).

These two researchers also studied changes in the rate of penetration of the domestic market by foreign patents and the trend of the numbers of patents registered in other countries by residents of Spain. The rate of foreign patents' penetration of Spain's internal market more than doubled between 1982 and 1988. Concurrently, the average annual rate of increase of the number of patents registered abroad by residents of Spain was the highest of the corresponding rates in the countries listed in Table 91.

*Table 92* Technological coverage ratios in Spain and selected OECD countries

| Country | Technological coverage ratio | |
|---|---|---|
| | 1982 | 1988 |
| German Federal Republic | 0.50 | 0.84 |
| United Kingdom | 1.21 | 0.92[1] |
| Italy | 0.27 | 0.54 |
| France | 0.86 | 0.80 |
| United States | 3.67 | 2.61 |
| Spain | 0.20 | 0.13 |

Source: Ibid., p. 51
Note: 1 1987

These writers also examined the evolution of the external 'technology balance' in Spain and in other OECD countries. Denoting the ratio of receipts from exports of technology not incorporated in productive factors to payments for imports of such technology as the 'technological coverage' ratio, Lafuente Félez and Oro Giral calculated these ratios for the years 1982 to 1988. As indicated in Table 92, Spain's technological coverage ratio declined between those years. The ratio increased however to 0.18 in 1989 and to 0.19 in 1990 (Ibid., 51). The decline in the technological coverage ratio throughout most of the 1980s was largely due to a rapid expansion of Spanish imports of foreign technology made possible by the opening of the national economy. Such imports also grew because of the strengthening of domestic investment during the latter half of the 1980s and because of their support by foreign investment in Spain. Table 92 shows the trends of the technological coverage ratio in Spain and in selected OECD countries from 1982 to 1988.

If we examine the technological coverage ratio for different industrial groups in Spain's secondary sector, we will observe that this ratio was lowest for Spanish technology-intensive industries. In the 1980s, the ratio was larger in lower technology-level industrial groups. Indeed, Spain's high technology industries showed less international competitiveness during the second half of the 1980s than domestic industries operating on the basis of lower levels of technology. The former group had to rely more than the other on imports of advanced foreign technology to meet foreign competition. However, the expansion of R & D funding helped to strengthen the competitiveness of some Spanish high technology industries. Though the country's electrical and electronic machinery industries had to face from 1986 an increasing penetration of rival foreign products into the domestic market, steadily expanding imports of foreign technology helped these industries to expand their

Table 93 Technological coverage ratios in high technology and other industries: 1987

| Country | Aviation | Electrical and electronic equipment | Computers and office machines | Manufacturing |
|---|---|---|---|---|
| German Federal Republic | 0.86 | 1.37 | 0.87 | 1.48 |
| United Kingdom | 1.73 | 0.71 | 0.83 | 0.83 |
| Italy | 1.19 | 0.82 | 0.70 | 1.15 |
| France | 1.62 | 0.93 | 0.71 | 0.95 |
| United States | 2.89 | 0.45 | 1.04 | 0.55 |
| Spain | 0.67 | 0.41 | 0.36 | 0.79 |

Source: Ibid., p. 54

exports during the second half of the 1980s. Table 93 shows technological coverage ratios in high technology and other industries in selected countries in 1987.

The Law for the Promotion of General Coordination of Scientific and Technological Research of 14 April 1986 gave the responsibility for the improvement of the national R & D effort to an Interministry Commission for Science and Technology, the CICYT. A General Council for Science was given the task of coordinating R & D activities pursued jointly by the central government and by autonomous community governments.

The National Plan for Scientific Research and Technological Development of 1988, commonly known as the National Plan for R & D, was to facilitate the improvement and expansion of R & D activities in Spain. This Plan, which was to be reviewed on an annual basis, allocated financial aid to various R & D programmes. The National Plan distinguished National Programmes, Sectoral Programmes, Horizontal and Special Programmes among which figured a Programme for the Development of Research Personnel, and Concerted Programmes dealing with joint public and private research efforts.

Various ministries had the power to propose research programmes containing national objectives. These programmes, once approved by the CICYT, were funded by a National R & D Fund. Autonomous community authorities could request funding for their own research programmes to be financed by this Fund if such programmes pursued goals of national interest. These programmes as well as proposed Sectoral Programmes had to be approved by the CICYT before they could obtain funds from the National R & D Fund.

The evaluation of the technological and economic interests of the various proposed research programmes was the responsibility of the

Center for the Development of Industrial Technology, CDTI. The CDTI evaluated concerted research programmes in which both public and private research centres participated. A Mixed Chamber of Deputies–Senate Commission for Scientific Research formed by twenty-two deputies and by sixteen senators was charged with the task of evaluating each year the industrial achievements attained with the aid of the National R & D Plan.

The National R & D Fund was endowed with 56.9 billion pesetas to fund R & D programmes between 1988 and 1990. Out of this budgetary allocation, over 13 billion pesetas were spent in expanding the numbers and enhancing the quality of Spain's research scientists. The CICYT approved the funding of 1,564 research projects in 1988 and 1989 whose aggregate cost amounted to 19.9 billion pesetas. Between 1988 and 1990 the National R & D Fund further spent 9.8 billion pesetas for the renovation of existing research facilities and for the acquisition of scientific instruments (Ibid., 56–69).

The expansion of concerted research programmes was encouraged by the authorities in order to stimulate the R & D effort of private industrial enterprises and to relate scientific and technological interests to economic interests more closely. The CDTI extended interest-free loans to private firms to facilitate their funding of R & D activities. Between 1988 and 1990, the CDTI spent 17.1 billion pesetas to finance concerted research projects. Nearly two-thirds of these funds were allocated to projects involving the technologies of production and communications (Ibid.).

The priority attached by the González government to the development of production and communications technologies in the distribution of public R & D financial assistance was particularly beneficial to Spain's technology-intensive industries which had to face from 1986 the competition of rival EC firms. Spain's technology-intensive industries were generally the country's strong-demand industries. Indeed, during the second half of the 1980s, internal demand grew most rapidly for the products of such industries and least rapidly for those of the weak-demand industries (Myro, R. 1990, 29). There were exceptions to this general trend. In a few cases, the demand for products of the medium- and weak-demand industries, such as mechanical machinery and transport materials, grew more rapidly than the demand for the products of the strong-demand industries. On the whole, however, the rise of consumption demand for the products of weak-demand industries was modest and the increase in the output of such industries was consequently relatively low. Production expanded most for those industries experiencing a rapidly rising demand for their products. Table 94 shows annual percentage production increases for the country's various industries during the period 1985 to 1988.

Table 94 Annual percentage production increases in Spain's industries: 1985–8

| Sectors | 1985 | 1986 | 1987 | 1988 |
|---|---|---|---|---|
| Energy | 3.1 | 5.2 | −1.9 | −0.4 |
|   Mining of energy minerals | −0.5 | −5.5 | −9.4 | −7.0 |
|   Petroleum products | 2.2 | 10.1 | −4.4 | −1.6 |
|   Electricity, water and gas | 5.5 | 1.5 | 3.7 | 2.8 |
| Non-energy mining | −5.3 | −3.4 | −13.9 | 8.9 |
|   Metallic minerals | −3.8 | −11.6 | −35.3 | 0.8 |
|   Non-metallic minerals | −6.0 | 0.3 | −5.4 | 11.1 |
| Strong-demand sectors | 2.8 | 11.5 | 12.2 | 9.3 |
|   Aviation | −2.1 | 19.0 | 5.3 | 13.1 |
|   Computers and office machinery | 18.0 | 18.4 | 21.7 | 13.2 |
|   Electrical and electronic machinery | −0.2 | 18.4 | 18.1 | 9.9 |
|   Precision instruments | 6.1 | 4.1 | 24.7 | −7.9 |
|   Chemicals | 2.5 | 6.3 | 6.5 | 9.0 |
|   Pharmaceuticals | 14.5 | 13.0 | 11.1 | 12.9 |
| Medium-demand sectors | 4.5 | 2.8 | 8.3 | 4.8 |
|   Cork and plastic goods | 4.8 | 3.3 | 7.5 | 4.1 |
|   Machinery | 9.1 | 6.0 | 7.0 | 6.0 |
|   Vehicles | 8.5 | 11.0 | 11.8 | 13.1 |
|   Railroad equipment | −33.5 | −16.2 | 25.6 | −10.0 |
|   Other transport materials | −5.1 | 6.0 | 20.6 | −25.2 |
|   Foodstuffs, beverages, tobacco | 4.8 | −1.0 | 7.9 | 3.2 |
|   Paper and printing | −2.5 | 6.5 | 4.4 | −0.2 |
| Weak-demand sectors | 0.1 | 1.5 | 3.4 | 3.4 |
|   Basic metals | 1.4 | −7.5 | −1.8 | 3.4 |
|   Steel | 1.4 | −10.6 | −3.3 | 3.2 |
|   Metallic products | 2.2 | 1.8 | 9.2 | 7.7 |
|   Shipbuilding | 4.7 | 27.6 | 8.8 | 31.0 |
|   Artificial and synthetic fibres | 6.0 | −2.5 | −3.7 | −2.7 |
|   Textiles | 3.5 | 9.3 | 3.9 | −7.1 |
|   Leather | −0.8 | 4.0 | −0.2 | −8.8 |
|   Footwear and apparel | −1.4 | −1.4 | −1.3 | −5.8 |
|   Wood and cork | −8.2 | 16.3 | 6.6 | 4.1 |
|   Other manufacturing | 8.0 | 1.6 | 6.3 | 2.0 |
| Construction | 2.2 | 5.9 | 10.0 | 10.5 |

Source: Myro, R., 'La recuperación de la industria española, 1985–1989', in Velarde, J., García Delgado, J.L. and Pedreño, A., La Industria Española, Recuperación, estructura y mercado de trabajo, Madrid, Economistas Libros, 1990, p. 33

Because the growth of internal demand centred on the products of strong-demand industries, industries which had already registered foreign trade deficits in 1985, the external trade deficit of such industries expanded during the second half of the 1980s as they expanded their imports to increase their output while the growth of their exports was hampered by their insufficient international competitiveness and by the rising internal demand. The trend in the foreign trade balance of such industries strengthened Spain's aggregate trade deficit. To maintain an unchanged trade balance during this period, Spain's medium- and weak-demand industries would have had to increase their foreign trade surpluses, a development which required a substantial increase in the exports of medium- and weak-demand industries. This was quite impossible to achieve, given the weak international competitiveness of the products of such industries. In addition, the growth of internal demand limited that of the exports of these industries. Exports of Spain's weak-demand industries, whose principal foreign markets were in non-EC countries, were further hampered by the real appreciation of the peseta in terms of the currencies of those countries.

The rapid growth of Spain's internal demand during the second half of the 1980s, the inability of the country's secondary sector to satisfy internal demand and the real appreciation of the peseta in terms of other currencies were factors which contributed to the increase of Spain's balance of trade deficit in the years of economic recovery. Part of this growing deficit was explained by expanding imports of foreign technology made possible by the government's efforts to intensify and modernize Spanish scientific and technological research. Such efforts promised to raise in the future the international competitiveness of Spanish industry, a development which would increase the country's export capacity and which would allow a gradual reduction of Spain's balance of trade deficit. The growth of the country's export capacity would also tend to offset the negative economic impact of a future weakening of domestic demand.

## GLOBAL ECONOMIC TRENDS AND THE SPANISH ECONOMY: 1987-90

### 1987

The economic historians of the industrialized countries will remember 1987 as the year of the American stock market crash of 19 October 1987, the memorable 'black Monday'. This Wall Street crash was transmitted to other stock markets in the industrialized countries and contemporary economic analysts in the Western world started predicting a serious international economic recession of a severity and a duration not yet ascertainable. Fortunately, such predictions proved to be erroneous. 1987 became the fifth consecutive year of global economic growth, the process of economic expansion in the industrialized countries being stimulated by a continuing rise of internal demand. However, the economic scenario of the Western world in 1987 included three black areas. Major industrial economies recorded continuing, if not worsening, external disequilibria. The United States' budgetary deficit had not been significantly reduced and the country's external deficit remained unchanged. External disequilibria ranged from an American current account deficit of US$156 billion to a Japanese external current account surplus of US$86 billion. The German Federal Republic recorded in 1987 an external surplus of US$44 billion, a figure exceeding its 1986 surplus by US$7 billion (Banco de Bilbao Vizcaya, 1988, 12).

Economic analysts worried about the possible worldwide impact of the American Gramm–Rudman–Hollings Law which imposed automatic cuts on United States federal spending in order to reduce the public deficit. It was feared that this Law could induce the American government to raise taxes, a development which would weaken American demand and reduce the exports of many countries.

Analysts were also alarmed by the effects of slow global economic growth. They pointed out that although global economic growth had still been able to give employment to the natural increases of most countries' active population, it had been unable to lower unemployment rates in such countries. An insufficient increase of the demand of industrialized nations had hindered the growth of world demand for the exports of the NICs at a time when the latter countries needed to expand their exports in order to be able to reduce their foreign indebtedness.

The economic performance of the OECD countries in 1987 was not similar. The rate of economic growth in the United Kingdom attained 3.75%; it was 3.50% in Japan. Australia, Iceland, Portugal and Spain recorded smaller but satisfactory rates of growth. The rate of economic growth in the German Federal Republic was a modest 1.50%. Austria, Belgium, Denmark, France and Greece experienced even lower rates. Table 95 shows rates of growth of real GNP in various OECD countries in 1986 and 1987.

Until the stock market crash of October 1987, the monetary policy of the industrialized countries remained moderately restrictive, largely because monetary authorities apprehended a possible rise of inflation in their countries caused by the failure of the American government to balance its budget. After the October crash, monetary authorities now feared the coming of economic recession and adopted a more expansive monetary policy.

Most OECD countries pursued a restrictive budgetary policy in the first ten months of 1987. Budgetary deficits in those countries, measured as a percentage of their GNP, declined. The aggregate budgetary deficit of the industrialized countries, measured in terms of their real GNP, fell

*Table 95* Annual increases in the rate of growth of real GNP in selected OECD countries: 1986 and 1987
(annual percentage change)

| Country | 1986 | 1987 |
|---|---|---|
| United States | 2.9 | 2.75 |
| Japan | 2.4 | 3.50 |
| German Federal Republic | 2.5 | 1.50 |
| France | 2.0 | 1.50 |
| United Kingdom | 3.3 | 3.75 |
| Italy | 2.7 | 2.75 |
| Canada | 3.3 | 3.75 |
| OECD–Europe | 2.7 | 2.25 |
| OECD–total | 2.8 | 2.75 |

Source: Banco de Bilbao Vizcaya, *Informe Económico 1987*, Bilbao, 1988, p. 14

by 0.5% from their 1986 levels. In the United States the implementation of the Gramm–Rudman–Hollings Act caused a decline in the public deficit from 3.8% of real GNP in 1986 to 2.4% in 1987 (Ibid., 18).

Employment in the European OECD countries increased by only 1% in 1987. In the United States employment strengthened, the increase attaining 2.75% in that year. In the European countries, the rate of unemployment in 1987 stood at 10.75%, remaining practically unchanged from its 1986 level. In the United States the rate declined from 7.0% in 1986 to 6.25% in 1987.

Throughout 1987 import prices of primary commodities, measured in dollar terms, rose by 7.5%. The rise of such prices was due to a number of factors: as the production of such commodities, including that of crude oil, came under tighter governmental controls, surpluses of such commodities started disappearing; concurrently, the demand for such commodities in the industrialized nations and in the NICs increased. The increase in the dollar prices of imported primary commodities strengthened inflationary pressures in those countries. Concurrently, real wages in the industrialized nations rose by 1.5% in 1986 and by 1% in 1987. As a result, consumer goods prices rose in most industrialized OECD countries. As shown in Table 96, the index of consumer goods prices in 1987 was 0.6% above its 1986 level. Analysts pointed out that should the industrialized economies experience stronger economic activity in 1988 while maintaining their external disequilibria, inflation rates in those economies would rise.

World trade in terms of volume expanded at the rate of 4% in 1987. In terms of US current dollars, the value of such trade rose by 15.6% over its 1986 value. The increase in the value of world trade in 1987 was due largely to both the depreciation of the American dollar in terms of other

*Table 96* Indices of consumer goods prices in selected OECD countries: 1986 and 1987
(percentage change from previous year)

| Country | 1986 | 1987 |
|---|---|---|
| United States | 2.2 | 4.0 |
| Japan | 0.6 | 0.25 |
| German Federal Republic | −0.5 | 0.75 |
| France | 2.5 | 3.25 |
| United Kingdom | 3.6 | 3.00 |
| Italy | 6.1 | 5.00 |
| Canada | 4.2 | 4.25 |
| OECD–Europe | 3.7 | 3.75 |
| OECD–total | 2.9 | 3.50 |

*Source*: Ibid., p. 22

currencies and to the increase in the dollar import prices of primary commodities, including the price of imported crude oil.

Although economists had feared that the stock exchange crises of late 1987 could have depressive economic effects in 1988, economic activity in the Western world proved to be surprisingly strong in the latter year. The growth of economic activity in the OECD area in 1988 was much stronger than predicted. In many industrialized nations, demand, investment and production growth strengthened the rate of inflation and their monetary authorities adopted a more restrictive monetary strategy during the second half of the year. All of the OECD countries recorded an increase of their real GNP. The average yearly rate of real GNP increase for the twenty-four member countries was 4%; for the European OECD nations, this average rate was 3.5% (Banco de Bilbao Vizcaya, 1989, 13).

## 1988

Various factors contributed to the dynamism of economic activity in the industrialized countries in 1988. During the first half of that year, the apprehension of a coming strong recession resulting from the financial crises of October 1987 induced national monetary authorities to adopt an expansive monetary policy. In all the OECD countries, the growth of domestic consumption and investment spending boosted aggregate internal demand at a rate which had not been foreseen in 1987. The rise in consumption spending was based on an increase in the disposable income of households and did not affect private saving. The strong rise in internal demand induced the secondary sectors of these countries to fully utilize their existing productive capacity; improving entrepreneurial

# ECONOMIC RECOVERY, 1985-90

*Table 97* Unemployment and consumer prices inflation rates in OECD countries: 1987 and 1988 (unemployment rate as percentage of active population, inflation rate as percentage change over previous year)

| Country | Unemployment rate 1987 | 1988 | Inflation rate 1988 |
|---|---|---|---|
| United States | 6.2 | 5.50 | 4.25 |
| Japan | 2.8 | 2.50 | 1.00 |
| German Federal Republic | 7.9 | 7.75 | 1.25 |
| France | 10.5 | 10.25 | 2.50 |
| United Kingdom | 10.3 | 8.50 | 5.25 |
| Italy | 11.0 | 11.25 | 4.25 |
| Canada | 8.9 | 7.75 | 3.75 |
| Spain | 20.5 | 19.50 | 4.50 |
| OECD–Europe | 10.7 | 10.25 | 4.75 |
| OECD–total | 7.9 | 7.25 | 3.75 |

*Source*: Banco de Bilbao Vizcaya, *Informe Económico 1988*, Bilbao, 1989, p. 15

*Graph 23* Annual percentage changes in the prices of consumer goods over their level in the previous year in major OECD countries: 1984–9

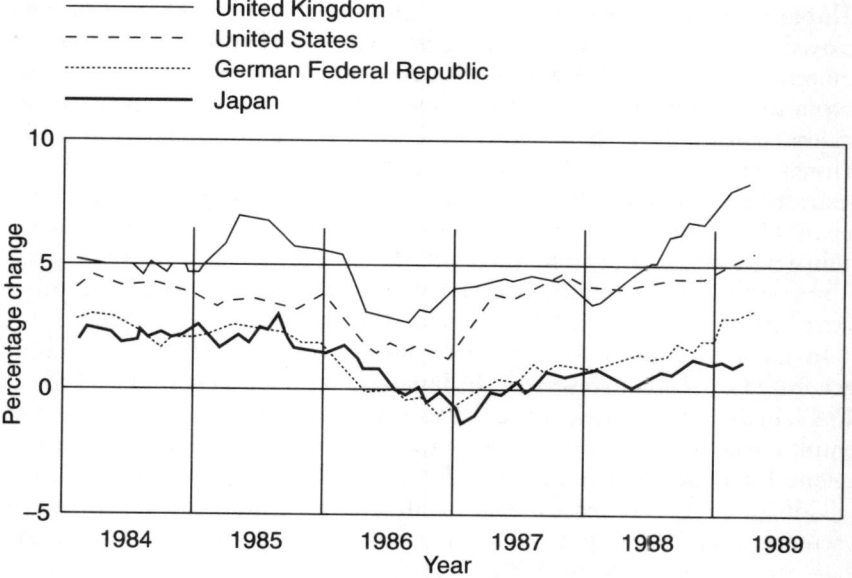

*Source*: Banco de Bilbao Vizcaya, *Informe Económico 1988*, Bilbao, 1989, p. 16

expectations caused an increase in productive investment. The expansion of such investment was the major factor explaining an increase of 1.0% in aggregate employment within the OECD–Europe area. This rise in employment reflected mostly an increase of part-time workers in the tertiary sectors of these economies; employment in the secondary sectors actually diminished. In most OECD countries, the unemployment rate showed a slight fall, as shown by Table 97.

Graph 23 shows the annual rate of change in consumer goods prices in major OECD nations between 1984 and the beginning of 1989. The strengthening of inflationary pressures in 1988 was due to a rise in the import prices of non-energy primary commodities and to the inability of domestic production to satisfy the rising domestic demand.

World trade experienced a strong increase in 1988. This trade increased by 8.5% in terms of volume over its 1987 level. The value of the trade in terms of American dollars rose by 14%. This increase in value was explained by the rising trade activity, a moderate increase in inflation in the trading nations and by the depreciation of the United States dollar (Ibid., 20).

## 1989

Global economic expansion continued in 1989. The pace of economic growth decelerated however in a few countries. The United States, the United Kingdom and Asiatic NICs recorded smaller rates of growth. Economists suggested that the growth trend OECD economies had followed since 1982 had finally reached a point of inflection in 1989. Monetary authorities, fearful of strengthening inflation, adopted a restrictive monetary policy which produced rising interest rates and acted as a brake on the pace of worldwide economic growth. Nevertheless, the industrialized nations remained on the whole on their growth path. Annual percentage changes in the growth of GNP in most OECD countries were however smaller in 1989 than in 1988, as shown by Table 98.

In most of these countries, economic growth in 1989 was mainly generated by rising investment. In Japan investment increased by 18% in 1989. In the totality of the OECD area investment rose by 9%. In that area employment increased by 1.7% in the same year, while the area rate of unemployment declined to 6.6% (Banco de Bilbao Vizcaya, 1990, 13).

Consumer goods prices rose in all OECD countries. Their rate of increase was 2.9% in the German Federal Republic. In Japan, this rate rose from 1.0% in 1988 to 2.6% in 1989. The increase in the rate of inflation diminished during the second half of the year as a result of higher rates of interest, moderate wage increases and a deceleration in the growth of internal demand. On the whole, the global 1989 economic scenario of the industrialized world showed a

Table 98 Annual percentage change in GNP growth in the OECD area: 1988 and 1989

| Country | 1988 | 1989 |
|---|---|---|
| United States | 4.4 | 2.9 |
| Japan | 5.7 | 4.9 |
| German Federal Republic | 3.6 | 4.3 |
| France | 3.8 | 3.7 |
| United Kingdom | 4.5 | 2.4 |
| Italy | 3.9 | 3.3 |
| Spain | 5.3 | 5.2 |
| OECD–Europe | 3.7 | 3.5 |
| OECD–total | 4.4 | 3.6 |

Source: Banco de Bilbao Vizcaya, *Informe Económico 1989*, Bilbao, 1990, p. 12

continuation of the economic growth trend which had started in 1982.

## 1990

The year 1990 appeared to bring an end to the long period of economic growth which the industrialized countries had experienced since 1982. The major political events of 1990, i.e. the unification of the two Germanies, the collapse of the political regimes of the Eastern European nations and the Gulf War affected the industrialized economies of the OECD in different ways. While the rate of economic growth declined in both the United States and the United Kingdom, it increased in Germany and in Japan. Averages of the values of key economic indicators for the entire OECD area no longer had much explanatory value.

Nineteen ninety could be divided into two distinct periods. Until August of that year restrictive monetary policies had little effect on generally optimistic entrepreneurial expectations. From August, however, the increase in the price of imported crude oil and the growing uncertainty about the global economic future brought about by the Gulf War started having an immediate negative impact on economic growth in the industrialized world. By the end of the year, the industrialized economies were experiencing rising inflationary pressures, increasing external deficits, a decline in industrial investment and rapidly deteriorating entrepreneurial expectations.

The major industrialized countries recorded dissimilar economic experiences in 1990. Real GNP increased by only 1% in the United States and by 0.6% in the United Kingdom. The German Federal Republic and Japan recorded the highest rates of economic growth they had attained since the mid-1970s. Japan's rate of economic growth was 5.6% and

*Table 99* Annual changes in the index of consumer goods prices: 1989 and 1990 (percentages)

| Country | 1989 | 1990 |
| --- | --- | --- |
| United States | 4.8 | 5.4 |
| Japan | 2.3 | 3.1 |
| German Federal Republic | 2.8 | 2.7 |
| France | 3.5 | 3.4 |
| United Kingdom | 7.8 | 9.5 |
| Italy | 6.3 | 6.5 |
| Spain | 6.8 | 6.7 |
| OECD | 4.4 | 4.9 |

*Source*: Banco de Bilbao Vizcaya, *Informe Económico 1990*, Bilbao, 1991, p. 14

that of the German Federal Republic was 4.5% (Banco de Bilbao Vizcaya, 1991, 12). The prospect of a long war with Iraq weakened the pace of economic growth in the United States and in the United Kingdom. The potential benefits of a Single European Market strengthened economic activity in the continental countries of the European Community.

All of the OECD countries experienced however an increase in their rates of inflation, largely the result of the increase in the price of imported crude oil from August 1990. Table 99 shows the annual change in the index of consumer goods prices in selected OECD countries in 1989 and in 1990.

Rising inflation and the deteriorating global political scenario caused the rate of increase of the volume of world trade to decline to 5% in 1990, a decline which increased the aggregate external deficit of the OECD area.

## The Spanish economy 1987–90

### 1987

In spite of the stock exchange crises in late 1987, Spain's economic growth in that year was stronger than the average growth in the developed countries. Spain's GDP increased in real terms at the rate of 5.3% in 1987, a rate of growth made possible by a number of developments, among them an improvement in the country's real terms of trade with the rest of the world, a significant decline in the rate of growth of consumer goods prices from 8.8% in 1986 to 5.2% in 1987 and a spectacular increase in domestic demand which rose at the annual rate of 7.9%, the highest rate of growth of real demand in the OECD area in 1987. Because the rise of domestic production could not satisfy the expanding internal demand, one-third of such demand had to be supplied by imports (Banco de Bilbao Vizcaya, 1988, 47).

Domestic investment demand expanded at the rate of 15.9%. Investment in fixed capital increased by 13.8%, with investment in industrial equipment and in transport goods rising by 18.9%; investment in construction expanded by 10.5% (Ibid., 48). This investment was used to modernize production facilities and to expand existing industrial capacity. Investment in industrial equipment surpassed by 22.7% that of 1986 and imports of such equipment in 1987 rose by 28% above their 1986 value. Investment in construction departed from its trend in earlier years with employment in that industrial subsector rising by 94,600 jobs, an increase of 11.4% in the numbers of persons employed in construction. These investments boosted the gross formation of capital to 21.7% of the GDP, a gain of 1.8 percentage points over the corresponding percentage in 1986 (Ibid., 49).

The growth of consumption spending in 1987 returned to the rates attained prior to the oil crises of the 1970s. Public consumption increased by 9% in real terms, an increase which mostly financed the acquisition of capital goods. Public salaries and wages and public transfers took a smaller part of public consumption spending than in earlier years. Real private consumption recorded a growth rate of 5.2%. Spanish consumers increased their spending on the acquisition of automobiles, electrical household appliances and electronic consumer goods. The import of foreign-made automobiles increased by 95%. Because the growth of consumers' spending slightly exceeded the growth of real household income, the latter being restricted by an increase in the household tax burden, gross household saving declined by −3.1%.

Domestic production responded to the strong rise in internal demand but was unable to satisfy it. Unlike the typical situation which existed during the years of economic crisis, in 1987 production rose most strongly in the primary sector and in the construction industry. The secondary and tertiary sectors expanded their output at the rate of 4.5%. The primary sector expanded its output by 9.5%, contributing thereby to the deceleration of internal inflation and to the growth of GDP. The output of cereals in 1987 was 23% larger than it had been in the previous year.

Industrial output increased at the rate of 4.7%, a higher rate than that attained in 1986 when this rate was 3.2% (Ibid., 46). Production growth was stronger in the equipment and transport goods industries. Table 100 shows changes in rates of industrial output growth in 1987.

Mining was the most depressed industry in Spain in 1987. Coal mining, as well as the mining of metallic and non-metallic ores, declined,

GROWTH AND CRISIS IN THE SPANISH ECONOMY

*Table 100* Annual changes in domestic industrial outputs: 1987 (percentages)

| Rates of growth over 5 per cent | | Rates of growth below 5 per cent | | Rates of decline | |
|---|---|---|---|---|---|
| Electronic components | 31.2 | Textiles | 3.9 | Leathergoods | −0.3 |
| Precision instruments | 24.7 | Mineral products | 3.8 | Metallurgy | −0.9 |
| Automobiles | 12.4 | Electricity, gas | 3.5 | Footwear, apparel | −1.2 |
| Electrical machinery | 10.7 | Chemicals | 1.8 | Petroleum products | −4.8 |
| Metallic products | 9.3 | Mechanical machinery | 0.8 | Mining of non-metallic ores | −5.2 |
| Shipbuilding | 8.8 | | | Coal | −9.1 |
| Foodstuffs, beverages, tobacco | 8.1 | | | Mining of metallic ores | −5.2 |
| Rubber and plastics | 7.3 | | | | |
| Wood and furniture | 6.4 | | | | |
| Paper, printing | 5.0 | | | | |

*Source*: Banco de Bilbao Vizcaya, *Informe Económico 1987*, Bilbao, 1988, p. 46

exposing Spain's industry to the risks of a greater dependency on foreign sources of energy.

The growth of industrial activity was not uniform throughout Spain. The regions of strong industrial growth were Andalusia, Aragón, the Balearic Islands, the Canary Islands, Catalonia, La Rioja, Murcia, Navarra and Valencia. The weakest growth of industrial activity centred in the northern areas of Asturias, the Basque region, Cantabria and Galicia.

A major achievement of the Spanish economy in 1987 was the narrowing of the price gap between EC consumer goods prices and those of Spain. This gap amounted to 5.5 percentage points at the end of 1986. It was reduced to 1.4 percentage points in December 1987 (Ibid., 55). This development was largely due to the deceleration of domestic inflation, to the relative stability of import prices in terms of pesetas and to a decline of −1.8% in the domestic prices of agricultural products.

In spite of a deteriorating trade balance, Spain's merchandise trade deficit of US$12.9 billion was covered by a services balance surplus of US$13.3 billion and by a transfers balance surplus of US$2.6 billion (Ibid., 53).

The rising trade deficit was the inevitable result of Spanish imports rising much faster than Spanish exports, both in value and in volume. In 1987, the totality of Spain's imports cif amounted to US$6 billion, the dollar value of Spanish exports attaining only US$4.2 billion. Spain imported in that year not only more industrial equipment than in 1986, but also more consumer goods. In terms of value, the import of industrial equipment rose by 41.3% in 1987; the import of foreign consumer goods increased by 44.8%.

An examination of the relative weight of Spain's exports in 1987 shows that Spain's industrial products were not sufficiently competitive in foreign markets in spite of the government's efforts to advance national industrial technology. The value of Spain's exports in terms of 1986 pesetas rose by 6.91% over its 1986 level. The export of foodstuffs showed a 17.6% increase in value; the increase in the corresponding value of exports of industrial products was only 4.9% (Ibid., 52).

In spite of a deteriorating balance of trade, Spain received in 1987 a massive net inflow of foreign, long-term capital exceeding US$8 billion. This capital inflow was financed by foreign and multinational commercial and industrial enterprises establishing themselves in Spain, a country which after its entry into the European Community offered excellent development potential. The immediate result of this foreign capital inflow was a dramatic increase in Spain's foreign exchange reserves which rose from US$16 billion in December 1986 to US$30.1 billion at the end of 1987.

The European Community remained Spain's best trading partner country in 1987. It absorbed 64% of Spain's exports and provided that country with 55% of its imports. Spanish imports from Japan and from the COMECON countries increased in 1987, as well as imports from Hong Kong, South Korea, Taiwan and Singapore. The latter group of countries supplied, however, only 2.2% of the totality of Spain's imports (Ibid., 53).

The main target of the government's monetary policy in 1987 was to limit the rate of inflation of consumer goods prices to 5%. The strong expansion of liquid assets in the hands of the people, the ALPs, threatened to increase the country's rate of inflation above its targeted level. In August 1987, the yearly rate of growth of the ALPs attained 20.6%, a rate which was about twice the targeted growth rate range of 8% to 11%. The high rate of growth of ALPs was largely the result of the government's substitution of short-term 'Treasury Letters' which were considered to be part of the ALPs for long-term public bonds, which were not classified as such. In order to restrict the growth of domestic liquidity, the country's monetary authorities adopted a number of measures: interest rates were increased at the risk of attracting to Spain an expanding flow of speculative short-term capital; bank deposits in foreign currencies were barred from earning interest; and financial institutions were compelled to hold a larger percentage of their cash holdings in the form of public securities. As a result, the ALPs' rate of growth declined to 14.2% at the end of the year (Ibid., 42).

## The success of restructuring and economic planning

There is no question that the remarkable achievements of the Spanish economy in 1987 were partly due to the strengthening of the world economy. Spain's entry into the European Community also boosted its economic activity. Such entry brought optimism to Spain's entrepreneurs and investors. Spain's economic performance in 1987 was however also due to the industrial policy pursued for some years by the PSOE government. The economic achievements of Spain's economy in 1987 were the result of earlier UCD and PSOE efforts to modernize the country's industrial sector and reflected the efforts made by the González government to expand public financial assistance for both private and public industrial research and development.

The early industrial strategy of the UCD governments had been centred on the granting of public financial assistance to industrial firms experiencing losses in order to prevent their collapse and the disappearance of the employment they supported. The PSOE government continued with greater vigour the policy of industrial restructuring and modernization. It published in May 1983 a White Paper on Reconversion and Reindustrialization which detailed its industrial policy goals. The achievement of these goals was given official recognition by the Royal Decree 831983 of 30 November 1983, and by a Law 27 of 26 July 1984. The White Paper examined three main aspects of industrial policy: the selection of measures needed to achieve the industrial plans of the government; the costs of industrial reconversion and reindustrialization and their finance; and the problem of declining industrial employment and regional economic difficulties. The Ministry of Industry and Energy was charged with the responsibility of implementing the government's industrial policy.

Industrial reform programmes could be initiated by the government acting alone, or by petitions to the Ministry of Industry and Energy presented by either employers' organizations or by trade unions. If the government accepted the inclusion of an industrial subsector or that of a group of industrial firms in a reconversion programme, the details of that programme were to be jointly formulated by the public authorities, the relevant employers' organization and the trade unions. The reconversion plan had to be worked out as a 'concerted action'.

If these parties were unable to agree on a joint reconversion plan, the government's experts could then submit their own proposed plan to a Select Commission for Economic Affairs which would decide whether or not the proposed plan should be presented to the Council of Ministers for its approval. If approved by this council, the plan proposed by the government's experts would acquire the force of law.

An important feature of the Law 27/1984 was the establishment of

Zones of Urgent Reindustrialization, the ZUR. The government was allowed to provide special development assistance to industries located in these ZURs. The latter covered industrial zones in Asturias, the Barcelona area, Cádiz, Madrid, Vigo–Ferrol and Vizcaya.

The Law purported to solve problems of sectoral excess capacities and redundant industrial labour forces. The implementation of this Law was quite successful. Economists who had participated in its formulation had estimated that by the end of 1989 excess labour in the industrial subsectors covered by the Law would amount to about 91,000 workers. The government succeeded in reducing this figure by 90% as of 31 December 1989. Necessary public investment in these subsectors was calculated at 756 billion pesetas. By the end of 1989, the government had invested 662 billion pesetas in the relevant industries, 87.5% of the targeted amount (Ibid., 254). A shortcoming of this policy was that such public financial assistance was only directed at a few industrial subsectors in order to maintain the viability of their industrial enterprises. Little was done to expand strong-demand industries.

It was only after Spain's incorporation into the European Common Market that the Spanish government became interested in adopting a horizontal industrial policy, i.e. a policy covering the entirety of the country's secondary sector. This policy was to raise productive technological levels, to improve the quality of Spanish industrial products and to give special assistance to medium- and small-size industrial firms. It was to promote and assist the merger of industrial enterprises.

A National Plan for Electronic and Information Science, PEIN I, was enacted in 1984; it was succeeded by a PEIN II which was to cover the period 1988 to 1990. The PEIN's objectives were to strengthen the domestic demand for electronic and information products, to expand Spain's exports of such products, to reduce Spain's dependence on foreign technology in its nascent electronics industry and to assist the development of an adequate infrastructure for this industry.

At the end of 1990, a PEIN III, covering the period 1991 to 1993, was enacted by the government. The principal goal of the new Plan was to facilitate the public financing of Spanish technological innovation. It purported to improve the adjustment of the R & D work of private enterprises in Spain's electronics industry to the needs of major consumers of advanced electronic technology such as the military establishment and the telecommunications industry. Another objective of PEIN III was to bring to Spain multinational enterprises and their advanced technological know-how (Ibid., 261).

A National Plan for Scientific and Technological Research covering the years 1988 to 1991 was endowed with a fund of 32 billion pesetas to finance the training of scientific researchers, to improve the country's scientific and technological infrastructure, and to approve and finance scientific research projects, particularly those related to concerted industrial renovation plans. As noted above, the Centre for Industrial Technological Development, CDTI, also funded R & D activities undertaken by private firms, particularly in the fields of communications, cybernation, new materials production and biochemistry.

A National Plan for Industrial Quality was enacted for the years 1990 to 1993. This Plan aimed to raise the quality of Spanish industrial products in order to strengthen the competitiveness of Spanish industry in the Single European Market which was to become operative in 1993. The Plan received a fund of 13 billion pesetas (Ibid., 265).

The government expanded its aid to small and medium-size industrial firms, known in Spain as the PYMES. An Institute for Small- and Medium-Size Enterprises, the IMPI, an agency operating under the direction of the Ministry of Industry and Energy, was to facilitate the dissemination of technological and commercial information to the PYMES, to promote greater cooperation and mergers between these firms and ease their access to financial markets. It was also charged with the task of encouraging the improvement in the design of domestic industrial products and the adoption by small and medium-size firms of more efficient methods of production. A Plan for the Promotion of Design, Quality and Fashion was formulated to provide producers of apparel and textiles, footwear and jewellery, furniture, ceramics and toys with extensive marketing information.

The PSOE government also decided to reprivatize or to partially privatize a number of public enterprises in order to provide the latter with greater managerial efficiency. Spain's socialist government proceeded to reduce the size of the national public sector and placed in the hands of private shareholders partial or total control of nationalized industrial enterprises. It took measures to prevent the INI from acquiring private firms facing financial difficulties and attempted to rid the public sector of unprofitable enterprises. A well-known partial privatization action taken by the government related to the large public enterprise REPSOL, a state-owned concern responsible for the import of crude oil, for its refining, for the production of oil-based products and for the acquisition of Spanish interests in oil extraction outside Spain. Of REPSOL's capital, 26.5% was made available to private investors. Sixty-five million shares of REPSOL's stock were sold to private purchasers and the company acquired through these sales 380,000 new shareholders (Martín Mateo, R., 1990, 447–60).

## 1988

Spanish economic growth remained strong in 1988. The country's GDP rose by 5.1% and internal demand increased by 6.8% above its level in

1987. A number of developments facilitated the continuation of economic growth. Spain's integration into the European Common Market induced foreign and multinational firms to start operations in the country. Net long-term capital inflows went on increasing and allowed the economy to benefit from expanding investment in fixed capital. Although rising foreign competition in the domestic market hurt a number of Spanish industrial subsectors, the opening of the Spanish economy boosted production and employment in the country. In addition, Spain's real terms of trade continued improving. Spanish economic growth was however not costless. Rapidly rising imports increased the external trade deficit. The Spanish balance of trade deficit had amounted to 2.55% of the GDP in 1985; it became equivalent to 5.19% of a larger GDP in 1988. Rising production and larger employment were also accompanied by rising prices and rising public spending (Banco de Bilbao Vizcaya, 1989, 48).

The strong growth of domestic demand in 1988 was explained by the growth of gross capital formation which rose at the annual rate of 14.6%. Private consumers' spending increased by 9.8% as a result of the growth of real disposable household income by 9.6%. Public consumption in real terms increased by 5%.

Domestic prices started rising more rapidly from mid-1988. The index of Spanish consumer goods prices, which in December 1987 surpassed by 4.5% its December 1986 level, was 5.8% above its December 1987 level at the end of 1988. Calculated in terms of an annual average, the rate of Spanish consumer prices increased by only 4.8% in 1988. In spite of the strengthening of inflation during the latter half of 1988, Spanish price trends in that year remained quite similar to those in the other EC countries. By the end of 1988, the differential in consumer goods prices between Spain and the rest of the European Community was only 1.6%, four percentage points less than in 1986 (Ibid., 52). The increase in Spain's rate of inflation during the second half of 1988 caused great concern to Spanish economists at the time. Table 101 shows the relative contribution of various cost groups to the general increase in prices in the period 1985 to 1988. For the latter period, the average annual increase of prices of goods and services constituting the GDP amounted to 7.74%.

Table 101 indicates that indirect taxes, largely the VAT, financial costs and the residual component played the largest role in the rise of the general price level. Per unit labour costs, with an average annual increase of 6.91%, also contributed to inflation. It was only the improvement in the country's real terms of trade which exerted a downward pressure on domestic prices.

The Banco de Bilbao Vizcaya study group analysed the percentage contribution of each cost group to the rise in prices in each year. Table

*Table 101* Relative contribution of various cost groups to the level of inflation: 1985–8 (annual percentage change in unit prices)

| Cost group | 1985 | 1986 | 1987 | 1988 | Average annual rate |
|---|---|---|---|---|---|
| GDP at market prices | 8.55 | 10.92 | 5.92 | 5.58 | 7.74 |
| Labour costs | 6.09 | 9.66 | 6.13 | 5.74 | 6.91 |
| Financial costs | 3.20 | 13.72 | 10.07 | 10.09 | 9.27 |
| Indirect taxes | 15.62 | 26.42 | 3.09 | 6.12 | 12.81 |
| Imports | 3.86 | −16.31 | 0.17 | 2.13 | −2.54 |
| Exports | 6.82 | −1.98 | 2.46 | 3.66 | 2.74 |
| Residual | 12.28 | 17.54 | 7.15 | 5.19 | 10.54 |

Source: Banco de Bilbao Vizcaya, *Informe Económico 1988*, Bilbao, 1989, p. 66

*Table 102* Percentage contribution of each cost group to the rate of inflation: 1985–8

| Cost group | 1985 | 1986 | 1987 | 1988 | Average annual rate |
|---|---|---|---|---|---|
| GDP at market prices | 8.55 | 10.92 | 5.92 | 5.58 | 7.74 |
| Labour costs | 2.88 | 4.47 | 2.80 | 2.63 | 3.19 |
| Financial costs | 0.19 | 0.77 | 0.58 | 0.60 | 0.54 |
| Indirect taxes | 1.41 | 2.55 | 0.34 | 0.65 | 1.24 |
| Foreign trade | −0.77 | −3.45 | −0.47 | −0.27 | −1.24 |
| Residual | 4.84 | 6.58 | 2.67 | 1.97 | 4.01 |

Source: Ibid.

102 shows that indirect taxes and the residual component acted most strongly on the rise in prices in 1985 and in 1986. In 1987 and in 1988, the increase in labour and financial costs were the main determinants of the increase in the rate of inflation.

In terms of pesetas, the prices of Spanish imports increased by 2.5% in 1988. In 1987, they had risen by only 0.9%. The peseta prices of Spanish exports increased by 5.2% in 1988, a rate exceeding that of 3.2% in 1987. These foreign trade price trends improved Spain's real terms of trade by 2.6%.

The aggregate value of Spanish imports, cif, amounted to US$57.6 billion in 1988. That of aggregate exports was only US$39.9 billion. The resulting trade deficit of US$17.7 billion was US$4.5 billion larger than it had been in 1987. As shown by Table 103, the surpluses recorded by the balance of services and rents and that of transfers did not cover the

Table 103 Spain's external accounts: 1986–8 (billion US dollars)

| External accounts | 1986 | 1987 | 1988 |
|---|---|---|---|
| Imports, cif | 33.46 | 46.30 | 57.60 |
| Crude oil | 4.04 | 5.02 | 5.34 |
| Other | 29.42 | 41.28 | 52.25 |
| Exports, fob | 26.95 | 33.40 | 39.95 |
| Trade balance | −6.51 | −12.90 | −17.65 |
| Services, other income | 9.34 | 10.23 | 9.58 |
| Services | 11.53 | 13.01 | 13.22 |
| Other income | −2.18 | −2.78 | −3.64 |
| Transfers | 1.13 | 2.61 | 4.47 |
| Current balance | 3.96 | −0.05 | −3.58 |
| Long-term capital balance | −3.35 | 8.87 | −10.61 |
| Basic balance | 0.61 | 8.82 | 7.03 |
| Accumulated reserves | 16.00 | 30.17 | 39.87 |

Source: Ibid., p. 63

trade deficit. Spain's current account deficit in 1988 reached US$3.6 billion.

The increased aggregate dollar value of Spanish imports in 1988 was mostly due to larger imports of manufactured goods and of consumer goods. Imports of consumer goods expanded by 27.1% in terms of their value in 1987; those of manufactured goods by 25.8% in terms of value. The import of energy products recorded, however, a decline of 18.7% in value (Ibid., 60).

Expanding imports of foreign capital goods of advanced technological content were undoubtedly beneficial to the future of the Spanish economy; they facilitated the growth of domestic production and a rise in the productivity of domestic industries. In terms of constant pesetas, Spanish imports increased by 13.9% in 1988; exports increased by only 6.2%. An indication of the industrialization of the Spanish economy was the fact that exports of industrial equipment increased by 24.9% in 1988 while the export of foodstuffs declined by 5.6% (Ibid., 61).

Spain's long-term capital balance recorded a surplus which rose from US$8.8 billion in 1987 to US$10.6 billion in 1988. As a result of the expanding inflow of foreign capital, Spain's basic balance showed a surplus of US$7 billion at the end of 1988.

The increase of the rate of inflation in the summer of 1988 induced Spain's monetary authorities to adopt stronger restrictive measures. Financial institutions were directed to hold a larger percentage of their cash holdings in the form of government securities, rates of interest were increased and new limitations were imposed on the inflow of foreign capital. By the end of the year, the average annual rate of interest charged by private banks for credits and loans of three years was 16.9% higher than it had been twelve months earlier (Ibid., 75).

The growth of the economy in 1988 expanded national employment by 2.9% over its 1987 level. Employment conditions in Spain in that year were favoured by the fact that the annual rate of growth of the young active population, i.e. persons between the ages of 16 and 24, was only 0.5%, whereas the total active population expanded at the rate of 1.5%. In spite of a decline in Spain's rate of unemployment from 20.5% in 1987 to 19.5% in 1988, Spain remained at the end of the latter year the EC country with the highest unemployment rate (Ibid., 68).

## Unemployment in Spain

A persistent high rate of unemployment remained Spain's major economic problem during the long period of economic crisis and during the years of economic recovery in the second half of the 1980s. Professor Andrés Pedreño Muñoz has examined the characteristics and the determinants of Spain's unemployment problem and the theories relied on by various economists to explain this phenomenon (Pedreño Muñoz, A., 1990a, 395–419, and 1990b, 387–419).

Professor Pedreño, observing the dramatic increase of Spain's unemployment rate from 2.6% of the active population in 1973 to 22.6% in 1986, noted that increasing unemployment affected the economies of most industrialized nations during the period of global economic crisis starting at the end of 1973. By 1985, most European Community countries recorded a two-digit rate of unemployment as shown by Table 104. Japan, the Scandinavian countries and the United States were the only industrialized countries able to maintain single figure unemployment rates. Within the European Common Market area, Spain not only had the highest rate of unemployment in this group of countries in 1985 and in 1988, but these rates dramatically surpassed corresponding rates in other EC countries.

This economist also observed that in Spain, just as in most OECD countries, the numbers of long-term unemployed persons, i.e. people who remained jobless for one year or more, constituted a large percentage of the totality of the unemployed. As shown by Table 105, next to Belgium, Spain recorded the highest percentage of long-term unemployed in total unemployment. In Spain, the percentage of persons remaining unemployed for a period exceeding two years rose from 4.2% of total unemployment to 36.1% in 1986 (Pedreño Muñoz, A., 1990a, 405). Long-term unemployment in Spain burdened most heavily women, persons with relatively low education or training and young people seeking their first job.

Economists have relied on two principal theories to explain Spain's

*Table 104* Rates of unemployment in various OECD nations: 1967–88 (numbers of unemployed as a percentage of the active population)

| Country | 1967–74 | 1975–9 | 1980–3 | 1986 | 1988 |
| --- | --- | --- | --- | --- | --- |
| Belgium | 2.6 | 7.02 | 11.5 | 11.3 | 10.2 |
| Denmark | 1.3 | 6.5 | 9.9 | 8.3 | 8.6 |
| France | 2.5 | 4.9 | 7.5 | 10.2 | 10.1 |
| German Federal Republic | 1.1 | 3.5 | 5.4 | 7.2 | 6.2 |
| Ireland | 5.6 | 7.0 | 9.7 | 11.5 | 16.6 |
| Italy | 5.6 | 6.8 | 8.6 | 10.5 | 11.8 |
| Netherlands | 2.2 | 5.3 | 9.9 | 10.6 | 9.5 |
| United Kingdom | 3.4 | 5.8 | 10.9 | 11.4 | 9.1 |
| Sweden | 2.2 | 1.9 | 2.8 | 2.8 | 1.6 |
| Norway | 1.7 | 1.9 | 2.4 | 2.6 | 3.2 |
| Finland | 2.5 | 5.1 | 5.4 | 5.0 | 4.5 |
| United States | 4.6 | 6.9 | 8.4 | 7.1 | 5.4 |
| Japan | 1.3 | 2.0 | 2.3 | 2.6 | 2.5 |
| Spain | 2.7 | 5.8 | 14.6 | 21.4 | 19.1 |

Source: Pedreño Muñoz, A., 'Análisis del desempleo español: necesidad de nuevos enfoques', in Velarde, J., García Delgado, J.L. and Pedreño, A., eds, *La Industra Española, Recuperación, Estructura y Mercado de Trabajo*, Madrid, Economostas Libros, 1990, p. 388

*Table 105* Percentage of long-term unemployed persons in total unemployment: 1979 and 1985

| Country | 1979 | 1985 |
| --- | --- | --- |
| Belgium | 58.0 | 68.3 |
| France | 30.3 | 46.8 |
| German Federal Republic | 19.9 | 31.0 |
| Ireland | 31.8 | 41.2 |
| Netherlands | 27.1 | 55.3 |
| United Kingdom | 24.8 | 41.0 |
| Finland | 19.3 | 21.1 |
| Norway | 3.8 | 8.3 |
| Sweden | 6.8 | 11.4 |
| United States | 4.2 | 9.5 |
| Japan | 16.5 | 11.8 |
| Spain | 27.5 | 57.3 |

Source: Pedreño Muñoz, A., 'Desempleo, fuerza de trabajo y mercado laboral', in García Delgado, J.L., ed., *La Economía Española de la Transición y la Democracia*, Madrid, CIS, 1990, p. 406

serious unemployment problems in the 1970s and in the 1980s. One study approach has relied on macroeconomic classical theory to identify the principal causes of Spain's persistent high unemployment rate. The 'classicists' have suggested that the main causes of the country's high unemployment level were continuing labour market rigidities and the excessive increase of real salaries and wages. The dramatic real wage increases which followed the first oil crisis exceeded rates of productivity growth and reduced profits. These writers pointed out that between 1970 and 1976, real labour costs in Spain increased by 60% and that between 1970 and 1983 the real cost of social security contributions paid by Spanish employers per worker rose by 122% (Ibid., 409). Growing unemployment could not be avoided in a situation in which real labour costs went on rising at a time of economic crisis. The rise of labour costs started decelerating only in the early 1980s. These classicists argued that the rise of real labour costs was the principal reason for the fall in investment during the years of economic stagnation and induced management to substitute capital for labour in that period. In their view only a drastic liberalization of existing labour market institutions and a containment of the pace of increase of real labour costs could solve the endemic high unemployment problem of Spain's economy.

Spanish 'Keynesians' have questioned the conclusion that the rise of real labour costs was the key factor producing the country's high level of unemployment during the decade 1975 to 1985. They also doubted that the institutional rigidities of the labour market contributed to the persistence of a high rate of unemployment in the years of economic crisis. These economists asserted that major reasons for the country's unemployment problem were the poor quality and the lack of dynamism of Spain's entrepreneurs, their obsolete skills and practices and their excessive dependence on governmental protection (Ibid., 410). For them, it was the lack of perception and the unwillingness of Spain's industrial managers to adopt more efficient methods of production which constituted the main reasons for the fall in domestic capital formation in this period. These writers felt that their country's high level of unemployment could only be reduced by an expansion of investment, investment which would be used to improve the economy's infrastructure and to advance industrial technology. They pointed out that the government's counter-inflationary monetary and fiscal policies increased rates of interest and discouraged investment.

Professor Pedreño believes that a large array of variables, both macroeconomic and microeconomic, have an impact on the level of unemployment in any economy and that their relative explanatory weight varies over time. He supports Professor R. M. Solow's conclusion that the trend in real wages does not necessarily reflect the trend in prices. Whereas prices are determined in commodity markets, wages are determined in a separate labour market where their trend is influenced by factors such as the strength of labour unions, possible mismatches between demanded and offered skills and the coverage level and time limitations of unemployment insurance. The larger unemployment insurance benefits are, the longer the job seeker may take to find the 'proper' job. The harsher the terms of the existing unemployment insurance system, the more rigorous will be the attempt by an unemployed person to find employment and the shorter will be his or her period of unemployment. This Spanish scholar also believes that significant increases in direct taxes may induce many workers to earn an income in the 'underground economy' while registering as unemployed in order to avoid paying income taxes. As the numbers of workers employed in the underground economy increase, the official level of unemployment will necessarily rise. Under such circumstance, the level of unemployment is determined by personal behaviour rather than by macroeconomic trends. A careful labour policy will have to pay particular attention in these circumstances to the micro-determinants of people's inducement to work officially. Professor Pedreño believes that a shortcoming of Spain's labour policy was that it was exclusively based on macro-interpretations of the country's unemployment problem and ignored the effects of microeconomic variables on the level of employment (Pedreño Muñoz, A., 1990b, 391–401).

## 1989

1989 continued the strong growth the Spanish economy had experienced since the summer of 1985. For the fourth consecutive year, Spain's real GDP increased at a higher rate than that of the entire EC. The study group of the Banco de Bilbao Vizcaya calculated the rate of annual growth of real GDP in 1989 at 5.2%. For the period 1985 to 1989, Spain's real GDP expanded by 21%, i.e. at an average annual rate of 4.9%. Spain's rate of economic growth in those four years exceeded that of the European Community. Aggregate EC real GDP increased by 13.2% in that period, i.e., at the average annual rate of 3.1% (Banco de Bilbao Vizcaya, 1989, 47). As a result of such growth trends, the differential between Spain's GDP per inhabitant and that of the EC was narrowed. Whereas Spain's GDP per inhabitant was 71.8% of that of the EC in 1985, it attained 75.9% of the EC average in 1989 (Ibid.).

Spanish economic growth in 1989 continued to be stimulated by a strong increase in real internal demand which recorded an annual rate of growth of 7.7%. Because domestic production was unable to satisfy the expanded demand, 44% of such expansion had to be covered by imports. The country's external deficit on current account increased by US$10.4 billion. At the end of the year, Spain's basic balance of payments recorded, however, a surplus of US$7.09 billion and that country's foreign exchange reserves rose from US$39.8 billion in 1988 to US$44.4 billion in 1989. This surplus was made possible by continuing large inflows of long-term foreign capital which surpassed those of the previous year by US$17.5 billion; in addition, net inflows of short-term capital in 1989 attained the sum of US$981 million (Ibid., 64).

The most dynamic component of aggregate domestic demand in 1989 was investment demand which increased at the annual rate of 14.5%. Investment in fixed capital expanded by 13.6%, with investment in industrial equipment and transport goods rising by 14.3% and that in construction by 13.1% (Ibid., 58). Gross domestic capital formation in 1989 represented 25.6% of the GDP, a gain of two percentage points over this figure in 1988.

Real private consumption spending grew by 5.6% while real public consumption rose by 5.5%. Spain's private consumers increased their purchases of automobiles by 6% and those of electrical household appliances by 9%. Because the rate of growth of disposable household income in 1989 was slightly lower than that of private consumption, household savings diminished.

The domestic production of Spain's economic sectors showed very different trends in 1989. While the real output of the construction industry expanded by 13.1%, that of the primary sector declined by 2.7%. The secondary and tertiary sectors of the economy recorded annual growth rates of 5.5% and 4.9% respectively. Within the secondary sector production performance varied sharply among industries. The strongest growth was recorded by the energy industries, i.e. those producing coal, coke, electricity, gas and petroleum products. Table 106 shows the annual percentage changes in the indices of domestic industrial production. As shown in Table 106, the output of processed foodstuffs, beverages, tobacco, footwear, apparel and of rubber and plastics products declined, largely as the result of rising foreign competition in the domestic market.

A major threat to the maintenance of Spain's strong pace of economic growth was the rise in the rate of inflation which started in the second half of 1988. The average annual rate of increase of consumer goods prices had been 4.8% in 1988; this rate rose to 6.8% in 1989 (Ibid., 65).

During the triennium 1987 to 1989, the prices of Spanish goods and services composing the GDP rose at the average annual rate of 6.09%. The principal factors contributing to such inflationary trends were the rise of per unit labour costs and the increases in financial costs and in the rate of gross profits. During this period of three years, per unit labour costs increased at the annual rate of 6.26%.

A more positive aspect of the development of the Spanish economy in 1989 was the increase in the level of employment by 4.2%, a growth rate which surpassed the 1.1% rate of growth of the active population. As a result, the rate of domestic unemployment diminished by two percentage points (Ibid., 48).

## ECONOMIC RECOVERY, 1985-90

*Table 106* Annual percentage changes in the indices of industrial production: 1986-9

| Index | 1986 | 1987 | 1988 | 1989 |
|---|---|---|---|---|
| General index | 3.0 | 4.7 | 2.9 | 4.4 |
| Energy | 0.7 | 0.0 | 0.5 | 5.9 |
| Coal, coke | -3.7 | -9.1 | -6.7 | 12.0 |
| Petroleum products | 10.1 | -4.8 | -1.7 | 7.2 |
| Electricity, gas | 1.4 | 3.5 | 2.8 | 4.9 |
| Basic industries, mining, chemicals | -1.2 | -0.3 | 3.6 | 5.8 |
| Metallurgy | -7.2 | -0.9 | 3.4 | 6.7 |
| Non-metallic minerals | 7.5 | 3.8 | 7.9 | 7.7 |
| Chemicals | 1.5 | 1.8 | 1.6 | 4.3 |
| Metals processing | 9.3 | 11.7 | 9.6 | 6.4 |
| Metal products | 1.7 | 9.3 | 7.8 | 9.3 |
| Mechanical equipment | 5.7 | 0.0 | 2.6 | 7.6 |
| Electrical equipment | 12.9 | 10.7 | 7.8 | 8.9 |
| Electronic equipment | 29.2 | 31.2 | 13.2 | -5.0 |
| Automobiles | 10.9 | 12.4 | 13.1 | 6.7 |
| Shipbuilding | 27.8 | 8.8 | 20.8 | 10.7 |
| Other manufactures | 2.9 | 5.0 | -0.4 | 2.1 |
| Foodstuffs, beverages, tobacco | -0.9 | 8.1 | 3.2 | -1.4 |
| Textiles | 8.1 | 3.9 | -7.1 | 4.9 |
| Leather goods | 4.0 | -0.3 | -8.8 | 3.0 |
| Footwear, apparel | -1.6 | -1.2 | -5.8 | 0.1 |
| Cork, wood, furniture | 16.2 | 6.4 | 4.1 | 3.8 |
| Paper, printing | 6.4 | 5.0 | -0.2 | 7.3 |
| Rubber and plastics | 0.8 | 7.3 | 4.0 | 1.1 |

*Source*: Banco de Bilbao Vizcaya, *Informe Económico 1989*, Bilbao, 1990, p. 56

The acceleration of economic growth since the second half of the year 1988 strengthened inflationary pressures and increased Spain's external current account deficit as rising internal demand caused domestic prices to rise and imports to expand.

The government's economists had planned to limit the rate of increase of real GDP in 1989 to 4% and had targeted for that year a rise of 3% in the domestic prices of consumer goods (Ibid., 77). In order to achieve such goals, the monetary authorities targeted a rate of increase for the ALPs of between 6.5% and 9.5% with a central rate of 8%. External deficits were to be covered by a continuing net inflow of foreign capital. Bank credit to the private sector was not to expand by more than 11.5%, a goal which was to be attained by means of an increasingly restrictive monetary policy supporting high interest rates.

This monetary policy was moderately successful. From August 1989, the rate of growth of bank credit to the private sector decelerated, though this rate averaged 17.2% in 1989. Between August and December, the ALPs expanded at the targeted rate of 8% after recording a rate of growth of 16% during the first seven months of the year. For 1989 as a whole, the ALPs grew at an average rate of 10.5%, a rate slightly higher than the targeted rate's upper limit of 9.5% (Ibid., 83).

A flaw in the government's strategy for the containment of inflation was that monetary policy alone was given the responsibility of maintaining an acceptable increase in domestic prices. The effectiveness of such policy was weakened by the growth of public spending.

The Gulf War of August 1990 clouded entrepreneurial predictions with uncertainties. The duration of the conflict and its possible effects on the prices of crude oil were not ascertainable at that time. The growth rate of the Spanish economy had started decelerating in July, partly as a result of restrictive measures taken by the government to correct internal economic disequilibria, partly because fewer foreign tourists entered the country and also because the pace of increase of domestic investment weakened. GDP, which had recorded a real rate of increase of 4.8% in 1989, expanded by only 3.7% in 1990. The rate of growth of real aggregate demand which had attained the annual average of 7.8% in 1989, declined to 4.3% in 1990 (Banco de Bilbao Vizcaya, 1991, 39–40).

The gap between the rate of growth of domestic demand and that of the GDP narrowed in 1990. Only 16% of the increase in national demand in 1990 was covered by imports. In 1989, real private consumption spending increased by 5.6% over its level in the previous year. In 1990, this rate was 4.3% (Ibid., 58). This decline in the growth of private consumption was mostly due to a fall in consumer spending on durable consumer goods. The purchase of automobiles in 1990 fell by 12.4% below its 1989 level. Imports of consumer goods which had grown at the rate of 20.3% in 1989, increased by only 13.1% in 1990 (Ibid.). Investment demand also declined in that year.

Domestic production followed the declining trend of internal demand. Spain's economic sectors recorded different rates of production growth in 1990. The primary sector's output increased at the rate of 2.8%. Industrial production rose by 2.5% and services grew at the rate of 3.4%. By comparison with these relatively modest growth rates, construction increased the value of its output by 9.7% (Ibid., 49).

Spain's balance of trade deficit was reduced in 1990 as the rate of growth of Spanish exports surpassed for the first time in the decade the rate of increase of the country's imports. In 1989, the strong growth of domestic demand had produced a trade deficit equivalent to 6.5% of the GDP. Only Greece and Portugal recorded in the EC area a balance of trade deficit at a higher percentage of their GDP. In 1990, the decelerating growth of Spanish internal demand reduced the percentage

Table 107  Spain's external accounts: 1989 and 1990 (billion US dollars)

|  | 1989 | 1990 |
|---|---|---|
| Imports | 67.38 | 83.08 |
| Exports | 42.54 | 54.29 |
| Balance of trade | −24.84 | −28.79 |
| Balance of services | 9.12 | 8.87 |
| Balance of transfers | 4.78 | 5.33 |
| Balance on current account | −10.94 | −14.59 |
| Balance of long-term capital | 17.51 | 18.59 |
| Basic balance | 6.57 | 4.00 |
| Accumulated reserves | 44.42 | 53.10 |

Source: Banco de Bilbao Vizcaya, *Informe Económico 1990*, Bilbao, 1991, p. 64

of the country's trade deficit to 5.9% (Ibid., 66). Spain's balance of services surplus, evaluated as percentage of the current GDP, fell from 3.5% of the GDP in 1989 to 1.8% in 1990. The country's balance on current account deficit rose from US$10.9 billion in 1989 to US$14.6 billion in 1990. As in the previous year, an expanding net inflow of foreign capital amounting to 10.5% of the GDP preserved a basic balance surplus, though the latter declined from US$6.5 billion in 1989 to US$4 billion in 1990. Table 107 shows Spain's external accounts in 1989 and in 1990.

## 1990

In 1990, the European Community continued to be Spain's best trading partner. Spain's trade with the EC expanded while Spanish exports to the United States declined. Table 108 shows that in terms of pesetas, Spain's exports in 1990 recorded a stronger annual growth rate than Spanish imports.

Consumer goods prices increased at the annual average rate of 6.7% in 1990, a rate identical to that of 1989. Because salaries and wages showed a real annual increase of 8.3% in that year, consumption spending expanded.

Table 108  Spain's foreign trade: 1989 and 1990 (billion pesetas)

|  | 1989 | 1990 | Percentage increase |
|---|---|---|---|
| Imports | 8,396.4 | 8,914.7 | 6.17 |
| Exports | 5,134.5 | 5,642.7 | 9.90 |
| Trade deficit | 3,261.9 | 3,271.9 | 0.31 |

Source: Ibid., p. 68

Spain's active population, i.e. the population over 16 years of age which was either employed or was seeking employment, increased by 1.2 million persons between 1985 and 1990, a growth equivalent to an annual increase of 1.7%. The growth of the country's active population was strengthened by a rising participation of women in the labour market.

In order to reduce the numbers of unemployed in 1985, i.e. nearly three million persons, net increases in the country's numbers of employed in the period 1985 to 1990 had to exceed the increase in Spain's active population in the same period. The active population increased by 1.2 million persons during those years. There were, however, 1.7 million new jobs created in this period and the numbers of unemployed persons consequently declined by 500,000 during these five years. Spain's rate of unemployment as a percentage of the country's active population fell from 21.5% in 1985 to 16.3% in 1990.

Spain's economic sectors experienced differing trends in their employment levels. Between 1987 and 1990, employment in the primary sector declined by 14.1%. Industrial employment increased by 7.8%; employment in the tertiary sector rose by 14.4% and that in the construction industry by 30.9%. In spite of a rising participation of women in the labour force, the male unemployment rate in the last quarter of 1990 was only 11.9% but the female rate of unemployment attained 23.8% (Ibid., 79).

Spain's employment difficulties greatly improved during the second half of the 1980s. In spite of an increase in the participation of women in Spain's total active population and although the latter expanded, the country's rate of unemployment steadily declined. A major problem faced by the PSOE government was to facilitate the continuation of this trend. This was a difficult problem. Only an annual increase of the real GDP at a rate exceeding 3% would allow an annual creation of new jobs which would be larger than the annual increase of the active population and thus allow a further decline of the unemployment rate.

## CONCLUSION: THE ECONOMIC ACHIEVEMENTS OF THE PSOE GOVERNMENT DURING THE SECOND HALF OF THE 1980s

The best evaluation of the effectiveness of the PSOE government's economic policies which followed in the latter half of the 1980s is a comparison of major economic trends in both Spain and in the neighbouring EC countries in that period.

The Statistical Department of the EC Commission has computed on an annual basis the ratio of discrepancy between the GDP per inhabitant in each of the twelve Community nations and the average GDP per inhabitant in the entire EC area. This ratio is adjusted to eliminate computation biases originating in changes in foreign exchange rates. Between 1985 and 1990, Spain's GDP per inhabitant narrowed its differential with the EC average by 4.9 percentage points (Ibid., 43). In 1990, Spain's GDP/inhabitant index still represented only 76.7% of the entire Community's average ratio. Spain's GDP/inhabitant index in that year amounted to only 70.7% of that of France.

To narrow this differential further Spain's GDP would have to grow in each subsequent year at a higher rate than the GDP growth rate for the entire Community. The study group of the Banco de Bilbao Vizcaya estimated that if Spain's GDP growth rate surpassed that of the European Community by only one percentage point in each year of the century's last decade, Spain's GDP/inhabitant in the year 2,000 would still represent only 86.4% of the Community's average figure (Ibid., 44). During the period 1986 to 1989, Spain's annual rate of economic growth surpassed the Community's average annual rate of growth by one and a half percentage points. This trend appeared to end in 1990 when Spain's rate of economic growth surpassed that of the Community by only 0.8%. Nevertheless, Spain's economic growth record in the second half of the 1980s constituted a great achievement of the González administration.

To continue narrowing the GDP/inhabitant differential between Spain and the Community, the Spanish economy had to maintain an annual growth rate of 3.5% in the 1990s without experiencing at the same time intensifying internal economic disequilibria. A potential danger to the growth of the Spanish economy was the pace of increase of domestic demand which remained larger than the rise of internal production. In 1989, the rate of increase of national demand surpassed by three percentage points that of the GDP. It was important for the government to narrow this differential in future years. The achievement of such a goal could weaken the country's annual rate of economic growth since a reduction of the rate of growth of domestic demand could adversely affect the level of investment.

A major factor explaining the strengthening of Spanish domestic demand was the strong growth of investment in fixed capital. During the triennium 1987 to 1989, domestic investment expanded by 47.8%, i.e. by an annual average rate of 14%. This rate declined to 6.7% in 1990. In that year, the Spanish ratio of investment in fixed capital to GDP represented 24.4% of the country's GDP, a rate which exceeded the corresponding average EC rate by 3.6 percentage points. A continuing, non-inflationary high investment ratio will force Spain's economic authorities to reduce the growth of both private and public consumption spending, a strategy difficult to pursue in a country whose residents are eager to come closer to the standards of living prevailing in the industrialized EC nations.

A major flaw in Spain's economic development was that per unit Spanish labour costs rose faster than the corresponding costs in other EC countries. The rate of increase of these costs in Spain in the years 1988 to 1990 remained 2.5% higher than that in the industrialized nations of the EC. Relatively high per unit labour costs in Spain maintained comparatively high domestic inflation rates, rates which resulted in relatively high interest rates, the latter strengthening in turn the continuing rise in domestic prices (Ibid., 46–7).

The expansion of employment in the period 1985 to 1990 was probably the strongest economic achievement of the PSOE government. During these five years, Spanish employment increased by 15.7%. The increase in non-agricultural employment in the same period attained 24.7%. In spite of such employment growth, Spain retained in 1990 one of the highest rates of unemployment in Europe. With an unemployment rate of 16.3% in 1990, Spain's unemployment rate was nearly twice as large as the average rate for the entire European Community.

## REFERENCES

Alonso, A., *España en el Mercado Común, Del Acuerdo del 70 a la Comunidad De Doce*, Madrid, Espasa Calpe, 1985.

Banco de Bilbao, Banco de Bilbao Vizcaya, *Informe Económico*, Bilbao (various issues).

Cuervo, A., *La Crisis Bancaria en España, 1977–1985*, Barcelona, Ariel, 1988.

Dorado, R., Triana, E., Rojo, J.M. and Martínez, F., eds, *Ciencia, Tecnología e Industria en España, Situación y Perspectivas*, Madrid, Fundesco, 1991.

Fundación Humanismo y Democracia, *El Decenio González*, Madrid, Ediciones Encuentro, 1992.

Gámir, L., 'Realidad y Política Económica Socialista: Una Interpretación', in *El Decenio González*, supra, pp. 171–95.

Granell, F., 'La Integración en la Comunidad Europea y sus Efectos sobre la Exportación Española', in *Información Comercial Española*, Nr. 588/89, Madrid, Aug./Sep. 1982, pp. 135–41.

Lafuente Félez, A. and Oro Giral, L.A., 'Evolución del Sistema de Ciencia y Tecnología en España, El Plan Nacional de I & D', in *Ciencia Tecnología e Industria en España, Situación y Perspectivas*, supra, pp. 33–123.

Martín Mateo, R., 'Revisión de la Intervención Pública en la Economía Española', in Velarde, J., García Delgado, J.L. and Pedreño, A. eds, *La Industria Española, Recuperación, Estructura y Mercado de Trabajo*, Madrid, Economistas Libros, 1990, pp. 447–60.

Myro, R., 'La Industria: Expansión, Crisis y Reconversión', in García Delgado, J.L., ed., *España, Economía*, Madrid, Espasa Calpe, 1988, pp. 197–230.

——, 'La Recuperación de la Industria Española, 1985–1989', in *La Industria Española, Recuperación, Estructura y Mercado de Trabajo*, supra, pp. 13–58.

Oller, V. and Conejos, J., 'Política Industrial', in Gámir, L., ed., *Política*

*económica de España*, Madrid, Alianza Editorial, 1993, pp. 249-67.
Pedreño Muñoz, A., 'Desempleo, Fuerza de Trabajo y Mercado Laboral', in García Delgado, J.L., ed., *La Economía Española de la Transición y la Democracia*, Madrid, CIS, 1990a, pp. 395-419.
——, 'Análisis del Desempleo Español: Necesidad de Nuevos Enfoques', in *La Industria Española, Recuperación, Estructura y Mercado de Trabajo*, supra, 1990b, pp. 387-19.
Petitbò, A. and Saez Barcena, J., 'El Papel de la Política Industrial en la Recuperación y Reestructuración de la Industria Española', in *La Industria Española, Recuperación, Estructura y Mercado de Trabajo*, supra, pp. 59-90.
Rodríguez Braun, C., 'De la Agonía a la Agonía', in Tusell, J. and Sinova, J., eds, *La Década Socialista, El Ocaso de Felipe González*, Madrid, Espasa Calpe, 1992, pp. 51-66.
Share, D., *The Making of Spanish Democracy*, New York, Praeger, 1986.
Torrero Mañas, A., 'El sector financiero: cambios y tendencias', in García Delgado, J.L., ed., *La Economía Española de la Transición y la Democracia*, Madrid, CIS, 1990, pp. 343-60.
Vázquez, J.A., 'Crisis, Cambio y Recuperación Industrial', in García Delgado, J.L., ed., *La Economía Española de la Transición y la Democracia*, supra, pp. 81-117.

# 6

# THE RETURN OF ECONOMIC CRISIS AND THE CHALLENGES OF THE EARLY 1990s

## THE SPANISH ECONOMY IN 1991

The Spanish economy continued to experience a deceleration of its rate of growth in 1991. The annual growth of its real GDP had started declining in 1989. This rate declined from 5.2% in 1988, to 4.8% in 1989, to 3.7% in 1990 and to 2.5% in 1991. This continuous fall in the annual rate of growth of GDP was due to a strong decline in the annual growth of internal investment whose rate fell from 13.8% in 1988 to 6.9% in 1990 and to 1.6% in 1991. Concurrently, gross national saving fell from 22.7% of the nominal GDP in 1988 to 21.7% in 1991. Spaniards were allocating an increasing share of their disposable income to the purchase of consumer goods to the detriment of productive investment and of the country's external current account (Banco de Bilbao Vizcaya, 1992, 7–14).

Following the Persian Gulf crisis, consumption demand expanded in Spain, while the growth of investment demand decelerated. Aggregate internal demand grew at the rate of 2.9% in 1991, increasing the external current account deficit. Private consumption demand expanded by 3.3% in that year; investment in fixed capital rose by only 1.8% (Ibid., 25). Departing from its trend in the previous year, the rate of growth of consumers' demand for durable consumption goods declined in 1991. On the other hand, imports of consumer goods, which had grown by 13.1% in 1990, rose by 18.7% in 1991.

The National Institute of Statistics estimated that domestic investment in industrial equipment and in transport goods declined by 2.5% in 1991. Spanish firms reported a fall of 41% in orders for new industrial equipment. Table 109 shows the significant decline in Spanish demand for industrial equipment and transport goods in 1991.

Investment in construction expanded by 2.5%, though the domestic consumption of cement grew by only 0.8% in the same year (Ibid., 28–30).

Table 109 Percentage annual changes in Spanish investment in industrial equipment and transport goods: 1990 and 1991

|  | 1990 | 1991 |
|---|---|---|
| Industrial production index, industrial equipment | −4.5 | −10.3 |
| Imports of industrial equipment | 6.2 | 2.2 |
| Purchases of transport vehicles | −4.2 | −9.5 |
| Orders for industrial equipment | −17.0 | −41.0 |
| Investment in industrial equipment | −3.8 | −6.4 |

Source: Banco de Bilbao Vizcaya, *Informe Económico 1991*, Bilbao, 1992, p. 29

Table 110 Structure of the Spanish GDP by sectors: 1970–91 (current prices, percentages)

| Year | Primary sector | Industry | Construction | Services |
|---|---|---|---|---|
| 1970 | 11.55 | 32.97 | 8.25 | 47.23 |
| 1971 | 12.31 | 31.91 | 7.77 | 48.01 |
| 1972 | 11.57 | 32.68 | 7.75 | 48.00 |
| 1973 | 11.26 | 32.39 | 8.29 | 48.06 |
| 1974 | 10.44 | 31.86 | 8.71 | 48.99 |
| 1975 | 10.26 | 30.54 | 8.49 | 50.71 |
| 1976 | 9.67 | 30.46 | 8.02 | 51.85 |
| 1977 | 9.34 | 29.82 | 7.78 | 53.06 |
| 1978 | 9.16 | 29.03 | 7.56 | 54.25 |
| 1979 | 8.17 | 28.62 | 7.59 | 55.62 |
| 1980 | 7.48 | 28.04 | 7.44 | 57.04 |
| 1981 | 6.57 | 27.95 | 6.87 | 58.61 |
| 1982 | 6.79 | 27.18 | 6.79 | 59.24 |
| 1983 | 6.54 | 27.38 | 6.27 | 59.81 |
| 1984 | 6.92 | 26.52 | 5.47 | 61.09 |
| 1985 | 6.39 | 27.90 | 6.28 | 59.43 |
| 1986 | 6.20 | 28.39 | 6.62 | 58.79 |
| 1987 | 5.98 | 27.51 | 6.83 | 59.68 |
| 1988 | 5.96 | 26.63 | 7.45 | 59.96 |
| 1989 | 5.43 | 25.78 | 8.36 | 60.43 |
| 1990 | 5.13 | 23.94 | 9.11 | 61.82 |
| 1991 | 4.64 | 22.99 | 9.38 | 62.99 |

Source: Ibid., p. 111

The growth of GDP at factor costs of 2.5% was based on the expansion of construction and of services, the latter recording a growth rate of 2.8% in 1991. Industrial output grew at the low rate of 1.6% and that of the primary sector declined by 0.2% (Ibid., 15).

Tables 110 and 111 indicate that over the long period 1970 to 1991, Spain's industrial sector lost importance in the domestic economy while

Table 111 Spain's employment structure and unemployment rate: 1970–91
(percentages)

| Year | Primary sector | Industry | Construction | Services | Unemployment rate |
|---|---|---|---|---|---|
| 1970 | 27.0 | 24.3 | 8.2 | 40.5 | 1.35 |
| 1971 | 25.9 | 24.5 | 8.3 | 41.3 | 1.79 |
| 1972 | 24.7 | 25.0 | 8.6 | 41.8 | 2.13 |
| 1973 | 23.6 | 24.7 | 9.1 | 42.7 | 2.50 |
| 1974 | 22.4 | 24.9 | 9.3 | 43.4 | 2.93 |
| 1975 | 21.8 | 25.1 | 9.3 | 43.8 | 3.74 |
| 1976 | 20.6 | 25.1 | 9.4 | 44.9 | 4.53 |
| 1977 | 19.4 | 25.5 | 9.5 | 45.7 | 5.25 |
| 1978 | 19.0 | 25.4 | 9.3 | 46.3 | 7.03 |
| 1979 | 18.8 | 25.1 | 9.0 | 47.1 | 8.67 |
| 1980 | 19.2 | 24.9 | 8.6 | 47.3 | 11.44 |
| 1981 | 18.5 | 24.8 | 8.2 | 48.5 | 14.15 |
| 1982 | 18.2 | 24.3 | 8.1 | 49.4 | 16.13 |
| 1983 | 18.1 | 24.4 | 7.8 | 49.8 | 17.70 |
| 1984 | 17.7 | 24.1 | 7.3 | 50.9 | 19.54 |
| 1985 | 17.4 | 23.4 | 7.0 | 52.2 | 20.75 |
| 1986 | 15.5 | 23.5 | 7.4 | 53.7 | 20.47 |
| 1987 | 14.5 | 23.1 | 7.8 | 54.6 | 19.82 |
| 1988 | 13.8 | 22.8 | 8.3 | 55.2 | 18.79 |
| 1989 | 12.5 | 22.7 | 8.9 | 55.8 | 16.73 |
| 1990 | 11.4 | 22.8 | 9.3 | 56.6 | 15.72 |
| 1991 | 10.3 | 22.0 | 9.7 | 58.0 | 15.82 |

*Source*: Ibid., p. 109

the tertiary sector became the foremost growth sector. During this period of 21 years, the secondary sector's contribution to the domestic economy, estimated either by its gross value added or by its employment, declined. This slow process of domestic deindustrialization was and remains a major concern to the country's political leaders and to its economists. During the 1980s, and particularly after 1986, it became increasingly apparent that Spain's relatively low levels of industrial productivity and rising per unit costs of production were seriously undermining the ability of the country's industrial firms to compete with foreign products in both foreign and domestic markets. An increase of 19.4% in Spanish imports of foreign consumer goods in 1991 revealed the weakening sales position of domestic industrial firms in their home market.

At the end of this period, the survival of many Spanish industrial firms was threatened by significant differences in domestic price trends. Prices of industrial products rose on the average by only 1.5% in 1991, while the prices of services increased by 9%. Wages rose by 9.2%. Such trends forced on many Spanish industrial firms the alternative of reducing their labour force and raising their productivity or ceasing operations. A few industries expanded their output in 1991. These were industrial subsectors producing processed foods and beverages, automobiles, electrical power and printing. Mining, metallurgy, textiles, footwear and apparel started experiencing conditions of economic recession.

In spite of an improving export performance, Spain's balance of trade deficit in 1991 attained US$32.9 billion, this deficit being equivalent to 6.3% of the country's GDP (Ibid., 40). The balance on current account deficit showed a small increase from its level in the previous year, rising from 1,851 billion pesetas in 1990 to 1,926 billion pesetas in 1991. A capital transfers surplus and an expanding net inflow of foreign long-term capital allowed the basic balance to maintain a surplus and the country's foreign reserves increased by US$13.18 billion.

The value of Spanish exports rose by 10.3%, a rate of increase which exceeded that of imports which amounted to 8.5% (Ibid., 31).

A negative aspect of such trade centred on Spain's rapidly rising imports of consumer goods, the rate of increase in the value of such imports attaining 18.7% while imports of industrial equipment in the same year grew by only 2.1%. Such import trends were a bad omen for the future of the Spanish economy.

The countries of the European Common Market continued to be Spain's best trading partners. In 1991, 59.9% of Spain's imports originated in EC countries and 70.7% of Spanish exports were acquired by the latter. The value of Spanish exports to Denmark increased by 76.7%. The value of these exports to Germany rose by 31.1% (Ibid., 40). Spain's export capacity would have been larger had the country's inflation rate and the rate of increase in its per unit production costs been those prevailing in the rest of the European Community.

The EC was not only Spain's best trading partner. It was also its most important financier. In order to finance the country's large balance of trade deficit, the Spanish economy needed annual large net inflows of foreign capital. During the years 1980 to 1985, the EC countries had supplied Spain with 52% of its foreign financed investment. This percentage dramatically increased following Spain's entry into the European Community. Between 1986 and 1990, the figure increased to 75%. France, Germany, the Netherlands, the United Kingdom and Switzerland provided over 50% of the foreign capital entering Spain (Ibid., 45).

During the period 1986 to 1990, foreign investment largely by-passed growth industries such as the production of automobiles, chemicals and pharmaceuticals (industries already saturated with foreign capital) to favour the production of energy, construction and, more particularly, banking and insurance.

At the start of 1991, foreign capital controlled 97% of Spain's information industry, 95% of the country's automobile manufacturing industry, 90% of its electronics industry and 41% of Spanish food processing industries (Ibid., 47).

The pace of increase of consumer goods prices decelerated in 1991, the average annual rate of increase in such prices attaining 5.9%, a decline from the 6.7% rate which prevailed in 1990. The decline in the Spanish rate of consumer goods prices inflation caused the rate of inflation differential between Spain and the EC to be reduced by one percentage point. Differing price trends in Spain's various economic sectors presented, however, a possible threat to the future growth of the country's tertiary sector. While the prices of domestic industrial products increased by only 1.5% and those of agricultural products showed a fall of 0.2%, prices of services rose by 10.2% (Ibid., 12).

Although the decline in Spain's rate of inflation was advantageous to domestic economic growth, the continuation of a large public deficit and an unfavourable balance of external trade remained major disequilibria in the Spanish economy, disequilibria which contributed to the deceleration of the country's GDP growth in 1991. Such deceleration explained a reduction in the rise of employment which in 1991 attained only 1.1%. Given the low annual increase in the country's active population of 0.3% in 1991, Spain's rate of unemployment, measured as a percentage of the active population, remained stable at 15.8% (Ibid., 11–12).

Professor Luis Gámir, a supporter of the opposition Popular Party, attributed the deceleration of his country's economic growth between 1990 and 1992 to the faulty economic policies of the PSOE government and particularly, to the continuing rise in public spending. For him, the socialist government was largely responsible for Spain showing the strongest deceleration of economic growth in the entire EC area, a deceleration which was accompanied by increases in the Spanish budgetary deficit which surpassed those in the other EC nations. He noticed that Spain had the highest unemployment rate of all the OECD countries and the second highest external trade deficit when this deficit was measured as a percentage of GDP (Gámir, L., 1992, 188).

Writing in support of his party's economic policy, Gámir pointed out that the Popular Party stood for a true free market economy, an economy the country needed to raise the economic efficiency of its industries and to strengthen the international competitiveness of the latter. He explained that the key agent of growth in that economy would be the Spanish 'Schumpeterian entrepreneur'. Gámir, like his illustrious Austrian mentor, asserted that only risk-loving, efficiency-seeking, employment-creating private entrepreneurs could inject new strength and vitality to the deteriorating Spanish economy. He chastised the Social Democrats for pursuing the goals of economic and social egalitarianism, goals which could be incompatible with a move to a freer domestic market economy. Condemning the González administration for trying to solve the country's economic and social problems by enlarging the public sector of the economy, Gámir advocated a growth of public spending which had to remain smaller than that of the nominal GDP, the privatization of public enterprises, the reduction of the public deficit and the immediate freeze and subsequent lowering of taxes (Ibid., 193).

Gámir failed to explain where the risk-assuming, competitiveness-conscious, innovative entrepreneurs could be found in Spain. Since the nineteenth century, Spanish businessmen and industrialists had relied on strong government protection to operate free of foreign competition in a domestic market in which they alone could sell. For too long, they clung to traditional methods of production, to traditional marketing policies and to traditional forms of investment. The Spanish industrialization spurt of the 1960s was generated by foreign firms, by foreign capital and by foreign technology. To the extent that industrialization in that decade had its roots in other countries, one cannot see in that phenomenon a late 'industrial revolution' developed by Spanish 'Schumpeterian entrepreneurs'.

For centuries, ever since the Catholic Kings strengthened feudal institutions in Spain at a time when they were decaying in most Western European nations, Spanish society remained anchored to aristocratic customs and values which ranked business and manufacturing activities as degrading for a Spanish *caballero*. Manual work was looked upon for too long as 'vile' and 'dishonourable' and a gentleman supervising or directing such workers moved down the rungs of the social ladder. Spain's élite simply lacked what Max Weber called the 'spirit of capitalism'. Spain's élite, the aristocracy, the Church and the large landowners despised business and industry. The entire society became permeated with their values. The traditionalism of this society did not suddenly end in 1959. Spain's resilient traditional institutions, firmly rooted in an institutional and cultural past, hindered the normal development of an innovative and perceptive entrepreneurial group in the country and gave to the evolution of Spain's economy unique parameters.

## THE SPANISH ECONOMY IN 1992

Nineteen ninety-two brought economic recession to Spain. According to the data of the National Institute of Statistics, the country's real GDP fell by 0.4% in the fourth quarter of 1992 below the level it had attained during the same quarter of 1991. Aggregate domestic demand followed the same trend. The deceleration in the growth of Spanish GDP had started in 1990, a year in which the GDP had expanded by 3.7%, a rate smaller than the average rate of growth of 5% that had been maintained between 1986

*Table 112* Evolution and structure of gross national saving: 1988–92 (percentage of GDP)

|  | 1988 | 1989 | 1990 | 1991 | 1992 |
|---|---|---|---|---|---|
| Private enterprises | 13.75 | 13.28 | 12.81 | 12.40 | 11.30 |
| Households | 7.07 | 5.70 | 6.94 | 7.80 | 6.97 |
| Public entities | 1.76 | 2.90 | 2.06 | 1.11 | 1.12 |
| Gross national saving | 22.58 | 21.88 | 21.81 | 21.31 | 19.39 |
| Gross capital formation | 23.66 | 25.11 | 25.50 | 25.13 | 19.39 |

Source: Banco de Bilbao Vizcaya, *Informe Económico 1992*, Bilbao, 1993, p. 26

and 1989. Economic growth continued to weaken in 1991 when the GDP grew by only 2.3%. This rate fell to 1.6% in the second quarter of 1992 and to 0.7% in the third quarter of that year to record a negative rate of –0.4% in the last quarter of the year. For 1992 as a whole, Spain's real GDP grew by only 1% (Banco de Bilbao Vizcaya, 1993, 13–14).

The poor performance of the Spanish economy in 1992 duplicated in part the weakening of economic activity in many developed nations in that year. The aggregate GDP of the total EC area grew by only 1.1% in 1992 and economists predicted that it would show a zero rate of growth in 1993. The deterioration of Spanish economic activity in 1992 was however also the result of endogenous economic problems: in 1992, Spanish wages rose by 8.7% in real terms; prices of services increased by 10.6%; and industrial prices on the other hand, rose by only 1.4%. The large differential in such price trends and the significant increase in labour costs created enormous difficulties for Spanish industrial firms which tried to survive by adopting labour-saving methods of production whose immediate effect was a fall in industrial employment (Ibid., 39).

As shown in Table 112, another important cause of the fall in economic activity was a redistribution of national income in favour of households which reduced the savings of private firms and lowered the level of national saving. Between 1988 and 1992 national gross saving declined by 3.2 percentage points of the GDP and this fall weakened internal investment and reduced the gross formation of capital.

Other reasons for the deterioration of economic activity were the continuing increases in production costs which adversely affected inflation, investment and employment, and the expansion of the budgetary deficit. Between 1990 and 1992, public revenue, as a percentage of GDP, rose by 2.8 percentage points. Public spending in that period increased by 3.5 percentage points. Spain's budgetary deficit increased from 4% of the GDP in 1990 to 4.7% in 1992 (Ibid., 26–7). In as much

*Graph 24* Evolution of Spain's GDP and industrial production: 1971-92

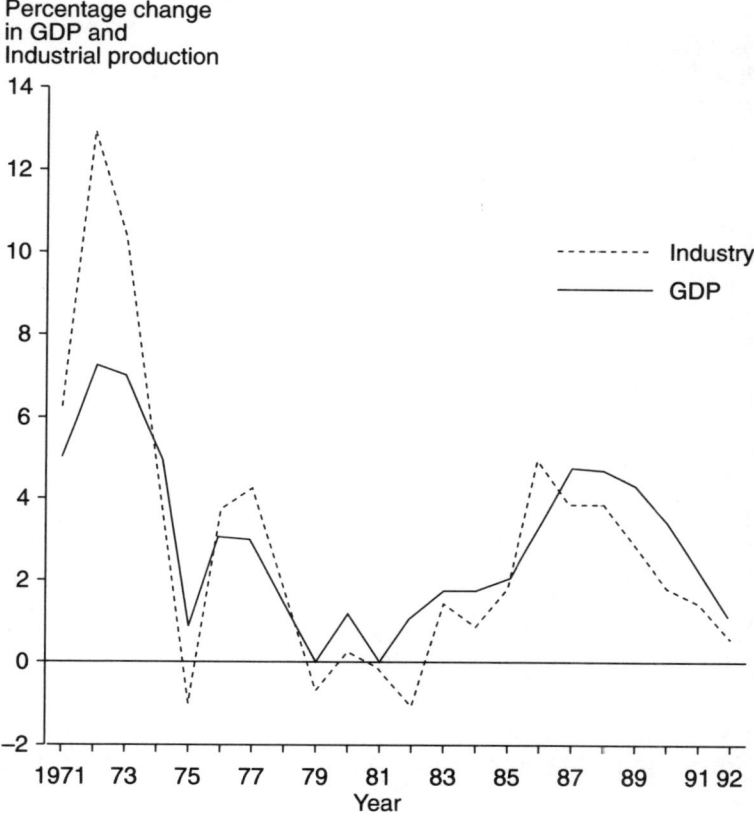

Source: Ibid., p. 35

as public spending took the forms of public consumption and transfer payments, it had an inflationary effect which contributed little to the growth of real GDP.

The growth of the GDP in 1992 was largely due to the expansion of the tertiary sector of the economy with the growth of public services accounting for more than 50% of the GDP increase.

The study group of the Banco de Bilbao Vizcaya estimated that in 1992 the output of the country's primary sector fell by 3%, with the production of crops diminishing by 4% and that of livestock products by 2% (Ibid., 33). The index of industrial production shows a decline of 1.7% from its level in 1991. The growth rates of Spain's GDP and industrial production are shown in Graph 24.

*Graph 25* Cyclical behaviour of the Spanish economy: 1972–92
(annual percentage change in GDP growth)

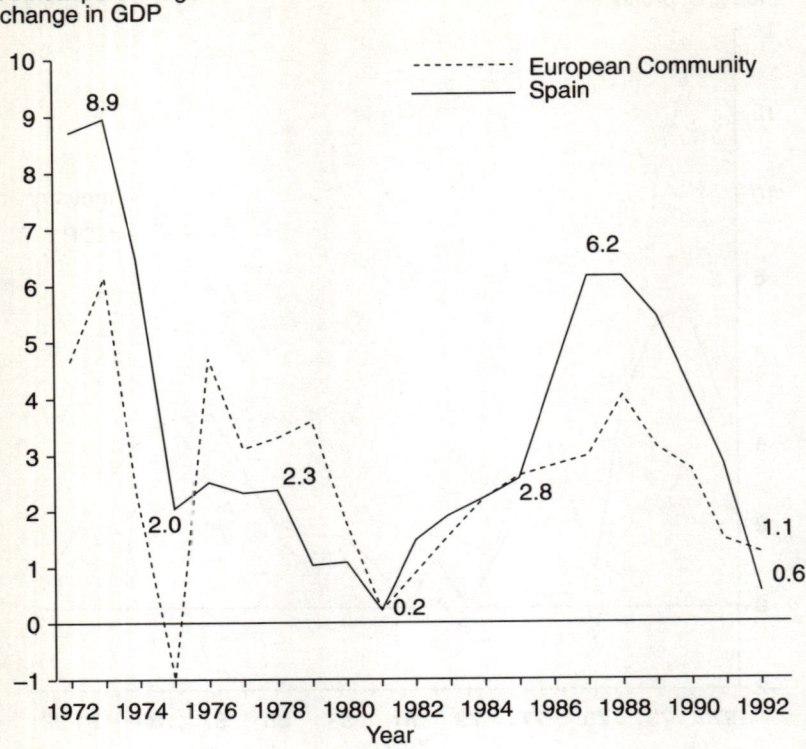

*Source*: Ibid., p. 16

The deterioration of Spain's secondary sector in 1991 and 1992 was further evidenced by a fall in industrial employment of 3% in both years. Compared to the level of industrial employment in the first quarter of 1992 such employment fell by 9.7% in the first quarter of 1993 (Ibid., 37).

The weakening of Spain's economy since 1990 has also been explained as reflecting the cyclical behaviour of the economy. Spain's economy experienced a rising trend between 1960 and 1974. From the latter year, the trend was reversed. A cyclical trough was reached in 1981. A new boom followed which reached a peak in the years 1987 and 1988. The Spanish economy appeared to experience a short cycle of about fourteen years. As shown by Graph 25, the economy peaked in 1973 when the rate of growth of real GDP attained 8.9%, and in 1987–8 when this rate was 6.2%. The trough of the first cycle was in 1981 when the rate of growth of real GDP was only 0.2%.

Graph 25 shows the effects of the oil crises in both Spain and the EC in the period 1973 to 1981, the adjustment period of 1981 to 1985, the strong Spanish growth phase from 1985 to 1988 and the renewal of economic recession in both Spain and the EC as of the latter year. In 1992 the Banco de Bilbao Vizcaya economists estimated that the domestic economy would bottom either at the end of 1993 or at the start of 1994.

The data published by the Statistical Office of the European Community, EUROSTAT, showing for each of the twelve member countries the ratio of every country's GDP per inhabitant to the corresponding EC average, adjusted for the real purchasing power of that country's currency, reveal that the Spanish ratio was 58.3% of the EC average in 1960 and increased to 79.2% in 1975. The oil crises of the 1970s reduced this ratio to 70.4% in 1985. Following Spain's incorporation into the EC in 1986, the ratio rose to 76.4% in 1991 as shown in Graph 26. The convergence of Spain's and the Community's real GDP per inhabitant which had been maintained between 1985 and 1991 appeared to be interrupted in 1992.

The most pessimistic projection of this convergence estimated by the Banco de Bilbao Vizcaya on the assumption that in the future Spain's real GDP growth would surpass that of the Community by only 0.5% per year, indicated that in the year 2020 Spain's GDP per inhabitant would still be only 88.5% of the average GDP per inhabitant level in the EC. The poor performance of Spain's economy in 1992 suggested that Spain would have great difficulty attaining even that goal.

Graph 27 shows that the Spanish economy tended to grow more rapidly than other EC economies in periods of economic upswing, but deteriorated faster than other economies in periods of economic recession. Such trends have been explained in terms of the stronger internal disequilibria of the Spanish economy.

A major Spanish economic disequilibrium originated in the dissimilar trends of domestic prices and of internal production costs. Between 1987 and 1992, per unit labour costs increased by 38.5%, i.e. at an annual rate of 6.7%. The economies of Belgium, Denmark, France, Germany, Luxembourg and the Netherlands recorded in the same period an average increase in their per unit labour costs of only 12.8%, i.e. an annual increase of 2.4% (Ibid., 23). Spanish inflation was also stronger than that of the central EC economies. As a result, the competitiveness of Spain's economy weakened. In addition, per unit labour costs rose more rapidly in Spain than domestic prices, particularly, the prices of domestic industrial goods. Such trend diminished the rate of profit of Spanish industrial firms. Table 113 shows the differences in the rates of

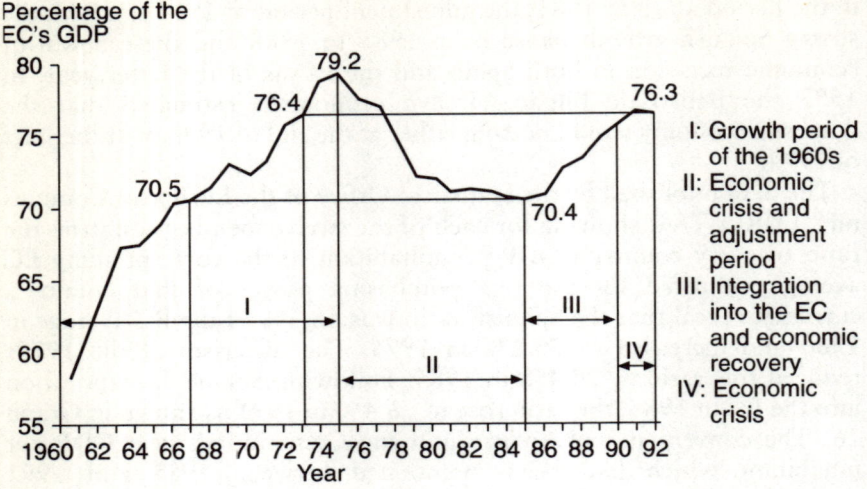

Graph 26 Spain's GDP per inhabitant as a percentage of the EC's GDP per inhabitant: 1960–92

Source: Ibid., p. 19

increase in the values of key economic variables in Spain and in the central EC countries between 1988 and 1991.

Spanish private consumption demand increased by 2.4% at constant prices in 1992. Spain's consumers increased their spending for the acquisition of durable consumer goods, particularly automobiles. Economic growth was, however, threatened by a fall of −1.3% in investment in industrial equipment and in transport goods. After continuously rising in the eight previous years, imports of industrial equipment declined by 9.5% in value in 1992. Graph 28 shows the evolution of Spain's real investment and of its GDP over the period 1983 to 1992. The sharp fall in investment since 1988 had various causes. Rising interest rates were a contributing factor, but more important were the decline in the entrepreneurial rate of profit and the deterioration of investors' expectations about the future of the economy.

According to the National Institute of Statistics, investment in construction fell by 4% in 1992, a decline which reduced employment in the construction sector by −6.1%, a decline which resulted in the loss of 77,200 jobs (Ibid., 52).

Spain's external position deteriorated in 1992. Though the trade balance deficit diminished as a result of an increase in the value of merchandise exports by 8.6% with imports rising by only 3.2% in value, the balance of services surplus was reduced by 163.2 billion pesetas; the

*Graph 27* Real GDP convergence trends, Spain–EC: 1984–92
(annual percentage growth)

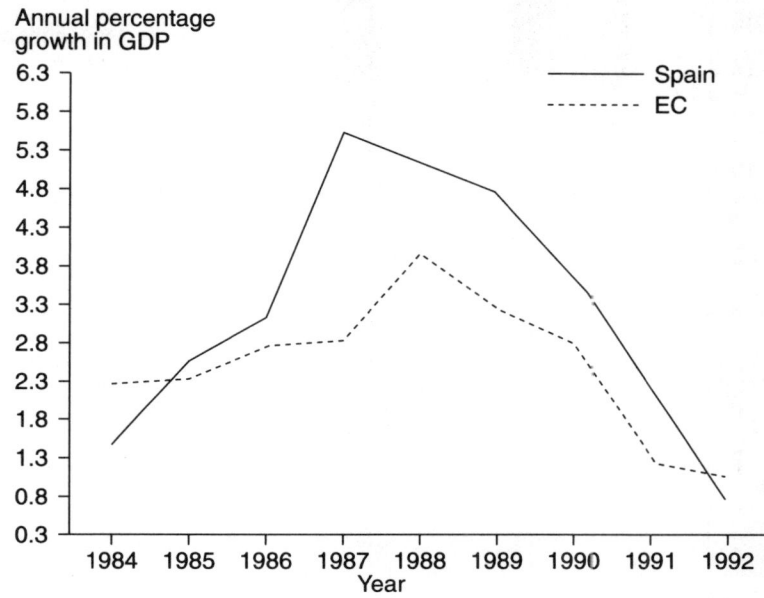

*Source*: Ibid., p. 23

*Table 113* Differences in the evolution of consumer prices and labour costs in Spain and the central countries of the EC: 1988–91 (percentage increase)

|  | 1988 | 1989 | 1990 | 1991 | Total of four years |
|---|---|---|---|---|---|
| Consumer prices | | | | | |
| Spain | 4.8 | 6.6 | 6.7 | 5.9 | 26.2 |
| Central EC countries | 2.0 | 3.2 | 2.7 | 3.2 | 11.6 |
| Differential | 2.8 | 3.4 | 4.0 | 2.7 | 14.6 |
| Unit labour costs | | | | | |
| Spain | 6.1 | 7.1 | 8.3 | 7.2 | 31.9 |
| Central EC countries | 0.8 | 1.2 | 2.7 | 4.3 | 9.3 |
| Differential | 5.3 | 5.9 | 5.6 | 2.9 | 22.6 |

*Source*: Ibid., p. 24
*Note*: Central EC countries: Belgium, Denmark, France, German FR, Luxembourg, Netherlands

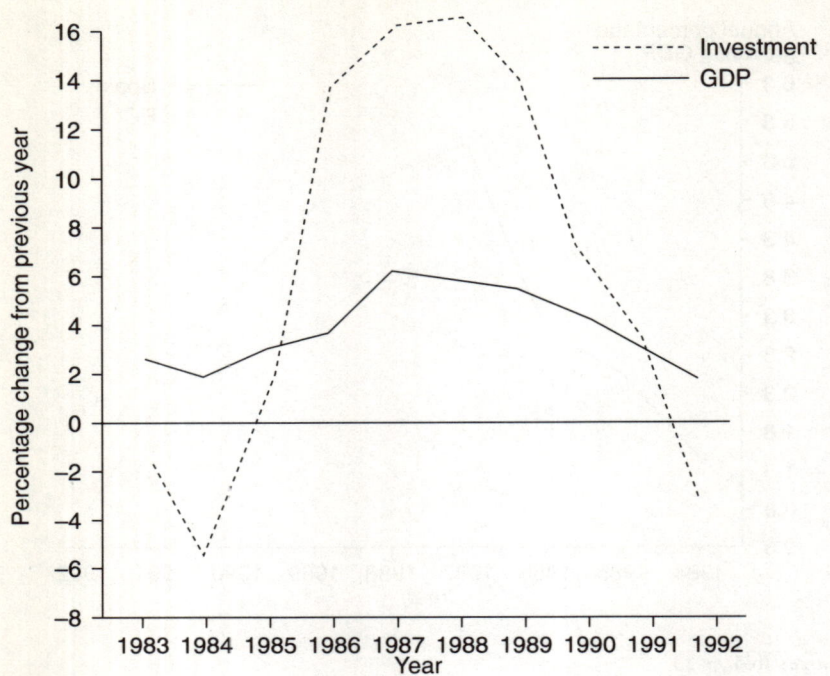

Graph 28 Evolution of Spain's investment and GDP: 1983–92 (percentage change from previous year)

Source: Ibid., p. 50

balance of transfers surplus declined by 20 billion pesetas. The effects of such trends was an increase in the country's current account deficit which rose from 1,736.3 billion pesetas in 1991 to 1,878.6 billion pesetas in 1992 (Ibid., 56).

The government decided to devalue the peseta in order to strengthen the country's external position. The peseta was devalued by 5% on 16 September 1992, and again by 6% on 21 November 1992. By the end of the year the peseta had depreciated by 11.2% in terms of the US dollar. Economists predicted however that unless the government succeeded in reducing the domestic rate of inflation, the beneficial effects of these devaluations on Spain's trade balance would be short-lived.

Of immediate concern to Spain's economists was the decline of foreign long-term investment in the country which fell from 3,499.4 billion pesetas in 1991 to 2,218.2 billion in 1992 (Ibid., 57). As a consequence, Spain's basic balance surplus diminished from 1,763.1 billion pesetas in

Table 114 Differentials between the Spanish rate of inflation and that in other countries and areas: December 1988–December 1992 (percentage changes at 12 month intervals)

| Country | Dec. 1988 | Dec. 1989 | Dec. 1990 | Dec. 1991 | Dec. 1992 |
|---|---|---|---|---|---|
| USA | 1.4 | 2.3 | 0.4 | 2.5 | 2.9 |
| German FR | 4.2 | 3.9 | 3.7 | 1.4 | 1.6 |
| UK | –1.0 | –0.8 | –2.8 | 1.1 | 2.8 |
| France | 2.7 | 3.3 | 3.2 | 2.5 | 3.5 |
| Italy | 0.3 | 0.5 | –0.1 | –0.5 | 0.7 |
| OECD–total | 1.4 | 2.0 | 1.0 | 1.8 | 2.5 |
| EC–total | 1.7 | 1.5 | 0.8 | 0.7 | 1.8 |

Source: Ibid., p. 73

1991 to 339.6 billion in 1992. In terms of the GDP, this surplus fell from 3.22% of the GDP in 1991 to only 0.58% of the GDP in 1992.

The countries of the European Community continued being Spain's best trading partners in 1992. Of Spain's exports 71.2% were sold in the Community area; the EC supplied 60.7% of Spain's imports.

Spain's rate of inflation in 1992 remained identical to that of 1991; consumer goods prices rose by 5.9% in both years. In the rest of the EC, such prices declined by an average of 0.6% in 1992.

Spain's agricultural prices declined by 6.8% in 1992; domestic industrial prices rose by only 1.4%. The relative stability of industrial prices together with increasing internal production costs and intensifying foreign competition imposed serious problems on the country's industrial firms. Prices of domestic services rose by 10.7%, maintaining the previously existing dichotomy in domestic price trends. The prices of transport, hotel and personal services, education and health care increased at a rate which exceeded the rate of increase of prices of consumer goods (Ibid., 66–75). A declining rate of growth of consumer goods prices in the rest of the EC increased the differential between the Spanish and the EC rates of inflation. The differential had amounted to 0.7 percentage points in December 1991; in December 1992, it attained 1.8% (Ibid., 7). Table 114 shows the evolution of this differential between 1986 and 1992.

Per unit labour costs rose by 5.8% in 1992, a larger rate of increase than the corresponding rate in most EC countries. The devaluations of the peseta in September and in November of the same year maintained for the time being the international competitiveness of Spanish exports. Public spending and the budgetary deficit continued to expand in spite of an increase in the tax burden.

Spain's active population increased by 1,315,000 persons over the

*Graph 29* Evolution of Spain's employment and unemployment between 1985 and 1992

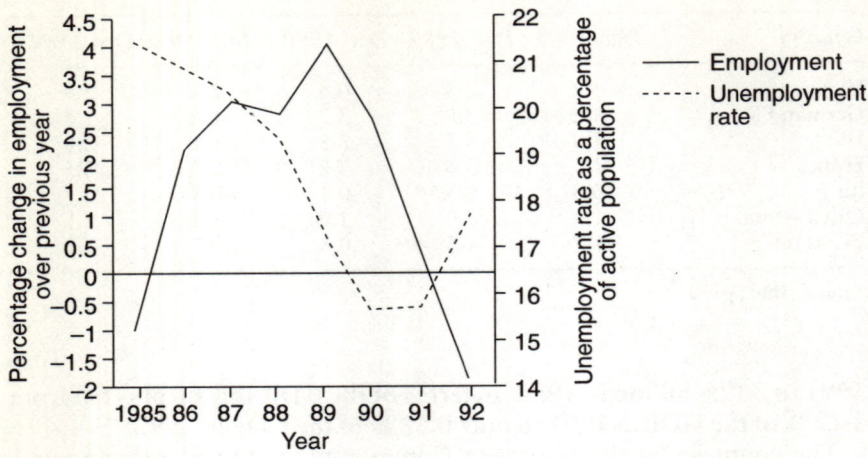

Source: Ibid., p. 86

seven year period 1985 to 1992, largely as the result of the increasing participation of women in the labour force. During this period the country's active population increased at the average annual rate of 1.3%. There had been 2,969,500 unemployed persons in the country at the end of 1985. To reduce this number in subsequent years, the net annual creation of new jobs had to exceed a rate of increase of 1.3%. The PSOE government succeeded in expanding sufficiently the number of jobs in the country during these seven years to reduce the country's rate of unemployment from 20.7% in 1985 to 18.4% in 1992 (Ibid., 83). Graph 29 shows the evolution of these figures.

## THE SPANISH ECONOMY IN 1993

For most industrialized countries, 1993 brought a continuation of the economic recession which had diminished growth in their economies since 1990. Economic trends differed however in the various industrialized nations. The United States, Canada, the United Kingdom and Ireland showed signs of economic recovery. Japan and the industrialized countries of Western Europe continued to experience deteriorating economies. The rate of unemployment rose in the Western industrialized world to such an extent that the Group of 7 called for an international conference on the prevailing world employment situation to be held in March 1994. At the same time the International Labour Organization (ILO) reported that 1.1 billion persons in the world lived in that year

*Graph 30* Rate of unemployment as a percentage of the active population: 1985–93

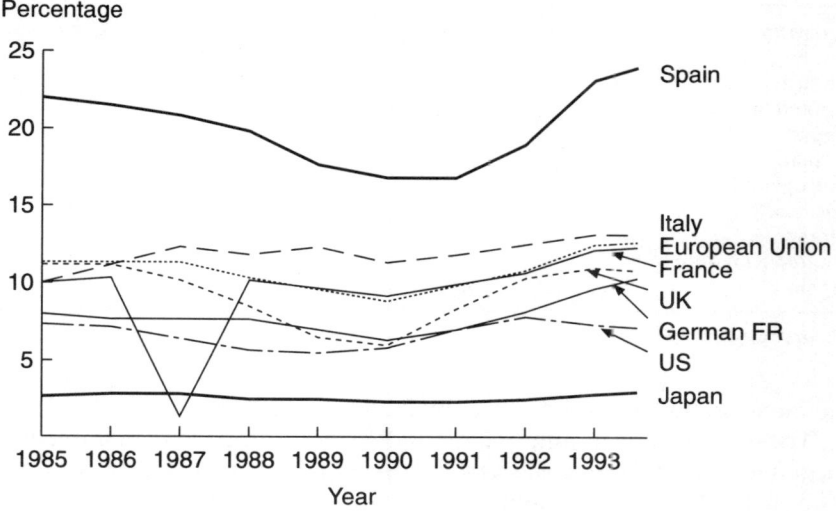

*Source*: Banco de Bilbao Vizcaya, *Informe Económico 1993*, Bilbao, 1994, p. 12

below poverty standards of living. It estimated that 30% of the world's labour force was unemployed in 1993 (Banco de Bilbao Vizcaya, 1994, 9).

Countries joined in international accords in 1993, or showed new interest in international economic agreements in the hope that they would facilitate an improvement in the existing economic climate. After seven years of negotiation, GATT succeeded in completing the Uruguay Round of tariff and of NTBs reductions. The United States Congress approved the formation of NAFTA, the North American Free Trade Association covering Canada, Mexico and the USA. Member nations expressed a new determination to implement the Central American Common Market agreement of 1961, though for more than two decades these countries had failed to take significant steps leading to the economic integration of that region. The thirteen small Caribbean nations invited Mexico, Colombia and Venezuela to join them in an Association of Caribbean States.

The economic scenario presented by the continental Western European nations deteriorated in 1993. Germany's GDP fell by –1.6% in that year; the GDP of ex-West Germany declined by –2.3%. German industrial output fell by nearly 8% from its 1992 level. The European Union's aggregate GDP fell by 0.2% in 1993 and its industrial production by nearly 4%. Only the United Kingdom and Ireland showed

Table 115  Percentage annual change in consumer goods prices in various countries: 1991, 1992 and 1993

| Country | 1991 | 1992 | 1993 |
|---|---|---|---|
| Industrialized countries | 4.6 | 3.3 | 3.0 |
| United States | 4.2 | 3.0 | 3.0 |
| Japan | 3.3 | 1.7 | 1.2 |
| Canada | 5.6 | 1.5 | 1.8 |
| European Union | 5.4 | 4.5 | 3.8 |
| Germany | 4.8 | 4.7 | 4.2 |
| France | 3.2 | 2.4 | 2.2 |
| United Kingdom | 6.8 | 4.7 | 3.2 |
| Spain | 5.9 | 5.9 | 4.6 |

Source: Ibid., p. 13

an increase in GDP by 2.5% and by 2.7% respectively (Ibid., 11–12).

The decline of economic activity in Western Europe had an immediate negative impact on the Western European labour market. As shown in Graph 30, the rate of unemployment rose in those countries experiencing a continuation of recession and remained unchanged or showed a slight decline in the countries undergoing economic recovery. Unemployment trends were affected by differences in the labour policies pursued by the various governments. In the United States, the Clinton government succeeded in raising the level of employment though the newly employed received a low level of remuneration while the gap between the poor and the rich widened in the country. In Germany, the government attached little importance to the creation of new jobs, but supported acceptable wage increases for the employed and maintained adequate unemployment insurance for the jobless.

The rate of inflation showed a decline in most industrialized nations in 1993. Table 115 shows the annual percentage change in the prices of consumer goods in various industrialized countries in 1991, 1992 and 1993.

The general decline in inflation rates was explained by a number of factors: the industrialized countries recorded low levels of utilization of productive capacity, per unit labour costs remained stable or showed moderate increases, rates of interest fell during 1993 and crude oil prices were falling. Graph 31 shows the trend of the spot US dollar price of a barrel of 'Arabian Light' between 1973 and 1993.

Governments employed an expansionary public deficit policy to strengthen domestic economic activity. Measured as a percentage of the GDP the budgetary deficit exceeded 10% in Greece and amounted to 9.8% in Italy, 8.1% in the United Kingdom, 8.1% in Portugal, 7.1% in Spain, 7% in Belgium, 6% in France, 4.5% in Denmark, 4.2% in the

*Graph 31* US dollar prices of a barrel of Arabian Light Oil: 1973-93

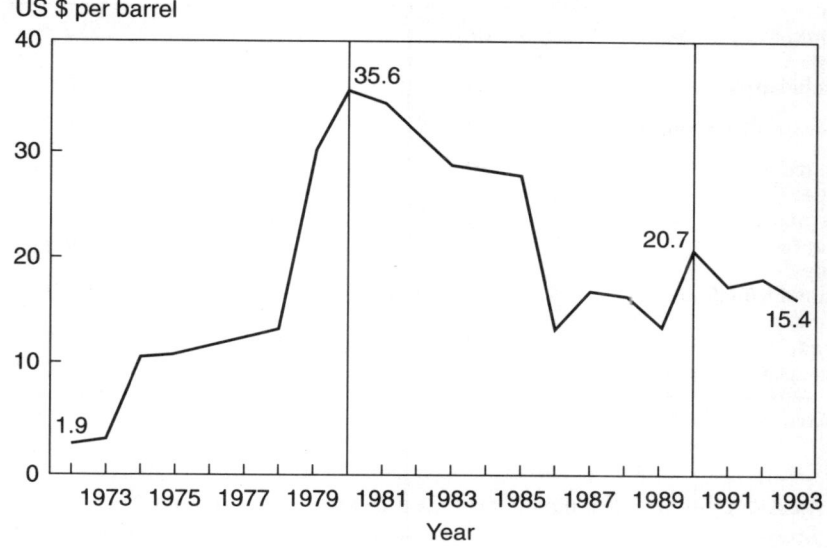

*Source:* Ibid., p. 14

Netherlands, 4% in Germany and 3.1% in Ireland. It attained 3.6% in the United States and only 1% in Japan (Ibid., 16).

The weakness of economic activity in the industrialized nations had an adverse effect on global foreign trade. The participation of industrialized Western European countries in the world trade of manufactured goods diminished from 54.1% of such trade in 1986 to 47% in 1993. That of Japan fell from 13.8% to 11% in the same period. The current account deficit of the United States increased from US$66.4 billion in 1992 to US$105.69 billion in 1993 (Ibid., 17).

The deterioration of economic activity in the area of the European Union in 1993 did not by-pass the Spanish economy. Spain's economic recession in that year was the worst the country had experienced in the twentieth century, whether measured in terms of domestic demand, of productive activity or employment. The trough of the cyclical downswing which had started in 1988 appeared to have been reached in the third quarter of 1993. According to the calculations of the National Institute of Statistics, real GDP fell by 1% in the latter year and domestic demand declined by 3.6% from its level in the preceding year (Ibid., 39). Spain's economic experience in 1993 did not simply duplicate the fall in economic activity in other industrialized countries and areas. As shown in Table 116, IMF calculations indicated that Spain experienced the

## GROWTH AND CRISIS IN THE SPANISH ECONOMY

*Table 116* IMF estimates of annual percentage GDP change in industrialized countries: 1991, 1992 and 1993

| Country | 1991 | 1992 | 1993 |
|---|---|---|---|
| Global growth | 0.6 | 1.7 | 2.2 |
| Industrialized countries | 0.5 | 1.7 | 1.1 |
| United States | −0.7 | 2.6 | 2.7 |
| Japan | 4.0 | 1.3 | −0.1 |
| Germany | 1.7 | 1.9 | −1.6 |
| France | 0.7 | 1.4 | −1.0 |
| Italy | 1.3 | 0.9 | 0.3 |
| United Kingdom | −2.2 | −0.5 | 1.8 |
| Canada | −1.7 | 0.7 | 2.6 |
| Spain | 2.3 | 1.0 | −0.6 |
| European Union | 0.8 | 1.1 | −0.2 |

*Source*: Ibid., p. 49

largest decline in GDP in the various industrialized nations.

Spanish economists explained the severity of Spain's recession in 1993 in terms of both the country's cyclical downswing and the worsening global economic environment. Graph 28 above shows that the rate of growth of the country's GDP started decelerating from 1988. In 1990, the GDP grew at the rate of 3.6%. In 1991, this rate declined to 2.2%. According to the calculations of the National Institute of Statistics, this rate was 2.5% in the first quarter of 1991 and declined to 2% in the last quarter of that year. In 1992, the rate fell to 1.4% in the second quarter of the year, to 0.5% in the third quarter and was a negative −0.6% in the last quarter. Spain's GDP fell at the negative rate of −1.3% in the first quarter of 1993, continued to fall by −1.4% in the second quarter and by −1% in the third quarter but grew by 0.3% in the last quarter of the year. The slight growth of GDP in the last quarter of 1993 induced economists to speculate that the recession had bottomed in the third quarter of the year and that a slow process of economic recovery could develop in 1994 (Ibid., 48).

The rate of growth of domestic demand had shown an annual decline since 1988. Real internal demand had increased by 7.78% in 1989; this rate fell to 4.67% in 1990 and to 2.82% in 1991. According to the calculations of the National Institute of Statistics, this rate was only 1.13% in 1992. The year 1993 recorded a negative growth rate of −3.63%.

In 1989, aggregate real consumption rose at the rate of 6.2% and investment expanded at the annual rate of 13.1%. In 1992, consumption demand still increased by 2.4%, but investment demand fell by 2.8%. In 1993, both public and private consumption demand declined by 1.5%

and investment demand showed a dramatic fall of 10.4% (Ibid., 83). The components of investment demand showing the greatest decline were the demand for industrial equipment and investment in construction. Real investment in construction fell by 9.2% and the construction industry lost 107,800 workers who represented 9% of the total employment in that industry (Ibid., 94–8).

The fall in real GDP in 1993 was largely the result of the decline in the industrial and construction outputs. The Spanish economic crisis which had started in 1992 was fundamentally an industrial crisis, as evidenced by the fall in the index of industrial production calculated by the National Institute of Statistics, a fall of 2.8% in 1992 and of 4.6% in 1993 (Ibid., 69).

The increasing deterioration of Spain's industrial activities, initiated in 1989, clearly showed the country's need for an efficient and competitive industrial sector, a sector able to generate employment and contributing to the financing of public spending. Without a well developed and modern secondary sector, Spain could not hope to achieve a continuing economic convergence within the area of the European Union. Even though most world economies were moving in the direction of freer market systems, Spain's government could not avoid taking new macroeconomic measures designed to facilitate the modernization and diversification of the country's industrial sector.

The acquisition of stronger international competitiveness by Spain's industrial firms required that the country's labour policy should follow more closely the labour policies of other European Union countries. Spain's industrial weakening in the early 1990s was largely due to labour, financial and fiscal costs rising at a rate which surpassed the average EU rate. In an international economic environment characterized by freer trade between nations and intensifying foreign competition, rapidly rising labour costs and slowly developing production technology could sound the death knell of Spanish industrial activity.

Spain remained a poorly industrialized country in the EU area in the early 1990s. Her industrial output represented only 7.54% of the EU's aggregate industrial production in 1993. Spain's industrial output per inhabitant attained only 63.3% of the EU's average figure in that year. Excluding construction, Spain's industry had contributed 27.9% of the GDP in 1985; in 1993, this percentage figure had declined to 21.5% (Ibid., 77–8). Spain's economic future depended, and continues to depend, on the country's ability to develop a more modern and efficient industrial sector, a sector in which high technology, strong-demand industries will acquire larger representation.

In 1993 it was, however, the tertiary sector which continued to be the strongest growth sector in the economy, showing a rate of increase of

2.8%, a rate largely based on the expansion of public services.

Spain's external sector played a major role in limiting the deterioration of the domestic economy in 1993. The growth of Spanish exports reduced the extent of the GDP's decline in that year. According to the data of the Spanish Customs Office, the country's balance of trade deficit in 1993 was equivalent to 4% of the GDP, and had declined by 30% from the corresponding 1992 percentage figure. While imports declined by 2% in value from their 1992 level, the value of Spanish exports increased by 14.7% in 1993. The expansion of exports was mostly due to a new devaluation of the peseta in June 1993, the third devaluation since September 1992; the peseta was devalued by 24.3% in terms of the US dollar, by 17.2% in terms of the German mark and by 12.4% in terms of the ECU.

Spain's trade with the countries of the European Union showed a slight fall in 1993 in spite of the devaluation of the peseta in that year. Although remaining trade barriers between Spain and the rest of the EU disappeared in 1993, only 59.1% of Spain's imports originated in EU countries in that year, a slight decline from the 60.7% recorded one year earlier. Imports from Japan and from the Asiatic NICs also declined. Spanish exports to the EU countries were 4.7% lower than their value in 1992, though exports to Ireland expanded by 65% and those to the United Kingdom increased by 24%. Spanish exports to non-EU countries showed significant increases. The value of Spanish exports to Brazil increased by 84%; the increase was 68% for Argentina, 66% for Mexico and 49% for Chile. Spain's exports to China increased by 196% in terms of value (Ibid., 110).

The decline in the rate of Spanish inflation in 1993 and the devaluation of the peseta restrained the fall of the GDP. The significant increase in the public deficit had the opposite effect. The decline in the rate of increase of domestic consumer goods prices from 5.9% in 1992 to 4.6% in 1993 reduced the differential between Spanish consumer goods prices and those of the central countries of the EU, i.e. Belgium, Denmark, France, Germany, Luxembourg and the Netherlands, by 1.6 percentage points. On the other hand, Spain's public deficit expanded from 4.4% of the GDP in 1992 to 7.2% in 1993.

The rate of increase of domestic industrial prices was accelerated by the devaluation of the peseta. These prices rose at the annual rate of 2.4% in 1993, though the prices of industrial equipment increased by only 1.3%. Concurrently, per unit labour costs recorded an annual increase of 3.9%, the latter surpassing their average rate of increase in the EU area by 0.7% (Ibid., 128).

Measured in terms of their percentage of GDP, public revenue declined from its 1992 level while public spending which had represented 4.45% of the GDP in 1992 increased to 7.25% in 1993.

## CRISIS AND CHALLENGE IN THE EARLY 1990s

*Table 117* Key economic variables in Spain and in the EU countries: 1990–3

| Variable | 1990 | 1991 | 1992 | 1993 |
|---|---|---|---|---|
| GDP per Spanish inhabitant: | | | | |
| compared to EU average | 77.8 | 80.5 | 80.0 | 79.6 |
| compared to EU central countries average | 68.4 | 70.3 | 69.8 | 69.3 |
| Consumer goods price inflation | | | | |
| Spain | 6.7 | 5.9 | 5.9 | 4.6 |
| European Union | 5.7 | 5.4 | 4.4 | 3.7 |
| Central EU countries | 2.7 | 3.2 | 3.5 | 3.1 |
| Balance on current account: Percentage of GDP | | | | |
| Spain | −3.7 | −3.6 | −3.8 | −1.3 |
| European Union | −0.4 | −0.8 | −0.3 | −0.9 |
| Central EU countries | −0.3 | −0.1 | −0.4 | 0.2 |
| Public deficit: percentage of GDP | | | | |
| Spain | −3.9 | −4.9 | −4.4 | −7.2 |
| European Union | −4.0 | −4.5 | −5.1 | −5.9 |
| Central EU countries | −2.3 | −3.0 | −3.6 | −4.7 |
| Long-term interest rates | | | | |
| Spain | 14.1 | 12.3 | 11.6 | 10.4 |
| European Union | 11.0 | 10.3 | 9.9 | 8.1 |
| Central EU countries | 9.5 | 9.1 | 8.4 | 6.6 |
| Per unit labour costs | | | | |
| Spain | 8.3 | 7.2 | 7.8 | 3.9 |
| European Union | 5.0 | 5.6 | 4.2 | 2.7 |
| Central EU countries | 2.7 | 4.3 | 3.6 | 3.2 |

*Source*: Ibid., p. 114

Spain's active population grew at the rate of 1.03% in 1993, a rate again resulting from the rising participation of women in the labour force. Total employment in that year fell however by 4.3%. Industrial employment recorded a fall of −9.43%; employment in the construction sector diminished by −9.01%. Employment in the tertiary sector fell by −1.43%. As a result of such trends, the rate of unemployment, measured as a percentage of the active population, increased from 18.4% in 1992 to 22.7% in 1993 (Ibid., 148).

The traditional restrictive monetary policy of the Bank of Spain came under strong attack in 1993. Economists claimed that such policy had given excessive priority to the stability of the external value of the peseta over economic recovery measures. Many of these critics believed that the Bank's restrictive policy was the fundamental cause of the economic crisis of 1993. They argued that the stubborn concern of the monetary authorities for the maintenance of the external value of the peseta had produced high domestic interest rates which had unduly depressed internal demand. Aware of such criticisms, Spain's monetary authorities appeared at first to be uncertain about what course of action they should follow. They were faced by the country's worst economic recession since 1959, a recession accompanied by excessive domestic inflation; they were troubled by the crisis affecting the European Monetary System, a crisis which had begun one year earlier and which had not been solved as yet. They finally opted for a significant policy change: the peseta was devalued in June and an expansive monetary policy allowed interest rates to fall. The key economic variables for 1990–3 are compared in Table 117.

## STOPPING SPAIN'S DEINDUSTRIALIZATION

Two major facts characterized the economies of the industrialized nations in the early 1990s. The ability of their industrial firms to survive in times of domestic economic recession depended increasingly on the ability of such firms to expand their sales in foreign markets. Efforts to maintain or to increase their shares of foreign markets forced these firms to face increasingly strong international competition in a world experiencing rapid technological advance. Their ability to incorporate into their methods of production and their products the most advanced technology became the deciding factor in their survival. Such ability depended in the last resort on their managers' capacity to perceive the potential economic benefits that they could receive by adopting new techniques and on their interest in acquiring new scientific and technological knowledge. The adoption by firms of new technological know-how also required that these firms should possess human resources having the necessary knowledge and skills to utilize new technologies efficiently.

When the domestic economy came close to national bankruptcy in 1959, Spanish business leaders suddenly realized that exports were the only means of their survival. To be able to export, they were forced to import foreign technology and suddenly Spain became one of the leading importers of technology in the OECD area. This did not mean however that the characteristics of Spain's entrepreneurial class changed overnight. The growing control of Spain's industrial sector by foreign firms and foreign entrepreneurs was clear evidence that too many Spanish industrialists were unwilling or unable to jettison traditional business methods and to invest in up to date methods of production and distribution.

The incorporation of Spain into the European Economic Community in 1986 impelled Spanish industrialists to give increased attention to the coming of intensified competition in their home market. The PSOE government attempted to strengthen the international competitiveness of the country's industrial firms by enacting a 'Science Law' whose main goal was to stimulate the expansion of domestic industrial research and development efforts. The government extended generous financial assistance to the private industrial sector to allow the latter to import needed foreign technology and to expand its own R & D efforts. Public aid particularly benefited domestic industries seriously affected by rapid technological development. The González administration channelled its financial support to the chemical, electronics, information, precision instruments and telecommunications industries.

Professor María Paloma Sánchez, president of the Science and Technology Policy Committee of the OECD, reported that in 1992 out of every 100 million pesetas of domestic industrial value added, 15.32 million pesetas were obtained from the technological component of industrial production. Of these 15.32 million pesetas, 12.24 million were due to the utilization of foreign technology and only 3.08 million pesetas were based on the use of national technology (Sánchez, M.P., 1993, 40).

In spite of the government's efforts to stimulate the private development of industrial technology and to facilitate the import of advanced technological know-how, the share of domestic industry in Spain's GDP continued to diminish in the early 1990s. Comparatively high increases in the financial, fiscal and per unit labour costs of Spain's industrial firms, particularly at a time when disappearing protection exposed such firms to increasing foreign competition in both their internal and external markets, subjected them to economic hardships which many found it impossible to surmount.

Reflection on Spain's industrial problems in recent years brings to one's mind the observations contained in Professor Harvey Leibenstein's landmark book, *Economic Backwardness and Economic Growth*, published in 1957. Leibenstein noticed that in any economic system, the process of economic growth is subjected to both stimulants and shocks. Economic stimulants of an inadequate magnitude may hinder or even prevent economic growth. As stated by this economist, 'in backward economies, long-run development does not occur because the magnitude of the stimulants is too small. That is to say, the efforts to escape from economic backwardness, be they spontaneous or forced, are below the critical minimum required for persistent growth' (Leibenstein, H., 1960, 94–5).

The writer pointed out that stimulants to economic growth generate both income-raising forces and income-depressing forces. For small values of such stimulants, their net effects on the economy may be negative because the impact of the income-depressing forces they generate may be stronger than that of their income-raising effects. For high values of the stimulants, the opposite will occur and the economy will be able to develop (Ibid., 98).

Leibenstein suggests that while the effects of income-depressing forces resulting from a given economic stimulant or shock may have an upper limit, the simultaneously generated income-raising forces may have no upper limit or a higher upper limit. If income-raising stimulants are expanded beyond a minimum critical level, their positive effects will outweigh the negative effects of their income-depressing consequences. If a backward economy can surpass the critical minimum value of the stimulant, it will be able to develop.

The author cites population growth as an example of an income-depressing effect of an economic stimulant such as an autonomous or induced increase in industrial investment. For small increases of such investment, population will grow in response to higher personal incomes and reduced mortality rates. The rate of demographic growth may exceed the rate of investment increase. In that case, average personal incomes would fall. Because there is a biologically determined upper limit to the growth of population varying between 3% and 4%, a similar rate of increase in industrial investment will, *ceteris paribus*, allow the economy to follow a path of economic growth. A rate of investment increase smaller than the rate of demographic growth will force the economy into greater poverty.

In spite of the Spanish government's efforts to boost private industrial investment, it appears that such investment, instead of rising to reach the 'minimum critical effort level' as defined by Leibenstein, has moved in the opposite direction. The income-depressing effects of Spanish industrial investment have taken the form of an excessive increase in private consumption spending with a large part of such spending financing growing imports of foreign-made consumer goods. The financial help extended by the government to domestic private industry has only led to an expanding foreign trade deficit and one of the highest unemployment rates in the OECD area. Using Leibenstein's terminology, Spain's economy has not received in the recent past the net benefit of stimulants whose magnitude surpassed the necessary critical minimum level.

It is very likely that Spain's tradition-oriented entrepreneurs will be most unwilling to finance the cost of sufficiently strong economic stimulants at a time when they are contemplating a fall in their rate of profit. In addition, at a time of globally weak economic activity, multinational enterprises and foreign firms operating in Spain will not expand their investments in the country in order to stop the process of Spanish deindustrialization. The Spanish government alone is in a position to act as the economy's agent of growth. No other institution will be able to mobilize sufficient investible funds to be used as industrial stimulants of adequate magnitude.

Any attempt by the Spanish government to act with necessary and sufficient strength to stop and reverse the process of internal deindustrialization will undoubtedly expose it to fierce political attacks. The government would be accused of reverting to old Francoist *dirigiste* practices and the conservative élite groups in Spain's society will claim that the government's new industrial policy was a road leading directly to socialism or communism.

The government will have to face this political risk because the continuing deindustrialization of the country's economy will bring catastrophe to Spain's economy in the near future. Though in recent years Spain's tertiary sector became the country's only growth sector, this sector too showed decline in 1993. In time, given the trend in the domestic prices of services, foreign tourists may decide to enjoy the Mediterranean sun lying on the beaches of the southern shores of that sea.

Gradual, partial and piecemeal industrial policy reforms, though probably acceptable to the conservative political opposition and to the country's economic interest groups, will not be effective in bringing to a timely end the process of domestic deindustrialization.

Rational and informed persons whose thinking is free of any ideological dogmatism, whether economic, political, religious or social, will recognize that neither recent neo-capitalist 'free market' economic systems nor the planned and controlled economies of the partially collapsed communist world have adequately performed in recent decades. The economic systems that have shown the most satisfactory internal equilibria have been the mixed economic systems which developed after World War II. These were the economies which combined to their maximum advantage the pursuit of private and public interests. It must be added, however, that even in the mixed economies the outcome of their industrial policies depended in the last resort on the competence, the foresight, the willingness to assume political and economic risks and the integrity of their public and private decision-makers. There can be good and poor leaders, both in the private and in the public sectors of any economy.

This author proposes that in order to revitalize Spain's industrial activity and to expand its industrial employment, the government should create, finance and operate for a limited time new industrial 'pilot plants' capable of diversifying the country's lines of industrial production and able to give stronger representation to strong-demand, high technology industries in the totality of Spain's industrial private and public sectors.

Unlike the industrial strategy followed in the past by the National

Institute of Industry, INI, the new industrial policy would prohibit the acquisition by the state of existing private industrial firms facing financial difficulties. Instead, the government would plan the creation, and finance the establishment, of new industrial enterprises which would produce high-demand products with a strong export potential. These would generally be new high technology products, some of which could be produced by labour-intensive methods. An example of the latter is the production of computer components.

A major effect of these pilot plants would be the generation of a 'demonstration effect' in the private sector which would be conducive to the technological advance of that sector. The pilot plants would also serve as training centres for Spanish managers, engineers and technicians. They would become W.W. Rostow-like 'growth industries' which would create external economies throughout the domestic economy.

These pilot plants would be kept in the public sector for only a limited period long enough to allow them to develop spread effects in the private sector. In time, they would be sold to private concerns. With the proceeds of such sales, the government would be able to finance the establishment of new and different pilot plants without unduly increasing the public deficit. This strategy would allow the government to direct domestic industrial activity toward strong-demand industrial activity without impairing the functioning of the country's market system.

What every Spanish citizen should realize is that the absolute level of the public deficit is not a significant economic variable. What is of major significance to the economic well-being of the people is the trend of the percentage of the GDP which the public deficit represents. If a rising public deficit generates a larger GDP increase, domestic production, incomes and employment will all expand and the internal economy will improve. Public investment in pilot plants may generate the increase in industrial production and in industrial employment Spain so badly needs.

## REFERENCES

Banco de Bilbao Vizcaya, *Informe Económico*, Bilbao (various issues).
Gámir, L., 'Realidad y Política Económica Socialista: Una Interpretación', in Rupérez, J. and Moro, C., eds, *El Decenio González*, Madrid, Ediciones Encuentro, 1992, pp. 171–95.
Leibenstein, H., *Economic Backwardness and Economic Growth*, New York, John Wiley and Sons, 1960.
Sánchez, M.P., ed., *Los Grandes Retos de la Economía Española en los Noventa*, Madrid, Ediciones Pirámide, 1993.

# BIBLIOGRAPHY

Abel, C. and Torrents, N., eds, *Spain, Conditional Democracy*, New York, St. Martin's Press, 1984.
Alonso, A., *España en el Mercado Común, del Acuerdo del 70 a la Comunidad de los Doce*, Madrid, Espasa Calpe, 1985.
Ardura Calleja, M.L., 'Dimensión y Concentración de Empresas', in Fraga Iribarne, M. et al., eds, *La España de los Años 70*, Madrid, Editorial Moneda y Crédito, 1973, pp. 337–448.
———, 'El Sector Industrial', in Fraga Iribarne, M. et al., eds, *La España de los Años Setenta*, supra, pp. 323–36.
Badosa Pagés, J., 'La Evolución de la Competividad de la Exportación', in *Información Comercial Española*, Nr. 544, Madrid, Dec. 1978, pp. 72–80.
Banco de Bilbao/Banco de Bilbao Vizcaya, *Informe Económico*, Bilbao (various issues).
Banco Urquijo, *El Crecimiento de la Industria Española, Evolución Reciente, Comparación Internacional y Expectativas*, Madrid, 1974.
Carr, R. and Fusi, J.P., *Spain: Dictatorship to Democracy*, London, George Allen & Unwin, 1979.
Carreras, A., 'La Producción Industrial Española, 1842–1981: Construcción de un Indice Anual', in *Revista de Historia Económica*, Nr. 1, 1984, pp. 127–57.
———, 'La Industrialización Española en el Marco de la Historia Económica Europea: Ritmos y Carácteres Comparados', in García Delgado, J.L., ed., *España Economía*, Madrid, Espasa Calpe, 1988, pp. 79–115.
Comisaría del Plan de Desarrollo, *I Plan de Desarrollo Económico y Social*, Madrid, 1963.
Coverdale, J.F., *The Political Transformation of Spain after Franco*, New York, Praeger, 1979.
Cuadrado Roura, J.R., 'Cambio Estructural, Terciarización y Remodelación Territorial', in García Delgado, J.L., ed., *La Economía Española de la Transición y la Democracia*, Madrid, CIS, 1990, pp. 169–91.
Cuervo, A., *La Crisis Bancaria en España: 1977–1985*, Barcelona, Ariel, 1988.
Donges, J.B., *La Industrialización en España, Políticas, Logros, Perspectivas*, Barcelona, Oikos-Tau Ediciones, 1976.
Dorado, R., Triana, E., Rojo, J.M. and Martínez, F., eds, *Ciencia, Tecnología e Industria en España, Situación y Perspectivas*, Madrid, Fundesco, 1991.

## BIBLIOGRAPHY

Fontana, J. and Nadal, J., 'Spain, 1914–1970', in Cipolla, C.M., ed., *The Fontana Economic History of Europe, Contemporary Economies*, Glasgow, Collins/Fontana Books, 1976, pp. 460–529.

Fuentes Quintana, E., 'La Crisis Económica en España', in Fundación Fondo para la Investigación Económica y Social, *Papeles de Economía Española*, Nr. 1, Madrid, 1979, pp. 84–142.

———, 'Tres Decenios de la Economía Española en Perspectiva', in García Delgado, J.L., ed., *España Economía*, Madrid, Espasa Calpe, 1988, pp. 1–78.

Fundación Fondo para la Investigación Económica y Social, *Papeles de Economía Española*, Madrid (various issues).

Fundación Humanismo y Democracia, *El Decenio González*, Madrid, Ediciones Encuentro, 1992.

Gallo, M., *Spain Under Franco, A History*, New York, E.P. Dutton & Co., 1974.

Gámir, L., ed., *Política Económica de España*, Madrid, Alianza Editorial, 1986.

———, 'Realidad y Política Económica Socialista: Una Interpretación', in Fundación Humanismo y Democracia, *El Decenio González*, supra, 1992, pp. 171–95.

Garayalde, I., 'El Desempleo como Mecanismo de la Salida de la Crisis', in *Información Comercial Española*, Nr. 588, Madrid, Feb. 1980, pp. 52–62.

García de Blas, A., 'Consideraciones sobre los Orígenes del Paro en España', in *Información Comercial Española*, Nr. 553, Madrid, Sept. 1979, pp. 7–13.

García Delgado, J.L., 'Estancamiento Industrial e Intervencionismo Económico Durante el Primer Franquismo', in Fontana, J., ed., *España Bajo el Franquismo*, Barcelona, Editorial Crítica, 1986, pp. 170–91.

———, ed., *España Economía*, Madrid, Espasa Calpe, 1988.

———, ed., *La Economía Española de la Transición y la Democracia*, Madrid, CIS, 1990.

Gerschenkron, A., *Economic Backwardness in Historical Perspective*, New York, Praeger, 1965.

González, M.J., *La Economía Política del Franquismo, 1940–1970*, Madrid, Editorial Tecnos, 1979.

Granell, F., 'La Integración en la Comunidad Europea y sus Efectos sobre la Exportación Española', in *Información Comercial Española*, Nr. 588/89, Madrid, Aug./Sep. 1982, pp. 135–41.

Guerra, A. and Tezanos, J.F., eds, *La Década del Cambio, Diez Años de Gobierno Socialista, 1982–1992*, Madrid, Editorial Sistema, 1992.

Hagen, E.E., *The Economics of Development*, Homewood, Ill., Richard D. Irwin, Inc., 1975.

Hornillos García, C., *Problemas de la Pequeña y Mediana Industria en España*, Madrid, Confederación Española de Cajas de Ahorros, 1970.

Hudson Institute for Europe, *El Resurgir Económico de España*, Madrid, Instituto de Estudios de Planificación, 1975.

Hull, A.H., *Charles III and the Revival of Spain*, Washington, D.C., University Press of America, 1980.

## BIBLIOGRAPHY

IBRD, *The Economic Development of Spain*, Baltimore, The Johns Hopkins Press, 1967.
Jovellanos, G.M. de, *Diarios*, Oviedo, Instituto de Estudios Asturianos, 1953.
——, *Informe sobre la Ley Agraria*, Madrid, Instituto de Estudios Políticos, 1955.
Kravis, I.B., 'Trade as a Handmaiden of Growth: Similarities between the Nineteenth and the Twentieth Centuries', *Economic Journal*, vol. 80, 1970, pp. 850–72.
Lafuente Félez, A. and Oro Giral, L.A., 'Evolución del Sistema de Ciencia y Tecnología en España, El Plan Nacional de I & D', in *Ciencia, Tecnología e Industria en España, Situación y Perspectivas*, Madrid, Fundesco, 1991, pp. 33–123.
La Rosa, T., *España Contemporanea, Siglo XIX*, Madrid, Ediciones Destino, 1971.
Leibenstein, H., *Economic Backwardness and Economic Growth*, New York, John Wiley and Sons, 1960.
Lewis, W.A., 'Economic Development with Unlimited Supplies of Labour', *The Manchester School*, vol. 22, 1954, pp. 139–91.
Lieberman, S., *The Contemporary Spanish Economy, A Historical Perspective*, London, George Allen & Unwin, 1982.
——, *The Economic and Political Roots of the New Protectionism*, Totowa, New Jersey, Rowman and Littlefield, 1988.
Linde, L.M., 'La profundización de la crisis económica, 1979–1982', in García Delgado, J.L., ed., *La Economía Española de la Transición y la Democracia*, Madrid, CIS, 1990, pp. 35–57.
Lluch, C., *La Industria Española del Futuro*, Madrid, Guadiana de Publicaciones, 1974.
Martín Mateo, R., 'Revisión de la Intervención Pública en la Economía Española', in Velarde, J., García Delgado, J.L. and Pedreño, A., eds, *La Industria Española, Recuperación, Estructura y Mercado de Trabajo*, Madrid, Economistas Libros, 1990, pp. 447–60.
Merigó, E., 'Spain', in Boltho, A., ed., *The European Economy, Growth and Crisis*, Oxford, Oxford University Press, 1982, pp. 554–80.
Ministerio de Industria, *La Industria Española*, Madrid (various issues).
Myro, Sánchez, R., 'La Industria: Expansión, Crisis y Reconversión', in García Delgado, J.L., ed., *España Economía*, Espasa Calpe, 1988, pp. 197–230.
——, 'La Evolución de las Principales Magnitudes: Una Presentación de Conjunto', in García Delgado, J.L., ed., *La Economía Española de la Transición y la Democracia*, Madrid, CIS, 1990a, pp. 527–58.
——, 'La Recuperación de la Industria Española, 1985–1989', in Velarde, J., García Delgado, J.L. and Pedreño, A., eds, *La Industria Española, Recuperación, Estructura y Mercado de Trabajo*, Madrid, Economistas Libros, 1990b, pp. 13–58.
OECD, *Economic Surveys, Spain*, Paris (various issues).
Palacio Atard, V., *Los Españoles de la Ilustración*, Madrid, Ediciones Guadarrama, 1964.
Pasinetti, L. and Lloyd, P., eds, *Economic Interdependence and World Development*, vol. 3, New York, St. Martin's Press, 1987.

## BIBLIOGRAPHY

Payne, S.G., *The Franco Regime, 1936–1975*, Madison, Wisconsin, The University of Wisconsin Press, 1987.

Pedreño Muñoz, A., 'Análisis del Desempleo Español: Necesidad de Nuevos Enfoques', in Velarde, J., García Delgado, J.L. and Pedreño, A., eds, *La Industria Española, Recuperación, Estructura y Mercado de Trabajo*, Madrid, Economistas Libros, 1990a, pp. 387–419.

——, 'Desempleo, Fuerza de Trabajo y Mercado Laboral', in García Delgado, J.L., ed., *La Economía Española de la Transición y la Democracia*, Madrid, CIS, 1990b, pp. 395–419.

Petitbò, A. and Saez Barcena, J., 'El Papel de la Política Industrial en la Recuperación y Reestructuración de la Industria Española', in Velarde, J., García Delgado, J.L. and Pedreño, A., eds, *La Industria Española, Recuperación, Estructura y Mercado de Trabajo*, Madrid, Economistas Libros, 1990, pp. 59–90.

Prados de la Escosura, L., 'El Crecimiento Económico Moderno en España: Una Comparación Internacional', in *Papeles de Economía Española*, Nr. 20, Madrid, 1984.

——, *De Imperio a Nación, Crecimiento y Atraso Económico en España, 1978–1930*, Madrid, Alianza Editorial, 1988.

Reventós, J., *Renovación Socialista*, Barcelona, Editorial Hacer, 1993.

Rodríguez Braun, C., 'De la Agonía a la Agonía', in Tusell, J. and Sinova, J., eds, *La Década Socialista, El Ocaso de Felipe González*, Madrid, Espasa Calpe, 1992, pp. 51–66.

Sainz Moreno, F., 'Historia de las Inversiones Extranjeras en España', *Boletín de Estudios Económicos*, Nr. 65, Bilbao, 1965, pp. 378 et seq.

Sánchez, M.P., ed., *Los Grandes Retos de la Economía Española en los Noventa*, Madrid, Ediciones Pirámide, 1993.

Sánchez Albornoz, N., *España Hace Un Siglo, Una Economía Dual*, Barcelona, Ediciones Península, 1969.

Sardá, J., *La Política Monetaria y las Fluctuaciones de la Economía Española en el Siglo XIX*, Madrid, Instituto Sancho de Moncada, 1948.

Sarrailh, J., *La España Ilustrada de la Segunda Mitad del Siglo XVIII*, México, Fondo de Cultura Económica, 1957.

Schwartz, P. and González, M.J., *Una Historia del Instituto Nacional de Industria, 1914–1976*, Madrid, Editorial Tecnos, 1978.

Segura, J., 'Del Primer Gobierno Socialista a la Integración en la CEE: 1983–1985', in García Delgado, J.L., ed., *La Economía Española de la Transición y la Democracia*, Madrid, CIS, 1990, pp. 59–77.

Segura, J. et al., *La Industria Española en la Crisis: 1978–1984*, Madrid, Alianza Editorial, 1984.

Share, D., *The Making of Spanish Democracy*, New York, Praeger, 1986.

Shneidman, J.L., ed., *Spain and Franco, 1949–1959*, New York, Facts on File, 1973.

Tamames, R., *Historia de España, La República, La Era de Franco*, Madrid, Alianza Universidad, Alfaguara, 1979.

Tortella Casares, G., *Banking, Railroads and Industry in Spain, 1829–1874*, New York, Arno Press, 1977.

Tusell, J. and Sinova, J., eds, *La Década Socialista, El Ocaso de Felipe*

*González*, 2nd edn, Madrid, Espasa Calpe, 1992.

Vázquez, J.A., 'Crisis, Cambio y Recuperación Industrial', in García Delgado, J.L., ed., *La Economía Española de la Transición y la Democracia*, Madrid, CIS, 1990, pp. 81–117.

Velarde, J., García Delgado, J.L. and Pedreño, A., eds, *La Industria Española, Recuperación, Estructura y Mercado de Trabajo*, Madrid, Economistas Libros, 1990.

——, *Apertura e Internacionalización de la Economía Española*, Madrid, Economistas Libros, 1991.

Velarde Fuertes, J. et al., *La España de los Años Setenta*, Madrid, Editorial Moneda y Crédito, 1973.

Zaldívar, C.A. and Castells, M., *España Fin de Siglo*, Madrid, Alianza Editorial, 1992.

# INDEX

*Abertzale* parties 176
Abril Matorell, Fernando 184, 186
accelerator and multiplier effects 61
*Aceros de Irura* 226
*Aceros de Llodio, S.A.* 226
Acheson, Dean 39
*Acuerdo Nacional de Empleo* (ANE) 244
AESA 227
agricultural machinery 20
agricultural sector 27, 59, 64, 81, 92, 182, 194, 201, 246, 253–5, 347
agricultural wages 202
aircraft production 212
airlines 32
Alcaide Inchausti, Julio 150
Algeria, 239
*Altos Hornos del Mediterráneo* 226
*Altos Hornos de Vizcaya* 226
Andreotti, Guilio 273
*Aperturista* 157, 168, 170
Arburua, Manuel 47
Ardura Calleja, María Luisa 123–5
Areilza, José Ma 168, 175
Argentina 354
Arias Navarro, Carlos 142, 156, 159–60, 167–8, 170, 173, 175
Arias Salgado, Gabriel 40
aristocratic work attitude 108–9
armaments 226
Arrese y Magra, José Louis 22
Association of Caribbean States 349
ASTANO 227
*Astilleros del Cantábrico y Riera, S.A.* 227

Australia 306
Austria 50, 52, 212, 306
autarky, (see economic, autarky)
automobiles 224, 229, 249, 269, 288, 297

*Babcock Wilcox, S.A.* 226
Badosa Pagés, Juan (Index of Relative Prices) 204–6
balance of Payments 203, 266, 269, 277, 282, 287, 288
   deficits 5, 44, 50, 65, 70, 83, 91–6, 126, 173, 177, 180, 183, 189–90, 192–3, 214–15, 219, 245, 252, 253, 256, 291, 304, 314, 328–9
   surplus 72, 81, 119, 140, 165, 183, 252, 253, 290
*Banco Coca* 276
*Banco de Bilbao* 181, 319, 325, 341
*Banco de Exportación* 276
*Banco de Valencia* 276
*Banco Ibérico* 276
*Banco Internacional de Comercio* 276
*Banco Rural y Mediterráneo* 276
banking 53, 106, 129, 276–7
Bank of Spain 22, 24, 50, 52, 53, 234, 244–5, 251, 252, 355
Basque 187–8, 226, 288
   rebellions and separatism 48, 141, 167, 178–80, 185, 209, 210, 282
   Nationalist Party (PNV) 176
Belgium 50, 121, 123, 125, 149, 233, 275, 306, 322, 343, 350, 354
Berreras de Irimo, Antonio 159
beverages 45, 49, 64, 80, 90, 122, 150

366

# INDEX

Birkelbach Report 127–8
'Blue Division' 41, 42
Boyer, Miguel 248, 281, 291
Bretton Woods monetary system 162–3, 223
budget or public deficits 215, 245, 250, 252, 254–6, 259, 281, 282, 340, 347, 350

Cabra, José Jerónimo de 112
Cabanillas, Pío 157, 159, 175
Cadiz, Diego de 112
Calvo Sotelo, Leopoldo 32, 176, 225, 241, 242, 243–4, 269, 296
Cumuñas, Ignacio 175
Canada 120, 212, 221, 282, 283, 284, 285, 286, 309, 349, 350, 352
capital flight 213
capital formation 194, 245
capital inflows 219
capital-intensive technology 60, 61, 202, 228
capital investments (see investments)
capital/output ratio 62, 199, 202
CARBOEX 215
Carr, Raymond and Fusi, Juan Pablo 38, 142
Carreras, Albert 18, 103–4
Carrero Blanco, Luis 26, 40, 48, 88, 114, 118, 141, 170, 171
   assassination 7, 17, 142, 156
Carrillo, Santiago 168, 187
Castiella, Fernando María 48, 88, 127, 141
Catalan Socialist Party 177
Catalan strikes of 1951 38
cement 37, 64, 65, 122, 148
Center Democratic Union (UCD) 176, 187–8, 208–10, 230, 242, 244, 296
Center for the Development of Industrial Technology (CDTI) 303
Central American Common Market 349
changes in domestic industrial output 314
chemicals 45, 64, 65, 80, 90, 100, 122, 150, 152, 194, 233, 288
China 354
Christian Democrats 68, 158, 171, 175–6
   *Tacito* 171
Chrysler 113
citrus fruit 44, 272, 273
Civil Guard 210
civil servant compensation 220
Civil War (see Spanish Civil War)
clothing 45, 49, 100, 122, 147, 212
coal 64, 65, 148, 215, 230
coefficient of indebtedness 236–7
*Colegios Mayores* 109
colour televisions 224
commercial policy 52, 195, 198
Communist Party of Spain (PCE) 158, 168, 210
Communist Party of Euzkadi 176
*Compañía Española de Petroleos* 32
comparative consumer price trends 214
competitiveness in international markets 199, 310, 305, 353, 357
*Continuismo* 160, 167, 175
construction 65, 100, 212–13, 214, 334
consumer electronics 212
consumer price index 291
consumption taxes 20
*Convergencia i Unió* 282
Council of Europe 269
Council of Ministers 316
cost of borrowing 237, 238
cost of living indexes 95, 155
cost push inflation 213, 220
crisis of 1967 89
*Cuadernos para el Dialogo* 68
Cuadrado Roura, Juan R. 246–7
*Cuadrogesimo Anno* 31
customs duties 270–2
customs union 128
Czechoslovakia, communist coup in 1948 39

data processing equipment 212
Decree 1775 (industrial policy 1967) 76

# INDEX

Decree-Law
  of June 1981 225
  9/1981 and 21/1982 228
deindustrialization 356–60
Delors, Jacques 272, 273–4
demand pull inflation 5–6
demand structure 194
democracy 7, 187, 210
Democratic Center (CD) 175–6
Democratic Pact for Catalonia (PDC) 177
'*Democratic Junta of Spain*' (JDE) 158
Denmark 70, 143, 154, 306, 323, 337, 343, 350, 354
deregulation and privatization 248, 296
development plans of the 1960s 4
development policies 199
direct taxes 251
*dirigisme* 4, 8, 15, 18, 24, 25, 27, 49, 67, 74–5, 77, 113, 290, 296, 359
*Divini Redemptoris* 31
domestic demand 93, 244, 251
Don Juan Carlos de Borbón, King of Spain 7, 88, 108, 142, 158, 167, 170, 238, 273
drought 217

economic
  and industrial backwardness 25, 58, 103, 110, 115, 149, 357–8
  autarky 1, 3, 7, 26–7, 29, 35, 39, 51, 108, 126, 150, 161
  crisis in the 1980s 192
  Development Plan (19645) 68–9
  liberalization 9–10, 17, 23, 25, 38, 60, 75
  'miracle' of the 1960s 5, 14, 26, 58, 61, 96, 143, 149
  recessions 160, 166
  reforms 46
educational facilities 202
education spending 94
Egypt 239
the *bunker* 157, 160, 171, 209
elections of 1982 210–11
electric machinery 37, 233

electric power companies 32, 37, 64, 231
electronics 212, 229
*El País* 171
employment trends 214, 217
energy and fuel 38, 64, 65, 80, 90, 100, 115, 152, 194, 215, 216, 250, 258, 275
energy crises (see also oil embargo) 194, 198, 211, 216, 223
energy price increases 215
ENSIDESA 32, 33, 115, 226
*Entente* 172
entrepreneurial expectations 151, 155, 193, 203, 224, 243, 245, 260, 262, 264, 308, 316
equal pay for women 46
euromissiles 271
European Community 101, 118, 122, 124, 126–30, 138, 143–4, 190, 196, 234, 242–3, 254, 265, 329
  agricultural policy 240, 241, 270–3
  as Spain's export market 8, 69–70, 214, 218, 224, 239, 287, 315, 337, 347, 354
  common tariff 272
  ECU 343
  EUROSTAT 343
  growth rates of real GDP per inhabitant 12
  on Spain's death penalty 238
  provisional accords 130
  signing the 1970 Commercial Accord 129
  Spain's full adhesion to (1986) 8, 14
  Spain's membership 10, 87, 118, 127–8, 240–3, 269–72, 273, 286–7, 292, 297, 315, 317, 343, 356
  Spain's Preferential Commercial Agreement with 8, 240
  tariff reductions 129
  trade accord with Spain 239
European Common Market 9, 10, 127, 287, 312, 317, 322
European Free Trade Association

(EFTA) 70, 126–7, 138, 143, 274
European Monetary System 9, 240, 356
European Parliament 238
European Payments Union 57
excess productive capacity 224
Executive Committee for Reconversion 229
external deficits 47, 83, 311, 321, 327, 329

Falangists 21, 22, 28, 40, 44, 46–8, 66, 140, 157, 167, 171
fascism 22
*Fasa Renault* 229
Federation of Democratic and Liberal Parties 175
Federation of Socialist Parties (FPS) 176
Feijóo, Benito Gerónimo 110
Fernández Cuesta, Raimundo 40
Fernández Miranda, Torcuato 141, 142, 170, 175
Fernández Ordoñez, Francisco 159, 175, 178, 188
fertilizers 20, 37
feudalism 110
financial and fiscal aid 225
Finland 323
firm sizes 123
fiscal and monetary policy 13, 93, 119–21, 192, 195, 219–20, 252, 256, 308, 310, 324, 327–8, 355
fishing 118, 273
Fontana, Josep and Nadal, Jordi 19–21, 27, 38, 57–8
foodstuffs 44–5, 49, 64, 65, 80–1, 90, 100, 122, 136–8, 152, 163, 194, 233, 249
   prices 20
   shortages 34, 38
footwear 45, 194, 269, 297, 337
Ford Motor Company 118, 229
foreign economic advisors 44
foreign exchange 37
foreign investments 53–4, 72, 104–7, 112, 119, 155, 198, 287
foreign relations treaties 118

Fraga Iribarne, Manuel 88, 141, 150, 159–60, 168, 175, 187–8, 208–9, 282–3
France 50, 70, 100, 103–5, 110–11, 120, 121, 123–4, 125, 149, 154, 158, 203, 212, 233, 238, 245, 275, 283–6, 298, 299, 300, 301, 302, 306, 308, 309, 311, 312, 323, 343, 350, 352, 354,
   *Midi* 271
Franco Bahamonde, Francisco 1, 3, 26–8, 86–8, 111, 157–8, 263
   and the 'Masonic leftist conspiracy' 160
   and the Roman Catholic Church 111, 159
   as an ally of Hitler 39
   as an anti-communist 22, 28, 39, 47
   Cabinet reorganization 48
   'Caudillo' 27, 28, 40, 42, 68, 86–8, 140, 157, 168, 172, 187
   commitment to industrialization 27, 34, 198
   conflicts with the EC Spanish delegates 127
   crackdown on demonstrations 46, 67–8, 87, 141
   death of 1, 7, 9, 15, 17, 26, 86, 157, 160, 167, 193, 211, 238
   dogma of 'Divine Right to Rule' 28
   first government formed 26
   fourth government 40
   'Generalissimo' 127, 142
   influenced by Mussolini's fascism 27
   last government, 'monocolour government' 118, 141, 143
   policy of autarky 1, 3, 9, 27, 29, 35, 161
   policy of the Nazi *Fuhrerprinzip* 28
   relations with the U.S. 42
   solicitation of U.S. economic and military aid 22, 41
   thirty-seven years of rule 26
Francoism
   after Franco 169–70

(also see Suarez)
authoritarianism 86
bureaucracy 6, 86
organic democracy 86, 88, 141
propaganda 51
Social Security 220
Syndical Organization 179
trade and market policies 17–18, 63, 198, 281
French Enlightenment 110
French Revolution 111
*Frente de Liberación Popular* 46
Fuentes Quintana, Enrique 3, 58, 59, 160, 161, 162, 164, 165, 177, 184
*Fuerza Nueva* (FN) 157
*Fundiciones Echevarría, S.A.* 226

Gámir, Luis 281, 338–9
García Delgado, José Luis 17–19, 21
Garrigués Walker, Joaquín 175
GATT 128–30, 274, 349
*Generalitat* 178, 180
General Labor Union (UGT) 158
German *Wehrmacht* 41, 68
Germany 50, 70, 100, 101, 103, 104, 120, 121, 124, 125, 139, 149, 154, 212, 216, 224, 233, 238, 275, 283–6, 298, 300, 301, 302, 306, 308, 309, 311, 312, 323, 337, 343, 350, 351, 352, 354
Gerschenkron, Alexander 58
Girón de Velasco, José Antonio 22, 40, 48, 157
glass 37, 45, 152
global recessions 183, 243
GNP deflator 92
González, Felipe 9–12, 15, 158–9, 175, 176, 187, 210, 248, 250–5, 257, 269, 270, 271, 273, 276, 282, 283, 290, 291, 296, 303, 357
González Gallarza, Eduardo 40
González, M.J. 42, 113
Gorría, Jesús Romeo 88
Government foreign exchange controls 36
Government interventionism and public spending 9, 24–5, 26, 36, 80, 94, 119–21, 130, 164, 219–20, 230–1, 244, 252, 290, 318, 340, 346, 350, 353
*acción concertada* 76–7
Gramm–Rudman–Hollings Law 306
Great Depression of the 1930s 1, 164–5
Greece 126, 143, 158, 212, 239, 240, 275, 306, 328, 350
gross capital formation 211, 251, 256, 288, 313, 340,
gross national savings 289, 340
Gross Value Added 217
Gual Villalvi, Pedro 50, 127
Guerra, Alfonso 176
'Guerrilleros de Cristo Rey' 157
Gulf War 248, 311, 328, 334
Gutiérrez Cano, Joaquin 26

*Hacia Dentro* 161
Hagen, Everett, E. 59
Herrera, Angel 47
Herrera, Leon 157
Herrero Tejedor, Fernando 171
high technology capital equipment and industries 37, 212
HISPANOIL 115
'Historic nationalities' 188
Historical Spanish Workers' Party 176
Hornillos Garcia, Carlos 123
housing 26, 48, 73–4, 213
Hull, A.H. 110
HUNOSA 115
hydroelectric energy 229

Iceland 306
Iglesias, Gerardo 282
import substitution 5, 31, 38, 44, 107–8
import liberalization 60, 81, 83
import duties and tariffs 81, 90–1, 187, 266
income per capita 34, 71
income redistribution 296, 340
Index of the Relative Value of the Peseta (IRVP) 204, 205, 206
Index of Trends of Spanish

## INDEX

Competitiveness (ITC) 204–6
indicative planning 6, 25, 74, 114–15
indicators of Spanish economic recovery 13, 132–3
indirect taxes 20, 219, 251
industrial
  competitiveness 243, 265, 267
  gross value added 152
  investments (see investment)
  machinery 20
  policy 215, 225, 230, 233, 316
  production and productivity 49, 50, 64, 74, 96–101, 108, 121, 146, 148, 149–50, 162, 167, 181, 192, 194, 195, 230, 258, 262, 294, 327
  privatization 258
  reconversion 215–16, 225–7, 228–9
  revolution 104
  sectoral distribution 45, 335
  size and structure 231–2
  stagnation 217
  'takeoff' 59, 148–9
inflation 5, 9, 26, 33–4, 36, 41, 43, 44–5, 49–51, 80–1, 92, 119, 136, 154, 155, 161, 165, 166, 180, 184, 192, 203, 206–8, 213, 217, 220, 221–2, 248, 250–1, 254, 277, 281, 311, 319–20, 340, 343, 345, 348
infrastructure development 25
Institute for Scientific Information 299
Institute for Small and Medium Size Enterprises (IMPI) 318
Institute for Technological Development (CDTI) 318
*Integristas* 159
Interconfederal Agreement 244
Interconfederal Framework Accord 296
interest rates increases 224, 263, 310
Interministry Commission for Science and Technology (CICYT) 302
internal aggregate demand 14, 217, 258, 288, 294
internal price stability 11, 198

International Bank for Reconstruction and Development (IBRD) 23, 76, 115
International Labour Organization 124
International Monetary Fund 23, 24, 51, 223
investments 70, 102, 105, 121, 134, 180, 202, 203, 236, 244, 249, 250, 264, 311, 313, 335, 344
investment/GNP ratio 70
'International Jewish Plot' 51
Ireland 143, 275, 323, 348, 354
iron and steel 35, 37, 44, 45, 63, 122, 123, 148, 212, 216, 224, 226, 265, 269, 271, 282
Israel 143, 153, 239
Italy 50, 100, 101, 104, 120, 121, 125, 143, 149, 154, 212, 233, 275, 283–6, 298, 300, 301, 302, 308, 309, 311, 312, 323, 350, 352
*Izquierda Demócrata Cristiana*, 46

Japan 120, 121, 122, 123, 125, 154, 212, 221, 224, 245, 283–6, 298, 306, 308, 309, 311, 312, 322, 348, 349, 350, 351, 352, 354
Jenkins, Roy 240
Jordan 239

key industrial indicators 293
Keynes, John Maynard 165
Keynesian economics 27, 324
Kohl, Helmut 269
Kravis, Irving 60

labour costs 199, 244
labour unrest and strikes 21, 45, 46, 48–9, 65–8, 86–7, 157, 159, 167–9, 179–80, 203, 282
labour productivity 197, 218, 264, 294, 336
labour laws and legislation 215, 252, 258, 282, 288, 324, 353
labour unions 46, 66, 258, 282
*La Compañía General de Crédito en Expaña* 105

371

## INDEX

Lafuente Félez, Alberto 297–9, 301
Lain Entralgo, Pedro 46
'*La Pasionaria*' 177
Larroque, Enrique 175
Latin America 221
Law for the Promotion of General Coordination of Scientific and Technological Research 302
Law of Collective Agreements (1958) 23
Law of Credit Societies (1859) 106
Law of December 4, 1855 105
Law of Protection and Development of National Industry (1939) 29
Law of Railroad Companies (1855) 106
Law of Regulation and Defence of National Industry (1939) 30
Law of September 9, 1857 106
Law on Intellectual Property 297
Law 152 (preferential interest, 1963) 76
Law 194 (government activity, 1963) 114
leather products 45, 49, 64, 65, 150, 212
Lebanon 239
Leibenstein, Harvey 357–8
Lequerica, José Felix 41
Lérida–Reus–Tarrogona railroad line 106
Lewis, W. Arthur 59
Liberal Party 175
López Bravo, Gregorio 75, 88, 113–14, 118, 144
López José María 118
López Rodó, Laureano 23, 25, 48, 69, 75, 88, 113, 142, 156, 176
Lora Tamayo, Manuel 69
low technology manufactures 37
Luxembourg 343, 354

machine tools 37, 122, 148, 224
Madrid–Zaragoza railroad line 106
Madrid–Alicante railroad line 106
Mahgreb countries 239
market economy or free markets 22, 113, 177, 358

Marañón, Gregorio 46
Marin, Manuel 271
Marshall Plan 2, 49
Martin Alonso, Pablo 88
Martin Artajo, Alberto 40
Marxian ideology and Marxism 176, 210
MATESA 140–1
medium demand industries 196–200, 265–9, 294, 295, 305
Medium Term Economic Program (1983–1986) 252
mercantilism 74
Merigo, Eduardo 14
middle class 112
minerals 35, 45, 64
'Minifundio' 123
mining 53, 64, 65, 80, 90, 100, 107, 152, 233, 313, 337
Ministry
  for the Planning of Development 25, 26
  of Economy and Commerce 229
  of Governance 28
  of the Interior 26, 28
  of Industry 226, 229
minimum hourly wage 46
Mitterrand, François 158, 291
Molière 112
money supply 66, 92, 219, 251
monetary policy (see fiscal and monetary policy)
Monreal Luque, Alberto 175
Morán, Fernando 269
Morocco 47, 143, 239
Multi-Fibre Agreement 224
Muñoz Grandes, Augustin 41, 47, 68, 88
Myro Sánchez, Rafael 194, 265, 292, 294

NAFTA 349
Napoleon Bonaparte 111
Napoleonic Wars 13
Natali, Lawrence 272
National Budget 1988–9
National Employment Accord 244, 296

INDEX

National Employment Act (ANE) 220
National Energy Plan 215, 217, 229
National Enterprise (EN) 31
national income
 redistribution 21
 and Spanish exports 43
National Industrial Institute (INI) 22, 30, 31, 32–3, 51, 114, 159, 227, 318, 360
National Institute of Statistics 245, 249, 250, 334, 339, 351, 352
National Movement 22
National Plan for Electronic and Information Science (PEIN I) 297, 317
National Plan for Industrial Quality 317
National Plan for Scientific Research and Technological Development 297, 317
national savings 252
National Stabilization Plan of 1959 2–3, 14–15, 17, 23–4, 50, 51, 58, 63, 74–5, 126, 150, 161, 195
natural gas 229
Navarro Rubio, Mariano 23, 48, 50, 69, 88
Negrin, Juan 47
Netherlands 50, 70, 121, 125, 149, 153, 233, 275, 323, 343, 354
New Democracy 187
NICs and NIC competition 200, 212, 220, 221, 223, 265, 310, 354
Nieto Antúnez, Pedro 88
North, Douglas 60
Norway 50, 70, 123, 143, 149, 212, 323
nuclear energy 230
Nurkse, Ragnar 60

OECD countries 74, 95, 123, 192, 211, 212, 213, 217, 218, 219, 220–1, 227, 251, 275, 283–6, 298, 306, 307, 310, 311, 338
OEEC countries 69
Office of the Presidency of Government 26
oil embargo and crises 152–3, 211, 216, 222, 247, 258, 324
oil import dependency 213, 218, 229
oil prices 7, 153, 163, 164, 189, 191, 198, 221, 250, 281, 286, 307, 350
*Olarra, S.A.* 226
OPEC 189, 218, 221, 248
*Opus Dei* 23, 47–8, 50, 68–9, 87–9, 118
*Orbegozo, S.A.* 226
Oro Giral, Luis A. 297–9, 301

Pact of Madrid (1953) 41
Pact of Moncloa (1977) 7, 12, 15, 178–9, 185, 187, 203, 296
paper and paper products 45, 64, 65, 100, 152, 194
*Partido Social de Acción Democrática* 46
particularism 103
'Party of Labour' (PTL) 158
Patent Law 297
Pasinetti, Luigi L. 62, 64
Payne, S.G. 40, 86–7
Pedreño Muñoz, Andrés 322, 324, 325
Pérez González, Blas 40
personal income taxes 251
peseta 24, 102, 320
 black market 37
 exchange rates and devaluation 24, 36, 48, 51, 92–4, 134, 195, 200, 204, 213, 216, 218, 245, 250, 265, 311, 346, 354, 355
 'free foreign exchange markets' 37
petro-chemical industrial complex 37, 45
petroleum (see also oil) 226, 228, 233
pharmaceutical industry 297
pilot plants 360
Plan for the Promotion of Design, Quality and Fashion 318
Plan of Economic and Social Development 115, 176
Plan of Reconversion of Electronic Components Industry 229
Planell Riera, Joaquín 41
'Platform of Democratic

# INDEX

Convergence' (PCD) 158–9
'Poles of Growth' and development 25, 77–9
political right 276
Pope John XXIII 47, 68
Popular Alliance 177, 187, 208, 210–11, 282
Popular Party 338
Popular Socialist Party (PCE) 158, 176
Popular Democratic Party 175
population increases 347–8, 355,
Portugal 70, 101, 158, 240, 269, 270, 274, 275, 306, 328, 350
Potsdam Conference 29
Prados de la Escosura, Leandro 103
Preferential Trade Accord 274
primary sector 194, 202, 213, 247, 307, 313, 341
price deterioration 217
price stabilization 24
private Consumption 221
*Procurador and Procuradores* 169, 173, 177
product specialization 267
production input prices 277
profit margins 214
pro-Nazism 28
protectionism 9, 43–4, 107–8, 195, 197, 220, 224, 356
'Provisional Accord' 128
public borrowing 219
public health facilities 202
public services 341
Pujol, Jordi 177, 282

raw materials 20, 34, 38
Raymond, José Luis 206–8
Reagan, Ronald 13, 222, 270, 291
'Reaganomics' 222
reconversion of steel industries 215–16
Reconversion Law of 1982 297
recession 224
Regentialists 88
regressive taxation 26
REPESA 32–3
REPSOL 318

Research and Development 123, 197, 234, 297, 299–303, 357
retirement income 202
Reventós, Joan 177
Revolutionary Socialists 68
'Revolutionary Tax' 180
Ricardian 'comparative advantage' 243
Ridruejo, Dionisio 159
Rodríguez de Sahagun, Agustin 184
Rodríguez Valcárcel, Alejandro 170
Roman Catholic Church 27, 28, 31, 40, 47–8, 68, 110–12, 159, 188
Rostow, W.W. 360
Rothschild Bank 106
Rousseau 111
Royal Decree
  643/1982 227
  971/1982 225
  2010/1981 228
  2206/1980 226
  of 17 November 1852 105
  of 3 October 1980
rubber 45, 194
Ruiz Giménez, Joaquin 46, 68
RUMASA 276–7, 282
*ruptura and rupturistas* 158, 159–60, 168
Russian blockade of Berlin in 1948 39

S.A. Echevarría 226
Saenz de Ynestrillas, Ricardo 210
Sánchez Covisa, Mariano 157
Sánchez, María Paloma 357
Sánchez Ramos, Juan 185
*'Saneamiento y reforma'* 252
scholasticism 110–11
Schumann, Maurice 144
'Schumpeterian entrepreneur' 338, 356
Science and Technology Policy Committee (OECD) 357
Science Law 297, 357
scientific output 299–300
SEAT 32–3
secondary sector 73, 125, 201–2, 220, 247, 294, 313, 336, 341, 353
Second Convention of Yaundé 126

Segura, Julio 231, 233, 237, 243
Select Commission for Economic Affairs 316
Serrano Suñer, Ramón, (Franco's brother-in-law) 28
shipbuilding 32, 53, 181, 212, 227, 255, 258, 282
Silva Muñoz, Federico 88
Sirvent Dargent, José 114
Smith, Adam 74
'Social Democratic Party' (USDE) 158–9, 175, 210
Social Security 93, 203, 220, 252, 262
Socialist Unity Coalition 176
*Sociedad de Crédito Mobiliario Español* 106
*Sociedad Española de Construcción Naval* 31
*Sociedad Española Mercantil e Industrial* 106
*Sociedad de Aluminio*, S.A. (ENASA) 32
Solchaga, Carlos 248, 281, 291
Solís Ruiz, José 88, 141, 168
Solow, Robert M. 324
SORENA 227
Soviet Union 103, 105
 launched *Sputnik* 42
Spaak, Paul Henri 128
Spain's
 external accounts 219
 first development plan 77, 79, 88
 judicial system 87
 infrastructure 94
 membership in
  the International Labour Organization 42
  the European Community (see European Community)
  the OEEC 23
  the United Nations 22
  the World Health Organization 42
 second development plan 79, 93–4
 third plan 79
Spanish
 agricultural sector 20
 borrowing abroad 257

Civil War 17, 26, 31, 49, 87, 111, 195, 208
Communist Party 177, 187, 273, 282
economic history
 Civil War to 1959 17
emigration 71, 73–4, 89–90, 121, 155, 201, 273
employers' association (CEOE) 244, 270, 271, 273
Democratic Union 171, 176
exports and industrial exports 38, 108, 138, 218, 249, 250, 252, 253, 267, 269, 274
fiscal policy (1975) 13
gross domestic product 3, 12, 34, 42, 97, 173, 181, 189, 193, 203, 213, 217, 219, 245–9, 260, 291, 312–13, 318–19, 327–31, 334, 351–3, 354
 per capita (1960–1974) 10–11, 12
gross industrial product 121, 145, 155
gross national product 25, 44, 61, 70, 94, 97–8, 119, 120, 153, 166
imports; import liberalization 24, 63, 64, 81, 90, 119, 128, 134–6, 194, 275
industrial production and growth 18–19, 22, 103–5, 262, 263, 291–2
'industrial revolution' 243, 339
industrial structure 268, 295
Institute of Foreign Currency 36
macroeconomic trends 211
multinational firms 233
Net National Income 174
Net National Product 183
Parliament (Cortes) 26, 32, 87, 93, 105–6, 142, 157, 168, 170, 172–3, 175, 177, 179, 187, 188, 208–11, 213, 215, 269
railway network 106–7
Socialist Workers Party (PSOE) 12, 158, 173, 175, 176, 209, 210, 242, 248, 250, 251, 257, 269, 282, 296, 316, 338, 348

# INDEX

special steel products 226
stagflation 26, 166, 188, 191
stagnating production 26, 34
standard of living increases 97
'Statute on the Right of Political Association' 159
stock market crisis 291, 305, 306–8, 312
stock prices 280
strong demand industries 196–200, 265–9, 295, 296, 304, 317
'Stuttgart resolution' 271
Suanzes, Juan Antonio, Director of the INI 31, 40, 114
Suárez González, Adolfo 167, 169–71, 173, 176–8, 184, 187–8, 191, 203–4, 209, 215, 225, 240, 242, 243, 296
'Supply Side' economics 223
Sweden 50, 101, 123, 149, 212, 323
Switzerland 70, 123
*Syllabus* 31
synthetic fibres 228
Syria 239

*Talbot* 299
Tamames, Ramón 42
tariffs 4, 108, 271–2, 356
tax reform 23, 188, 215
tax reductions 165
technology and technological backwardness 43–4, 49, 122, 123, 126, 195, 199, 224–5, 231, 233–4, 263, 264, 301, 356
technological coverage ratios 235
technological-intensive industries 301
technological unemployment 61
Tejero, Antonio 210
    coup attempts of 1978 and 1981 210
*Terna* 170
telecommunications 212
terms of trade 288
terrorism 157, 167, 175, 185, 209
tertiary sector 73, 194, 201–2, 214, 246–7, 257, 288, 313, 336, 341, 353, 355
textiles and textile machinery 37, 45, 49, 64, 80, 122, 150, 152, 181, 194, 212, 224, 228, 265, 337
Thatcher, Margaret 222, 291
Thorn, Gaston 272
Tierno Galván, Enrique 158, 176, 187
tobacco 45, 64, 80, 90, 122, 150
Torrejón de Ardoz 41
Tortella Casares, G. 106
totalitarianism 31
tourism 4, 36, 71, 73, 81, 97, 155, 159, 181, 213, 217, 218, 245, 249, 288
trade union organization 258, 263
transition to democracy 175, 187
Treaty of Adhesion 273–4
Treaty of Rome 57, 128
Trias Fargas, Ramón 177
Truman, Harry 39
Tunis 277
Turkey 126, 143, 239

Ullastres Calvo, Alberto 23, 48, 50, 68, 240
'underground economy' 325
unemployment 34, 154, 161–2, 166, 191, 200, 213, 216, 224, 244, 247, 249, 250, 254, 255, 257, 282, 290, 291, 322, 348, 355
unemployment insurance 46, 325
Unified Socialist Party of Catalonia (PSUC) 177
UNINSA 115
*Unión Naval de Levante, S.A.* 227
'Union of the Spanish People' UPDE 160, 167, 168
United Nation's General Assembly 39–40
United Kingdom 50, 70, 100, 101, 103–5, 120, 143, 149, 150, 153, 212, 216, 233, 275, 283–6, 298, 300, 301, 302, 306, 308, 309, 311, 312, 323, 348, 350, 352
United States 120, 124, 125, 139, 153, 216, 224, 298, 300, 301, 302, 308, 309, 311, 312, 323, 348
    aid 22, 41
    budget deficits 306

military bases 22, 41, 103–4
prime interest rates 216
Universal Declaration of Human
 Rights of the United Nations 171

Value Added Tax 241
Veblen, Thorstein 58
Vigón, General Jorge 88
Vila Reyes, Juan 140
Voltaire 111
voluntary restraint agreements 224


weak demand industries 196–200,
 228, 265–9, 294, 295, 296, 303,
 305

wholesale price index 34, 83
wine 273
wood and cork products 45, 73, 100,
 233, 265
'Workers' Commissions' (CC.OO.)
 158
World War II 2
worldwide recession 222–3

Yugoslavia 239

Zapatero, Juan 110
zinc mining 229
Zones of Reindustrialization (ZUR)
 317

## DATE DUE

| | | | |
|---|---|---|---|
| ~~TA 8676~~ | | | |
| | | | |
| | | | |
| | | | |
| | | | |
| | | | |
| | | | |
| | | | |
| | | | |
| | | | |
| | | | |
| | | | |
| | | | |
| | | | |
| | | | |
| | | | |
| | | | |

Demco Inc. 38-293